CONTOURS OF WHITE ETHNICITY

YIORGOS ANAGNOSTOU

Contours

POPULAR ETHNOGRAPHY

of White

AND THE MAKING OF USABLE PASTS

Ethnicity

IN GREEK AMERICA

Ohio University Press

Athens

Ohio University Press, Athens, Ohio 45701
www.ohioswallow.com
© 2009 by Ohio University Press

To obtain permission to quote, reprint, or otherwise reproduce or distribute material
from Ohio University Press publications, please contact our rights and permissions
department at (740) 593-1154 or (740) 593-4536 (fax).

Printed in the United States of America
Ohio University Press books are printed on acid-free paper ∞ ™

16 15 14 13 12 11 10 09   5 4 3 2 1

Library of Congress Cataloging-in-Publication Data
Anagnostou, Yiorgos.
  Contours of white ethnicity : popular ethnography and the making of usable pasts in
Greek America / Yiorgos Anagnostou.
    p. cm.
  Includes bibliographical references and index.
  ISBN 978-0-8214-1820-8 (cloth : alk. paper) — ISBN 978-0-8214-1821-5 (pbk. : alk.
paper)
  1. Greek Americans—Ethnic identity. 2. Whites—Race identity—United States. I.
Title.
  E184.G7A53 2009
  305.809—dc22
                          2009038443

In memoriam

Eleni Anagnostou

(1930–2007)

What more appropriate image for the art of criticism: the tightly closed fist, the open and relaxed hand? The one concerned with defining boundaries, passing judgment, inflicting punishment; the other with presenting the subject sympathetically, pushing beyond boundaries, a predilection for appreciation and praise. Contrary to what might be assumed, it is far easier for the critic to revile than to reveal; to deride and dismiss than to illuminate.

——Joyce Carol Oates

CONTENTS

Contents

ACKNOWLEDGMENTS

Books bear countless imprints of those critical communities and institutions that contribute to their making. This book is no exception. It is animated by the eddies and currents of intellectual and material sustenance that I have received throughout years of teaching and writing in my intellectual home, the Modern Greek Studies Program at the Ohio State University. I have been fortunate to find myself in the company of scholars who encouraged the kind of critical scholarship that drives this work. I am indebted to Gregory Jusdanis for stressing the importance of interventionist scholarship, and of academic prose unencumbered by jargon. I am equally indebted to Vassilis Lambropoulos for teaching me the meaning of scholarly commitment and for nurturing critical inquiry and interdisciplinary research. With boundless generosity Artemis Leontis created environments for intellectual exchange beyond the classroom. I am grateful to her for taking the time to read my manuscript numerous times, gently encouraging me to keep asking better questions.

The writing of this book has been made possible by the material and intellectual support that I have received from various academic institutions. I express my appreciation to the College of Humanities of the Ohio State University for granting me generous research leaves that helped formulate my ideas and bring this book into fruition. A Stanley J. Seeger Visiting Research Fellowship in Hellenic Studies (fall 2005) made available crucial time for uninterrupted thinking and writing. I thank Dimitri Gondicas, the affiliated faculty, and the staff at the Program in Hellenic Studies at Princeton University for their warm hospitality and for offering a critical forum for the discussion of my ideas. I have also benefited from invitations to present my work in modern Greek programs at Columbia University, San Francisco State University, Yale University, and the Center for Folklore Studies at the Ohio State University. I thank both my hosts and the audiences for engaging with and providing insights on my work. All along, my home Department of Greek and Latin has been supportive of research on modern Greece and its diaspora. I would like to express my appreciation particularly to the chairs, David Hahm and Fritz Graf, for their guidance and unflagging backing. To all those institutions and individuals I extend my gratitude for encouraging an interdisciplinary research project whose aim has been to interrogate disciplinary assumptions and practices.

Numerous individuals lightened the arduous process of writing with their friendship and intellectual presence. Since my graduate years, Martha Klironomos has been a constant source of support and a reminder that along with an unwavering commitment to research, one must have an uncompromising dedication to teaching. I cannot thank her enough for the advice she has given me about how to manage this dual investment. I have greatly benefited from the analytical acumen of Eric Ball and Anthony Kaldellis, who have been tireless in supporting my work. They have provided the critical ear that listens well, leaving no premise and no assumption unexamined. What an invaluable intellectual companionship they have offered! In addition to offering his editorial expertise, Gerasimus Katsan was the one to supply a cheerful outlook when difficulties cast a heavy weight on my shoulders. From far away, Vangelis Calotychos, Stathis Gourgouris, Yiorgos Kalogeras, Smaro Kamboureli, Neni Panourgiá, Penelope Papailias, David Sutton, and Bonnie Urciuoli all crucially contributed through their intellectual support, their conversations, and their work. They have served as an inspiring compass to critically navigate the territory of ethnicity and ethnography. From the start, my editor Gill Berchowitz exhibited an unwavering faith in this project. I express my profound appreciation for her crucial support in critical times of its development. I am also thankful to Rick Huard, whose editorial assistance greatly contributed to the improvement of this work. Last, but not least, I thank the unsung heroes of academic life, the administrative associates. I cannot thank enough the late Mary Cole, as well as Suzanne Childs and Wayne Lovely, for creatively solving all kinds of problems and for creating a welcoming sense of home away from home.

I am devastated that my mother is no longer with us to see this book come to fruition. The fact that I cannot share the joy with her, the person to whom I owe the strength to persevere in the face of extreme adversities, weighs unbearably upon me.

With Ana, we have journeyed the last twenty-three years along contours that have been hospitable to all kinds of differences and yet familiar with the commonalities that inhabit the spaces of the margins. I couldn't have written this book without her—she was always near, even when geography kept us apart.

PARTS of this book were published in early versions as follows: "Metaethnography in the Age of 'Popular Folklore,'" *Journal of American Folklore* 119, no. 474 (2006): 381–412; "Forget the Past, Remember the Ancestors! Modernity, 'Whiteness,'

American Hellenism, and the Politics of Memory in Early Greek America," *Journal of Modern Greek Studies* 21, no. 1 (2004): 25–71; and "Model Americans, Quintessential Greeks: Ethnic Success and Assimilation in Diaspora," *Diaspora: A Journal of Transnational Studies* 12, no. 3 (2003): 279–327.

Why White Ethnicity? Why Ethnic Pasts?

> [T]he search or struggle for a sense of ethnic identity is
> a (re-)invention and discovery of a vision, both ethical
> and future-oriented. Whereas the search for coherence
> is grounded in a connection to the past, the meaning
> abstracted from that past, an important criterion of
> coherence, is an ethic workable for the future.
>
> —Michael Fischer, "Ethnicity and the Post-modern
> Arts of Memory"

> As more of us anthropologists from the borderlands go "home"
> to study "our own communities," we will probably see
> increasing elisions of boundaries between ethnography and
> "minority discourse," in which writing ethnography becomes
> another way of writing our own identities and communities.
>
> —Dorinne Kondo, "The Narrative Production of
> 'Home,' Community, and Political Identity in
> Asian American Theater"

IN THIS WORK I explore the social category of "white ethnicity" in the United States. A classification that emerged and gained currency during the civil rights era, white ethnicity refers to hyphenated populations that trace their origins to Europe but also to countries and areas in relative proximity to it. This ascription incorporates both ethnic and racialized dimensions, attaching to these populations both cultural attributes and inescapable racialized overtones. It indicates, therefore, how white ethnics are placed in multiple, yet interrelated, systems of difference within the nation. On the one hand, groups such as Armenian Americans, Greek Americans, Jewish Americans, Irish Americans, Italian Americans, and Polish Americans are recognized as distinctly ethnic, claiming unique cultures, histories, and religions. The Americanization of these populations, on the other hand, has entailed a specific kind of assimilation, their eventual incorporation into whiteness. It is this racialization that marks these groups in counterdistinction to "nonwhite" racial minorities. Therefore, the ethnoracial label "white ethnic" simultaneously accomplishes two distinct classificatory functions. On the one hand, the racialized ascription places these collectives within the boundaries of whiteness, pointing to their current entrenchment as white in the national imagination. On the other hand, the ethnic marker attaches a cultural hue that differentiates these populations from unmarked whiteness. It is often thought that white ethnics possess culture, in contrast to the cultureless whiteness of the general population. Racially denigrated and classified as nonwhite in the past, people now designated "white ethnics" define themselves against the backdrop of complex social and political struggles over assimilation and cultural preservation, and histories of brutal symbolic and physical violence over their racial and ethnic place in American society.

In this book I analyze the ways in which one specific group of white ethnics, Greek Americans, represent themselves, undertaking this task from a specific vantage point: I examine how their past is made to matter in the present. I probe, in other words, the enduring relevance of ethnic pasts for the contemporary social imagination. Specifically, I investigate how practices and values associated with the past and glossed as "tradition," "folklore," "heritage," "custom," or "immigrant culture" are endowed with significance today. I analyze how various pasts are used to create identities and communities and to imagine the future of ethnicity. I identify specific texts and practices where such pasts are produced, and I investigate their social and political valence. I ask why and how selective pasts are retained, reworked, dismantled, discarded, or contested in the making of ethnicity. I illuminate the visions of social life that these engagements with the past endorse and what all of this tells us about present-day white ethnicity.

My aim here is to provide an analysis of how these pasts are produced and by whom, of what interests they advance and for whom. I am interested, that is, in the poetics and politics of white ethnic pasts. In this analysis, I wish to initiate a critical discussion that investigates academic and popular understandings of ethnic whiteness. I frame this category as a contested, heterogeneous cultural field whose complexity and relevance for social life has been downplayed, even maligned, in larger debates about diversity. I argue that bringing the past into the present to produce *usable ethnic pasts* illuminates dimensions of white ethnicity that discussions on American pluralism cannot afford to ignore.[1]

I strive to focus attention on the notion that ethnic pasts are always plural—not singular or monolithic—and inform the present in ways that are not always clearly discernible. Such perspective demands a bold critical intervention. I intervene in dominant academic and popular representations of ethnicity that tend to erase this diversity and, in the process, take a step toward mapping how multiple pasts give texture to the contours of the field of ethnic whiteness in the United States.

My project emerges from and participates in a number of intersecting academic conversations in anthropology, cultural studies, ethnic and racial studies, folklore, modern Greek studies, sociology, and women's studies. One common thread in these discussions involves the cultural politics framing the social production of the past. As a domain made rather than found, the past generates passionate struggles over its meaning. Ownership of the past is an important power relation, one grounded in the ability of particular social groups to establish those versions of historical truth that serve their own interests. One must therefore pay attention to the political and social implications associated with questions about who narrates the past and who is excluded—and for what purpose. These are but a few of the important issues discussed by the current burgeoning academic interest in cultural memory, tradition, heritage, and historical consciousness. The stakes in the way in which critical scholarship engages with these questions are high. The construction of usable pasts today guides how ethnicity is imagined tomorrow. Ethnic memory, as Michael Fischer (1986) puts it, is "or ought to be, future, not past, oriented" (201). Or, in the words of Raymond Williams (1977), those traditions selected to "ratify the present" powerfully "indicate directions for the future" (116).[2]

In this introduction, I explore through various paths the significance of the past for white ethnicity. One such path leads to a recent debate over the depiction of early twentieth-century immigrants and illuminates the point that what could count as a past is a contested, problematic site within an ethnic collective. In revisiting this dispute, I bring to the fore a concept often forgotten in popular thought about ethnicity, namely that a white ethnic group is never a uniform, homogeneous entity. But because this heterogeneity is often contained, I pursue a discussion of how dominant narratives of American multiculturalism manage the boundaries of ethnic diversity. Having established white ethnicity as a terrain of contested meanings about the past, I continue exploring its constructions, this time focusing on how this category is discussed in the academy. This mapping helps me situate my own contribution to the debates. I identify the specific terrain of my analysis—Greek America—discuss my methodology—critical readings of what I call "popular ethnography"—and acknowledge my politics of knowledge—an interventionist critical scholarship that emanates from a minor academic field, modern Greek studies.

Who Are the White Ethnics?

One of my aims is to destabilize the understanding of white ethnicity as a uniform category. I do not, of course, neglect the racial privileges enjoyed collectively by white ethnics, and I closely analyze the dominant narratives that seek to fix the meaning of a group as a homogeneous collective. But I am also interested in mapping pluralities, marginalized perspectives, and the struggles over which pasts count as meaningful in the present. As a way of entering the complexity of this terrain, I trace here a specific contour of this struggle as it was expressed in the conflict over ethnic self-representation in a highly visible cultural institution, the Ellis Island Immigration Museum.

In her cultural history of Greek America, *An Amulet of Greek Earth: Generations of Immigrant Folk Culture* (2002), historian, folklorist, and fiction writer Helen Papanikolas features an archival photograph whose exhibit in the Ellis Island Immigration Museum stirred heated controversy. Posing for the camera is a group of immaculately dressed male immigrants in Utah in 1911. They are coal miners from the island of Crete. Gazing defiantly at the photographer, they conspicuously display their prized possessions: elegant suits, brand-new guns, and bottles of alcoholic beverage. Destined for consumption by relatives, or possibly prospective brides in the ancestral homeland, the snapshot captures a particular moment in the complex encounter between the immigrants and American modernity. In relation to the economy of labor, the photograph exemplifies a specific kind of performance. The laborers have meticulously scrubbed off those markers that scar their working-class bodies. The experience of dangerous, low-paying, dirty, and physically taxing labor associated with mining and railroad construction is rendered invisible. The body politic of labor is bracketed off for the sake of a photographic inscription that flaunts material possessions, showcases well-being, communicates vitality, and advertises economic progress. Paradoxically, as the men sport American modernity, they simultaneously declare their defiance to it. The brandishing of guns and alcohol stands as a potent symbol of competitive Cretan masculinity, proclaiming that local culture remains central to immigrant identity. In one crucial aspect, modernity does not compromise the past but enhances it. Surely, the signs of prosperity in the New World legitimize the immigrants' break from the agricultural past, specifically their subjection of the self to migrant labor under conditions of industrial capitalism. At the same time, this material success amplifies the defiant male performance of enduring transnational continuities, a posture destined for domestic visual consumption.

A document of regional and gender pride in the past, the snapshot has sparked contemporary controversy. Its meaning has become contested. An obstinate artifact of a bygone immigrant era, the image currently appears in a variety of places (including the cover of this book). Readers of literature may be familiar with it from the novel *Days of Vengeance,* whose author, Harry Mark Petrakis, "[admired] the photo so much that he used it" to illustrate the cover (Georgakas 2003a, 46).[3] Through this literary venue, the photograph has gained prominence as a document of Greek immigrant social history. Yet its display in the Ellis Island Immigration Museum in New Jersey—credited to Papanikolas's curatorial decision—has stirred fanatical intraethnic dissent. Ever sensitive to the politics of cultural representation, some Greek Americans approach the photograph as a site of memory that is better forgotten than nationally commemorated. A New York–based lobbying group has "for years" been pressing the museum "to get the photo taken down and replaced with a wedding or some other conventional scene. They feel the photo is defamatory to the Greek image and not at all representative of ethnic values" (ibid.). The specific objection, as reported by Nick Smart (2005), is that it makes Greek America "'look like a Greek Mafia,' violent and intemperate" (119), a criticism that invokes the museum's exhibition politics: the museum "makes no reference to the immigrant underworld of Sicilian mafiosi and Jewish prostitutes" (Lowenthal 1996, 160). The dissenters' tactics have been aggressive and have included personal harassment. Commenting on this discord, Zeese Papanikolas (2003) offers the following testimony about his mother's experience: "For years, wherever . . . [she] spoke and read on the East Coast she was shadowed by a Greek American woman who expressed her outrage at this horrible view of Greek immigrants with guns in their hands like *mafiosi,* and who insisted that my mother have the photograph removed" (13).

In a symbolically loaded commemorative monument such as the immigration museum—which "has become a status symbol" for families descended from immigrants who arrived in the United States through Ellis Island (Welz 2000, 67)—the lay public takes it upon itself to legislate the exhibition of the immigrant past. Vigilant in the politics of representation, it reacts against a portrayal that may blur the distinction between the Greek Americans, often construed as model ethnics, and the Italian American underworld, an image that has been partially responsible for turning the Italians into the "symbolic villains in the American imagination" (Novak 1971, 3).[4] If "any historical narrative is a particular bundle of silences" (Trouillot 1995, 27), here is an attempt at silencing the production of Greek American history at "the moment of fact retrieval (the making of narratives)" (26).

What is at stake when a photograph of working-class men who flaunt their new-found success—and who advertise, one might say, the magnanimity and freedoms of America by hiding the signs of labor exploitation—stirs passions as an improper sign of the past? We witness here the mapping of the past as a terrain of contested meanings. White ethnicity, a social category to which Greek America is commonly assigned by social discourses, unmistakably slips away here from its alleged cultural superficiality into an array of contested issues ranging from institutional representation to collective memory, authority, conflict, and agency. The friction over exhibiting the past directs ethnicity into the fray of heated cultural politics. It foregrounds the notion that the manner in which the past is made known to the public is not harmonious but is shaped at the intersection of competing views of identity in the present. Helen Papanikolas's commitment to historical documentation and her authority to represent Greek America clash with the ideology of the model ethnic, the desire to construe an idealized positive image of ethnicity.[5] Furthermore, how the past is made meaningful illuminates the kinds of identity that are desired today. As Jonathan Friedman (1994) observes, "the past is always practiced in the present, not because the past imposes itself but because subjects in the present fashion the past in the practice of their social identity" (141).

Who are the white ethnics here? Individuals committed to the realist representation of the past, or those determined to silence aspects of the historical record? Those who invest in exhibiting the past, or those who threaten to censor it? The public controversy over the proper display of immigrant ancestors reveals that there can be no single answer to these questions. By no means a transparent social category, white ethnicity is a construct of social practices and narratives that compete over the significance of the past in defining contemporary identity and the ways in which this identity is portrayed in the public. Of course, the idea of ethnicity as "invented, imagined, administered, and manufactured" (Bendix and Roodenburg 2000, xi) is a truism in critical scholarship, antagonizing the popular—and even sometimes academic—view of ethnicity as biologically innate and therefore immutable. Consequently, the critical responsibility becomes to investigate how pasts are made to matter in the production of ethnic meanings today: who produces usable ethnic pasts, how, and for what purposes?

In the remainder of this introduction, my task is to probe the production of usable pasts as a process crucial for identity making but also as an instrument for containing difference. I discuss this dual function in relation to white ethnicity, pointing out how the immigrant past is deployed as a resource not only to construct identity but also to sustain racial hierarchies. The discussion moves on to identify the analytical focus of my work—namely Greek America—the textual corpus that enables this analysis—popular ethnography—and my methodological locus—a metaethnography of the politics and poetics of these ethnographic texts. In the process, I map the broad contours, past and present, of Greek American popular ethnography and its relation to professional anthropology. The conclusion lays open my politics of interpretation, outlining the aims of my interventionist scholarship.

The Significance of the Past: Making Difference and Similarity

The past has emerged as a crucial social and political resource in the making of contemporary ethnicities. Ethnic pasts are politically charged because they are invariably deployed to legitimize collective belonging. Claims to identity, cultural ownership, and in the case of nationalism, territory, all build on arguments about common ancestry, heritage, tradition, and indigeneity.[6] Status and prestige hinge on the possession of glorious pasts. The controversy over the right to own the Elgin Marbles—a legacy that is both Greek *and* global (Lowenthal 1996, 244)—for instance, rests on a logic that equates the past with biology, "heritage with lineage" (200). From the Greek perspective, if one wishes to appreciate this global heritage, one should do so in terms dictated by those who claim a pedigree from the classical past: visit Athens, not the British Museum, where they are currently exhibited. Possession of a past anchors claims to identity. Even in the most visible cases of constructed panethnicity in the United States, that is, when distinct ethnic identities submerge themselves in politically and socially expedient collectivities, the past continues to mark cultural specificity. Such was the case during the inaugural festivities of the National Museum of the American Indian in 2004 at the Smithsonian Institution. In celebrating the establishment of this panethnic museum, commemorative events stressed a history of European-inflicted persecution and loss shared by all native people in the Americas; at the same time, the narrative of cultural perseverance necessitated the highly visible performance and exhibit of an astounding native cultural heterogeneity. Dances, music, dress, and crafts differentiated the Aztecs from the Cherokees and Potawatomis; the Otomis (central Mexico) from the Chippewas (Lac du Flambeau band, Lake Superior Chippewa in Wisconsin); and the Cheyenne River Lakota Akicitas (South Dakota) from the Seminoles (Florida), to mention a few. Rather than eclipsing specificity, the celebration of a common pan-Indian history brought it to the fore. Discourses on and performances of ethnic pasts bring about a dazzling proliferation of identities; their particularizing function counters the homogenizing processes of globalization.

But even as heritage and tradition communicate distinctiveness, they have also turned into venues that, paradoxically, spread global uniformity.[7] Ostensibly staged to showcase ethnic particularity, heritage sites such as the genre of the ethnic festival in the United States, a commodified performance of urban ethnic tourism, tend to homogenize the global experience of ethnicity. The rhetoric of difference often produces a flattening uniformity as to what merits display and preservation. A brief survey of ethnic spectacles in the United States illustrates the unfailing predictability of what counts as a valued past in the multicultural agora. Can there be an American ethnicity without food, dances, music, costumes, or personal research into roots and family genealogy that offers recourse into an ethnic past? *Polka* and *kalamatianos* may differ in style and symbolically differentiate the Poles from the Greeks on the dancing stage, yet both function as *indispensable* markers of respective ethnic identities. Cultural commodification reduces ethnicities to selectively predictable expressions, applying a hue of aesthetic diversity and exoticism over routinely enacted uniformity. Belly dancers in Cairo, Istanbul, and Athens; Zorba-dance in Crete and ethnic festivals in Columbus, Ohio. Sameness is showcased as an emblem of ethnic distinctiveness for the benefit of international and domestic tourism. As the past is commodified, cultural standardization contains diversity; increasingly, local heritage circulates across national borders in a prepackaged uniformity.

Worldwide homogeneity now extends to the realm of values and ethics, a phenomenon contributing to what Michael Herzfeld (2004) calls the "global hierarchy of value" (2). Globalization in this formulation entails "the hidden presence of a logic that has seeped in everywhere but is everywhere disguised as difference, heritage, local tradition" (ibid.). Adopted globally by states, elites, and the bourgeoisie, a set of values "such as efficiency, fair play, civility, civil society, human rights, transparency, cooperation and tolerance" is normalized via an "increasingly homogeneous language of culture and ethics" (ibid.). As Bonnie Urciuoli (1998) argues, the cultural definition of the model ethnic American citizen resonates with this universalizing process. Immigrant and ethnic traditions are given premium value insofar as they contribute to what is seen as the moral betterment and socioeconomic mobility of ethnic subjects (178). "'Family solidarity,' 'work ethic,' 'belief in education,'" she writes, "provide the moral wherewithal" that meets the culturally entrenched requirements of Americanization: in the age of multiculturalism, immigrants are classified as desirable Americans-in-the-making, and racial minorities are ethnicized on the basis of middle-class criteria, achievement, and progress. Those attributes serve as a powerful instrument of social control, given that the "worth of one's ethnicity hang[s] in the balance: good Italian-American or low-class Sicilian? Hardworking African-American or undesirable black?" (179). Morally upright, family-centered, and successful Greek American or lazy, morally corrupt Greek immigrant (Karpathakis 1994)? Such a model, Urciuoli comments, sanctions specific forms of "acceptable difference" (1998, 178), "mak[ing] it easy to imagine that, despite categories of difference, the same embracing social truths must hold for everyone" (179).[8] As American society celebrates the diversity of ethnic identities—"it has become almost a civic duty to have an ethnicity as well as to appreciate that of others," writes Robert Wood (1998, 230)—the past is contained, and the centrifugal tendencies associated with the proliferation of specificities is managed.

The ideology of the model American ethnic sustains racial and ethnic hierarchies based on what anthropologist Micaela di Leonardo (1998) calls an ethnic report card: the positive valuation and public flaunting of those traits that are seen as leading to mobility. Such a "report card mentality," di Leonardo writes, explains class divisions in terms of "proper and improper ethnic/racial family and economic behavior rather than by the differential incorporation of immigrant and resident populations in American capitalism's evolving class structure" (94). The explanation of prosperity merely in terms of ethnic propensity for entrepreneurship or for hard work, for instance, denies the function of economic policies to sustain stagnation or bring about downward mobility. In this instance, ethnicity works as a mystifying process, allowing ubiquitous political and economic policies responsible for the plight of the poor to escape interrogation. In di Leonardo's evocative phrase, it allows material processes responsible for poverty "to be hidden in plain sight" (22). In doing so, it sustains a deeply entrenched American ideology regarding the ability (and responsibility) of ethnics to pull themselves up by their own cultural bootstraps.

Culturalist explanations of mobility serve the interests of dominant classes. As Raymond Williams (1977) argues, the selective consolidation of the past into a single aspect "passed off as 'the tradition,' 'the significant past'" (115–16), entails an interpretive process "within a particular hegemony" (115) in which a whole range of diverse meanings and practices is neglected, discarded, muted, or marginalized. Here, dominant traditions regulate the present; in fact, they become an essential "aspect of *contemporary* social and cultural organization, in the interest of the dominance of a specific class" (116). This is why every time middle-class white ethnics publicly wave their report card as an explanation of their success, scholars working on race-based poverty see in it a weapon of antiminority politics. Therefore, to write about usable white ethnic pasts means to find oneself at the center of a politicized debate that connects the past with racial and class hierarchies in the present.

The twin functions of the past as a resource for organizing ethnic identity and as a venue of containment and domination require the observer to focus on the enabling power of the past to sustain meaningful lives without losing sight of it as an "actively shaping force" (Williams 1977, 115) of hegemony that excludes alternative practices and meanings. This standpoint brings into sharp relief the notion of ethnicity as a contested field of meaning, not a uniformly shared culture or a bounded homogeneous community. I am interested here in exploring the tension between hegemonic renderings of the past and alternative cultural practices, a juxtaposition that advances the conceptualization of ethnicity beyond its present regulation as celebratory and acceptable difference. Here I am in full agreement with anthropologist Michael Fischer (1986), who frames ethnicity as an "ethical (celestial) vision that might serve to renew the self and ethnic group as well as contribute to a richer, powerfully dynamic pluralist society" (197). But the view of the past as a future-oriented ethical resource must be supplemented with a concern for cultural politics. This is to say that I wish to examine the material and political interests served in the name of the past. Specifically, I situate any claim on the past—invariably glossed as a time-honored tradition, a legacy of a work ethic, a heritage of entrepreneurial acumen, or a cultural trait of perseverance—within historically specific political economies that sustain class-, gender-, and race-based inequalities.

The present cannot be seen apart from its pasts. The regulation of ethnicity as acceptable difference in the present invites investigation of the historical processes that brought about the hegemony of white ethnicity in the first place. Now selected as celebrated signs of inclusion to the multicultural polity, the pasts of white ethnics have undergone a dramatic social and semiotic shift in relation to their transnational histories. American modernity has historically treated Old World expressive culture with suspicion, ambivalence, contempt, outright hostility, or a cautious acceptance often supplemented by strategies of containment. Immigrant customs have been objects of intersecting discourses that have constructed immigrants as primitives, exotics, savages, and inferior folk irreducibly unfit for American citizenship. Powerful racial hierarchies and relations of domination were sustained on the basis of representing immigrant cultures as embodiments of an inferior way of life. A host of immigrant activities, such as political activism directed toward social and racial justice, were excluded from American modernity. This particular immigrant engagement with social issues was fiercely persecuted and demonized as unpatriotic. What is more, bilingualism was seen as anathema and a menace to the nation. Even today's reclaimed ethnic cuisine and dancing were at some point subjected to scorn, ridicule, and even disgust. The present celebratory packaging of the past often forgets these histories of oppression and intimidation. The glorification of selective aspects of the past is wrapped in a bundle of silences.

In view of the struggles over the place of the immigrant past in the present, it would be erroneous to treat the past as a known, fixed entity waiting to be retrieved at a moment's notice. It would be false to approach it as a resource that merely awaits discovery by disinterested researchers: the past is a domain made rather than naturally found. What we recognize as the past comes about as a process of exclusions, displacements, and forced forgetting. It entails, in other words, an ideological construct. Attention to how the past is defined in specific social and temporal contexts enables the identification of continuities and discontinuities, but also helps recover those practices and meanings of the past that have been erased from public memory in the present. In this examination, we must take into account the strategies, interests, and investments that motivated the production of specific usable pasts. For if we take seriously the notion of the past as a dynamic and historically contingent process, we should agree with Vladimir Propp (1984) that our inquiry should center on "what happens to old folklore under new historical conditions and trace the appearance of new formations" (11). For my purposes, the inquiry into the ways in which the past is appropriated under new conditions must exhibit a strong historical component. The principal task becomes to explain why certain pasts are privileged, why some pasts resonate better than others with present conditions, and why certain pasts are relegated to the margins.

"Who Are the White Ethnics"? Whiteness, Racial Hierarchies, and Ethnic Identity

To frame my topic in relation to whiteness, might seem counterintuitive. An obvious alternative strategy is to privilege the cultural component of ethnicity at the expense of its relation to systems that organize difference in racialized terms. One might even suggest that the examination of *ethnicity* as culture cancels a claim to whiteness because of the normative understanding of whiteness as an invisible domain devoid of culture (Frankenberg 1993). As Pamela Perry (2001) shows, white identity is construed as a culturally empty category associated with the explicit refusal to seek "ties or allegiances to European ancestry and culture, [and having] no 'traditions.'" To the white high school populations that she studied, "only 'ethnic' people had such ties to the past" (58). For these youth, ethnic traditions were not merely meaningless but undesirable as well.

In fact, this construction sustains powerful hierarchies that rest on the implicit duality between whiteness as "good, controlled, rational, and cultureless, and otherness . . . [as] bad, out of control, irrational, and cultural" (85). "It connotes a relationship of power between those who 'have' culture (and are, thus, irrational and inferior) and those who claim not to (and are, thus, rational and superior)" (86).

But this should not lead to the erroneous assumption that an ethnic location necessarily distances one from whiteness. Hyphenated ethnic identities are not merely cultural signifiers; as I noted in the opening of this introduction, they are deeply entrenched in racialized categories. Popular classifications confer upon Italian Americans, Irish Americans, Polish Americans, Greek Americans, and Jewish Americans a specific racialized status because "the second part of the compound [in these identities] . . . always emphasize[s] whiteness" (Trouillot 1995, 133). It is precisely the incorporation of these groups into whiteness that affords them a contextual self-manipulability of identity. One could self-identify as a Greek in one context and as a white American in another.

As the scholarly project of whiteness studies has demonstrated, the whiteness of the ethnics can no longer remain unexamined, an invisible norm that evades critical scrutiny. Making its operation visible becomes a first-order analytical priority in order to reveal how it confers privilege and to disrupt its reproduction of relations of inequality. As a category historically associated with systems of domination, the whiteness component of ethnicity must be examined in order to identify practices and social discourses that contribute to its making.[9]

A thread within whiteness studies explains the historical transformation of the so-called new immigrants of the 1900s—a category that classified southeastern Europeans and a host of other collectives such as Syrians and Armenians as nonwhite—into the celebrated middle-class white ethnics of the 2000s. It becomes crucial for its practitioners to demonstrate how this reconfiguration in racial meaning gradually endowed white ethnics with those social privileges that were denied to people of color: entry to unions, the ability to secure loans, the right to live in certain neighborhoods, and eventually high rates of intermarriage with members of the dominant population. In a society in which complex political and social developments led to the redrawing of the boundaries of whiteness to accommodate the formerly despised immigrants, privileges accrued to those who most closely approximated its cultural, physical, and aesthetic standards.[10] But the political import of whiteness studies lies in their capacity to link white ethnic empowerment with race-specific inequalities. As a center of racial and cultural normativity, whiteness does not merely represent the standard against which other categories of people were measured and evaluated. In addition, it stands for "an oppressive ideological construct that promoted in the past and maintains in the present social inequalities" (Newitz and Wray 1997, 3); as such, it is constituted by practices that consent to racial domination. Nobel laureate (1993) and distinguished professor Toni Morrison (1994a) speaks about these practices as "race talk," the "most enduring and efficient rite of passage into American culture": "The explicit insertion into everyday life of racial signs and symbols that have no meaning other than pressing African Americans to the lowest level of the racial hierarchy" (98). Consenting to race talk means embracing whiteness. The failure to challenge "negative appraisals of the native-born black populations" (ibid.) was the single most important variable that opened the immigrant path of opportunity. In his autobiography, labor historian Dan Georgakas (2006) affirms this position, showing how it was immigrants' fear of stigmatization and retribution by white society—not inherent racism— that led to their passive consent to whiteness:

> [I] ask[ed] my father why his bar was racially segregated. I knew he had no personal animus toward blacks, so I wanted to know why blacks were not welcomed at his bar. He replied that The Sportsman's Bar, like all the worker bars on Jefferson Avenue, was already segregated when he arrived in the city. Greek bar owners, even if they had wanted to do so, were in no position to challenge the color line. The result would have been empty stools and tables at the least, more likely broken windows, smashed heads, and possibly worse. (263)

Whiteness studies have been effective in showing that race talk permeates social discourse even when not making explicit references to race or racism. The notion of model ethnicity, for instance, stigmatizes African Americans and works against their political interests, such as affirmative action, though it abstains from directly mentioning race. By explaining mobility on the basis of cultural values, it masks institutional practices that historically have limited or taken away opportunities from racial minorities. Anthropologist Karen Brodkin (1998) makes this point forcefully in regard to Jewish whiteness: "The construction of Jewishness as a model minority is part of a larger American racial discourse in which whiteness, to understand itself, depends upon an invented and contrasting blackness as its evil (and sometimes enviable) twin" (151). Giving "rise to a new, cultural way of discussing race" (145), ethnic pluralism eschews the burning issue of the role played by the political economy of race in structuring hierarchies. Similarly, avoiding consideration of how white ethnics commonly disassociate themselves from whiteness and instead privilege their ethnic identities fails to interrogate how white ethnics are still immersed in white privilege. As Annalee Newitz and Matt Wray (1997) make clear, "[m]aking whiteness visible to whites—exposing the discourses, the social and cultural practices, and the material conditions that cloak whiteness and hide its dominating effect—is a necessary part of any anti-racist project" (3–4).[11]

The "white ethnic community, since the late 1970s, is no longer a hot topic for academic papers and popular cultural accounts," stated one of its most authoritative interpreters in the 1990s (di Leonardo 1994, 181). Its "transformed construction . . . remains 'on hold.' . . . [It] stands backstage, ready to reenter stage left or right on cue" (ibid.). Of course, white ethnics still possess academic cachet within whiteness studies, in which they are analyzed in terms of their historical incorporation into whiteness, as I earlier pointed out. A thread in this scholarship rightly interrogates those social structures that treated European immigrants and their descendants preferentially, while it criticizes the historical complicity of assimilated ethnics in the oppression of racial minorities. It calls attention to the political implications of early immigrant discrimination as a means of white ethnic participation in the discourse of racial victimization. Asserting "that no single group has a monopoly on being a victim" (Gallagher 1996, 349) carries political valence, as it contests race-based affirmative action policies. Construed in this manner, white ethnicity and its expressive cultures are out of vogue in departments of ethnic and racial studies presently preoccupied with alterity oppression, minority status, and marginality. But the construction of white ethnicity has been gaining momentum in popular culture, representing the intensification of an ongoing trend in numerous venues engaging with ethnicity, such as narrative and documentary film, standup comedy, television series, autobiography, fiction, ethnography, and history. No longer on hold, this production of white ethnicity has attracted increasing scholarly interest, particularly in the context of ethnic revival and roots (Jacobson 2006).

On another academic front, it was sociology, notably the work of Herbert Gans (1979), that launched white ethnicity to the forefront of research as "symbolic ethnicity," a situational deployment of "easily expressed and felt" cultural symbols (9). Ethnicity was seen as a choice, a fleeting attachment, a nostalgic return to the immigrant past. It was discussed as a matter of sorting through the closet of one's ancestral memorabilia, family traditions, and the available stock of ethnic manifestations to *choose* those aspects that most suited an individual's needs. Symbolic ethnicity subsequently received its most systematic examination and exposition by Mary Waters (1990), and, embraced by prominent sociologists of ethnicity in the United States, most notably Richard Alba (1990), it became a powerful interpretive tool to explicate identity among middle-class, assimilated white ethnics.

The academic success of thinking of ethnicity as choice is due, in no small measure, to the capacity of its practitioners to tap into and authoritatively interpret an enduring social phenomenon: the persistence of ethnic identification among the highly assimilated descendants of European immigrants in America in the post–civil rights era. Symbolic ethnicity effectively addressed a pressing sociological question, namely why ethnicity persisted among middle-class white suburbanites. The answer privileged the notion of ethnicity as an individual's voluntary connection with selective aspects of ethnic culture—professional organizations, parades, and festivals—that suited the need for personal fulfillment through temporary ethnic belonging. Such largely unforced belonging counteracted alienation, and its ephemeral nature freed individuals from the traditional experience of ethnicity as an all-encompassing obligation. This conceptualization marked a fundamental shift in understanding the form and function of ethnicity. It signaled a drastic departure from the classic understanding of ethnicity as a force that determines an individual's biography (occupation, selection of spouse, place of residence, behavior). Practitioners of symbolic ethnicity reversed this model, assigning to the individual the power to exploit ethnicity, now seen as a cultural resource that could be manipulated almost at will. White ethnics, then, embodied a historical transformation in the way ethnicity was experienced and practiced. Unlike their grandparents, who followed the dictates of ancestral ways, they were endowed with the agency to script their own ethnic repertoires. Having no need of ethnicity for purposes of adaptation, generations of assimilated ethnics expressed their identities in ways quite different from those used by previous generations, this time in readily available and contextually activated ethnic symbols. Ethnicity "takes on an expressive rather than instrumental function in people's lives," Gans (1979, 9) suggested, framing symbolic ethnicity as a matter of enjoyment and leisure, a set of "easy and intermittent ways of expressing" identity (8). Ethnicity entailed manipulation of culture for the purposes of temporary belonging to a collective and of connecting—most often nostalgically—with the immigrant past. Individual choice was emphasized, and the significance of ethnic structures in the making of identities was severely downplayed.

Powerful academic narratives invite scholars and the wider public to think of white ethnics in terms of a polarized duality. On the one hand, these populations are known as previously stigmatized entities that eventually were granted access to whiteness; subsequently, the question of how these populations utilized white privilege to become complicit in the subordination and exclusion of nonwhites becomes of paramount importance. On the other hand, white ethnics are represented as the apotheosis of ethnic celebrationism, parading their distinct hyphenated ethnicities in public and treasuring them privately, albeit in a fleeting, superficial manner. While neither of these accounts is incorrect, one is confronted with an urgent question: is that all there is? If we uniformly hold white ethnics hostage to the notion of oppressive whites or, alternatively, treat them as innocuous ethnic caricatures, we simplify a heterogeneous constituency and neutralize its progressive politics. For, although assimilated into whiteness to a large degree, segments of these populations have not ceased to contest racial oppression or to create culturally textured worlds.[12] White ethnics creatively explore their past, define their values, perform their culture, contest or reproduce whiteness, and seek connections with ancestral homelands. Still, academic writings often represent them as lacking enduring cultural moorings; they are increasingly dismissed as superficial and trivial and are relegated to the sphere of leisure and consumption. The complex web of embodied practices that organize individual action is ignored, not because of inconsequentiality in an individual's life but because of the lack of an adequate model to accommodate their complexity and relevance.

It becomes imperative, then, to undertake a critical project that takes into account multiple facets of white ethnicity and to address their social implications in the present through an explicit politics of knowledge. This includes the interrogation of academic work that culturally caricatures and imposes an unfounded homogeneity on white ethnicity. Long overdue is a critical study of texts and practices that engages with often-cited academic topoi of white ethnicity: identity as choice, cultural superficiality, panethnicity, assimilation, and antiminority politics. Such a critical venture must undoubtedly contest white ethnic constellations that, under various guises and emerging configurations, have a negative effect on vulnerable collectives. It must expose and criticize white ethnic narratives that explicitly or implicitly contribute to the devaluation and domination of racial minorities. But such a scholarly project should not conveniently forget to identify instances in which those who have been already inscribed as whites interrogate the category from within and imagine alternative social futures for themselves and others.

White Ethnicity through the Lens of Popular Ethnography

In this work, I explore white ethnicity in a specific site of cultural production, popular ethnography. I closely analyze texts and practices whose authors, all nonacademics, deploy idioms and build on methodologies associated with the academic discourses of anthropology and folklore. For their data collection these authors depend on ethnographic methods of documentation: participant observation and interviewing. Drawing material from autoethnography and family biography is common. The authors invariably refer to and engage with anthropological and social science concepts, some in vogue, others outdated: folklore, tribe, native, ethnicity, diaspora, and heritage, for example. Their analytical concerns resonate with the ethnographic interest in local culture, transnational ties, personal testimony, and identity politics. Though interdisciplinary in scope, the body of works that I consider exhibits the ethnographic imagination to translate social realities—in this case ethnic, immigrant, or preimmigrant pasts—in terms meaningful in the present.[13]

None of the authors whose work I analyze are professional anthropologists or folklorists, though some style themselves ethnic historians-cum-lay-folklorists and are recognized as such in academic and professional circles. Others situate themselves as feminists, or pilgrim ethnographers. They initiate oral history projects, publish essays on immigrant folklore, curate exhibits of material culture, or even undertake fieldwork and write popularly and academically acclaimed ethnographies. Their work reaches wide-ranging audiences—both the lay public and scholars—through a wide variety of publishing venues and genres of writing—journal articles, monographs, popular essays, academic and popular books, documentaries, and museum exhibits.[14]

Its accessibility to wide audiences makes popular ethnography of particular analytical importance. The extensive circulation of popular accounts is in no small measure due to the saturation of the public sphere with ethnic commodities targeting niche audiences, a process that I discuss in chapter 2. Public sites of multiculturalism—including ethnic festivals or parades, children's entertainment, museum exhibits, television programs, films, documentaries, the ethnic studies section in bookstores, as well as ethnic studies programs in universities—bring ethnicity into national consciousness. Ethnic marketers and producers are in a position to reach consumers of ethnic products in the "sacred" space of middle-class life, the entertainment center. Under these conditions, popular ethnographies become key texts through which the public encounters and acquires knowledge about ethnic and immigrant Others. They also work as venues through which audiences may reflect on practices, ideas, and images of ethnicity and race. As Anna Karpathakis and Victor Roudometof (2004, 279) report, Helen Papanikolas's family biography *Emily-George* shapes how Greek immigrants in New York City explain ethnic mobility and race-based socioeconomic stratification. In the "age of ethnography" (Lambropoulos 1997, 199), market forces and the ideology of multiculturalism intersect to intensify the valence of popular ethnography about ethnicity in the American public sphere. Therefore, popular ethnographies urgently demand scholarly attention precisely because of their capacity to bring ethnicity deep into the cultural fabric of the nation.

In the broadest terms, my work examines how popular ethnography produces accounts about ethnicity in relation to immigrant pasts. I engage with this production and circulation by asking how popular ethnography intersects with the transnational and intranational movement of people, values, and ideas. I am interested in analyzing how nonprofessional ethnographers map the specific political and social geographies where cultures take root or become rerouted, are dismantled, reworked, or revived at given historical moments and under identifiable relations of power. In other words, how does popular ethnography produce ideas and traditions that have traveled across space and through time—specifically across transnational fields, through generations, within immigrant collectivities, or in the psychic and social worlds of individuals—and beyond the boundaries of ethnicity in conversation with dominant discourses, all in identifiable historical moments.

Popular Ethnography and Professional Anthropology: Flows and Circulations

Popular ethnographies are venues through which American ethnics imbue the past with value and make or unmake whiteness; they therefore lend themselves to addressing the central question of this book, namely the manner in which the production of usable pasts illuminates contours of white ethnicity. To investigate this process, I turn to a social space widely perceived as white ethnic, Greek America. A complex, variegated terrain, Greek America resists a single definition. Since its formative years, arguably in the early twentieth-century mass labor migration, Greek America has built upon a variety of pasts for different purposes. At various times, institutions or individuals have appropriated the past to accommodate both progressive working-class politics and middle-class conformism; radicalism as well as political conservatism; pioneering, boundary-crossing gender activism along with gender oppression; model ethnic success together with social failure; advocacy on behalf of minority interests alongside practices of antiminority politics; dense transnational connections with preimmigration regions of origin and Greece as well as patterns of reorientation away from the ancestral homeland.

Popular ethnography is a convenient point of entry into Greek America. The cultural archive facilitates inquiry because individuals variously connected to it have long been taking the interpretation of ethnicity into their own hands. They translate the current fascination with memory, roots, identity, and personal testimony into a rich ethnographic record. These authors regularly enjoy participation in mainstream institutions and access to academic knowledge. They exploit folklore methods to collect and analyze oral histories, to script and produce nationally circulated documentaries, to curate exhibits, and to write their own ethnographies based on long-term participant observation. Educated and attuned to the cultural politics of ethnic representation, nonprofessional ethnographers of Greek America have created a corpus of ethnographic texts— sometimes uncomplicated, often highly sophisticated, and invariably ideologically charged. The majority of these ethnographers have capitalized on the enabling conditions of multiculturalism. Their work has been supported by ethnic, national, and commercial institutions: festivals, academic and popular presses, universities, state cultural organizations, preservationist societies, community organizations, museums, and public television are among the institutional spaces that contribute to and even finance their production.

By way of introducing the complex ethnographic terrain of Greek America, I offer here the broadest possible historical survey of cross-fertilization between professional and popular ethnographies. In 1911, Henry Pratt Fairchild, a Yale-trained anthropologist, relied on social Darwinism and cultural evolutionism to deny Greek immigrants an immediate place in American modernity. His findings were confronted in the early 1920s by a self-reflexive popular anthropology generated by a Greek immigrant elite (see Anagnostou 2004a). Professional folklorist Richard Dorson (1977) argued that folk beliefs survived among Greek Americans during the nascency of multiculturalism in the mid-1950s. In contrast, popular folklorist Helen Papanikolas (1984) reached the opposite conclusion; she declared the total disappearance of Greek immigrant folk culture in post–World War II America. Feminist popular ethnographer Constance Callinicos (1990) drew on anthropological studies of gender in Greece and Greek America, including the work of noted professional ethnographer Ernest Friedl, to subvert ethnic patriarchy and reclaim tradition for Greek American women. In the process, Callinicos's politics of transgression reproduced the evolutionist assumptions of Fairchild's colonialist anthropology. More recently, in 2003, popular ethnographer Michael Kalafatas, an admissions officer at Brandeis University, conducted fieldwork on his ancestral island of Symi in order to examine the political economy of the sponge-diving tradition in Greece and in Greek communities in the United States and Australia. Well versed in the anthropology of Greece— carrying into the field, so to speak, Michael Herzfeld's *Poetics of Manhood* (1985) and David Sutton's *Memories Cast in Stones* (1998)—he advanced an allegorical reading of sponge diving.

Usable pasts are often produced through collaboration between—or juxtaposition of—professional and popular ethnographers. Anna Caraveli for instance, well known for her work on ritual laments in Greece, collaborated with professional *and* nonprofessional folklorists to bring to fruition "Scattered in Foreign Lands: A Greek Village in Baltimore" (1985), an exhibit on the transnational circulation of tradition. The now defunct periodical *Laografia: A Journal of the International Greek Folklore Society* regularly published articles on Greek folklore by both professional and popular ethnographers. Ethnographers have contested one another's interpretations, as well. For example, professional historian Theodore Saloutos (1956) conducted a popular ethnography among repatriated immigrants, traveling throughout Greece to collect oral accounts about the experience of repatriation between 1908 and 1924. A respected scholar in the American academy, Saloutos identified but never resolved the methodological challenge of establishing the reliability of the information he collected. Dully noting the partiality of the data, he nevertheless showed no hesitation in drawing authoritative conclusions about the negative consequences of what he saw as underdevelopment in the lives of the repatriated immigrants. Yet he abstained from claiming to a total truth, "trust[ing] that future scholars" would build on his findings and "adduce new information to provide the fuller story" of the repatriated immigrants (xv). Almost half a century later, professional anthropologist Penelope Papailias (2005) cast an entirely different methodological net through the archive of immigrant repatriation to reach a conclusion contrary to that of Saloutos. In her ethnography on the poetics of historical production in Greece, she analyzed the writing, circulation, and reception of a diary written in 1951 by a certain Yiorgos Yiannis Ilias Mandas, an immigrant who ultimately returned to Greece in 1922 after a painful working-class experience in the United States. In her analysis of this account, written by a subject who might well have served as the historian's informant, Papailias questioned Saloutos's underdevelopment thesis. The professional historian-cum-popular ethnographer had posited underdevelopment in Greece as the source of alienation and disenchantment among repatriated immigrants. In contrast, the professional anthropologist pointed to the contingencies of history, specifically the German occupation and the Greek Civil War, as the causal factors disrupting the socially and politically meaningful life of a repatriated immigrant.

The more closely one examines the ways in which popular ethnography intersects with professional anthropology, the richer the implications about their convergences and divergences become. Take, for instance, a specific textual example,

Papanikolas's (2002) reading of Herzfeld's (1986a) analysis of Greek folklore as a national institution. Here one witnesses how a nationalist reading of Greek identity overdetermines the popular ethnographer's reading of the professional anthropologist, whose analysis she closely follows and generously quotes:

> "Folklore studies" in other countries "played an important part" in forming a national identity "before statehood," but "the Greek scholars were unusual in having folklore studies virtually forced on them by events" [Herzfeld (1986a, 12)]. . . . The Greek folklorists were intent on showing that classical Greek civilization was the foundation of European culture and that contemporary Greek culture was directly descended from ancient Greece. They set out to prove Greeks were European, not Asiatic as was commonly believed. (47)

Such a reading comes close to recognizing Herzfeld's main thesis, namely that folklorists work ideologically and that the folk are a social construct rather than the embodiment of a national essence. But, in fact, Papanikolas reads the professional anthropologist's analysis literally, as an objective datum that validates the idea of a racially inherent national character. This is made clear once we juxtapose Herzfeld's point about the folkloristic construction of Greek individualism with Papanikolas's interpretation of it:

> Stressing the ethnic purity of the Greeks, she [folklorist Dora d'Istria] argued that this was revealed in a unique combination of heroism and, as the quoted passages show, individualism. (Herzfeld 1986a, 59)

> The remarkable folklorist Dora d'Istria, a Romanian princess of Albanian origin, said the ethnic purity of the Greeks was "revealed in a unique combination of heroism . . . and individualism" (Herzfeld 1986[a], 59). (Papanikolas 2002, 49)

The two quotes are brought to bear on two divergent understandings of folklore. For Michael Herzfeld, the writings of Dora d'Istria drew selectively upon nationalist folklore and misconstrued indigenous cultural categories to present the Greek folk as unadulterated heirs of the ancient Greeks. Such a construction made d'Istria—whose work on Greek folklore gained her "Hellenic nationality by a special decree of Parliament" (55)—the ideological kin of nineteenth-century Greek nationalist folklorists. For these scholars, discovering expressions of individualism among the folk meant that this trait, which was seen as the defining attribute of Homeric heroes, had persevered as an essential element of the

Greek race and, therefore, as pure national character, in spite of foreign occupations. Individualism functioned as a mirror of racial continuity that reflected the Hellenicity of the peasants (*laos*). Moreover, its relative abundance or lack established proximity or distance from a prized, authentic European connection. Hence Greek folklorists established a hierarchical scale of Balkan individualisms, in which the Greeks were accorded the crown of its most genuine, pure form. Because Greek individualism signaled identification with ancient Hellas, and Hellas, in turn, was "the cultural exemplar of Europe" (5), the survival of individualism underscored the Hellenic origins of European civilization. "If Greece had been the *fons et origo* of all Europe," Herzfeld (1986a) writes, "then Greek folklore would enshrine the quintessence of the European spirit" (55).

In contrast to the social constructivists, Papanikolas (2002) reads Herzfeld's quote of d'Istria as a literalist would, as evidence that Greeks *are* in fact individualists "to the depths of their being" (49). Ironically, an analysis that aims to expose the constructedness of national character is relied upon as evidence that substantiates that character. In this instance, the nineteenth-century folklorists become the ideological ancestors of a twentieth-century popular folklorist in Greek America. In this model, the immigrant folk *are* natural heirs of undiluted Hellenic culture. The identity of Greek Americans as staunch individualists, an ideological claim in Greek America that I will discuss in chapter 2, is sustained.

This close reading of a specific juncture of popular ethnography and professional anthropology gives shape to a crucial contour of white ethnicity: the power of the immigrant past to constitute ethnicity. Instead of vanishing with the dissolution of the folk *Gemeinschaft,* as Papanikolas has elsewhere argued (see Anagnostou 2008a), ethnicity continues to exercise a powerful grip beyond the immigrant cohort, well into the second generation. In fact, in this instance, social discourse, namely nationalism, determines an ethnic reading of anthropological scholarship. Furthermore, the popular ethnographer approaches ethnicity in the same way that a nineteenth-century Greek nationalist folklorist would approach the nation, but with one crucial difference: if early Greek folklorists produced an idealized image of the folk for the purposes of nation building, Papanikolas faced a different predicament. As we will see in chapter 3, her narratives on folkness and the degree of her connection with the vernacular were mediated by her own social proximity to ethnic traditions, which induced her to draw rigid boundaries between herself and aspects of the immigrant culture. At the same time, as I will show, her experience created an ambivalent location of identification with and disassociation from the folk, furnishing the background of a popular ethnographer's particular investment in the making of usable pasts.

Popular Ethnography and Ethnic Roots

The quest for ethnic roots in the ancestral homeland produces yet another nexus of popular ethnography, this time in the transnational plane of Greece, America, and Greek America. In surveying the accounts of "ethnic travelers" born outside Greece—Theodore Saloutos, a social scientist; Daphne Athas, a fiction and travel writer; and Elias Kulukundis, a writer—Yiorgos Kalogeras (1998, 703) identifies a profound identity crisis that defines the encounter with the preimmigration homeland in the 1960s. This anxiety arises when the returning ethnic subject experiences the site of travel as both familiar and alien, as both known and foreign. The discourse positing Greece as the origin of the West frames the cultural literacy of the ethnic travelers. What is more, their ethnic descent qualifies them to claim the ancestral culture as authentically their own. But the actual encounter generates the crisis. Everyday social realities are alien and alienating. They pollute the Western image of Greece, accentuating the distance between the ideal and the real. The travelers have arrived too late to partake in the genius of Greece and so suffer "the anxiety of belatedness" (705). Repatriation, therefore, foregrounds a crisis of identity; it triggers a reflective process about cross-cultural connection and the representation of otherness. Greeks through filiation and Americans through affiliation, the ethnic travelers negotiate the disorienting experience of Greece as a familiar alterity largely through the lenses of ahistoricity and Orientalism. The cultural distance between Greece as a literary and an ethnographic topos is understood hierarchically. The United States is seen as the pinnacle of progress and cultural completion, whereas Greece is seen as corrupt and irredeemable, generating contempt in the observers. Greece's own distinct modernity is not recognized by the returnees and is therefore denied. The resolution of the crisis lies in the narrative identification of the travelers with the source of affiliation, with dominant narratives about what it means to be an American. The reinvention of identity, as Kalogeras argues, "implements neither the masking of a Greek American nor the expression of a displaced American identity; it simply consolidates their sociopolitical 'reinscription' in US culture" (721). "It should come, then, as no surprise," he writes, "that ethnic writers so often . . . perceive that their political and cultural empowerment lies in their ties to the US, rather than in other spaces, even if they are designated as pre-American mother/fatherlands" (722). But still, the quest for roots yields alternative representations of peasant life in Greece. Visiting the ancestral village in the hope of discovering clues that could explain his grandfather's life, James Chressanthis (1982) created a popular ethnographic documentary on the experience of those who never followed their immigrant relatives to the United States. The documentary's stark realism records the annual cycle of economic activities as well as poverty, hardship, ritual, expressive culture, and narratives about loss and separation. But unlike the ambivalent ethnic travelers, the popular ethnographer turns into an admiring witness of human beings struggling to sustain meaningful lives amid adversity. It is more this focus on the present than the effort to retrieve fragments from the past that guides the concluding humanistic message, namely the praise of the village's human vitality.

From this broad outline, Greek America emerges as a social field crisscrossed with transnational and intranational flows of people and knowledge, one replete with contradictions, competing interpretations of ethnicity, and intellectual affinities but also with significant disjunctures. This circulation relates to all sorts of all sorts of movements: the traffic of anthropological methodologies and knowledge between the academy and the public sphere; fieldwork and the international circulation of ethnographic texts; the appropriation of the politics of feminism for the purpose of representing gender and ethnicity; American multiculturalism and the quest for ethnic roots; preimmigration traditions animated through the work of ethnics-turned-ethnographers; and the work of scholars who translate academic concepts to ethnic constituencies. Though largely produced in the United States, this cultural archive has been the result of dense transnational permutations and the permeability of boundaries between specialized professional knowledge and generalized popular interpretation. This traffic of meaning has produced a true interpretive polyphony. At any one time, Greek immigrants have been variously represented as outside the boundaries of whiteness but also at the center of it; as vanishing but also enduring folk; as successful but also failed white ethnics; and as politically invested but also apolitical subjects. The ethnographic richness of the field of Greek America makes the reading of popular ethnography a fruitful point of analytical departure.

This proliferation of popular ethnography contrasts with the embarrassing dearth of academic Greek American anthropology and folklore. Whereas in Greece a vital political function turned folklore into a socially and politically instrumental and autonomous academic discipline (Herzfeld 1986a), anthropological and folklore studies in Greek America have never enjoyed the visibility and prestige of their transnational counterparts in institutions of higher learning. The reasons for such marginality in the academy are complex. They include historically variable academic ideologies of what counts as a legitimate ethnographic subject, the lack of economic and cultural capital that would have enabled early immigrants to gain access to the university and to dominant cultural institutions, and the immigrants' instrumentalist view of education as a means for socioeconomic mobility. Until very recently, this investment in producing "professional entrepreneurs" resulted in a historical reluctance to invest in education in the social sciences and the humanities (Kourvetaris 1989, 125).[15] On the other hand, the abundance of popular ethnography on Greek America can be explained in relation to histories of controlling matters of ethnic self-representation. As a group of internal Others within the United States who were subjected to negative representation by the mainstream, including disparaging anthropological accounts, the first wave of early twentieth-century Greek immigrants to the United States deployed their own narratives about the place of their traditions vis-à-vis the nation's history. Lacking access to institutions of higher learning, they relied on their own intellectual elite, who targeted mainstream and immigrant audiences to articulate at a popular level a theory about ethnic origins, culture, identity, and belonging. The fact that such cultural politics of controlling self-representation proved an effective tool for acceptance, power, material gains, and prestige may partially explain the tradition of popular ethnography currently in full swing in Greek America, a tradition boosted, as I mentioned earlier, by the current fascination with ethnic identity and roots.

Metaethnography as Critical Intervention: Managing the Ethnographic Field

A vexing issue remains. How does one manage this metaethnographic field? More precisely, what kind of politics must guide one's metaethnographic reading of the vast multitude of texts and practices that vie for inclusion under the rubric of popular ethnography? For in an era of blurred genres (Geertz 1983), ethnic festivals, popular periodicals, ethnic and immigrant family biographies, autobiographies, folk dance performances, documentaries, and museum exhibits on ethnicity are all components of generalized ethnography. The producers of these ethnography-centered cultural products (self-proclaimed folklorists, oral-history collectors, community archivists, librarians turned ethnic preservationists, authors of immigrant narratives, documentary makers, or "folk" folklorists) are literally everywhere. Under these conditions, sorting out what to analyze and what to exclude from analysis becomes an acute methodological challenge. What are the criteria that will allow the displacement of some texts and the privileging of others? What are the politics of reading that will position a metaethnographer to negotiate responsibly this fuzzy, anarchic, and vastly complex field? Inherently ideological, contested, and infused with relations of power, this terrain requires methodological management, a strategic containment through an explicit politics of knowledge.[16]

I do not claim to read Greek American popular ethnographies from a position of disinterest. The "remaking of social analysis" (Rosaldo 1993) has made it epistemologically and politically impossible to claim a detached Archimedean point from which an omniscient scholar surveys the social field independent of power relations, material and ideological interests, and prior knowledge. Critical reflexivity demands the explicit recognition of the analyst's subject position rather than a pretension to objectivity. It goes without saying that my current institutional location in a modern Greek studies program motivates my "choice" of Greek America as the focus of my analysis. Teaching and research in this academic field require that Greek-related topics become an indispensable component of my interest in producing and disseminating knowledge. The explicit recognition of this position helps me further sharpen the focus on my politics of knowledge. I draw my critical agenda from a body of scholarship that consistently reflects on the critical function and relevance of modern Greek studies, an academic field that operates at the institutional fringes of the American academy.

As Gregory Jusdanis (1991, 11) writes, "Disciplines like modern Greek, though marginalized at the university, need not be irrelevant. . . . Instead of bewailing their banishment to the fringe they can benefit from their ostracism by conducting a critique of the center." Writing from such a position demarcates my critical vantage point. I interrogate hegemonic academic practices whose unexamined disciplinary assumptions or politics contain the range of available meanings associated with white ethnicity or, alternatively, promote its social and political trivialization. From this angle, I wish to intervene strategically and to confront influential scholarly trends in sociology and race studies that represent European ethnicities in terms of dissolution, closure, and disposability.[17] My aim is to survey the complexity of Greek America and to select for analysis those texts that make accessible a set of meanings not otherwise available in dominant academic narratives about white ethnicities. While I do not shy away from interrogating dominant white ethnic narratives for their complicity in generating ahistorical accounts of diversity, I also showcase those usable pasts that challenge hegemonic interpretations in the sociology of ethnicity. In this respect, my work raises broad interpretive questions and redraws the conceptual boundaries in the study of white ethnicities. For instance, whereas scholars who privilege race as an analytical category project the weakening of collective ethnic identities, I illuminate usable pasts constructed to forge enduring group commitments. In addition, if symbolic ethnicity privileges choice in the making of ethnic identities, I demonstrate the importance of social discourses and history in determining identities. In my analysis, white ethnicity emerges as a heterogeneous social field constituted by agency and cultural determination, ambivalence and certainty, open-endedness and closure, private creativity and collective belonging—an uneven field marked by contested cultural boundaries and defined by alternative social meanings.

The organization of this book reflects my aim to intervene and problematize current academic discussions of white ethnicity. In chapter 1, I introduce the core analytical framework of this work. I discuss how a selective corpus of narrative and visual texts (professional folklore, an inchoate popular ethnography, a photograph, a newspaper editorial, and the writings of an intellectual) produces usable ethnic pasts, and I situate these texts in relation to history and social discourse. It is at this point that I demonstrate the pitfalls of analyzing ethnicity on the basis of texts alone and instead make a case for the utility of a discourse-centered, historical approach to ethnicity. I show, in other words, how texts intersect with history and discourse. To this end, I include an analysis of an inchoate popular ethnography, a text extracted from an interview that a professional folklorist conducted with members of an ethnic family. By reembedding this textual fragment in history and examining its relation to various social discourses, I show how this method helps interrogate scholarly and popular constructions of the folk and to enrich our understanding of the production of usable ethnic pasts.

In chapter 2, I continue to critically probe scholarly works that produce generalized meanings about ethnicity. I specifically take to task claims about the uniform decline of deep cultural commitments among white ethnics. Here, I turn on its head the common view of assimilation as cultural loss and examine assimilation—paradoxically—as production of ethnic particularity. For this purpose I analyze a documentary film as a narrative that assimilates Greek America into ethnic whiteness while simultaneously reproducing ethnicity as enduring collective obligation to a specific form of cultural affiliation.

In chapter 3, I further interrogate the notion of the dissolution of collective ethnicity and therefore complicate the proposition of entirely privatized white ethnic identities. Tracing the historical contour of gender construction in Greek America, I illuminate why and how two specific popular ethnographers produce competing versions of ethnic community and, therefore, polyphonies of collective Greek American belonging. Taken together, these constructions challenge the ideology of ethnicity as a homogeneous culture.

In chapter 4, I enter the political minefield of popular ethnography as cultural critique. I probe popular ethnographies that decidedly and unambiguously indict Greek America from within, leveling charges of racism and complicity in ideologies of whiteness. Sensitive to the significance of these internal critiques—but also vigilant as to the implications—I carefully discuss their politics and poetics, illuminating the consequences of white racial domination of vulnerable minorities.

Within this context, I showcase an ethnic intellectual who advocates an antiracist politics based on social solidarity between white ethnics and racial minorities.

In chapters 5 and 6, I undertake a long-overdue critique of the ideology of white ethnic identity as choice. In chapter 5, I examine one popular ethnographer's quest for roots, analyzing this ethnography of travel as a site of identity formation. I show how culture and history powerfully mediate if not partly determine this narrative construction of identity. In chapter 6, I continue this critical polemic through an alternative reading of the popular ethnography of travel, this time focusing on the historical routes of ethnic meanings. The analytical shift from roots to routes enables me to situate the current production of usable pasts historically and to place ethnicity in terms of cultural domination and power relations. I show that a historical approach to white ethnicity directs one away from the mystifying ideology of choice and toward a view of whiteness as a process of contextual negotiation and oppression, in which certain ethnic "options" become available or privileged (or, more precisely, are produced as options) while others are displaced, stigmatized, or even eliminated.

The conclusion points to a dramatic tension in how popular ethnographies construct white ethnicity. Ethnicity may be seen as a richly textured social terrain but also as a culturally impoverished landscape. It may be seen as a site that requires historical memory for its realization or, alternatively, as a site that affords the opportunity to actualize without it. And it may sustain antiracist politics or appropriate for itself social privileges at the expense of racial minorities. This polyphony complicates the current thinking of ethnic whiteness as a culturally superficial and uniformly antiminority field. My work identifies those usable pasts offering an enticing model that ratifies a progressive present and shapes a promising future. A corpus of popular ethnographies rewrites pasts as contemporary resources that inspire commitment to social justice, drive an ethic of care, shape meaningful lives, counter amnesia, and inform creative performances of identity. As they do so, they convey a powerful critique, expressed as structure of feeling that interrogates the relegation of ethnicity to the realm of a cultural wasteland. Certain popular ethnographers writing within Greek America caution us that histories of assimilation and cultural caricaturing jeopardize the obligation of ethnics to remember historically, urging us not to forget that dominant groups crush minorities and exclude the most vulnerable of the population. And the ethnographers powerfully feel that this act of domination must not be repeated in the present, now that white ethnics are perhaps closer than ever in their aspiration to hegemony.

CHAPTER ONE

The Politics and Poetics of Popular Ethnography

Folk Immigrant, Ethnic, and Racial Pasts in History and Discourse

> We must therefore read the great canonical texts, and perhaps
> also the entire archive of modern and pre-modern European
> and American culture, with an effort to draw out, extend,
> give emphasis and voice to what is silent or marginally
> present or ideologically represented . . . in such works.
>
> —Edward W. Said, *Culture and Imperialism*

IN THIS SCHOLARLY intervention, I rely neither on statistical data to tabulate objective patterns of cultural retention or loss nor on interviews and surveys to identify degrees of subjective attachment to ethnicity. The aim is not the collection of statistically significant evidence that disrupts conventional interpretations of white ethnicity. Instead, I build on the close reading of texts. I undertake the critical reading of a selected corpus of popular ethnographies to examine how ethnic meanings are produced and what this production tells us about white ethnicity. In other words, I explore how and why these ethnographies construct ethnicity by asking the following broad questions: Who defines usable pasts, where, for what purpose, and under what conditions? What are the uses of the past in each case, and how do they reproduce or contest ethnic whiteness?

I analyze this textual corpus by foregrounding ethnicity as a heterogeneous social field defined by similarities but also by internal differences, conflict and consensus, consistency and contradiction, resistance and accommodation, negotiation and consent. That is, I offer a venue to investigate ethnicity not as a shared culture, but as a field of contested meanings. Here I draw on a particular Gramscian thread of cultural studies that examines culture as a field "marked by a struggle to articulate, disarticulate, and rearticulate particular meanings, particular ideologies, particular politics" (Storey 2003, xi). If "[m]eaning is always a social production, a human practice," white ethnicity must be seen in terms of texts and practices that contribute to its making. And white ethnicity cannot generate a single, authoritative interpretation of the past: "because different meanings can be ascribed to the same thing, meaning is always the site and the result of struggle" (ibid.).

I have already identified my object of analysis: popular ethnography. As interpretive descriptions of social life, these ethnographic accounts conveniently offer an opportunity to explore the multilayered contours of white ethnicity. In reading ethnographies, I do not assume that these texts offer transparent reflections of reality, faithful mirrors of the worlds they depict. As foundational work on the politics and poetics of ethnography has shown (Clifford and Marcus 1986), ethnographies are narratives that rest on rhetorical strategies of persuasion to establish authority and to produce convincing representations of social life. What this means, of course, is not that ethnographies are lies—and therefore illegitimate sources of knowledge about white ethnicity—but that they tell only partial truths (Clifford 1986a). I draw from this anthropological tradition the insight that attention to how ethnographies make meaning is of particular analytical value in the textual production of usable ethnic pasts. This method of reading becomes useful for interrogating narratives that claim absolute truths about Greek America or white ethnicity. I also use it to recover textual ambiguities, contradictions, silences, and the muting of alternative meanings within a text. Thus, I am interested in the manner in which the politics of ethnicity intertwines with textual poetics. My compass includes the interests that texts serve and the ways in which textual meanings are made rhetorically in the first place. I undertake all this with the goal of writing against culture (Abu-Lughod 1991), that is, disrupting tendencies to represent white ethnicity as a unified whole, a single demarcated culture.

I do not merely analyze texts. Ethnographic truths are embedded in broader impersonal structures and must be situated in relation to wider social discourses. I consider, therefore, textual politics and poetics as well as discourse and history. Attention to history and discourse allows me to conceptualize the terrain of ethnicity not in terms of a neatly delineated and already known past. Pasts are not natural facts; instead, they entail knowledge produced at specific moments in history. It becomes of primary analytical importance, then, to identify the specific political and cultural geographies where pasts were created, where they took root or were rerouted, were rejected or revived, were activated or silenced, at any given point in time. In other words, we must carefully scrutinize how tradition or heritage traveled across specific social fields and through identifiable historical moments. For the "recovery of discarded areas, or the redress of selective and reductive interpretations [of tradition]" has little value "unless the lines to the present, in the actual process of selective tradition, are clearly and actively traced" (Williams 1977, 115).

This mapping is necessary if we wish to understand the current modification, preservation, elimination, valorization, or deprecation of the past as a *historical process*. It is an enormous task, this comprehensive excavation of a multitude of relations, and it lies beyond the scope of this book. I merely make a gesture toward initiating this project; I *start* mapping only some dimensions of this process. In this chapter, for example, I enter this terrain through the analysis of *selective* representations in which claims about the past intersect with discourses and power relations to produce the meaning of ethnicity. I discuss four key, yet arbitrarily selected, historical moments of ethnic representation.[1] First, I reflect on an ethnographic encounter between a folklorist and a Greek American family in 1955. I move on to analyze a public performance of Greek immigrant identity from a few decades earlier, as captured in a photograph taken during a national commemorative event in Washington, D.C, in 1917. I then discuss a 1907 editorial in the *San Francisco Chronicle* that situated Greek immigrants in relation to racial categories in the United States, in order to reflect on the racial politics of that era vis-à-vis southeastern Europeans. And I continue with an autobiographical narrative by an ethnic intellectual in the 1970s that gave voice to the descendants of southeastern European immigrants in the context of white ethnic revival in America during the civil rights era.

My discussion of these representations demonstrates the utility of combining textual, historical, and discourse analysis to illuminate the complex interrelationships among various discrepant historical constructions of Greeks in the United States as ethnic, folk, white, and white ethnic. I begin this discussion by exploring how, in a specific historical moment and in the writings of a specific scholar, the discourse of folklore constituted Greek ethnicity as folkness. The text here is an extract from an ethnographic depiction of a Greek American family by folklorist Richard Dorson. It comprises excerpts from interviews that members of the family granted to the visiting folklorist. These textual fragments stand as a nascent popular ethnography, neither fully fledged nor textually autonomous. But once they are situated in relation to history and discourse—a task that I undertake in detail below—they foreground the idea that folklorists may miss or misrepresent the perspectives of the people they study.

Ethnicity as Folkness? Academic Constructions

Intellectuals and academics function as crucial agents in assigning significance to the culture of common people—their dances and riddles, songs and lullabies, jokes and celebrations. In fact, as John Storey (2003) shows, they have been instrumental in constituting the categories of the "folk" or "popular." In the context of eighteenth- and nineteenth-century romantic nationalism, for example, it was the learned middle class—book editors, collectors, publishers, artists, and academics—who introduced and subsequently valorized the category of folk culture. Such a classification, Storey notes, extracted from the cultural complexity of peasant experiences an idealized version, which it subsequently posited as the authentic core, the essence of the nation. In this enterprise, intellectuals "discovered" the folk, not because ordinary people did not previously exist but because the learned classes attached to them a historically specific meaning as the embodiment of national virtues and used the state apparatus to disseminate it. By stripping peasants of the authority to function as guardians of their own traditions, the educated bourgeoisie assumed "control of folk culture on behalf of the nation" (5). In the context of a nationalist ideology that posited folk culture as an eternal spirit that connected the present with the authentic origins of the nation, such an appropriation enabled the middle class to assume sole guardianship of the national past. The British Folk Song Society, for example, included among its members distinguished artists, academics, and professionals, but it was not a place where one "could expect to meet members of the folk" (122). Peasants could be interviewed and observed, invited to perform and documented, but they were excluded from membership in prestigious institutions established to preserve folk heritage.

The process of peasant folklorization outlined by Storey underscores an issue central to this book, namely how the past is used to promote social and political interests. "The idea of folk culture was a romantic fantasy," Storey writes, "constructed through denial and distortion. It was a fantasy intended to heal the wounds of the present and safeguard the future by promoting a memory of the past which had little existence outside the intellectual debates of the late eighteenth, nineteenth, and early twentieth centuries" (13). The implications of such cultural engineering were far-reaching. Intellectuals conjured an idealized pastoral folk culture as an "alternative to the rather troublesome specter of the urban-industrial working class" (14). In the context of rapid industrialization and urbanization, the culture of the uneducated masses was seen in terms of a sharp duality. On the one hand, the positively valued folk represented a site of authentic unity and peasant conformity, now threatened by widening class distinctions and labor unrest. On the other hand, the expressive culture of the urban proletariat was stigmatized as vulgar and debased, a potent force that threatened the social order. Such a bifurcation in the meaning of popular culture served as a strategy to discipline the unruly working class. Folk culture, elevated to the status of national heritage, was seen as a pedagogical and political instrument to restore morality and to civilize the masses. It was embraced as a means of creating national unity out of class and cultural disunity. This portrayal of common people, however, bore no resemblance to the rural folk, as it said nothing about the social realities of the peasants. As Charles Keil insisted in his acerbic exchange with Richard Dorson (1978b) regarding the utility of the term "folk," the process of "'folking over' people's lives" (Keil 1978, 264) works as an ideological tool to "mystify the class forces and power differences that structure inequality (Keil 1979, 209). No one but the bourgeoisie and the folklorists need the folk, Keil continues: "[T]here were never any 'folk,' except in the minds of the bourgeoisie. . . . A world of misery and stolen pleasures can become a staged world of song and dance and ever so colorful costumes, . . . a fantasy, a lie, that the bourgeois world needs to believe" (1978, 263).

In this reflexive moment in the history of social sciences, academic folklore can no longer be defined descriptively, as a set of scholarly activities that record and analyze everyday activities—conversations, jokes, dance performances, superstitions, forgotten songs, tales about past heroic deeds. Rather, the discipline is understood as a practice that constitutes the quotidian occurrences that it documents as "folk." In the words of Barbara Kirshenblatt-Gimblett (1998), folklore becomes a "mode of cultural production" that is actualized at the moment when "particular objects and behaviors come to be identified, and understood, as folklore" (305). This process of naming and classifying "create[s] our disciplinary subject, even if those caught in our disciplinary drift net protest" (ibid.). Here, the old metaphor of the ethnographic discipline as an ocean still holds: "Ethnology is like the ocean. All you need is a net, any kind of net; and then if you step into the sea and swing your net about, you're sure to catch some kind of fish" (quoted in Clifford 1988, 134).

The folk are not, then, to be naturally discovered during a folklorist's forays into communities, places of ordinary sociability, and sites of expressive culture. The category "folk" may be alien or irrelevant to the individuals who share a story, worship, or recall a proverb for the benefit of the visiting folklorist. They may manipulate or resist it. Aspects of the everyday behavior of people acquire significance as folklore through social processes often removed from their immediate social experience. It is the discipline of folklore that folklorizes the quotidian.

Producing Greek America as "Folk" (Mid-1950s)

The metaphor of a "disciplinary drift net" points to folklore as an ever-expanding academic field in search of disciplinary subjects. It was such a search that led

Richard Dorson, a neoromantic folklorist vested in the function of immigrant folklore in American modernity (Del Negro 2004, 44), to direct his attention to Greek America. When Dorson made arrangements to interview the Coromboses, an extended Greek family that resided in Iron Mountain, Michigan, he was pursuing a lead he had discovered while teaching a folklore class at Michigan State University. As a site of folklorization, this course was crucial in encouraging Peter (Ted) G. Corombos, a student in the class, to recognize his ethnic family as folk and to contribute material on Greek tradition. The Corombos family was caught in the folklorist's net. His interest sparked, Dorson took it upon himself to continue the process of folklorization through fieldwork. On a fall day in 1955, he set out on the five-hundred-mile drive to Iron Mountain for a pilot study of the family, which spanned three generations.

This field trip was part of a larger academic project. Dorson was invested in demonstrating the resilience and relevance of the premodern past in modernity. He polemically defended the position that urbanization and industrialization did not signal the extinction of this past, which he, like his fellow neoromantics, treated "as a discrete category of culture"—folklore (Del Negro 2004, 47). Maintaining that folkness endured because it functioned as a crucial source of meaning in an alienating modernity, Dorson organized his research around the question "Is there a folk in the city?" (1978a, 29). His fieldwork in rural Michigan was a precursor of future ethnographic work in urban settings, such as Gary and East Chicago, Indiana, where he pursued "the multigroup targets . . . [he] had aimed at in the Upper Peninsula of Michigan in a remote, rural, and small town situation" (ibid.). The emphasis was on ethnicity, and the thrust of the research was to explore how memories among ethnic people help elucidate "the relation of memory culture to New World hyphenated folk culture" (31). Discovering evidence of durable folk cultures was imperative, therefore, to lend credence to his project. To locate "folklore's canonical subject" (Kirshenblatt-Gimblett 1998, 306) in Iron Mountain, that is, to show that the Corombos family had retained its folkness, would prove that premodern ethnicity represented a vital counterforce to modernity. Rather than being obliterated by modernity, immigrant folkways took root in the New World as vital living traditions.

Dorson surveyed major Greek American institutions—the church, the press, community language schools, and voluntary associations—from the position of an omnipotent observer. The circulation of printed material, the practice of institutionalized worship, and teaching in the classroom made Greek America a modern society only in appearance, he argued. Below the modern surface, the folklorist identified a vital folk community. For Dorson, ethnic communities acted as "forces for conservatism" (1977, 156) that enabled the preservation of folkness that he equated with tradition. As he wrote elsewhere, "layer upon layer of folk-cultural traditions lie heaped up in the metropolis" (1978a, 29). He then summarily dismissed as error a rival interpretation advanced by Dorothy Demetracopoulou Lee's "Folklore of the Greeks in America" (1936), a study of Greek immigrant acculturation in the Boston area. Responding to her argument that Old World culture was a functionless vestige of the past, already on the verge of being swallowed by modernity, he wrote:

> [Demetracopoulou Lee's essay] errs in its gloomy forecast for the ancient legacies. Lee fails to consider the forces for conservatism operating in new-fangled America. A solid and cohesive Greek-American community takes root within the metropolis, buttressed by its Greek Orthodox church, parochial schools teaching modern Greek, Greek social and religious clubs, Greek language newspapers distributed from New York. Ties with the homeland remain strong and constant, a fact easily overlooked by the outsider. . . . In such an atmosphere, certain folk traditions endure and prosper. This was my discovery when I visited the Corombos family in northern Michigan one fall day in 1955. (1977, 155–56)

In this account, ethnicity fragments American modernity into coherent patches of enduring folk entities. Cohesive and deeply felt, interethnic ties operate invisibly in proximity to unsuspecting outsiders, as an alternative to modern anomie. The trained folklorist then identifies the folk in the city and reports a case of effective cultural transplantation. Dorson viewed ethnic communities as face-to-face organic entities that, along with transnational ties, assure ethnic traditionalism. Curiously, Dorson asserted the resilience of folk custom in the cohesiveness of the urban enclave but sought evidence of it among immigrants in the relative isolation of rural Michigan. This paradoxical shift impelled him to elaborate on the poetics of his quest for the folk.

"Insofar as one family can represent a national folk heritage, the Coromboses indeed qualify," Dorson wrote. "In spite of their isolation in Iron Mountain, where no other Greek families live," he assured his readers, their natal village of "Bambakou and the saints and the icons in Greece remain a powerful reality in their lives, to which they return on occasion" (164–65). Isolated in a remote small town, the family is seen as a carrier of national, regional, and religious folk heritage. For a folklorist who at the time of his fieldwork was keen on searching for functioning cultural remnants of a bygone past in the present, the Corombos family represented a "folkloristic gem." In fact, the discovery of the Greek folk in rural America stands as an instance of "folkloristic surrealism," the effect produced by "the gap between the folkloristic gem and the unlikely circumstances in which it is harbored" (Kirshenblatt-Gimblett 1998, 301). Though living in Iron Mountain, the family was foreign to it. Though a part of Greek America, it was far removed from Greek ethnicity's customary site of social organization, the urban community. Dramatically alien to its surroundings, Greek immigrant folkness powerfully wrought its surrealistic effect.

Dorson refrained from representing the Greek immigrants as frozen relics of the past. His research was guided by the assumptions (1) that selective traits of the folk past can be found in the lore and activities of contemporary peasants and (2) that they furnish evidence not merely of the survival of folkness but of the vitality of its function in modernity. Dorson's search for coherence, for a "typical form or theme" that defines a group or period, led him to the conclusion that "the epitome of immigrant folklore is the duality of Old Country mores in a New World context" (Ben-Amos 1989, 55). This analytical framework accommodated both the preservation of folklore in the tradition of romantic nationalism (Wilson 1989) and integration, which precluded the total folklorization of the family. Dorson represented the Coromboses as being partially folk and in a state of intergenerational flux. Its male members were described as mobile and acculturated, holding various degrees of attachment to folklore. The son, Ted, who was college-educated and "had taken a course in comparative folklore . . . handled Greek and English with equal facility, and [while] he listened with respect to the family tales . . . he could look at the traditions with some degree of detachment" (Dorson 1977, 157). His father and uncle, who had immigrated to America in 1903 and 1907, respectively, "spanned the two cultures, speaking fair and rapid-fire English, adapting themselves to American business ways, but withal respecting the old heritage" (ibid.). In contrast, "their wives, residing in the home and not meeting the public like their husbands, spoke only broken English, and appeared timid and withdrawn" (ibid.). Ted's late grandmother "represented the fountainhead of ancient lore. When Ted was stricken by the evil eye, she knew the proper formula detecting the culprit" (156–57).

The folkloric value of the family lay precisely in its porous boundaries. There was evidence in the immigrant narratives that despite acculturation and extended contact with American modernity, the male Coromboses still preserved a memory culture of meaningful folklore. For a scholar like Dorson, who was invested in showing the functional contemporaneity of folklore, this was a delightful discovery. It demonstrated the tenacity of folk culture among ethnics who had effectively adapted to American modernity. It furnished evidence for defending the terms "folk" and "folklore" as all-inclusive categories, a position that his trenchant critic Charles Keil effectively captured in the statement "We all need the folk because we are all folk" (1979, 209).[2]

But discovering folklore's canonical subject in ethnicity is hardly an innocent enterprise. By underscoring the persistence of elements commonly associated with lower stages of cultural evolution—magic and superstitions—Dorson inevitably, though unwittingly, attached a dimension of primitivism to Greek immigrants. Dorson's own discussion (1968) of Edward Tylor's evolutionist work *Primitive Culture* (1871) underscores the hierarchical implications of his findings:

> According to the doctrine of survivals, the irrational beliefs and practices of the European peasantry, so at variance with the enlightened view of the educated classes, preserve the fragments of an ancient, lower culture, the culture of primitive man. Consequently these survivals not only illuminate the past history of the race but also confirm the broad theory of development, as opposed to the theory of degeneration, which Tylor vigorously counters. While the main march of mankind is upward, from savagery through barbarism to ascending levels of civilization, relics of savagery, such as witchcraft, still survive among civilized peoples, and occasionally burst into revivals, as in the fad of spiritualism, a revival of primitive society. (Dorson 1968, 193)

"We have but to scratch the rustic," said evolutionist and president of the British Folk-Lore Society Edward Clodd in 1895, in order "to find the barbarian underneath" (quoted in Dorson 1968, 250). In evolutionist thought, there lies behind the modern veneer of the Greek immigrant a functioning and inescapable layer of primitivism. The folklorization of the family makes Dorson an unintentional participant traversing a historical minefield, the representation of immigrants as primitives in our midst. Did the Coromboses represent primitive folkness, as the professional folklorist maintained? Or did they stand for something else, entirely missed by Dorson? To fully explore this question it is necessary to shift the frame of analysis from the folklorist's conclusions to the statements made by members of the family—the textual fragments to which I alluded earlier—during the course of the ethnographic interview. The question "Who are the folk?" will yield unexpected insights once we foreground ethnic self-representations and situate them in relation to the practice of collecting ethnographic data and to historical discourses on national identity.

Who Are the Folk?

Viewed through the lens of the anthropology of Greece, the encounter between Richard Dorson and the Corombos family raises a number of key questions. What kind of cultural assumptions informed the family's self-representation to the folklorist? Did the immigrants have prior knowledge about the place of the folk in Greek national history? If so, how was this expressed? Were they the functioning folk, as Dorson portrayed them, or were they self-consciously performing a specific kind of folkness, obliging the expectations of an educated outsider? If one member of the family exhibited "the broad insight of a folk historian" (Dorson 1977, 157), wasn't this member also familiar—through exposure to mainstream as well as ethnic print media—with the history and politics of immigration? In my attempt to nuance Dorson's conclusions, I turn to studies in anthropology and folklore, which have cast light on the complexities of doing ethnography with Greek people. In the context of Greek ethnography, Michael Herzfeld (1986b) has emphatically identified the ethnographic interview as a rhetorical construct. When he writes, "the villager's ability to situate any ethnographer in a particular ideological framework must affect the recording of data" (222), he frames the problem in terms of a politics of ethnographic location. Similarly, Margaret Alexiou's pioneering (1984–85) insight had earlier debunked the myth of pure ethnographic facts. "The 'folk,' however defined," she wrote, "will often provide information they think is expected, or even deliberately mislead. Neither they nor we are 'innocent'" (11).[3]

Following the internal development of folklore in Greece as a discipline "committed to the presentation of an idealized view of national culture," the peasants expected folklorists to be urban, educated *Greeks* whose high position and perceived prestige "caus[ed] reluctance among rural informants to disclose their local traditions" (Herzfeld 1986b, 222). Through self-censorship, they sought to conceal those aspects of vernacular culture—obscene songs and ribald jokes for example—that would have compromised the idealized view of the folk promoted by official folklore. On the other hand, what were construed as ancient Greek (Hellenic) elements of folk culture were performed for the benefit of foreign anthropologists. The latter were seen as ideal interlocutors for whose benefit the peasants deployed the outward-oriented model that showcased the Hellenic dimensions of Greekness. "The Romeic model might have slipped through the crack," Herzfeld notes, "had the ethnographers not been receptive to the often all-too-vague suggestions of its importance in the villagers' own scheme of things" (221). Extending credit to the astuteness of anthropologists of Greek culture here safeguards the legitimacy of ethnographic knowledge.[4]

Herzfeld presents the peasants as being both fully aware of the debates on the place of the folk in national history and in a position to manipulate this knowledge. For my purposes, the question is whether the placement of Dorson in the rural taxonomy of ethnographers affected the ethnographic data and, if so, in what way. Undoubtedly, the family did not disappoint Dorson's quest for ethnic folkness. It not only generously displayed its folk knowledge in narratives about the past, but it also performed tradition while hosting the folklorist. Because the male informants assumed center stage in the encounter—their wives appearing "timid and withdrawn"—we can safely deduce that the professional folklorist was accorded the gendered rituals of formal Greek hospitality. The "architectonic distinctions between formal/male and familiar/female" that organized social experience in Greece also informed the customary reception of the distinguished guest (Herzfeld 1987, 118). Paradoxically, the women, who function as guardians of ethnicity according to patriarchal ideology, are marginalized in this ethnographic encounter. They are twice removed from the center stage of knowledge production about the folk: once on account of the customary decorum of ritualized hospitality and again because of insufficient acculturation, their limited English language skills.

A crucial passage documented and reported by Dorson, however, complicates the performance of the Coromboses as folk subjects:

> Besides their myriad accounts of saints' legends and miracles and black magic, the Corombos brothers spouted forth lighter tales of entertainment from the old wonder stories to modern jests. A prize specimen from George showed an American veneer coating the venerable European tale of the valiant hero overcoming the stupid ogres. George introduced the story as an account of how baseball was invented in Greece two thousand years ago. Giants eight and ten feet tall then lived in Greece and from them the New York Giants took their name. A weak, lazy fellow joined the giants and outwitted them in trials of strength. When night fell he placed his overcoat over a pile of stones, to simulate a man sleeping, and hid in the hills. The giants attempted to kill the little fellow by pounding his bed with an ax. But in the morning the youth, whom they had presumably chopped in a thousand pieces, reappeared, complaining that the bedbugs had been scratching him all night long. Impressed and overawed, the giants named him captain. And thenceforth carried out his orders. The Americans picked up baseball from this adventure, and the New York Giants began swinging bats two thousand years after the Greek giants had swung axes. (1977, 164–65)

To recognize the irony in Dorson's interpretation of the Greek claim to the origins of baseball, we must place this narrative in the historical context of Greek identity. The folklorist bypasses the national significance of the narrative, treating it as a "lighter tale." From his longstanding interest in motif analysis, he draws on "comparative folklore theory" (Georges 1989, 7) to place the narrative on the origins of baseball in relation to the European tale tradition. But had Richard Dorson read the work of Nikos Politis (1852–1921), the founder of the discipline of folklore in Greece, that knowledge would have constrained him to interpret the interview material differently.[5] Folk references to *Hellenes,* a giant race of mythical ancestors of superhuman size and strength, served for Politis as irrefutable evidence of the continuing use of the word as a term of national self-ascription, a name that he favored over that of *Romii.* Whether these references in popular tradition "represent the survival of a true self-designation" or whether they "may be metaphorical in origin" is a moot point (Herzfeld 1986a, 127–28). Of relevance here is the realization that popular circulation of Hellenic markers of identity cannot be treated as evidence of an authentic folk knowledge but only as a site of cross-fertilization between popular and literary sources (Herzfeld 1986a, 125; Alexiou 1984–85, 20). This realization shifts the analysis of folk tradition from "pure orality" to "literary orality," toward the contextual analysis, that is, of the interaction between the textual and the oral (ibid.).[6]

Dorson's folk historians appropriated an item of popular and literary tradition to create a usable past in the context of the ethnographic encounter. I suggest that the narrative on the Greek derivation of baseball functions to inscribe the ethnic folk within American modernity, not outside it. Establishing the modernity of the folk in turn averts the hierarchical impulse to classify ethnics as less modern and, by implication, less American. The narrative does not merely claim ethnic origins for a quintessentially national (American) pastime. The Greek invention of an American sport additionally works as a claim to beginnings, in the sense that it views the Greek past as an *active* cultural force that shapes the present (see Said 1975). The national past of the folk is afforded supreme value in that it functions as a model worth emulating. This narrative of beginnings establishes continuity between the Greek past and the American present as it underwrites Greek cultural authority over a quintessential American pastime, baseball. It collapses the distinction between the premodern and the modern, the ethnic and the national. It therefore authorizes the family to identify itself as authentically Greek (by virtue of ancestry) and American (by virtue of shared culture). If the interview points to the family's folkness, the narrative decidedly illuminates the family's Western (and by implication white) pedigree. It deflects, therefore, the

Orientalist and primitivist gaze that any reference to irrational beliefs ostensibly invites. To put it differently, if the ethnic family is indeed premodern by the virtue of its beliefs in superstitions, so is the entire baseball community, a network of players, coaches, and audiences who thrive on the practice of superstition (Gmelch 1984). As popular theoreticians, the Coromboses shatter the hierarchical dichotomy between ethnic folk and modern national subjects.

The Coromboses responded to Dorson's romantic nationalism with a folk version of its Greek counterpart, one that reverses the historical devaluation of the immigrant folk. The fact that immigrants indeed possess folklore makes them neither alien primitives nor devalued Orientals, but equal participants in America. The ethnic folk and the inquiring folklorist inhabit a common temporal civilizational plane; a claim to origins establishes a fundamental coevality between the family and their prestigious visitor as it simultaneously subverts the structural hierarchy between the educated academic and the ethnic folk.[7]

To fully grasp the implications of the story's claim to beginnings, we must place it in relation to Greek immigrant negotiations with American modernity. Neither an idiosyncratic nor a merely creative cultural appropriation, the narrative about the Greek invention of baseball belongs to a foundational identity narrative. In fact, the text produced by the Coromboses constitutes a component of early immigrant historiography, which located Greek America within "the 'illustrious' history of Classical Hellenism attributing a semi-divine origin to Greek Americans" (Kalogeras 1992, 17). These historical narratives are in turn part of a wider social discourse that encompasses them. Whether claiming Greek ancestry for Christopher Columbus, as historian Seraphim Canoutas did in *Christopher Columbus: A Greek Nobleman* (1943), or whether designating Greek immigrants in America as the racial inheritors of the classical legacy while simultaneously positing ancient Greece as a cultural and political archetype of white America, as an early immigrant elite did, a dominant Greek American discourse has consistently presented (and continues to present, as I will show in chapter 2) Greek Americans as active *participants* in the making of American political and cultural life. Not unlike the Corombos narrative, this discourse of beginnings attempts to reverse deeply ingrained hierarchies between the immigrants and the American hosts. It seeks to subvert the historical devaluation of the Greeks as primitive folk who were rendered unworthy (and incapable) of equal participation in early twentieth-century American modernity.[8]

Who are the Coromboses? Or, more precisely, who are they made to be in this ethnographic encounter? Once we analyze the exchange between folklorist and family through its textual politics and poetics and situate it in history and in relation to extratextual discourses, we see that no single answer can capture the identity of these individuals. Caught in the disciplinary net of folklore, they are made to possess a premodern folkness. As subjects entangled in a specific historical negotiation with the discourse of Western Hellenism they represent exemplary modern Greeks. But in their performance of folk knowledge, they stake a claim not only to a Greek identity but also to an American affiliation. Simultaneously folk, white ethnic, modern Greek, Greek American, and American, they inhabit a plurality of subject positions and advance a complexity that interrupts any scholarly attempt to fix them as persevering folk or as ethnics on the verge of assimilation. The ethnographic encounter between Dorson and the Corombos family foregrounds the importance of history and discourse in the negotiation over the meaning of ethnicity. The poetics and politics that construe the ethnic family as Greek and American, folk and modern, ethnic and white, cannot be appreciated in its complexity without delving into the historical discourses that framed immigrant negotiation with American modernity. The family produces ethnic meanings at the intersection of the discipline of folklore, popular ethnography, and social discourses such as Hellenism.

This is, then, how this book will proceed, paying attention to texts and contexts, to history and discourse, to popular ethnography and professional anthropology and folklore, to intellectuals, academics, and the "folk" as they contribute to making usable pasts and situate themselves in relation to whiteness. It will look at the making of selective dimensions of the past and the way in which these structures of the old are given a new life, an animating ethnic purpose, today. My reading, then, of the transmutations of the past into the present finds inspiration in the critical project described by Said (1994) and introduced in the preface of this chapter, to examine, that is, dominant discourses "with an effort to draw out, extend, give emphasis and voice to what is silent or marginally present or ideologically represented" (66). In the remainder of this section, I proceed to discuss the three historical moments of representation that I outlined earlier in order to illuminate further intersections between the immigrant vernacular *and* modernity, and to identify additional ways in which canonical texts contain the plurality of ethnic pasts.

Transnational Pasts and the Making of the Modern Folk (Late 1910s, Early 1920s)

A photograph of early Greek immigrants taken in 1917 on the occasion of the Fourth of July celebrations in the nation's capital dramatizes how the immigrants visually narrated their national pasts for public consumption (see Warnke 1996). In it, a Greek delegation poses in front of the U.S. Treasury, a neoclassical building located at the civic heart of the city. Strategically staged, the picture is rich in meaning; it showcases ethnic particularity as it simultaneously communicates cultural affinity with and political loyalty to the host nation. Variously dressed as ancient Greek soldiers standing on guard and as folk in dancing postures, the immigrants display their costumed bodies as signs of the temporal continuity of the Greek nation. They appear to embody the uninterrupted continuation of the *ethnos,* encapsulated around the two symbolic poles that historically organized Greek national identity: Hellas, the golden age of ancient Greece; and the dia-chronic heritage of the folk.[9] The common people, according to the principles of Herderian romantic nationalism, were the vessel that preserved the authentic national spirit up to modern times, despite intervening and interfering foreign invasions and conquests.

But the photograph does not record a mere unreflective transplantation of Greek ethnicity into the host national space. It represents not the intrusion of a foreign body, but a negotiation that becomes evident once one decodes the additional signs that nuance the visual enactment of cultural and ethnic (racial) continuity. Posing in front of the neoclassical government building serves two functions: it showcases the political and cultural currency of ancient Greek cul-ture in the United States while simultaneously advancing the immigrant claim to ownership of the cultural capital of classical Greece.[10] The narrative of con-tinuity and the adoption of ancient Greek political culture by the host society support the articulation of an ideological commonplace in Greek America: the persistent claim of the compatibility, even confluence, of American and Greek cultures. As the racial descendants and, by the principles of biological determin-ism, the cultural inheritors of classical Greece, Greek immigrants not only were endowed with the potential to embrace "Americanness" but also had access to "Ur-Americanness."

The popularization of a resonance between an immigrant minority and its host, however, becomes politically possible on the basis of discontinuity. A banner announcing the "Upcoming Victory of the Allies"—conspicuously displayed at the upper center of the photograph—subtly redirects the interpretive frame-work. Read in the context of war politics, which promoted assimilation and framed the immigrant desire for political and social inclusion in American soci-ety, this sign marks a shift in the way in which immigrants saw themselves as po-litical subjects. As historian Ioanna Laliotou (2004) shows, immigrants eagerly capitalized on Fourth of July parades as ideal public forums in which to recon-figure their political identification and proclaim their loyalty to America during a time of war. In this manner, the ideology of ethnic continuity was retained, but the narrative of national continuity was disrupted. On the one hand, the visual display of ancient Greek and vernacular forms pointed to "the cultural and civilizational value inherent in Greek descent" (124) and, therefore, to ethnic filiation. The performance of immigrant loyalty and belonging to the adopted homeland, on the other hand, served a denationalizing function. The declaration of political and social commitment to U.S. interests denationalized Greek history, since the display of Greek cultural symbols in the parades ceased to "operate as symbolic representations of national existence and sovereignty" (ibid.). Rather, their meaning was contained as depoliticized ethnic manifestations "of high cultural and ideological traits that were supposedly inherently embodied by Greek migrants" (124–25). Until the postwar rise of American nationalism, it was possible for the immigrants to publicly deploy a dual mode of identification for popular consumption. This investment in making the ethnic past conform with political expectations of Americanness was "based on the condition that America could accommodate transnational forms of identification" (125). But soon a militant assimilationism and exclusionist nativism coerced immigrants to rewrite their connections with their cherished pasts.

The site represented in the photograph is one among many—the home, the coffeehouse, the church, the workplace, the community, theatrical plays, regional societies, histories and folklore monographs, ethnic media, literature, intellectual and artistic societies—where early Greek immigrants negotiated the place of their pasts in America. The photograph simultaneously represents an instance of transnational continuity and a rupture from the ancestral nation-state as the primary site of attachment. The visual expression of ethnic continuity certainly imports the Greek state's ideology, which, in the context of nation building, sought to integrate unlettered peasants into the grand narrative of the nation. Often told, most notably by Michael Herzfeld, this story of producing the folk as national subjects who embody the glorious ancient past redirects how we gaze at the photograph.

The immigrants at the U.S. Treasury perform a scripted version of the past, as it was produced at the time by Greek academic discourses, such as folklore, and by cultural movements, such as demoticism, both of which nationalized the vernacular. As folklorist and classicist Margaret Alexiou (1984–85) observes, the elevation of the peasants into a crucial component of national history must be seen in relation to political contingencies associated with the foundation of the modern Greek state early in the nineteenth century. "Only after the establishment of the Greek state, was the word *laos* used increasingly to mean 'people' in the Herderian sense of *Volk,* as carriers of the eternal spirit (*pneuma*) of the

Greek nation (*ethnos*), whose values are transmitted 'in the blood'" (14–15). The performance of immigrants posing in folk costumes constituted a modern folk-ness embedded in complex political histories and struggles to establish a nation-state and nationhood. It is necessary, therefore, to situate the representation captured in the photograph both historically and in relation to social discourses on Greek identity. In what follows, I will take a brief detour to discuss how the academic discipline of folklore construed the place of folk culture and the classical past in narratives of national identity and, in turn, how these narratives sought to contain the variability that defined peasant cultural expressions.

In the context of nineteenth-century Greek nation building and European power relations, turning the folk into national subjects served key political pur-poses. This explains the ideological significance of Greek folklore as a national institution whose production of truths about ordinary people was placed at the service of the state's cultural politics. The systematic study of peasant culture was politically crucial at the time because it sought to legitimize the newly es-tablished nation-state. Greek folklore scholarship was staunchly empirical, yet ideologically invested in establishing an uninterrupted continuity between the ordinary people of the Greek countryside and ancient Greece. Selective customs and folk beliefs became the functioning link between the so-called golden past and the present, the latter envisioned by Western-trained Greek intellectuals and statesmen as a resurrection of the former. Long scorned and derided by the urban bourgeois, the practices of the folk, the *laos,* served as irrefutable evidence of racial purity, a sign that the spirit of Periclean Athens was transmuted into the greatness of folk poetry and song. Hence the name of the new discipline, *laogra-fia,* the study of people (the Volk), instead of *ethnografia,* the study of the ethnos (the nation). As Michael Herzfeld (1986a) points out in his groundbreaking work on the politics of Greek folklore studies, it was necessary for the new discipline to prove that the folk constituted an organic part of the nation, that they "indeed belonged to the Hellenic *ethnos*" (13). "The *ethnos,*" Herzfeld writes, "did not need a branch of study of its own: it was one of the eternal verities, an absolute moral entity against which the *laos* could be matched and measured" (ibid.). By establishing the Hellenicity of the peasants, folklore scholarship legitimized the claim of the Greek nation-state to the cultural and intellectual legacy of ancient Greece. Such reasoning carried far-reaching political implications. If Hellas stood "as the cultural exemplar of Europe" (5), to claim that modern Greeks were racial and cultural descendants of ancient Greece was to declare their access to an Ur-European identity. The prestigious pedigree of the peasants carried inherent political implications. "Against the background of the Greeks' dependence on

European patronage" (6–7), Herzfeld writes, the claim to racial and cultural ancestry substantiated the European identity of the Greeks and made them eligible for European political and material support.

Seen against this historical background, the photograph testifies to the power of the discourse of Western Hellenism to shape the national and transnational expression of Greek immigrant identity. But it also demonstrates the immigrant performance of a larger, preemigration process of cultural containment. In nineteenth-century Greece, the state-sponsored nationalization of folk culture assaulted regional variation in order to domesticate its fragmentary potential.[11] It imposed homogeneity in yet another sense, when it purged vernacular practices that deviated from the construction of an ideal, virtuous folk. Thus, the photograph's orderly symbolic arrangement edits out the variability and messiness of the social realities that defined the lives of immigrants who were fleeing the poverty of the Greek countryside for the promises of material prosperity in the United States.

Enabled by the labor demands of transnational capitalism, the movement of poor peasants to the centers of American industrial production set in motion the mass flow of immigrant vernacular cultures.[12] Greek immigrants imported to the New World highly variable folk practices consisting of multilayered secular and religious elements. On the broadest level, staples of the immigrant vernacular included, among others, storytelling, songs and dances, ritual laments, hospitality, traditions and beliefs associated with Orthodoxy, superstitions, folk healing, oral poetic traditions, and divination. The vernacular offered a rich, culturally expressive repertoire of oral genres that reproduced central community values. Didactic folk practices savored proverbs and tales that communicated moral values and folk wisdom. On the ethnographic level, the cultural field was crisscrossed by regional, class, and gender variation. Certainly, tradition functioned ideologically to reproduce the moral order. Patriarchy loomed large, expressed in vernacular forms, including proverbs, that represented women as weak and sexually vulnerable and that regulated their spatial and social movement in everyday practices. Socially constraining customs often sanctioned violence, most paradigmatically honor crimes, to enforce the traditional order.

But the vernacular also provided a venue for subversive language and activities resisting, to the degree possible, domestic centers of power as well as the encroachment of state structures and peasant exploitation.[13] Anthropologists and folklorists have documented powerful subversive elements among the folk. Jokes challenged the authority of the priests (Orso 1979). Peasant protests challenged and ridiculed the landholding class and the authority of the state (Gallant 2002). Ribald jokes told within the intimate social circle of relatives and female friends challenged the stereotype of female timidity in rural Greece (Clark 1983). And vernacular poetry, as we will see in chapters 5 and 6, was deployed in local struggles against the intrusion of capitalism.

Furthermore, the vernacular never represented an insulated, singular culture. As historical anthropologist Thomas Gallant (2001) points out, "The view of the Greek village as isolated in space and frozen in time . . . at best is misleading and at worst inaccurate" (97). This observation is supported by a regional approach in scholarship that examines villages in relation to the histories and the political economy of their surrounding settlements and that challenges the assumption of Greek villages as fixed, stable, and uniform entities. The emerging consensus represents settlements in the Greek countryside as fluid and dynamic social units (see S. Sutton 1994) characterized by outward movements of seasonal emigration, networks of social relations in the context of regional festivals, and flows of repatriated immigrants. Moreover, rural populations were differentially exposed to modernity and urban lifestyles because of the uneven modernization of the Greek countryside and each group's relative geographic proximity to or distance from towns and cities. Peasants therefore are best understood as national subjects enmeshed not only in a local symbolic universe and moral order but also in national discourses of identity and citizenship, the flow of extralocal symbolic resources, material culture, and economic networks of transnational capitalism in the industrial periphery.[14] What is more, Greek-speaking refugees who fled Ottoman Turkey because of nationalist conflicts in the region (culminating in the 1923 compulsory exchange of populations between Greece and Turkey) represented a heterogeneous population, sectors of which were cosmopolitan and appreciative of high culture. Their presence in Greek America adds yet another layer, one largely unexplored, between the rural and the urban, and between the popular and the elite cultures, where the illiterate, the literate, the vernacular, and the literary intersected.[15]

The foregoing discussion helps me position the staged performance of identity at the U.S. Treasury in terms of transnational negotiations over the signifiers of Greek identity. The photograph captured a scripted presentation: it sought to synthesize the Hellenic and Romeic aspects of Greek identity in a highly stylized form for the immigrants' nascent public presentation of the ethnic self to the American public. But it also signaled, as I have already pointed out, a moment of discontinuity. It announced a process in which the definition and expression of Greek vernacular culture were increasingly understood as a negotiation between ever-vigilant immigrant constituencies and the cultural and political demands placed upon them by their hosts. In other words, the encounter between the immigrants and American political modernity made the past not merely an issue of transnational connections *but also* a reflective ethnic process that was mediated by powerful national (American) discourses on the proper place of foreign pasts in the nation. To put it succinctly, narratives of national belonging in the United States shaped the content and boundaries of what could be counted by the immigrants as usable Greek pasts. To illustrate how immigrant folkness was understood and performed under these conditions, I now turn to another point of rupture: the racialization of the Greek immigrants in the United States. The following section shows how the making of transnational usable pasts in Greek America in the early 1920s took place in response to a social discourse that relegated immigrants outside proper whiteness.

Racial Pasts: The Rewriting of Transnational Pasts in the 1920s

"[T]he descendants of the undesirable Greeks may become loyal and useful American citizens," asserted a 1907 editorial in the *San Francisco Chronicle*. Unlike "the Asiatics," it added, Greek immigrants "do not differ from us so radically in all essential particulars as they can never assimilate, but must always remain a race apart" (quoted in Karampetsos 1998, 66). In its succinctness, this passage crystallizes the racialized logic of its era, identifying the Greek "new immigrants" as a distinct race and subsequently locating the newcomers within the hierarchical racial fault lines of American society (Almaguer 1994). Placed between unmarked American whiteness and "the Asiatics" commonly demonized as the "yellow peril," the immigrants are relegated to an ambivalent position of simultaneous privilege and exclusion. Occupying a racial space higher than that of immigrants from Asia, they are deemed potential national subjects, their phenotype (the likeness in "all essential particulars") conferring on them the privileges of citizenship from which Chinese immigrants were barred. Classified within the underbelly of whiteness, the undesirable immigrant is subjected to the disciplinary gaze of the dominant, his coevalness with American modernity denied, his national inclusion set tentatively in a remote future.

During the early twentieth century, Greek immigrants occupied a marked and unstable location, a potential component of the racialized nation yet outside it. The unmarked enunciation "us" naturalizes whiteness as the racial center and regulates national belonging. If whiteness, understood in contrast to blackness and to Native American "savagery," stood as an undifferentiated monolithic category in the early years of the republic, the immense waves of immigrant laborers in the nineteenth and early twentieth centuries challenged those fixed racial categories. Largely a source of cheap labor for America's burgeoning industrial capitalism, immigrants occupied an ambiguous racial location. Their phenotypical whiteness enabled their entrance into the polity as "free white persons," making them eligible for citizenship under the reigning naturalization law. In this sense, "[i]t was their *whiteness,* not any kind of New World magnanimity, that opened the Golden Door" of immigration (Jacobson 1998, 8). Beneficiaries of racialized citizenship, the immigrants also partook in the privileges of whiteness, for example, becoming eligible under the 1905 homestead law to acquire property in what formerly had been Ute Indian reservation territory in Utah (Papanikolas 2002, 114).

Yet the immigrants also posed an anomaly in the political space of whiteness. Although they were legally white, their status as distinct national groups undermined their full inclusion in whiteness. As "in-between peoples" (Barrett and Roediger 1997), or "probationary whites" (Jacobson 1998), these Greek, Italian, Jewish, Polish, and Slovak immigrants fractured whiteness into a hierarchical plurality of races, fuelling debates over their capacity to participate in the racialized polity. Were southeastern European immigrants fit for the rigors of democratic government? Were they capable of exercising self-discipline? Did they posses the moral character necessary for making a constructive civic contribution to the republic? Or did their allegiance to ancestral ties and Old World political traditions threaten the smooth functioning of the polity? Did custom undermine modernity? Even worse, was it not the case that immigrant biological inferiority posed a genetic threat to the nation, promising nothing short of racial degeneration and chaotic disorder? How was it possible to test the immigrants' fitness for self-government? Popular magazines and prestigious research centers, congressional debates and political speeches, immigration laws and civic institutions all generated a discourse classifying, assessing, measuring, evaluating, and predicting immigrants' fitness and potential for assimilation. Phenotypes, genotypes, customs, habits, health, appearance, intelligence, cranial capacity, and work habits were all factors in locating immigrant groups in relative proximity to or distance from the center of whiteness, which in turn determined degrees of national exclusion and inclusion.

As Gunther Peck (2000) has shown in his impressive work on racial categories in the early twentieth-century American West, immigrant racial status was far from stable or permanent. Immigrant laborers, as well as established communities, were caught in shifting racial locations. While participation in labor unions, such as the Western Federation of Miners, could render immigrants white (220), discrimination in residential accommodations through city covenants refuted their whiteness. Transience "was almost always a marker of nonwhiteness in the West in 1900," although "being a member of a residentially persistent community did not guarantee one whiteness" (166). Conversely, middle-class respectability bestowed the privileges of whiteness, though these rights were withdrawn to punish immigrants belonging to politically active nationalities. Whiteness, therefore, functioned as a coveted social space whose boundaries were tightly regulated:

> There is much similarity between the case of the negroes and that of the modern immigrants. To be sure, the newcomers are for the most part white-skinned instead of colored . . . yet in the mind of the average American, the modern immigrants are generally regarded as inferior peoples—races he looks down on, and with which he does not wish to associate in terms of social equality. . . . The business of the alien is to go into the mines, the foundries, the sewers, the stifling air of factories and work shops, out on the roads and railroads in the burning sun of summer, or the driving sleet and snow. If he proves himself a man, and rises above his station, and acquires wealth, and cleans himself up— very well, we receive him after a generation or two. But at present he is far beneath us, and the burden of proof rests with him. (Fairchild 1911, 237)

Incorporating racist assumptions in assimilationist thought, this passage is paradigmatic of the kind of "progressive racism" (Michaels 1995) that was directed against turn-of-the-century southeastern European immigrants. Moreover, by linking race, class, gender, and the nation, this commentary underlines the pervasiveness of social Darwinism in narratives of assimilation. The assimilation of the immigrant is framed generationally, as a test to biological fitness. The author builds on a central motif of what Werner Sollors (1986) calls the "genetics of salvation." According to this concept, American identity is "safely and easily received" by the native-born by virtue of birth and descent, "but [it is] something that foreign-born workers would have to strive long and hard to achieve" (88). Here, the labor conditions of industrial capitalism test racial immigrant fitness. The transformation of wage labor, a class location associated with nonwhiteness, into middle-class respectability, a sign of republican whiteness, mirrors racial inclusion. Not unlike the Protestant covenant with God, material wealth guarantees immigrant national salvation.

The making of usable ethnic pasts at the time constituted a precarious cultural project, one undertaken in the face of severe constraints imposed by the dominant society. This was especially true in the turbulent years following the

First World War, when the volatile contingency of racial meanings and the fluidity of cultural and political immigrant affiliations in the early years of immigration turned into rigid patterns of identity ascription. American nationalism increasingly turned to militant strategies of conformity and racist policies of exclusion. Confronted with an acute domestic economic crisis, the rise of communism abroad, an increasingly powerful domestic unionism, vast cultural diversity, extensive urban riots, and homegrown terrorist acts, the federal government politicized ethnic identity. Appointing directors of Americanization to the Bureau of Education and the Department of the Interior and establishing a National Americanization Committee, the state launched a "crusade" of "intense Americanism" known as 100 percent Americanization (King 2000, 90). Aggressively embraced by such civic and patriotic organizations as the Daughters of the American Revolution, the National Security League, and the American Legion, the movement castigated immigrants for retaining their cultures. In addition, it also branded working-class unionism, which it often conflated with communism and anarchism, as un-American. This deployment of Americanism as an ideology to extinguish diversity and neutralize working-class activism demarcated the boundaries of whiteness in relation to Americanness, understood as uncompromising cultural and political conformity to the middle-class values of 100 percent Americanism. A state-sponsored "class vigilance" (Jacobson 1998, 72) endorsed by Congress and the media culminated in the arrest and eventual deportation of alleged foreign immigrant radicals, in violation of their civil rights and due process of law (Archdeacon 1983, 169).

This discourse of whiteness challenged immigrant narratives of continuity like the one performed at the U.S. Treasury. Greek exceptionalism, the claim that the Greeks were heirs to the ancient Greek civilization and, as such, were distinct from their southeastern counterparts (Anagnostu 1999), was dismissed by racist nationalists:

> The modern Greeks like to have visitors believe that they are descended straight from the true Greeks of the days of Pericles; but if they are, then every Greek bootblack in New England is descended straight from Plymouth Colony. The Greeks of to-day—except on some of the Greek islands, which have been comparatively free from invasion and immigration—are descended from Asiatic and African slaves, Italians, old Bulgarians, Slavs, Gepidæ, Huns, Herulians, Avars, Egyptians, Jews, Illyrians, Arabs, Spaniards, Walloons, Franks, Albanians, and several other races. History has an unfortunate but incurable habit of repeating

itself—and a word to the wise ought to be better than a jab with an eight-inch hatpin. (Roberts 1922, 232)

Popular classifications similarly placed the Greeks as undifferentiated members of a racially inferior Mediterranean race. "The driver mounted his quickly emptied wagon, with a curse upon the 'Dagos,' and the crowd informally discussed for a while the immigration question; its verdict being that it is time to shut our doors against the Greeks, for they are a poor lot from which to make good American citizens" (Steiner 1906, 283). The racialization of the new immigrants was convenient for those racists who appropriated anthropological typologies of European morphological variations and turned them into racial hierarchies. The strict morphological classification of the European people into three races—the Teutonic, or Nordic, race (which included northern Europeans), the Alpine race (which included southern Germans, Celts, and Slavs), and the Mediterranean race (which included the people of southern Europe) produced by the "scientific gospel" of the era, Ripley's *The Races of Europe* (1915)—was appropriated by racist thinkers to reflect inherent racial inequalities (Bendersky 1995, 137). Thus, in the terminology of the era, the Nordic "long-headed dolichocephalic races from the zoological zone of Northern Europe" were posited as the superior type of all European races (ibid.).

While the narrative of progressive racism provided a location, albeit an ambiguous one, for southeastern European immigrants in the political economy of whiteness, nativist racism, in contrast, systematically denied them one. Racist nationalists drew immutable boundaries between racialized citizenship and the immigrants, barring the latter from participation in the polity. Access to whiteness here became a utopian impossibility, for the immigrants were seen as organically alien substances to the national body: "An ostrich could assimilate a croquet ball or a cobble-stone with about the same ease that America assimilated her newcomers from Central and Southeastern Europe" (Roberts 1922, 4). Racist nationalists dehumanized Greek immigrants, fixing them outside whiteness, even outside common humanity. The following announcements, which appeared in restaurants and newspaper advertisements, speak volumes to the extent of Greek humiliation: "No sailors, dogs, or Greeks allowed" (Akrotirianakis 1994, 26) and "John's Restaurant, Pure American. No Rats, No Greeks" (Leber 1972, 104).

The link between whiteness and citizenship has been central to constructions of American identity. While this complex connection has been historically contested and, in the process, transformed, racial understandings of citizenship dominated the political establishment of the young nation and remained a pre-occupation well beyond the arrival of successive waves of European immigration in the nineteenth and early twentieth centuries. Though implicit in colonial discourse and framed in opposition to the alleged savagery of the Indians, the relationship of whiteness to citizenship was enshrined in the laws of the new republic. As codified in the 1790 naturalization law granting citizenship to "all white free persons," whiteness increasingly came to be understood not solely in terms of citizenship but most importantly in relation to moral and cultural values. An understanding of citizenship as practice, rather than mere political ascription, defined civic participation as the performance of certain related duties. Self-reliance, rationality, self-discipline, the ownership of property, temperance, and restraint, were essential ingredients of the civic contract between the state and a new type of republican citizen. Unlike the submissive, docile subjects associated with the monarchical dynasties that republicanism sought to replace, the new citizen was a reflective participant whose rationality and self-reliance were necessary for the proper functioning of the democratic process. Unlike feudal peasants, whose actions depended on royal decrees, custom, superstition, kin, and community obligations, the modern citizen was encouraged to act as an autonomous individual, exhibiting rational initiative in the making of the society over compliant submission to the traditional status quo.

Forgetting the vernacular past, then, a past that was understood in evolutionary terms as inferior premodern irrationality, debasement, dependency, backwardness—in short, as antithetical to American modernity—functioned as a necessary condition for the making of immigrants into citizens of the republic. The following recollection illustrates the connection between coerced cultural amnesia, whiteness, and Americanization:

> [In the American Hellenic Progressive Association] you met people your age who had the same goals. To become American. You became American by giving up your parents' ways because they also had to give them up so they wouldn't stand out like a sore thumb. By giving up the Old World ways. We ran away from being Greek. We married non-Greek blonde women. . . . We made a conscious effort to forget Greece. (Anonymous interviewee quoted in Karpathakis 1999, 62)

In its association of forgetting the ancestral homeland, abandoning tradition, and embracing blondness—the icon of whiteness—the above passage illustrates immigrant acquiescence in the discourse of Americanization as total cultural, political, and racial assimilation. Because the immigrants' past is understood as a source of pollution, the immigrants themselves were expected to undergo a profound transformation by surrendering their past to a new historical location. They were asked to abandon their memories and bury their ancestral ties in the landfills of history in order to cultivate new identities.

This vocabulary of radical rupture and discontinuity, pervasive in political discourse as well as in narratives of personal transformation, indelibly marked the immigrant encounter with American modernity in the nineteenth and early twentieth centuries. Academic monographs, popular magazines, immigrant diaries, research reports, immigration policies, and political speeches repeatedly refer to the forgetting of ethnicity as a condition necessary to reconstitute immigrants as American subjects. National belonging required de-ethnicization: the liberation of newcomers from ancestral ties, loyalties, and obligations through a process of social amnesia. Forgetting, as Ernest Renan's (1990) often cited statement makes clear, "is a crucial factor in the creation of a nation" (11).

I have analyzed one specific Greek American response to the foregoing conditions in more detail elsewhere as a reflexive project of disembedding the self from traditional structures in order to claim full participation in modernity (Anagnostou 2004a). There, I showed that political and racist nationalism worked dialectically to make race and cultural forgetting crucial components of immigrant Americanization. In response to this predicament, a sector of Greek America's middle class embraced whiteness as an institutional policy of racial exclusion as well as an everyday practice that sought to obliterate habits of thought and conduct that could be traced to the immediate Greek past. At the forefront of this emerging configuration was the American Hellenic Progressive Association (AHEPA), an organization that made a spectacle of the Hellenic past while purifying its vernacular counterpart. In public performances that staged the newly constituted American Hellenic identity, immigrants performed usable pasts that stressed their racial and cultural compatibility with Americanism. In ritual commemorations of the nation, this identity generated a visual economy that was intended to ingrain into newcomers a cultural and racial whiteness: draped in American flags, dressed in ancient togas or in the alternatively uniform costumes of Masonic lodges, immigrants marched in arrangements tailored to the expectations of their new national affiliation. Through their physical discipline and standardization of dress, they came to embody the values of the racialized nation. Highly stylized, the folk past was relegated to the margins, still holding symbolic significance as a link with antiquity—folk dances, for example, continued to be featured at AHEPA events—but being largely devalued as incompatible to American modernity. The configuration on the steps of the U.S.

Treasury was superseded by a body politic that performed its ethnic ancestry in a manner that privileged "the externally directed model" of ideological Hellenism over the Romeic model of Greek identity (Herzfeld 1986a, 23). It visually inscribed the narrative of Greek cultural continuity in the political economy of American whiteness.

Mapping Ethnicity onto Race: From New Immigrants to White Ethnics (1970s)

I now move forward to the 1960s and 1970s to focus on a period that witnessed the articulation of a new social category, that of the white ethnic. A product of the volatile racial politics during the civil rights era, this classification sought to impose cultural coherence on and, in turn, to harvest the political potential of the descendants of the new immigrants. On the one hand, it advocated antiassimilationism, ethnic revitalization, and a return to the roots. On the other hand, coming "into existence as a labeled group in response to the civil rights and black power movements and the allied organizing of Latinos, Asians, and Native Americans" (di Leonardo 1994, 170), it operated as a potent political force in the competition for cultural and material resources.

"I am born of PIGS—those Poles, Italians, Greeks and Slavs," Michael Novak (1971, 53) provocatively framed his confessional narrative, in an apparent intermeshing of personal and collective politics. A pioneer account in the now popular genre of growing up ethnic, this autobiographical work provided a testimony of how subtle and not-so-subtle coercion—by peers and institutions—and gentle encouragement—by wary immigrant parents bearing the scars of racism—led to ethnic self-effacement. An intellectual who professed a politics "rooted in the social and earthy sensibility of Catholic experience" (70), Novak claimed to give public voice to a collective that had been forced into silence. "The PIGS are not silent willingly" (53), he wrote. "The silence burns like hidden coals in the chest" (ibid.). The son of Slovak immigrants, Novak shattered this silence with all the intellectual might, eloquence, and political acumen that he had mastered in the corridors of the academy as a professor of philosophy and religious studies. He adopted the position of an intellectual committed to advancing the interests of white ethnics by articulating a sense of profound rage and discontent. "Such a tide of resentment begins to overwhelm the descendant of the 'new immigration' when he begins to voice repressed feelings about America," he wrote. "[A]t first his throat clogs with despair" (61). The authorial exposé of private thoughts and feelings becomes a necessary step toward collective empowerment. "So the risks of letting one's own secrets out of the bag are rather real," he noted, casting his testimony as a vital crossing of boundaries between the private and the public.

The category "white ethnic" was crucial for Novak's function as an intellectual who wished to advance the interests of an underrepresented and maligned population, the PIGS. The self-ascription PIGS itself—"an insulting, self-polluting label" (Abrahams and Kalcik 1978, 233)—makes the claim of "belong[ing] to the margins of society rather than [being] part of the center or establishment . . . [and] reverses the assimilation process and brings down on ethnics' heads the charge of being different, non-Anglo" (233–34). This politics drew from a textbook case of panethnic identity construction: the making of a common cultural and historical experience and the subsequent construction of uniqueness through difference. White ethnics were assigned a shared history of discrimination, a cultural content, national and familial loyalties, close-knit solidarity, neighborliness, work ethic, attachment to locality, patriotism, and modesty. And, as the title of one section attests—"Neither WASP nor Jew nor Black"—this entity was sharply differentiated from what the author construed as rival social groups. Presented as different from "'middle America' (so complacent, smug, nativist, and Protestant)" (Novak 1971, 57), white ethnics were also removed from an arrogant and privileged liberal establishment. But they also kept a safe distance from radicalism, abstaining from interfacing with Jewish and black politics.

"Confessions of a White Ethnic" intervened in the ethnic politics of its era, purporting to represent white ethnics from an insider's viewpoint. Novak wrote bitterly: "If you are a descendant of southern and eastern Europeans, everyone else *has* defined your existence. A pattern of 'Americanization' is laid out. You are catechized, cajoled, and condescended to by guardians of good Anglo-Protestant attitudes. You are chided by Jewish libertarians. Has ever a culture been so moralistic?" (62). Boldly entering into the fray of polemic ethnic politics, Novak spoke on behalf of the working-class and lower-middle-class ethnics—the laborers, "small businessmen, agents for corporations perhaps" (56), shoving their raging discontent in the face of 1970s America. Conscious of their parents' humiliation as immigrants and forced to hide their ethnicity, the story goes, white ethnics played the WASP game, only to discover that the game was rigged. Their struggle to escape social marginality and economic stagnation was "blocked at every turn" (ibid.). Excluded from liberal-black political coalitions, denigrated as parochial, conservative, and racist by intellectuals, oppressed by middle America, silenced and misrepresented by the media, excluded by curricula and preservation societies, the white ethnic emerged as a profoundly resentful collective subject. "[F]eeling cheated" (ibid.) and abandoned, white ethnics witnessed the liberal sympathy extended to racial minorities while they themselves absorbed the scorn of East Coast intellectuals, who failed "to engage the humanity of the modest, ordinary little man west of the Hudson" (59).

Novak's victimizing populism articulated ethnic dissatisfaction and resentment to subsequently harness it for a specific antiassimilationist and antimodernist agenda: the return to ethnic roots. His "politics of cultural pluralism, a politics of family and neighborhood, a politics of smallness and quietness" (8), sought to revive what he saw as the communitarian ethos that was stripped away from the immigrant Gemeinschaft. Indicting modernity for this outcome, he enumerated its ills. The culprit in this polemic was the modern individual, culturally disconnected and alienated, incapable of long-term ties and commitments, who resigned himself to the mercy of the free marketplace. Novak tenuously connected atomism, transience, and corporate capitalism. "Becoming modern," in his view "is a matter of learning to be solitary," to experience a life where "nothing [is] permanent, everything [is] discardable" (68). The assault on immigrant traditions—effected by militant assimilationism in the past and secular humanism in the present—devalues roots and disdains "mystery, ritual, transcendence, soul, absurdity, and tragedy" (67) in the name of rationality and progress. What this reconfiguration enables, according to Novak, is the making of ethnic subjects amenable to the demands of rational and individualized corporate culture. White ethnics—an inherent component of "network people," as "socially textured selves, not individuals" (68)—functioned as a bulwark against this specific kind of assimilation. "Part of Americanizing the Indian, the slave, or the immigrant [was] to dissolve network people into atomic people. Some people resisted the acid. They refused to melt. These are the unmeltable ethnics" (69).

"[L]osing the sharp lust to become 'American'" (4), the sons and daughters of the new immigrants are transformed here into white ethnics. Anthropologist Micaela di Leonardo (1994) has dissected the emergence of this category in the 1960s, illustrating its relation to the social and political currents of the time and to the specific interests it served. She bluntly maintains that the construct of "white ethnic community" as a homogeneous, working-class, close-knit set of coherent urban communities constituted an invented American tradition in that it falsified the social realities of the people who were made known through the category. What media, scholars, politicians, and ethnic leaders presented as a neatly demarcated collective was, in fact, as di Leonardo points out, an assortment of diverse, shifting, mobile, and residentially dispersed populations. Widely disseminated in popular culture, this was an ideological construct created as a political strategy to address profound social rifts. Represented as law-abiding, orderly, patriotic, and hardworking, white ethnics composed the silent majority that stood opposite the collectives pressing the federal government, the states, and social institutions toward reform and, often, radical change. The image of the white ethnic as social exemplar further polarized divisions in a society shaken to the core by the vocal activism of racial minorities, including the black power, civil rights, antiwar, and feminist movements. The ideology of the white ethnic was consciously embraced and promoted by the political establishment, di Leonardo (1994) maintains, outlining this dynamic:

> The Nixon administration in particular sought to exploit and enhance these social divisions through the use of the polarizing discourse of the silent majority—as opposed to the protesting anti-administration "minority." . . . [B]etween administration rhetoric and the media's response, an image grew of this stipulated entity: the silent majority were white (implicitly, white ethnic), largely male, blue-collar workers. They were held to be "patriotic" and to live in "traditional" families—ones in which males ruled, women did not work outside the home for pay, and parents controlled their children. (175)

It is noteworthy that in the writings of ethnic intellectuals such as Novak, the making of the white ethnic followed the template of black nationalism. Di Leonardo, once again, notes: "[K]ey expressions of white ethnic resentment were couched in a language consciously and unconsciously copied from the blacks themselves. Notions of the strength and richness of white ethnic cultures and their repression by WASPs, for example, mimicked black cultural nationalist celebrations of black culture's endurance despite white domination" (ibid.). But if the immigrant past served as a reference point for the ensuing white ethnic revival or new ethnicity—tentatively in the beginning, and with an increased ethnic confidence later—it was a past that had been seriously reworked for public consumption by the dominant society and the assimilated progeny of the immigrants. In the 1920s, the Chicago School of sociology and anthropology construed urban immigrants from southeastern Europe as caught in the duality "noble versus nasty peasant" (di Leonardo 1998, 87). They were seen "both as the inheritors of Gemeinschaft—the simple, humanly satisfying, face-to-face, traditional rural world that was giving way to the complex, anomic, modern urban world of strangers—and as rude, uncivilized peasants who must modernize, assimilate, Americanize in order to rise to the level of work and social life in the new industrial city" (di Leonardo 1994, 171). As we will see in chapter 2, the highly scripted ethnic festivals in the 1970s and 1980s, sanitized that past.

Community closeness and access to an authentic folk past furnished evidence of exotic, domesticated otherness, while the rational management of the festival place implicitly communicated the modernity of the folk, neutralizing in the process the negative image of the uncouth peasant.

White Ethnicity as Contour

It is time to identify interconnections among the practices and moments of representation discussed above and to reflect on how specific intersections help us understand the making of ethnic pasts in relation to whiteness. The ethnographic encounter between the folklorist and the ethnic family; the staged performance of ethnic/racial continuity in front of the U.S. Treasury; the racialization of the immigrants as interstitial whites; and their ethnicization/racialization as white ethnics—all point to ethnicity as a contested terrain of cultural representations. We witness in these examples the power of dominant narratives to displace or marginalize nonhegemonic alternatives. The perspectives of the "folk," immigrant rejection of whiteness, the anticapitalist function of the vernacular, and nonpopulist views of white ethnics are contained or rendered invisible by professional folklore, assimilationism, and populism. The analysis of these moments of representation in discourse and history makes it possible to illuminate struggles over the production of ethnic meanings and to rehabilitate what has been historically relegated to the margins. It will therefore provide the critical compass throughout this work.

Attention to history and discourse also brings to the fore the notion of ethnicity as a social field crisscrossed with historical junctures and disjunctures. My discussion identifies some continuities and discontinuities at work in Greek America: an ideology central to the constitution of Greek national identity in the eighteenth and nineteenth centuries, the continuity between modern and ancient Greeks proved once again crucial for constructing Greek immigrants, this time as white Americans in the early 1920s. What is more, the continuity thesis was deployed to negotiate the dominant discourse of folklorization in the 1950s and to represent Greeks as white ethnics, not simply ethnic folk. Further historical links abound. The civil rights era representation of white ethnicity intersects with Dorson's folkloric interest in ethnicizing the descendants of immigrants. But this construction of American ethnics as folk refrained from situating the ethnics in relation to American racial categories. It was the ethnics themselves who in their interaction with the folklorist articulated a view of themselves as white ethnic folk and quintessentially American, a location that escaped Dorson. And it is in the writings of an ethnic intellectual, Novak (among others), that the category of white ethnicity acquires cultural and political va-lence, becoming entrenched in the national imagination. In this intertwined web of representations, it is critical scholars such as di Leonardo but also occasionally the "folk" themselves that nuance the tendency of social and academic discourses to impose uniformity on the subjects they constitute.

The task here becomes one of finding ways not to allow dominant narratives—the historically privileged and therefore magnified contours of ethnicity—to hide from view a social landscape punctuated by enforced silences, marginalized alternatives, and muted political visions. And the more remote the pasts we in-vestigate, the greater the risk of missing discordance, contestation, and protest. If the way in which dominant Greek American historiography treated that past serves as a guide, the telling of narratives that demarcate Greek America as a cultural whole in linear progression (toward success or assimilation, for example) makes itself vulnerable to charges of being a history of exclusions. Until recently, the immigrant and ethnic left, women's perspectives, artists, non-Orthodox Greek Americans, civil rights activists, or homosexuals were treated as insignificant historical footnotes.

The analysis of ethnicity in terms of spatial and temporal interrelationships invites the metaphor of ethnicity as a social terrain crisscrossed by contour lines. The image of ethnic contours that I have in mind does not match the logic of a topographical map, where each contour marks a line of equal elevation and where contours never cross. In my view of ethnicity's map, contours connect texts, statements, and practices that claim to represent ethnicity; because these representations are interrelated in vastly complex ways, ethnic contours inter-sect, tangentially touch each other, or converge in dense hubs. Ethnic contours meander through history to create unexpected connections and make their ways around dominant representations to open previously untraced links. Despite these fundamental differences between the metaphor of ethnicity as contour and the actual contours of the topographical map, I retain the topographer's preoccu-pation with painstakingly charting the unevenness of a terrain through time. This attention to the ways in which contours are shaped diachronically foregrounds the potency of history to shape the terrain of ethnicity, the way in which past and present intertwine. This is why I favor the metaphor "contours of ethnicity" over the other frequent contender, "ethnicity as network." The latter fails to capture the constitutive dimension of history in charting contemporary ethnic-ity. A cultural topographer pays paramount attention to the detailed mapping of differential altitude—that is, uneven historical depth—so unlike the even plane sug-gested by the image of the network. Densely packed contours represent steep slopes, while widely spaced contours indicate slight differences in elevation. The emphasis is on representing differences, irregularities, and complexities while not ignoring consistencies and similarities. With this image as a guide, the researcher becomes aware that in entering the terrain of white ethnicity, what is readily visible from one angle becomes invisible from another perspective; what appears to be a horizontal vista may in fact be punctuated by deep trenches. And one is made mindful that dominant representations of ethnicity may obscure the better point of vantage from which to consider minute features of the landscape. Those who wish to explore the complexity of this terrain must not lose sight of ethnic representations shadowed by dominant discourses.

In this book, I defer my ambition to undertake an inclusive mapping of Greek America's contours of continuities, discontinuities, junctures, and disjunctures. I discuss here only those contours of the past that my specific interventions guide me to explore. I trace the continuing importance of the Greek classical past as a source of identity, community, and distinction in Greek America. I bring into focus a particular node where this past intersects with nostalgia for the preimmigrant folk and the discourse of New Age beliefs. One contour takes me to a feminist reading of the immigrant past. Another one leads me to consider the appropriation of the vernacular to advocate solidarity between Greek Americans and minorities. I sketch such contours in painstaking detail to show how and why the immigrant pasts that I outlined in this chapter continue to exert a powerful force on contemporary popular ethnographers.

Within this framework, I identify dominant views on ethnicity, contradictions, and contestation. I pay close attention to the incongruities that take shape every time a narrative about ethnic perfection is confronted by a countermemory about ethnic failure. In my mapping I attend to contours that exhibit unexpected twists and turns and intersect at surprising coordinates, having escaped the charting of specialized or amateur topographers. I am interested therefore in recovering ethnicity as a heterogeneous, uneven social field, an interpretive polyphony that is crisscrossed by languages of success and failure, loss and preservation, decline and reconfiguration, historical memory and ahistorical nostalgia, self-affirmation, and self-critique. The next chapter introduces such unanticipated contours. It outlines assimilation as ethnic production—not cultural loss—that simultaneously locates Greek America at the complex, fractal intersection among whiteness, the discourse of heritage, model white ethnicity, collective identity, and European Americanness.

CHAPTER TWO

Whither Collective Ethnic Identities?

White Ethnics and the Slippery Terrain of European Americanness

> The twilight [of ethnicity] metaphor also allows for the
> occasional flare-ups of ethnic feelings and conflicts that give
> the illusion that ethnicity is reviving, but are little more than
> flickers in the fading light.
>
> —Richard Alba,
> *Italian Americans: Into the Twilight of Ethnicity*

> From "power feminism" to libertarian gay rights to
> assertions of "ghetto nihilism," we are awash in a petit
> bourgeois politics that simultaneously caresses the better-
> off female, gay, and/or minority self while consigning its
> working-class and impoverished sisters and brothers to their
> "richly deserved" misery, lecturing them, for all the world
> like some twentieth-century Gradgrind, to pull themselves
> up by their bootstraps.
>
> —Micaela di Leonardo, "White Ethnicities, Identity
> Politics, and Baby Bear's Chair"

WHAT IS HAPPENING to American white ethnicities in the era of multiculturalism? A significant number of scholars tend to think about white ethnicity
in apocalyptic terms, writing, if not of its imminent extinction, certainly of its
dramatic weakening. Key words such as "atrophy," "twilight," "superficiality," and
"thinness" increasingly frame a research perspective that is unwilling to probe
beyond the vocabulary of white ethnic cultural decline, the celebratory display
of symbols in parades and festivals, forgetting, and the dimming of tradition.
White ethnicities are seen as attenuated to such a degree as to become fleeting and
shallow. Their communities are portrayed as verging on dissolution, a monumental fragmentation that will lead to the proliferation of an infinite variety of

private and tenuous ethnic identities. And the fusion of distinct ethnic identities of Americans of European ancestry into a (white) European American identity is predicted, inevitably diminishing the importance of particular ethnic collectives. Whereas elsewhere in scholarship racial minorities are represented as embodying richly textured cultural lives, white ethnics are made to stand for a transparent people on the verge of losing culture.

The work of Richard Alba (1990), one of the most influential sociologists of white ethnicity in the United States, exemplifies a powerful contour of this scholarship. Alba argues that distinct white-hyphenated identities are undergoing a dramatic transformation, morphing into an emergent panethnic European American identity. Crucial to this argument is the notion that high degrees of cultural loss among ethnics of European ancestry have dissolved the differences that have historically separated them from one other—say Italian Americans from Polish Americans. This collapse of ethnic boundaries makes possible their assimilation into an emerging European American group, which is brought together by a shared narrative of immigrant hardships followed by a hard-earned experience of social and economic mobility.

Alba identified and sought to tackle a "paradoxical divergence" in the expression of white ethnicity (290). On the one hand, his findings pointed to the "long-run and seemingly irreversible decline of objective ethnic differences" (ibid.) among populations of European ancestry, a process he explained as the end product of inexorable acculturation and structural assimilation. The resulting cultural dilution of ethnicity becomes sociologically quantifiable, measured in high rates of language loss, the diminishment of ethnically marked behavior, and the "great extent and ease of intermarriage," which tellingly reveals "the growing extent of social integration among persons with European ancestry" (291).[1] On the other hand, the sociologist is confronted with recurrent evidence underlining "the continuing subjective importance of ethnic origins to many white Americans" (290). Although white ethnics have departed radically from the immigrant generation's behavioral patterns, they continue to observe family-based ethnic traditions, explore roots, undertake trips to places of ancestral origins, and voluntarily participate in the activities of ethnic associations.

What is more, the persistence of individual ethnic identity correlates positively with high levels of education and social mobility. "[I]ncreasing education tends to heighten awareness of ethnic background," Alba writes (308), accounting for this persistence as the outcome of rational choice. He suggests that ethnic identification among mobile, highly educated white Americans works beneficially "as a form of cultural capital" (ibid.) in that it enhances an individual's economic and social interests by facilitating access to social networks of power. This position "presumes that ethnic symbols and references can be of use in the complex signaling by which individuals establish relationships to one another" (ibid). Its salience in upper-class circles requires that such an identity "need not occupy more than a small portion of the identity 'masks' individuals present to others, and need not be deeply felt" (308). Assimilated white ethnics do not return to behavioral ethnicity; instead they display a romanticized, nostalgic, and sentimental connection to it, a nonthreatening association that carries no social stigma whatsoever. In other words, total assimilation, in the manner predicted by traditional assimilation theory, has not occurred. What has taken place instead is a radical transformation of old-style identities and communities (determined by an ethnic culture) into voluntarily chosen, malleable ones that weaken and even situationally dissolve internal cultural boundaries among whites.[2]

Because the overall thesis of his landmark book *Ethnic Identity: The Transformation of White America* rests on the notion of a tenuous ethnic identity, Alba expends a great deal of intellectual labor to establish white ethnic identities as weak in salience, ultimately shallow, and superfluous. He argues that the dissolution of ethnically based social structures that have historically shaped and sustained collective identities results in a fundamental transformation: the formation of largely private, family-centered identities, whose extreme variability makes the maintenance of meaningful ethnic collectives impossible. The weakening and de-centering of the "available collective expressions of ethnicity" or the "supply side of ethnicity" (303) results in ethnic fragmentation and gives rise to highly personal and culturally tenuous identities. The prevalence of voluntary (and fragile) ethnic affiliation comes about as a result of social disintegration, as ethnic structures determining identity recede or even disappear from the public sphere.

In Alba's model, weak ethnic identities furnish the conditions for "the formation of a new ethnic group"—European Americans—"based on ancestry from anywhere on the European continent" (293). Drawing from Max Weber's classical definition of an ethnic group, he identifies—as he must in order to justify this new formation as an ethnic collective—the ethnic myths of European Americans (ibid.). Having lost their deep cultural anchoring, expressions of ethnicity exhibit fundamental commonalities across European ethnicities.[3] Although ethnic-experience narratives of identity do retain the specificity of hyphenated labels, they are uniformly scripted around a common plot. Shared by all is a history of "immigration and mobility" (314) and "social honor" based on an ethos of hard work and heroic sacrifice. "Identities that once separated the English, Irish, Italians, Jews, and Scots now bring individuals with these ancestries together, based on the putative memories of ancestors who contributed to this common history" (ibid.). And, Alba concludes, the sharing of these essential components is intimately connected with ethnic politics and racial polarization. The European American narrative of immigrant origins marred by discrimination, the ensuing struggle for social integration, and eventual self-made success through a persistent work ethic validates the hegemonic narrative of America as an open and inclusive democracy. "The thrust of European-American identity is to defend the individualistic view of the American system, because it portrays the system as open to those who are willing to work hard and pull themselves over barriers of poverty and discrimination" (317). It defines, therefore, "a prototypical American experience, against which non-European minorities . . . are pressured to measure themselves" (316). In addition, "the European-American identity provides a way for whites to mobilize themselves, bridging what were once their own ethnic divisions, in opposition to the challenges of non-European groups" (ibid.) in the competition for social and economic resources in a multicultural agora.[4]

The import of such a European Americanness is worth elaborating upon. The dissolution of meaningful internal boundaries among historically distinct ethnic groups does not totally eliminate hyphenated identities but results in the production of rigid external boundaries of racial differentiation between whites and nonwhites. Therefore, the continuing circulation of weak but specific ethnic identities carries crucial racial implications. For Alba, cultural thinness among white ethnics returns social and political dividends, translating cultural loss into racial privilege. On the one hand, the redrawing of internal ethnic boundaries facilitates solidarity around shared whiteness. On the other hand, the claim of ethnic affiliation among socioeconomically successful white ethnics enables them to eschew the language of race, even as this claim fundamentally participates in race talk. Ethnic identity is put into the service of whiteness because it explains hierarchies and economic inequality in terms of culture, not social structure, as I will discuss in detail in the conclusion of this chapter. The persistence of (thin) ethnic identities supports, inescapably, an ideology of racial domination.

The strengths of Alba's model lie in its explication of ethnicity in relation to racial privilege and in its reliance on statistically significant cultural trends to navigate a complex terrain and tap into an emergent phenomenon. But the model skirts around a number of social realities that could have troubled its neat coherence. Alba is aware of variability within and across ethnicities and is conscious of the pitfalls of predictive social science: his analysis cautions against a uniform treatment of white ethnicity and a teleological approach to identity formation. But, ultimately, his discussion brackets the crucial question of how diversity within white ethnicity may complicate the model of European American whiteness. One could take serious issue with a number of convenient exclusions and factual inaccuracies in his book. Although his approach acknowledges the operation of religion as a corporate body producing ethnicity for the Jews and the Greeks (304), for example, this admission is conveniently forgotten when the moment comes to argue about the privatization of white ethnic identities and their strong disassociation from determining collective structures. If "religious affiliation tends to reinforce ethnicity" (Bakalian 1993, 48) among certain white ethnics, such as Armenians and Greeks, how exactly does the continued operation of a corporate ethnoreligious body, such as the Greek Orthodox Church, square with the alleged dominance of privatized identities and the concomitant weakening of social structure? This question acquires particular poignancy in Greek America because, according to Charles Moskos (1990), "for the American born, even as the immigrant past fades, the church community becomes the prime definer of Greek ethnicity" in the United States (67). Moreover, Alba's (1990) inattention to institutions fostering at least some degree of ethnic cohesion leads to empirically false assertions. "[T]here is little evidence," he writes, "of ethnicity functioning as a form of mutual assistance. Rare are the whites who claim to have received any special professional or economic assistance from fellow ethnics" (306). This claim cannot possibly hold up against empirical scrutiny; its falsity becomes evident from any cursory glance at the long list of ethnic descent-based scholarships or coethnic mutual aid organizations currently at work in Greek America.[5]

Therefore, Alba's model of privatized identities can easily be problematized by pointing to ethnic practices—dance groups, mutual aid societies, festivals, and community functions, including language schools—that continue to produce collective identities within the space of Greek America. But in this chapter, I opt for an alternative, less obvious, and therefore more challenging critical route. I focus my critique on an ethnic narrative that *most closely approximates* the main contours of Alba's model of identity. Through this strategy, I wish to join Alba and the wider circle of scholars who interrogate the bootstrap ideology of white ethnicity. But my analysis will show that it is possible to argue that a distinct ethnicity can be complicit in the European American narrative of struggle and self-made success and still call for a strong ethnic identity. I will illustrate the continuing power of social discourses, specifically Hellenism, to constitute Greek American identity and to fashion it as a duty and obligation, not as a fleeting superficiality.

Inevitably, this requires a move away from a core notion of the sociological model that frames white ethnicity in terms of cultural loss. Instead, I understand ethnicity as a multidimensional practice in which ethnics continuously reinvent, rework, abandon, negotiate, and resignify their relation with the past. Although cultural surrender is an unquestionable aspect of this dynamic process, ethnicity is infused with new meanings or selectively reattached to old ones within a contested field of cultural production. I do not approach ethnicity in terms of its departure from the "immigrant generation's cultural and behavioral patterns," which are "taken as the statistical baseline" measuring ethnicity (Bakalian 1993, 5) and leading inescapably to the so-called white ethnic crisis of authenticity (Steinberg 1981, 63). Neither do I approach it as an ethnic revival intended to reinstitute a lost culture.[6] Instead, I understand it as constituting any narrative or practice that invokes a past or ancestry to sustain various kinds of cultural affiliations, which may include material and symbolic support of ethnic institutions. Rather than confine my view of ethnicity to the reproduction of immigrant behavior, I expand it to include all sorts of actions that generate cultural connections in new and reinvented ways. Once white ethnicity is viewed through these lenses, it is no longer feasible to frame it in terms of decline, loss, or triviality. Instead, the reverse can be illuminated once one enumerates the multiple ways through which ethnicity is realized. The writing of ethnic autobiography, the establishment of museums, the practice of dance, the production of archives and the preservation of the past in general, the support of university ethnic studies programs, and the writing of popular history, fiction, and ethnography are in full swing in Greek America but also in other white ethnic fields.[7] Once these practices are recognized as powerful forces constituting—or even inventing—new forms of ethnic expression, then white ethnicity is seen to represent a vibrant cultural production deserving of analysis that ventures beyond choice and rational interest. These new forms are erroneously understood as weak and trivial because they signal a fundamental departure from the classical model of ethnicity-as-behavior and ethnicity-as-replication of an originary immigrant culture. It is true that sociologists of white ethnicity have successfully identified a historical transformation in the form and function of ethnicity in postmodern multicultural democracies, a shift from "being ethnic" to "feeling ethnic." But in holding the experience of the former as authentic and real and the latter as shallow and often disposable, they have fumbled an opportunity to probe the depths and complex contours associated with this new way of experiencing ethnicity.

Furthermore, positing the reduction of ethnic difference as evidence of assimilation presents a problem because it fails to interrogate why assimilation should be framed solely in terms of cultural loss in the first place. Why should assimilation be reduced to a one-dimensional process of loss instead of a multidimensional one characterized not only by cultural relinquishment but also by selective retention and transmutation, even ethnic invention? The answer to this question, as Roger Waldinger (2003) points out in his incisive review of Richard Alba and Victor Nee's *Remaking the American Mainstream: Assimilation and Contemporary Immigration* (2003), lies in a resonance between this kind of sociology of assimilation and popular views on ethnic difference. He observes that "for both [the popular imagination and this sociological theory], ethnic differences are fundamentally imported by the foreigners, whose intrusions disrupt what would otherwise be an integrated whole" (256). According to this logic, the preservation of national integrity is predicated on the nationalization of the immigrants, which is measured in turn by degrees of ethnic forgetting. The reproduction of nationalist ideology by laypeople is fortified here by the confluence of academic and popular views that understand assimilation as cultural loss. In this respect, a sociological paradigm purporting to explain assimilation becomes complicit, albeit unintentionally, in a specific ideology of the nation as a homogeneous whole. Inevitably, the analysis of assimilation as ethnic reduction functions "not so much [as] a theory [but] as a part of the [assimilationist] process itself" (ibid.). Thus, if assimilation into dominant discourses and practices indeed occurs, as I agree it does, it should be examined through a series of additional questions: who assimilates and specifically to what?

I organize this chapter, therefore, around the following question: in what way does ethnicity produce usable ethnic pasts that serve assimilationist purposes? To this end, I analyze a specific site—the PBS documentary *The Greek Americans* (1998)—and I proceed to argue that, paradoxically, assimilation to European American whiteness is claimed through a narrative that posits ethnic identity as a powerful collective attachment. In other words, assimilation in this instance takes place as a process of ethnicization, not one of cultural decline. I discuss this popular ethnography to show how its specific production of usable pasts participates in a wider social discourse that posits identity in Greek America as a collective commitment and obligation. I argue that the documentary constructs Greek ethnicity in conformity to an Occidental model of identity—Western-Greek—without compromising the specificity of a strong ethnic element. So construed, ethnicity is subsequently assimilated into the model of liberal multiculturalism and the ideology of pan-European Americanness, as Alba's model would have predicted. But crucially, *The Greek Americans* becomes a site of assimilation into this hegemonic ideology of white ethnic identity via ethnicization, *not* de-ethnicization. My conclusion demonstrates that while the documentary advances a claim to whiteness, it does so without shedding its strong commitment to an ethnically marked *collective* identity.

Before I scrutinize the documentary, I will take a detour that examines the social and economic conditions enabling the production of collective and private ethnic identities in the United States in the post–civil rights era. This is necessary in order to illustrate how the making of white ethnicity—as it pertains to Greek America—is defined at the intersection between the struggle to maintain stable, collective identities and the postmodern drive to encourage fluid, highly personalized identities. I suggest that it is this tension, not an inexorable drive toward the privatization of identities, that best captures the present moment in the making of usable ethnic pasts in reference to at least one white ethnic field that falls outside the purview of Alba's analysis, Greek America.

White Ethnicity, Multiculturalism, and the Heritage Industry

Current representations of white ethnicity are historically embedded in the discourse of liberal multiculturalism that emerged from the civil rights movement in America. Sponsored by the state, embraced by the corporate world, and promoted by ethnic intellectuals and community leaders, the cultural production of ethnicity brought about a profound historical reconfiguration of American society as a multicultural society. Enabled by what is commonly called the heritage industry—a term denoting the production of ethnic pasts at the intersection of political, social, cultural, and economic interests—multiculturalism provided the conditions for the public visibility of ethnicity.[8] Forced for so long to practice their ethnicity backstage, within the interior, invisible spaces of private and family lives and hidden within their communities, the descendants of the formerly despised southeastern European immigrants came out, inundating the public sphere with folksy images and performances. If the immigrant past signified premodern ties unfit for a modern America and had been coerced into oblivion in the assimilationist 1920s, by the 1960s, it began to command wide national attention. If new immigrants had been subjected to and had acquiesced in coercive assimilation—if in fact they "render[ed] to Caesar while maintaining a kind of underground ethnicity" (Abrahams and Kalcik 1978, 232)—now white ethnics capitalized on multiculturalism to self-consciously perform, exhibit, narrate, document, preserve, and take pride in their past.[9] Heritage production in the form of dance, museums, archives, exhibits, university ethnic studies programs, festivals, cookbooks, culinary exhibitions, parades, language schools, and cultural centers circulated ethnicity in the public sphere, adding value to what once was "the obsolete, the mistaken, the outmoded, the dead, and the defunct" (Kirshenblatt-Gimblett 1995, 369). Conceived as "a new mode of cultural production in the present that has recourse to the past" (370), heritage gave the past "a second life," infusing it with new meanings (369). Heritage meant that traditional costumes *on display* no longer stood for folk backwardness but represented an authentic repository of identity, cultural ownership, and the value of preserving the past. Reconstructed ancestral villages in festival spaces represented not embarrassing folk origins but exclusive access to a meaningful past lost to nonethnic modernity.

This "coming-out party for white ethnics" (Abrahams and Kalcik 1978, 227) produced more than community-centered forms of cultural vitalization. It brought ethnicity into the orbit of national consciousness, promoting it as a public spectacle and popular destination. Working synergetically with domestic tourism, the heritage industry capitalized on folklorization to promote the "local for export," representing white ethnics as traditional enclaves within modernity (Kirshenblatt-Gimblett 1995, 373). The commodification of ethnicity-as-folklore proved valuable to ethnic collectives, which appropriated folkness as a central component of their self-representations as tightly knit, culturally rich communities. Enabled by multiculturalism and domestic tourism, white ethnics staged reflexive, highly scripted cultural spectacles centered on authentic folkness and community solidarity that appealed to the public taste for exotic, nonthreatening Others. Recourse to vernacular roots became a route that bridged modernity's sharp break from the folk past.

In this regard, the ethnics stole a page from the folklorist's notebook. In Richard Dorson's folklore, for example, a Greek family represented neither a frozen relic from the preimmigrant past nor a case of inward immigrant insularity. Simultaneously folk, ethnic, transnational, and national—by virtue of its participation in American cultural, economic, and educational institutions—the family is best described in terms of cultural syncretism. In this case, aspects of the folk past were remembered, and even partially practiced, in coexistence with the family's modernity. Inescapably though, its folkness in the present was seen by the folklorist as a continuous thread, so to speak, that connected acculturated ethnic Americans with a premodern past. Folklore's disciplinary net foregrounded the folkness of ethnicity. Similarly, the heritage industry's folklorization demanded that ethnic modernity (organizational and business skills, savvy public relations, reflexivity in matters of cultural representation that were in full force in the planning, organizing, and promoting ethnic displays of difference) were dressed up, so to speak, in the costume and language of folk authenticity.

Heritage made the folk past hypervisible. If the heritage industry relies on exotic realness to turn a locality into a tourist destination, skillful translators of ethnicity built on the notion of authenticity to stage spectacles of Otherness. They produced images of a cohesive, harmonious ethnic community that could claim legitimate access to the group's premodern past and boast the virtuoso competence to perform it. Highly scripted cultural displays staged the inauthentic authenticity that Dorson (1950) would find objectionable as "fakelore."[10] Ironically, if the discipline of folklore "has been constituted to seek the authentic" (Bendix 1997, 14), American ethnics have played a key role in self-consciously manipulating authenticity to establish cultural visibility. Across the nation, sites of folk performativity, such as festivals, parades, and ethnic theme towns, were particularly effective in naturalizing ethnic folk practices as an integral component of the dominant symbolic order. Endorsing an integrationist version of pluralism that marked ethnic distinctiveness but also rooted ethnics in a vision of unified America, these spectacles were readily turned into signs of the nation's cultural openness. The popularity of public performances and their extensive media coverage have made step dancing, polka, spanakopita, and feta common household words, turning the foreign into a familiar idiom of an expanded American culture.[11]

The national domestication of ethnicity and its commercial appeal as heritage performance are associated with a wider expansion of the culture industry. Ethnicity has become an integral component of corporate planning and marketing strategies because of the increasing purchasing power of ethnic and minority consumers and the enormous profit potential that this development represents. Upwardly mobile consumers loyal to specific ethnic brands create an irresistible niche market for the food, clothing, housewares, entertainment, and leisure industries.[12] Writing about the relationship between ethnic identity and consumerism in the United States, Marilyn Halter (2000) illuminates the intersection of culture and commerce. Ethnicity, she argues, has become interwoven with a consumerist ethos that makes the purchasing of certain ethnic-related products an integral component of identity. This "shopping for identity," she suggests, replaces "traditional neighborhoods and community affiliations as the connective tissue of postmodern life" (13). It has become a key practice for experiencing and expressing identity at the individual level. "In a society in which individualism is so highly valued," she proposes, "this type of 'convenience' or 'portable' ethnicity works very well" because it disassociates ethnic affiliation from obligations and ties to a collective (9). Such a commodified identity, in turn, sustains a devoted ethnic clientele that, in economic terms, gives shape to a segmented market consisting of diverse yet readily identifiable ethnic constituencies defined by specific tastes and preferences.

The wide circulation of nonprofessional ethnographies in the popular culture should be understood in this context. A culture industry, consisting of publishers

and other information- and entertainment-related businesses, packages and circulates a wide range of popular ethnographies catering to specific ethnic niches
as well as to mainstream audiences. The great number of ethnic products (books,
toys, magazines, DVDs, and CDs) in a wide range of genres—literature, folklore,
standup comedy, music, community history, satire, films and documentaries,
ethnography, family biography, and autobiography—testifies to a vital cultural
production that targets ethnic audiences. Presses with little national visibility—
such as Five and Dot Corporation, Tegea Press, and Arcadia Publishing—as well
as the enduring Pella and the increasingly visible Cosmos Publishing produce
handsome volumes on ethnic autobiography, the immigrant family, and community
histories. Alternatively, community-based organizations, the educated public,
and self-appointed ethnic gatekeepers take the initiative in producing and marketing documentaries, magazines, cookbooks, and popular ethnographies. This
trend also extends to prestigious sites of national cultural production. Television
networks, established academic presses, and the state are increasingly financing
the making and the marketing of popular ethnographies. The Public Broadcast-
ing System, for example, promoted the ethnographic documentary *The Greek
Americans* (1998) as part of its Heritage Specials Series, and Brandeis University
Press published the transnational ethnography of Michael Kalafatas (2003), a
nonprofessional ethnographer, to critical and popular acclaim.

Private Identities in Postmodernity

Thus, while the heritage industry encourages the production of collective ethnicity embedded in community structures, it simultaneously drives the reconfiguration of the collective into scattered, highly individualized identities. Consumed
in the privacy of one's home, ethnic products, such as music, books, and films,
constitute resources that make possible the solitary consumption of ethnicity and
provide a forum for the self to fashion its own private identities. Ethnic audiences
could read Michael Kalafatas's personal quest for family roots, for instance, and
draw inspiration to initiate their own idiosyncratic, highly personal projects of
ancestral discovery. Commodified heritage requires no community for the performance of ethnicity; it is available for an individual's creative appropriation.

Alba's model accords one-sided privilege to this process of identity privatization. In this regard, it owes an intellectual debt to symbolic ethnicity, a paradigm
that theorizes white ethnicity in terms of individual choice, malleability, and
creative self-fashioning. It situates ethnic identity in relation to postmodernity,
a connection effectively discerned by Gregory Jusdanis, who views symbolic
ethnicity as "an extension of the postmodern proclivity to self-invention, the

tendency to regard the self as a synthesis of various traditions" (2001, 174). Ethnicity becomes yet another resource in the cultural repertoire of lifestyle options, which the self reflexively sieves to fashion itself as it sees fit. Capturing the association between symbolic ethnicity and the aesthetics of the postmodern self, Jusdanis writes:

> The questions "How shall I live?" and "Who am I?" have to be faced in daily decisions since they are *not* determined by kinship and traditions. These questions have to be answered with regard to fashion, diet, health, profession, the family, and, of course, ethnicity. In other words, the postmodern individual conceives of identity as a reflexively maintained enterprise rather than a set of duties and obligations. The difference between the white immigrants and their great-grandchildren (and between whites today and racial minorities) is that ethnic identification has become largely a life-style choice. (174)

Postmodernity certainly produces flexible identities and promotes self-reflexive creativity. Ethnicity is seen as a resource disembodied from the subject, which is largely accorded autonomy to effect its own, voluntarily chosen ethnic identity. But significantly, it is "the postmodern individual [who] conceives of identity" as a self-determining project of self-fashioning. This concept operates in the domain of popular belief, and scholars do not miss the resonance between the ideology of identity-as-choice and what Herbert Gans (1988) calls popular or "middle American individualism" (1). Alba draws on this concept to recognize the extent of the popular disassociation of ethnicity from social obligation. "[T]he ethos of individualism," he writes, shapes "the belief, evident throughout our interviews, that there is little obligation to identify in ethnic terms and also little obligation to behave in specific ethnic ways" (1990, 300).

Practicing ethnicity as self-invention is therefore culturally determined. Lifestyles do not take place in a social vacuum but are constituted by powerful discourses, such as New Age beliefs, primitivism, antimodernism, multiculturalism, individualism, and health and fitness, among others, that determine how and when ethnicity is situationally enacted. Alluringly seductive, the play of identities is ubiquitous in the cultural marketplace, pulling subjects beyond ethnicity or, alternatively, channeling and multiplying ethnic options. Postmodernity antagonizes those social forces, including religion and ethnicity, that historically required conformity to the dictates of collective culture. It assaults subjection to the authoritative command of ethnicity as it hides its own determinative function through the ideology of choice.

Although scholars pay due attention to processes of cultural fragmentation, ethnic amnesia, individual agency, and self-invention, they often neglect or minimize the importance of the simultaneous operation of practices and narratives that anchor or seek to ground individuals in enduring structures of collective belonging. They fail to recognize that the individual is still partly enmeshed in familial and ethnic determinations and that the postmodern self, therefore, escapes the determining grip of ethnicity only partially. In the current environment of rapidly changing expressions of ethnicity, cultural decentering, the scattering of meaning, fluidity, and contingency—all in a context of rampant cultural commodification—one witnesses the dense circulation of alternative narratives that posit coherence, stability, and continuity as central features of ethnic collectives. Far from marginal, these constructions of identity largely replicate the ideology of liberal multiculturalism, compartmentalizing complex and overlapping cultural affiliations, ambiguity, and contradictions into discrete ethnic identities. In claiming an essential identity defined by a shared set of cultural traits, they posit a stable, deep contour of collective attachment; they function in a centripetal manner, countering the centrifugal social forces that scatter stable meanings and promote ethnic superficiality.

Let us then dissect the politics and poetics of this kind of contour by focusing on a specific narrative site of Greek America, the PBS documentary *The Greek Americans,* and examine why and how it constructs a sense of collective identity and belonging. Produced by a national institution whose power lies in bringing ethnicity into representation at a national scale, the documentary comes to life at the intersection of national and ethnic interests. It arose out of the union between state-sponsored multiculturalism—and particularly the heritage industry—and the economic power of Greek America, willing at that specific time to financially support the production of ethnicity for national consumption.[13] The link between national and ethnic interests was strengthened through the mediation of the documentary's author and producer, who is biographically and socially connected with Greek ethnicity and deeply entrenched in the corporate world of the arts, entertainment, and the television cultural industry. For all those reasons, a nationally important institution, PBS, opted to work with and function as a key site for ethnic, economic, and cultural networks to produce a narrative of ethnic identity and collective belonging.

Such a point of departure is consistent with the interventionist politics of this book. In my effort to complicate the model of white ethnic identity as a primarily private, ethnically superfluous lifestyle expression, I turn to this nationally visible site that constructs white ethnicity as a collective whole whose existence hinges on attachment to community and commitment to cultural reproduction. I examine both how this documentary series, a narrative of community and identity, manufactures ethnic homogeneity and what it excludes in the process. I look, therefore, at how and why an identity narrative produces ethnicity around a set of specific meanings. At the same time, I situate *The Greek Americans* in history and in relation to dominant representations of white ethnicity.

The Poetics of Ethnic Homogeneity

At a historical juncture when the heritage industry bifurcated the production of ethnicity between private and collective identity, the documentary *The Greek Americans* produced a narrative of ethnic coherence and deep belonging. Promoted as "the first ever, definitive television work that . . . tells our fantastic [Greek American] story," it builds on the discourse of authenticity to enunciate an insider's representation of ethnicity. *The Greek Americans* appropriates authenticity, but it does so in a manner that inscribes ethnic folkness within the narrative of Western identity. As a site for constructing ethnic meanings, it assimilates Greek America into an Occidental model of ethnicity. And it does so while retaining ethnic hyphenation and, in fact, explicitly aiming to produce usable pasts and preserve cultural specificity for the future. It can be said that the documentary publicly articulates an often-told narrative of Greek identity—a popular version of which the Corombos family sought to impart to the folklorist Dorson—this time addressed to a national audience in the context of institutionalized American multiculturalism.

The Greek Americans was part of the network's much-advertised Heritage Specials Series, which featured a wide range of ethnic and racial groups: Armenian, Chinese, Cuban, German, Greek, Italian, Jewish, Mexican, Polish, and Puerto Rican Americans, among others. This serialization of cultural diversity signals the increasing inclusion of representations of ethnicity in the public sphere and the popularization of ethnic images that, through television, reach deep into the cultural fabric of the nation. In addition, it exemplifies a particular moment in the way in which ethnic groups make themselves known to a wide audience. They adopt mass technologies as a strategy for authoring and disseminating widely accessible self-representations.[14]

A component of the heritage industry, the documentary employs the ethnic topos of struggle and success. In accordance to Alba's model, it presents Greek Americans as contemporary Horatio Algers who "started at the bottom," overcame nativist hostility and discrimination, and while playing fair in a system that did not always do the same, earned through hard work "a special place on the

American dream scheme."[15] References to Greek America's comparatively high educational and income rankings are common. In the words of Senator Paul Sarbanes, "[Greek Americans] came over here as immigrants, and now they are the number one educated group in this United States, [and] number two group financially."[16] In this typical rags-to-riches narrative, Greek Americans are portrayed as model ethnics: "Super Americans" (*Passing the Torch*) and "disciple[s] of the American Dream" (*The Greek Americans*). They represent modern agents who successfully build on the legacy of the immigrant and classical past and ensure a future for Hellenism, whose guardianship they claim. *The Greek Americans* anchors a group of people to a past, a classic gesture of ethnic identity formation. The second part of the series, *Passing the Torch,* addresses issues of cultural preservation to fashion possible ethnic futures.

Like an ethnic festival, the documentary claims access to authenticity. But as scholars have shown, authenticity is not an inherent quality, but "a struggle, a social process, in which competing interests argue for their own interpretation of history" (Bruner 1994, 407). The prize for which these interest groups jostle and contend is the privilege of speaking for Greek America. In so doing, the prevailing group displaces alternate perspectives. It is necessary, then, to examine who speaks for Greek America in the documentary, what kinds of pasts are authenticated, and whether the production of these usable pasts makes or unmakes whiteness.

The documentary intersperses popular interpretations with the perspectives of artists and academics. The views of nonspecialists about ethnicity are particularly privileged. Restaurateurs interpret immigration for the audience, for example, not sociologists, anthropologists, or historians. According to the owner of Milos restaurant in New York City, "out of a deep appreciation for the United States for accepting them during their times of hardship . . . the Greeks were very ready to accept the demands of American society." Similarly, corporate executives are also authorized to interpret ethnicity: "[Participation in ethnic networks] is a way of reaffirming their tribe . . . . [I]t is totally cultural; it is anthropological, Greeks do that a lot." "[*Filotimo*] is a uniquely Greek trait. It is [a] combination of perhaps unreasonable pride, a powerful beyond description force [propelling you] not [to] appear bad in the eyes of other people" (*Passing the Torch*). Actors and political celebrities join this interpretive chorus. Actress Olympia Dukakis and political maverick Arianna Stassinopoulos Huffington, for instance, articulate the golden mean of Greek Americans as bon vivant natural entrepreneurs: "There is an adventurous spirit, and there is an entrepreneurial spirit in Greeks." And "the best Greek quality is a passion for life, . . . the

Zorba, the Greek quality of enthusiasm . . . to be full of life, to really live life to the fullest."

The ethnographic orientation of our times is evident here. As Greek Americans anthropologize Greek America, the audience witnesses the current immersion in the practice of "generalized ethnography" (Bazin 1999). In a multicultural society, Jean Bazin writes, "everyone participates as his neighbor's ethnographer, representing the other's identity in terms of typical behavior. With everyone becoming someone else's native, modern (or postmodern) society must itself become a space of ethnographic inscription" (31). The documentary participates in this process to produce and legitimize, as I will argue, an ideological consensus on what constitutes a Greek American identity. For this purpose, it represents Greek America as a single cultural whole. Aspiring to an ethnographic holism, the camera visits a wide range of diverse sites where ethnicity is produced. It zooms in on the dancing stage of a Greek festival, represented as the inclusive space where the Greek flair for celebration is realized, where the "zest for life" and Zorba-like spirit are performed and shared. It surveys the interiors of Byzantine-style Greek Orthodox churches in the United States as "time capsule[s]" in which the "ritual and the moods all reflect ancient traditions." It dwells on narratives about overcoming hardships, ethnic pride, and success, juxtaposing them with images of Greek immigrants at work. The camera visits eating establishments, from fine restaurants to Greek-owned diners, as archetypal icons of Greek American entrepreneurial success. It features working-class immigrants and artisans, though it favors interview segments with Greek American celebrities, politicians, and business executives. It delivers on its claim to inclusiveness by representing the views of women and men across generations. In the process, the documentary assembles definitions of Greek American identity ("Greeks have been a powerful force for some basic values: the emphasis on family, on education, on the church, and on hard work"), which it supports through corresponding visual images.[17]

Although the documentary relies on numerous ethnographic interviews and features a variety of perspectives, it ultimately regulates the meaning of Greek America. It manufactures ethnic homogeneity by creating from its various sources a collage that tells a single ethnic story. An initial strategy of representation entails establishing the truth of the oral accounts. The documentary adopts the conventions of realist representation and plots its narrative through an unfolding sequence of photographs, video footage, newspaper clips, interviews, and commentary. Photographs and video footage—from family gatherings and community festivities, for instance—provide the visual evidence to support narrative content. Footage depicting an exuberant performance of a solo male dance, for example, works as indexical evidence to substantiate the earlier-quoted statement on the Zorba-like passion of the Greeks. The making of homogeneity here becomes possible through a "synecdochic fallacy" (di Leonardo 1998), in which samples of images and statements are taken to represent the whole. This narrative mode functions as a metalanguage that naturalizes certain cultural expressions as an ethnic essence. It invests itself, therefore, with the narrative power to cancel Greek American heterogeneity.

The documentary produces ethnic meanings through the authoritative interjections of the omniscient narrator. It is his voice, ultimately, that interprets collective experience on behalf of the group. Take, for example, the assertive rendering of a painful historical experience, discrimination: "It wasn't easy but we [the Greeks] overcame [discrimination] with grace and humor." Offensive in its ideological oversimplification of a traumatic experience that shattered immigrant lives and humiliated their progeny, this statement is not only an example of blatant historical amnesia but also an example of a narrative posture of detachment that, following the conventions of objective journalism, legitimizes representations as unequivocally true. The documentary thus regulates how the working class, for instance, experiences America. It is through the intervention of the objective narrator that immigrant laborers are depicted as adhering uniformly to the ideology of the American dream. Thus, a hot dog vendor shown at work represents a step in a process of inevitable progression. His views are never aired. He is made known to the audience only through the narrator: "Every slap of mustard means another book in the hands of a well-educated and hardworking disciple of the American dream." In other instances, the documentary showcases spoken testimony but controls its meaning. A young Greek American's statement, "I don't believe in ever losing Greece, the Greek spirit in me," is followed by the narrator's interpretation of what the "Greek spirit" is all about. He says, "Working six days a week, twelve hours a day, he [the father of the interviewee] tries to give that spirit back to his daughter: the spirit of work, the spirit of family."

The effort to tightly script Greek America as a uniformly successful American ethnic group leads to a selective editing of those who speak on behalf of the collective. A range of scholars, chroniclers, commentators, and artists who have critiqued the views presented in the documentary or who have articulated alternative interpretations of Greek America are nowhere to be found in the documentary. They have no place in this definitive rendition of Greek America.[18]

What is more, the documentary advances the paradigm of ethnicity as a single culture through a particular politics of knowledge: the reproduction of the narrative of Greek America as an ethnoreligious Greek Orthodox collectivity with an idealized immigrant past. Such a scripted narrative demands that only those intellectuals who legitimize dominant ideologies in the public sphere become the spokespeople for the group. It also relies on the confluence of selective academic and popular knowledge to present the hegemonic script as self-evident and natural. For example, the view of Greek identity as an ethnoreligious one is achieved when a chorus of popular voices is complemented with that of a scholar, conflating Greek and Greek Orthodox identities:

> We have the uniqueness of having a heritage and a church that match.

> The church has been very responsible for maintaining the Greek culture.

> And then we get the irony that Anthony Quinn, of Mexican Irish descent, becomes the prototypical Greek. . . . I understand he converted to Greek Orthodoxy a few years ago. So the greatest Greek of them all has become a Greek.[19]

The selective omission of intellectuals and artists who advance an alternative interpretation of Greek ethnicity indicates the documentary's emphasis on producing a coherent, unitary narrative out of a diversity of perspectives and disjointed visual fragments. The circumscription of Greek America's heterogeneity and complexity is apparent in the editorial strategies used to regulate the production of meaning and to manufacture consensus out of popular representations of Greek America. Generalized ethnography functions as the glue that holds together an ideology pervasive in Greek America: the rags-to-riches narrative of struggle and success and its corollary, the ideology of an inclusive American society.

The positive reception of *The Greek Americans* by ethnic media and institutions testifies to the documentary's success in winning the support of leading Greek American circles. Numerous awards and wide social recognition placed its writer-producer in the media limelight and elevated him as an authoritative speaker on matters Greek American. A community is configured through consent to a narrative produced by a popular ethnographer. What is remarkable about the maker of this documentary is his enmeshment within a web of multiple economic, social, and cultural functions. A board member of a professional football team, an owner of a communications company, an NBC consultant, a community speaker, an ethnic promoter for the film industry, and a producer of scores of documentaries, George Veras has emerged as a powerful broker in the production of Greek culture in the anglophone world.[20]

Significantly, the documentary's ahistorical representation of Greek America as a homogeneous whole bears a remarkable resemblance to the practices of corporate multiculturalism, in which its producer is intimately implicated. In remarking how corporations practice diversity management of their multiethnic workforce, Avery Gordon and Christopher Newfield write: "Diversity management explicitly dehistoricized culture, race, and gender in order to offer *management* itself as the instrument for organizing differences. Employee differences would be encouraged but employee sovereignty over the use of difference would not. Multiculturalism alternately encouraged and suppressed the use of cultural difference to expand political democracy" (1996, 6). The documentary regulates the meaning of Greek America, extending its managerial containment into history. It portrays ethnic history as a process of cultural perfection, grafting the dominant narrative of Greek America as an American ethnic group of a prestigious Greek pedigree onto the discourse of multiculturalism.[21]

Immigration as Redemption in Canonical History and Popular Ethnography

Prestigious origins imbue ethnicity with social distinction. It comes as no surprise, therefore, that the legacy of ancient Greece organizes the documentary's account of modern Greek immigration to the United States. Immigration brought about a paradoxically familiar encounter with this legacy in the host society. Restlessly wandering since the era of Alexander the Great, the descendants of the ancient Greeks found redemption in America, a completion made possible by the ancient Greek democracy transplanted in American society.

> We've made our impact on the world over the centuries, but we've only been in America since the 1800s. For us, coming to America meant you could take care of your family. We've always been searching for new challenges since the time of Alexander the Great. We found it in America, even though the journey at times has been painful.
>
> The roots of what this country has become were set in Greece. And America took it, opened the doors, opened the opportunity and made a contract with everyone that said if you work hard, if you play fair . . . the sky is the limit. And that's the ultimate culmination of democracy.

Here, the perpetual quest of an ethnic group to reconnect with its achievements in the past (re)discovers in America the fallen Greek classical world restored. The people are bound to find redemption not in the natural soil of birth, the Greek peninsula, but in the host society. Emigration, in this perspective, entails not a movement away from a homeland, but instead a journey toward a reterritorialized home. It embodies the culmination of ethnic history toward cultural perfection as it sets in motion a project of (re)acclimatization. Here, creating a home in diaspora becomes as important as tracing past origins (see Bakalian 1993). As Avtar Brah (1996) observes, "diasporic journeys are about settling down, about putting roots 'elsewhere'" (182). Greek America capitalizes on the American political identification with the principles of ancient Greek democracy by reconfiguring this "elsewhere" into the restored originary homeland.

The historical quest of an ethnic group to make the United States its intrinsic home on the basis of an ancient heritage and the reclaiming of cultural excellence in alignment with the dominant values of the host society is an enduring theme in the making of Greek American identity. It entails a foundational narrative (see chapter 1) connected with an early twentieth-century middle-class cultural project that posits America as the natural location of the Greek immigrants and reconfigures their identities in relation to *normative* whiteness. Reformulated in order to foreground the immigrant era—and not the preimmigrant past—as the beginnings of Greek America, this narrative was deployed once again in the tumultuous 1960s, in the seminal ethnic history *The Greeks in the United States* (Saloutos 1964). An impressive research achievement, this canonical text endowed with scholarly legitimacy the ideology of assimilated Greeks as American Hellenes, modern American citizens of Hellenic descent. In dissecting the ideological implications of this history, Yiorgos Kalogeras (1992) identifies textual constructions of Greek ethnicity that have an astonishing resonance with the documentary's telling of Greek America's redemptive history. For the author of *The Greeks in the United States,* American-born Theodore Saloutos (1910–1980), "immigration to America came to represent . . . a more feasible objective of Hellenic rebirth and achievement" and "a different route for the fulfillment of Hellenic Destiny" (Kalogeras 1992, 20). According to Kalogeras, Saloutos's history was written "at a critical time in the 'life' of the ethnic group" when "the Greek American community seemed to him at least well-established and on its way to full assimilation" (16). The historical construction of Greek Americans centered on the linear cultural evolution from the impoverished peasant to the respected middle class and from a biologically based immigrant group into a voluntarily affiliated ethnic collective with civic and political loyalty to America. The overwhelming magnitude of rebirth—economic, social, political, and cultural—marked a dramatic departure from the immigrant and pre-American past. But if Saloutos saw Greek Americans as "a universe of Americans in the making and on the make" (20), he did not entirely erase the presence of the past in the Americanized present. Instead he saw Greek immigrants as possessing inherent attributes—a "pioneering spirit" and an individualism that "was to blend admirably with the native American variety" (Saloutos 1964, 20)—that made Greek America fundamentally compatible with American modernity.

The juxtaposition of Kalogeras's reading of *The Greeks in the United States* with my own reading of *The Greek Americans* reveals the continuities and discontinuities between Saloutos's and Veras's texts. It specifically illuminates a contour connecting Saloutos's construction of the ethnic past in the 1960s with Veras's appropriation of that past to serve the needs of the 1990s. The interconnections are multiple. Both narratives are organized around the model of Greek American embourgeoisement and both exclude working-class struggles against abuses of labor by capital. Both project America as a redemptive place that delivers ethnic fulfillment, and both posit an ethnic essence that makes this realization possible, a topic about which I will have more to say in the following section. At the same time, the divergences are telling. The historian places the beginnings of the ethnic group in the immigrant era, whereas the popular ethnographer and documentary maker situates the group in relation to the Greek classical past.

We can explain this incongruity if we take into account the histories and discourses that framed each narrative production. If Saloutos's claim "that he had seen the beginning as he had seen the end of the Greeks in the U.S." (Kalogeras 1992, 33) was somewhat legitimate in midcentury assimilationist America, the documentary rewrites ethnicity under a different set of social conditions, multiculturalism. In the 1960s, the professional historian eschewed the significance of the prestigious classical past, seeing no need to legitimize a group that had already reached "the era of respectability" (Saloutos 1964, 362), having successfully claimed the ancient Greek legacy as its rightful ethnic property. In the 1990s, the popular ethnographer, in contrast, returned to that past at a historical moment shaken by the force of culture wars, the intensification, that is, of competition among ethnic and racial groups for material and symbolic resources. As a component of this struggle, the contest over the cultural ownership of prestigious ethnic and racial pasts in the United States presented a formidable challenge to Greek America. Martin Bernal's *Black Athena,* in particular, provocatively refuted the Greek origins of Western culture, assaulting the social distinction that Greek America has historically enjoyed as the rightful heir of the ancient Greeks. Triggering heated charges about Western arrogance, racism, and Africa's "stolen legacy"—but also about African American reverse racism and chauvinism—the caustic debate did not fail to mobilize Greek America in defense of its ethnic interests, in fact "forc[ing] Greek Americans' formal entry into American race politics and debates" (Karpathakis and Roudometof 2004,

277). In an echo of this cultural politics, the documentary visits this controversy, if only obliquely, to once again claim the legacy of ancient Greece as Greek America's own, regrafting a prestigious pedigree to Greek ethnicity in the multicultural agora in which ethnicities compete for cultural capital. It is in this function that we witness an important disjuncture between *Greeks in the United States* and *The Greek Americans.* Each narrative, nonetheless, assimilates Greek America into the hegemony of its own time. The historical text assimilates ethnicity into ethnic Americanism, whereas the popular ethnography assimilates ethnicity into a specific narrative of American diversity, liberal multiculturalism.

Assimilating Ethnicity into Liberal Multiculturalism

The Greek Americans organizes itself around the ideology of liberal multiculturalism. It celebrates such values as attachment to roots, ethnic food, education, dancing and singing, family, hard work, entrepreneurial determination, and community ties. Held up as signs of ethnic difference rather than narrated as richly textured practices, these attributes domesticate ethnicity into what I discussed in the introduction as "acceptable difference" (Urciuoli 1998). By placing their dances, costumes, songs, music, and food on display, white ethnics assimilate into what Barbara Kirshenblatt-Gimblett calls the "banality of difference": the "proliferation of variation has the neutralizing effect of rendering difference and conflict inconsequential" (1991, 433). Colorfully exotic and nonthreatening, depoliticized, celebratory, familiar, and commercialized, difference in this context works to affirm the notion of America as an inclusive cultural democracy. This construction of identity resolves the classic American dilemma of how to create unity out of plurality, singularity out of diversity, oneness out of manyness (Walzer 1992). If ethnic belonging becomes the dominant mode of group affiliation and collective mobilization, it threatens to fracture the nation into distinct, mutually exclusive groups. In a society confronted by the potential conflict between oneness and manyness, the centering of identity on dominant middle-class values enables ethnic and racial groups to stand metonymically for the American cultural whole. A semantic closure against potential fragmentation, American pluralism is achieved as ethnic groups organize their particular identities around values that are ethnic and at the same time national.

The documentary forges an ideology of inclusion, a claim that there is a fundamental compatibility between national and ethnic identity, by making permeable the boundaries between Greek ethnicity and American culture. Greek Americans can simultaneously be model Americans and quintessential Greeks. A crucial strategy toward this end is the depiction of Greek America as a cultural entity rooted in the West. In America, where the Occident is posited as the cultural model of preference, originary *Western* Greekness integrally belongs to cultural Americanness, the documentary tells us. This move expands the scope of what is considered American to encompass ethnicities compatible with Western values. Greek Americans in this manner are represented as active participants in the society, as contributing to its cultural enrichment. Such a construction of identity assimilates Greekness into Western Americanness without sacrificing the ethnic component. Here the resonances between Theodore Saloutos's history and George Veras's popular rendition of identity are astounding. The documentary posits a rebirth of Greeks in the United States, establishes an ethnic identity compatible with the national one, and delineates specific boundaries of differentiation between Greeks in America and Greeks in Greece. Let's examine these contours in detail.

A recurrent point of view throughout the documentary, expressed most explicitly in part two, *Passing the Torch,* appropriates the concept of *palingenesis* (rebirth) and associates it with cultural perfection. Emigration initiated an unspecified process of cultural selection by which Greeks in America "brought the best of the Greek culture," such as commitment to hard work, charity, and community—"these . . . wonderful things that we should keep up"—while they "forgot the worst" (*Passing the Torch,* videotape version). This narrative resonates remarkably well with Saloutos's own understanding of immigration as a selective break with the Greek past. For the historian, Greek ethnicity in the United States represented a "new era for Hellenism" (Kalogeras 1992, 20). The "passage to America" signaled full entry to modernity, "with a subsequent 'fall' from history. History here was equated with a continuity that in the New World was neither desired nor feasible for the immigrant. It was a continuity of civil disobedience and ecclesiastical strife, cultural provincialism, and marginalization" (ibid.). In contrast to the provincialism of the past, Saloutos saw American modernity as a topos of perfection, "as 'the completion' of Modern Greece" that led to "the full realization of the immigrant as a historical subject" (Kalogeras 1998, 706).

The undesirable past that remains largely unnamed in the documentary becomes visible once one identifies its counterpart, those attributes that the documentary celebrates. Selective forgetting establishes a cultural distance from the past by exclusively aligning Greek America along values privileged by Occidentalism—individualism, discipline, the work ethic, order and equality.[22] Thus images of Zorba the Greek—the embodiment par excellence of undisciplined emotionality, spontaneity, lack in organizational skills, and nonproductive sensual abandon—are repeatedly tempered with an emphasis on the Greek

American work ethic. Assertions such as "[we are] good at work, great at play," "at the root, we're all about hard work," "Greeks, as much as we like to have fun, we're also workaholics" point to the "taming" of an Orientalist stereotype through the appropriation of Occidental values.[23]

Furthermore, the documentary's Occidental orientation is expressed through a critique of those cultural dispositions that tend to counter it. If Greek individualism has been consistently deployed as an argument for Greek immigrant fitness in America, the "negative variety" of *eghoismos* (competitive self-regard) brings to the fore disruptive atomism (see Herzfeld 1995, 224). In this instance, immigration as a new beginning is associated with a particular interpretation of eghoismos. According to Herzfeld, the term captures at once two meanings, positively valued individualism and negatively valued disruptive atomism. This semantic coherence fractures into an Occidental and Orientalist model of national identity when the cultural orientation of Greece (Western or Eastern?) is at stake (ibid.). *The Greek Americans* criticizes eghoismos as "the Greek ego, our Achilles heel." Threatening collective action, it becomes an element of unruliness and uncivil divisions. As a result it is singled out as an unwanted anomaly in the Greek American self.

The critical singling out of eghoismos points, of course, to the incompleteness of the Occidentalization of Greek Americans. Yet merely articulating this cultural critique works to differentiate Greek Americans from Greeks in Greece. Unlike the latter, whose Western self is said to be confronted by an internal Oriental Other—marking, therefore, a historically constituted ambivalence that makes Greeks less-than-authentic Occidentals (Herzfeld 1995)—Greeks in America are constituted as emerging Occidentals whose identity is constructed in relation to ur-Western (white) America. Because the Occident is prized as the cultural model of preference in America, Occidental perfection enables Greek Americans to disavow any association with minority status and therefore to claim the label of honorary Americans, in fact "America's ambassadors in the world." According to this logic, the indigenous ethnic identity that emerges as the result of a diasporic journey guarantees a privileged location devoid of non-Western, Oriental, polluting, and therefore corrupting elements. Such a location, furthermore, disrupts the view of Greek Americans as a transnational community organically connected to Greece. The will to Occidentalism works as a transnational boundary and a national integrative mechanism, making Greek America an American ethnic group whose loyalty, cultural affiliation, and sense of belonging make for a uniquely American entity. The documentary concurs that Greek American identity is "not that of a transplanted Greek, but rather the sensibility of an American ethnic" (Moskos 1990, 146).

In its integrationist politics of difference, ethnic Occidentalism opens a discursive space to expand the range of Americanness: "What is more American than having a delicious slice of lamb gyro at the festival?" the narrator asks, pursuing a politics of assimilating Americans into Greeks. "It makes you feel like one of us. . . . The Greek food, dancing, cooking, talking and singing . . . we want you to be part of us." In this dialectic, ethnic practices become American, as Americans assimilate to ethnic culture. The discourse of liberal pluralism enables ethnic representations to expand the cultural vocabulary of the host nation. In expanding the cultural category "American," the power relations inherent in the process of assimilation seem to balance somewhat, as ethnics can now sponsor their own politics of countercultural assimilation. In this instance, ethnic culture, long subjected to assimilative pressures, becomes the site of American assimilation into ethnicity. This relative leveling of the playing field, however, does not come without ideological implications. Commodified liberal multiculturalism manufactures cultural equality as it defers addressing inequality in the social and political realm. Greek America's participation in the discourse of multiculturalism is consistent, therefore, with a long tradition of fortifying the position of the ethnic middle class in relation to hegemonic formations. What could be perceived as a counterassimilationist politics of difference may indicate, in fact, another stage of assimilation, this time in the new historical bloc of liberal multiculturalism (Jusdanis 2001, 171). Though the practice of this kind of multiculturalism takes place through highly idealized, nonthreatening cultural scripts, the challenge remains, as we will see, to validate the value of diversity to those sectors of the national and white ethnic audience who are often ambivalent or even hostile to difference.

Ethnic Futures: The Poetics and Politics of Heritage

The Greek Americans creates usable pasts to anchor a vision for the ethnic future. The authoritative voice of former CIA director George Tenet in the documentary calls attention to preservation, understood as the challenge of the intergenerational transmission of culture: "We love being Americans. But we also love our heritage. We love our culture, we love our language. Will we be able to translate all of that to our children and to their children?" Enunciating a collective affective connection with the American nation and ethnicity, this passage endorses the integrative model of liberal multiculturalism. Furthermore, it deploys the language of heritage to mesh the past with the present while grasping a fundamental issue that confronts ethnic collectives: to invent ethnicity anew for their future survival. Consistent with the position that the making of usable pasts is "future, not past, oriented,"Tenet's statement advances a remarkable insight that pervades academic thinking: transmission of culture hinges on effective translations, which, in the case of ethnicity, render the past and the present meaningful across generations. As Anny Bakalian (1993) notes, "It is impossible for American-born Armenians to find Armenianness meaningful or functional if they are not taught how to appreciate it" (9). In the absence of a "role model for becoming" ethnic in America (Fischer 1986, 196), the passage above posits the reconfiguring of the past into a meaningful present as ethnicity's greatest challenge.

As Tenet presents the challenge to generate new translations, his own portrayal of Greek America as an entity realized by enduring, emotive connections ("We love our culture, we love our language") is itself an act of translation. It casts the tumultuous history of contradictory and even self-deprecating sentiments toward Greek ethnicity into a uniformly positive valuation. Adopting an unambiguously affirmative stance toward the Greek language, for instance, has not been the historical norm in Greek America, despite considerable individual and institutional investment on language retention. During the height of American nativism, for example, an immigrant elite in Ohio thought it necessary to invite American scholars to Greek communities in order to defend the value of the Greek language. In an era when the public use of immigrant languages was stigmatized as un-American, these scholars made a case for the preservation of Greek linguistic identity, pointing to the universal prestige of Greek, and in turn admonishing assimilationist immigrants that "have underestimated the power their [Greek] native tongue yields to the world" (Alex 1974, preface). Counteracted by assimilation pressures, this strategy for language preservation has not been historically effective. Even in the multicultural present, American-born Greek Americans are often embarrassed by aspects of immigrant culture, and their sensibilities are offended when Greek is spoken in public (Chock 1987). Despite some attempts at language maintenance, a consistent shift away from Greek language retention (Demos 1988), particularly in suburban Greek America, offers evidence of a linguistically declining community.[24]

Similarly, Greek America has exhibited a historical ambivalence, if not outright hostility, toward immigrant culture. Since the turn of the twentieth century, folk culture has been a source of ethnic embarrassment as it interfered with the quest for inclusion in American modernity. Superstitions, dream-books, folk healing, haggling, collectivism, and parental authority may have meaningfully organized aspects of immigrant life, but they were perceived by the dominant culture and by many immigrants as signs of belonging to a lesser stage of cultural development: backward remnants of a traditional life that needed to yield to modern habits of prescribed contact, individualism, rationality, and science. In an age obsessed with total conformity, the accents of immigrant parents only reinforced feelings of inferiority in their children, adding to the sense of Otherness they endured at school. Regulation of adolescent behavior by vigilant, authoritative parents buttressed the notion that immigrant culture stood for constraining tradition, in stark contrast to the American ideal of liberty and choice. Many Greek Americans were caught between the obligations exerted by immigrant traditions and visions of self-determination promised by American modernity.

Furthermore, sectors of Greek America erect symbolic boundaries to disassociate themselves from perceived immigrant "foreignness." Post–World War II Greek immigrants, for example, were designated as "displaced persons," a "generic expression [used] by the second and third generation to describe negatively recent arrivals from Greece" (Moskos 1990, 60). Labeled with the Orientalist stereotype "lazy" (Karpathakis 1994), immigrants were also seen as a potential threat to Greek American morality (Patrinacos 1982). Even within coethnic communities, they may be viewed as the embodiment of radical difference, vulnerable to the stigma that America attaches to its nonassimilated minorities.[25]

Thus, Tenet's pronouncement makes a case for the value of the past to an insider audience often skeptical about the relevance of Greek culture. Silencing the historical devaluation of language, forgetting the capacity of immigrant culture to injure and oppress, and skirting around conflicts and struggles over what counts as properly ethnic, it attaches an overwhelmingly positive value to the ethnic past. This is congruent with the documentary's politics of palingenesis and its association of ethnic rebirth with partial memory and historical exclusion. But the drive to preserve ethnicity—pervasive throughout the narrative—extends beyond mere selective retention; it undertakes the transvaluation of Greek culture. It adds value to practices, such as language, that are in danger of disappearing and to an immigrant culture that has been devalued and scorned. This preservationist agenda is anchored in a particular discourse of the politics of heritage. As David Lowenthal (1996) reminds us, "[H]eritage has always twisted the past for some present purpose" (101) by "rel[ying] on antithetical [to history] modes of persuasion. History seeks to convince by truth and succumbs to falsehood. Heritage exaggerates and omits, candidly invents and frankly forgets, and thrives on ignorance and error" (121). It "is immune to critical reappraisal because it is not erudition but catechism; what counts is not checkable fact but credulous allegiance" (ibid.).

As my analysis shows, the making of usable pasts violates the historical record for the sake of specific ethnic interests.[26] The point is to persuade audiences of the value of ethnicity, a necessity that explains why the documentary resorts to rhetoric designed to convince—rather than to describe or identify the truth—and employed to legitimize and induce attitudes and dispositions to act on behalf of ethnic preservation. This is because "[h]eritage ... attests our identity and affirms our worth," writes Lowenthal (122). It "privileges action . . . [and] . . . [a]ctive involvement." Therefore, "'[m]aking history' and 'steering its course' are quintessential *heritage* activities" (125).

The project of steering the course of history to partake of Greek ethnic preservation rests on positive stereotyping and on the authority of professionals recognized in public life as both American and Greek to underwrite it. Paradoxically, the stereotypical discourse of Greek America as a model ethnicity ("super Americans" [*Passing the Torch*] and "disciple[s] of the American dream" [*The Greek Americans*]) that values ethnic heritage operates within the logic of minority discourse. As JanMohamed and Lloyd (1990) note, minorities coerced into a "negative generic subject-position" invest in a cultural politics that aims to transform this location "into a positive collective one" (10). The documentary's emphasis on collective success exemplifies once again Greek America's vigilance in matters of representation. This alertness cannot be viewed independently from histories of exclusion and denigration. Along with other minorities, early Greek Americans were subjected to negative stereotypes and felt their powerful material and psychological consequences. They are historically situated, then, to recognize that it is vital to fashion positive identity narratives in relation to changing definitions and criteria of national belonging. Stereotypes, Michael Herzfeld writes, "are both instrument and symbol of hegemony" (1995, 222). Greek Americans have learned this lesson well. As I will emphasize in chapter 4, in spite of their eagerness to conform and to distance themselves from a position of alterity, Greek Americans can always be subjected to the power of the dominant society to define for its own interests who can count as American and who can be excluded as foreign.

Overall, the narration of ethnicity around tightly controlled scripts of positive valuation establishes the conditions for heritage production both within communities and in the wider public sphere. In other words, it recognizes that the making of usable pasts must be thought of in relation to social discourses about difference. In this project of cultural engineering, stereotypes become instrumental: they operate as powerful rhetorical tools capable of inciting action and demarcating moral boundaries. Therefore, the documentary may be seen in terms of rhetorical strategies that construct a positively valued past as a necessary condition for ensuring an ethnic future. In this perspective, *The Greek*

Americans and *The Greek Americans II: Passing the Torch* generate dialectical identity narratives. Ethnic affirmation is constructed through a positively valued past and present focused on the middle-class values of family, work ethic, and church. In turn, this becomes the necessary condition for opening up future possibilities of cultural becoming.[27] In order to inspire and convince, this dialectic extracts from the complexity of history a thread of socially approved values and pre-dispositions that subsequently are highlighted as *the* components of a distinct Western Greek American identity. Not unlike Orientalism, which chokes Asian America in a "deathly embrace" (Ma 2000), Occidentalism stifles Greek America as it circumscribes ethnic identity exclusively in terms of normative American expectations of Otherness and, as a result, marginalizes alternative definitions of Greek American identity and success. *The Greek Americans* produces an ideal community, endorses an ahistorical perspective, and inserts Greek Americans into the space of white ethnicity via the discourse of model ethnicity.

Model Ethnicity as White Ethnicity

The valorization of usable pasts that centers on the ideology of acceptable difference makes a case for continuity between the immigrant past and the ethnic present. A narrative contour in this sanitized discourse of heritage elevates im-migrant hard work as a source of affective intergenerational ties. The immigrant fathers and mothers, grandmothers and grandfathers are represented as modern Greek heroes whose work ethic molded future generations of Greek Americans and laid the foundations of mobility. This is a historically appropriate homage to individuals who experienced immigration as sacrifice. But the tribute must not distract attention from the role of the wider political economy in contributing to ethnic success. Affective appreciation of past hardship and deprivation should not be confused with the erroneous assumptions of immigrant values as the sole explanation of ethnic mobility.

The notion that specific groups were able to turn "sweat into capital" (Sowell, quoted in Takaki 1987a, 6) because of their ethnic culture's compatibility with dominant norms (hard work, discipline, perseverance, industry) is routinely employed by certain think tanks and the public alike to explain differential economic success among ethnic and racial collectives. It is at the core of what Stephen Steinberg calls the "Myth of Ethnic Success" (1981, 82), the ideology that posits "cultural values as the fulcrum of success" (86–87) and organizes what Sylvia Lazos Vargas (1998) labels the "White ethnic immigrant narrative," the claim that immigrant virtues alone were crucial in the overcoming of ethnic prejudice (1493). The political stakes in this kind of argument are high. To argue that values inherent in a group explain that group's mobility is also to suggest that poverty can be explained in terms of lack of effort and cultural predisposition, not in terms of constraints imposed by racial and political economies.[28] Such a reading privileges a view of America's attitudes toward its Others in terms of an "American ethnic pattern" of inclusion, not in terms of a history of colonization and discrimination and oppression, an "American racial pattern" of exclusion (Takaki 1987b, 36). It provides the "theoretical justification" that fuels "the intellectual assault on affirmative action" (26). The affirmation of Greek America as a model ethnicity that was lifted to success by its own bootstraps is therefore far from innocuous. Although the documentary operates at the level of ethnicity and makes no explicit reference to race, in fact it powerfully inserts ethnicity into the domain of whiteness. This is because "ethnic pluralism," as Karen Brodkin perceptively observes, "gave rise to a new, cultural way of discussing race" (1998, 144–45). Since the 1960s and under the rubric of "ethnicity theory," academics, intellectuals, and political bandits have encouraged Americans "to view race as a variety of ethnicity, and to apply to racially defined groups certain standards and values whose pioneers and exemplars were European immigrants" (Omi and Winant 1986, 5). This paradigm imagines America as a universe of ethnic groups, explained differential socioeconomic mobility on the basis of value compatibility with WASP ideals, and blamed racial minorities for their poverty as a self-inflicted, cultural phenomenon. In Brodkin's (1998) wonderful metaphor, "model minorities and deficit cultures are like two hands clapping; they are complementary parts of a single discourse of race as a cultural phenomenon" (150–51). She continues, "[T]he Jewish ethnicity that intellectuals claimed for themselves as model minorities was an immigrant version of bourgeois patriarchal domesticity characterized by values of hard work, deferred gratification, education, and strong two-parent families with the mothers full-time at home. It was the invention of a deficient African American culture that illustrated its exemplariness" (ibid.).

To summarize, ethnicity as whiteness promotes a particular national ideology, what Ruth Hsu (1996) calls a "rehabilitative concept of ethnicity" (37). Such an ideology depends on the belief that "this nation is open and inclusive, that it is democratic and egalitarian, and that it welcomes any race, creed or religion" (38). The concept buttresses the ideology of the American dream because it "functions first as proof that America works, that its principles and beliefs are well-founded" (39). The hegemony of such a worldview springs from its capacity to bolster the discourse of liberal multiculturalism. In this case, ethnicity becomes an ideology legitimizing hegemonic narratives, such as the American dream, individualism, and America as progress, ideas that have become part of American self-imagining. At the same time, this narrative "elide[s] the fact that acceptance into this society is actually restricted and contingent upon one's racial and ethnic identity. … [T]he Dream has 'worked' more readily for white people than for people of color" (ibid.). As Alba (1990) suggests, claiming a place in whiteness via the route of rehabilitative ethnicity does become a common topos in the making of middle-class white ethnicity. It does not necessarily, however, require the surrender of a distinctly ethnic powerful identification. Thus, the idea that European Americanness is about to minimize the importance of specific ethnicities has to take into account the proliferation of ethnicized narratives, such as Veras's documentary. As I explained, the Occidentalist model of identity enables a white ethnic group simultaneously to claim access to "authentic" cultural Americanness, Western Europeanness, *and* ethnic Greekness. That this discourse establishes compatibility between a Western identity on the one hand and Greek ethnicity on the other obviously does not mean that collective ethnic identity is about to dissolve any time soon into monolithic panethnicity. Moreover, and contrary to Alba's view of white ethnics as lacking "any deep commitment to ethnic social ties" (306), the discourse of Hellenism, which drives the ideology of the documentary, produces among Greek Americans binding obligations that are readily observable, in what follows, as ethnic cultural activism.

Racial Hellenism, Whiteness, and Ethnic Identity

The ideology of model ethnicity is one implicit route toward inclusion in whiteness. An additional, explicit path to ethnic whiteness offers itself to Greek America via racialized interpretations of Hellenism. As in the case of early twentieth-century immigrant assimilation (Anagnostou 2004a), a number of American-born Greeks today continue to claim access to the coveted white status by positing a biological link with the ancient (and white) Greek civilization (Karpathakis and Roudometof 2004). The idiom of ancient Greece as white and Greek Americans as its natural heirs affords access to whiteness and serves a dual function: it reproduces ingrained racial hierarchies in American society while generating an internal racial pecking order. The consciousness among Greek Americans that nonwhiteness confers inferior social status and "fears . . . [of] be[ing] seen as anything but 'white'" (282) lead to identity positions that conveniently distance Greek American ethnicity from nonwhiteness. On the other hand, such a racialized appropriation posits Greeks as "superior to these 'biological whites' who are simply white because of their skin tone," not because of their cultural achievement (283). This production of racial hierarchies heightens intergroup antagonisms in the context of American race politics. The debate over *Black Athena,* for instance, pitted African Americans against Greek Americans in an acrimonious public dispute to ascertain rights over the ownership of Hellenism. This racialization of heritage generated a further conduit for grafting Greek America onto whiteness. One counternarrative, among the many that sought to rebuff Bernal's thesis, enmeshed Greek identity into American racial categories, as a number of commentators, including classicists, cast Greek ethnicity in terms of whiteness. As Anna Karpathakis and Victor Roudometof (2004) indicate, "the Hellenic identity constructed as the end-product of the *Black Athena* debate in the community became a 'white' identity; i.e. Hellenes are 'whites'" (278). This racial reduction of Greek ethnicity represents yet another reified identity location among the numerous essentialisms—both ethnic white and African American—that were produced by the reductive racial politics of the *Black Athena* controversy (see Lefkowitz 2001).

Racialized Hellenism, then, provides a route for Greek America to gain access to whiteness. But this does not occur universally because not all claims to Greek American connections with ancient Greece necessarily take on a racial hue (see Anagnostou 2004c). What is of significance for my argument here is that to identify with ancient Greece means to make it impossible to deploy weak ethnic identities. For its legitimation, the link between ancient and modern Greeks requires an ethnic of obligation toward preserving that past. To put it differently: whether or not Greeks in the United States utilize the discourse of Hellenism to graft themselves onto whiteness, they are nowhere near giving up their claim to ownership of the ancient Greek legacy. And this assertion is not activated independently from a set of cultural responsibilities. Historically, this relationship to the past has represented cultural, political, and economic capital for this ethnic group, but it has also exacted duties and obligations imposed by the West and experienced as the "burden of antiquity" (Clogg 1992, 1). In an exercise of Western hegemony, Greeks have been invariably required to substantiate, in action and deed, in appearance and behavior, in language and physique, their Hellenic identity. The incisive and often hostile question commonly raised in popular and literary culture, "What have the Greeks done lately?" highlights the continuous comparison with the ancients that modern Greeks have been subjected to. It brings forth the concomitant idea that the ancient Greek legacy equals achievement and distinction, whereas neo-Hellenism stands for a cultural regression from this illustrious past.[29] This logic carries over into the documentary. "How would you like to have the responsibility for your actions measured against one of the world's greatest civilizations?" the narrator concludes in *The Greek Americans.* "Thousands of years of Hellenic culture. . . . How do you compete with Aristotle and Plato and Aristophanes, and all these cats?" and "We expect the highest level of accomplishment; it is the standard for Greek Americans." George Stephanopoulos legitimizes it: "To be Greek is to be good in what you do."

Entrenching Greek America in ancient Greek heritage produces centered identities that become substantiated through practices of commitment. Wholly contrary to present celebrations of postmodern identity as unconstrained choice, Greek Americans do *not* disassociate their identities from a set of culturally constituted set of duties and obligations. Both privately and *collectively,* vast symbolic and material resources have been invested in a wide range of civic, educational, and cultural activities that aim to preserve and disseminate classical Greek culture. The list is exceedingly long. In 2004, Kyriakos Tsakopoulos, president and CEO of KT Communities, "presented a generous gift to Columbia University to establish" a chair in Hellenic studies and to inaugurate an annual lecture, "On Aristotle and the Moderns." Offered as "a tribute to his grandfather for whom the Chair . . . [and the lecture are] named," the endowment paid homage to both family and ancient Greek heritage, seen as inseparable. "My grandfather exemplified what it was to have character and [to] be a good man, and that's what Aristotle teaches," the donor said (brochure promoting the 2006 "On Aristotle and the Moderns" lecture). Further examples abound. AHEPA and community organizations fund the making of floats with Greek classical themes (a rose-covered Parthenon, ancient Greece as the birthplace of democracy) in the annual Rose Parade for an estimated cost between $100,000 to 200,000 (Niarchos 2001). In addition, Greek Americans in Ohio have been mobilized to "ensure the success of 'The Cleisthenes Project,'" which is a plan to "bring state recognition to persons who have had a significant impact on democratic governance" (promotional brochure). Chaired by a Greek American, the project's executive committee will finance the making of plaster busts of the "Greek statesman Cleisthenes, the Father of Democracy," and of Thomas Jefferson. It will also support the unveiling ceremony at the Ohio Statehouse in Columbus and civic programs designed to promote education about Ohio's "shared cultural and political history." The project, which "provide[s] a linear connection to the system of government that the free world enjoys today," symbolically positions Greek Americans as heirs of classical Greek culture and as exemplary American citizens. What is more, the Greek American connection to classical Greece also has been expressed in terms of material and symbolic support to departments of classics. Recently,

Greek Americans lobbied intensively against a plan to eliminate the Department of Classics and its curriculum at Wayne State University. The Greek American "Hellenic Society *Paideia* of Michigan" raised funds to benefit the department's plan to establish an endowed chair. In this kind of practicing cultural identity, Greek America exhibits affinities with diasporic Armenians during an era when the claim to a transnational Armenian identity was linked with demanding duties and obligations: "[B]ut the dominant view was that just as being the citizen of a nation-state had a cost (taxes, the draft, obedience to laws), so also membership in a diasporic branch of the transnation must have a cost, a demonstration of loyalty that undertook the responsibility of sacrifice" (Tölölyan 1996, 15).

My analysis demonstrates that some white ethnic identities are neither wholly privatized nor weak and readily disposable. Identity narratives script ethnic obligations, which are also practiced as expressions of enduring *collective* belonging. Thus, although *The Greek Americans* represents Greek ethnicity in a manner that conforms to aspects of Alba's model, it does so through the production of a strong ethnic identity, which translates into a powerful commitment to continue to claim ancient Greece as an integral component of Greek America. In one important sense then, the making of a usable ethnic past through the discourse of Hellenism sustains narratives of collective identity that translate into enduring material and symbolic allegiance. Today the ancient Greek heritage is as vital for Greek America's cultural politics as it was in the early immigrant years. Thus the close analysis of even the single ethnic narrative that most closely approximates Alba's view cautions against scholarly attempts to neatly demarcate and fix the meaning of white ethnicity as a singular entity. The category of white ethnicity cannot be treated as uniform; it is fractured by the distinct histories and modes of adaptation of particular ethnicities. Furthermore, each ethnicity is internally differentiated along class, gender, and cultural fault lines. The next chapter builds on this point to demonstrate the plurality of meanings that popular ethnographers attach to Greek America as an ethnic community. In contrast to the claims of *The Greek Americans,* I bring attention to how the making of usable pasts cannot possibly be seen as a singular enterprise, but only as a plural enterprise generating intra-ethnic differentiation. I discuss how these internal rifts are expressed through cultural projects to generate collective—not privatized or solely family-centered—identities and how attention to ethnic plurality helps us start discerning the contour of ethnicity as cultural self-critique, one that challenges the ideology of the model white ethnic.

CHAPTER THREE

Whose Ethnic Community?

Gendered Pasts and Polyphonies of Belonging

> Community, then, is the product of work, of struggle; it
> is inherently unstable, contextual; it has to be constantly
> reevaluated in relation to critical political priorities; and it
> is the product of interpretation, interpretation based on an
> attention to history.
>
> —Biddy Martin and Chandra Mohanty,
> "Feminist Politics: What's Home Got to Do with It?"

> The author [George Pelecanos] has his own deep bonds of
> family involvement. "We've got this kind of rainbow family.
> I've started from an early age with my children. I've taken
> them to church every Sunday, got them indoctrinated into
> the Greek community, and they definitely know who they are.
>
> "My sons are black, but they also consider themselves to
> be Greek, and they dig it, because it's cool to [be] something
> else other than just a white American."
>
> —Robert Krause, "Heart Murmurs from Home"

THE MODEL OF white ethnicity as cultural loss equates the dispersal of ethnics in the suburbs with the depletion of cultural resources that promote collective belonging. Thus it sustains the notion of the dissolution of meaningful ethnic collectivities and the fragmentation of ethnicity into a domain of largely privatized identities. Yet, contrary to this view, popular ethnographies illuminate practices and narratives that anchor individuals into collectives; they posit common experiences and values that construct specifically situated communities. This is not to say that the corpus of these ethnographic texts construes a uniform ethnic culture. On the contrary, because some ethnographies pay attention to differences within the collective, they fracture the ethnic domain of Greek America into diverse and sometimes competing constituencies. In other words, the texts I discuss here counter the notion of ethnicity as a homogeneous culture without abandoning the idea of collective belonging. Read against each other, these popular ethnographies help us recognize the expanse of ethnicity as an uneven terrain punctuated by features of internal diversity.

One cannot stress enough the notion of internal differentiation of ethnicity. The reduction of ethnicity to a uniform entity serves specific hegemonic interests by excluding or silencing alternative meanings. Therefore, attention to intraethnic differences—based on class, gender, or sexuality, for example— necessarily illuminates all sorts of counterhegemonic perspectives. Hegemony is never a completed process. As previously silenced constituencies vie for public recognition, it becomes increasingly difficult to contain diversity. The critical aim, therefore, is to reframe the analysis of ethnicity away from invariable sameness and toward heterogeneity and the struggle to contest hegemony. As a configuration of contested meanings about origins, roots, ancestors, group membership, and cultural affiliation, ethnicity cannot be thought of apart from internal conflict, dissent, and exclusion. It becomes necessary, then, to sift through popular ethnographies to bring into sharp focus the way in which they build on the past to construct a plurality of ethnic belonging. In this chapter, I complicate the notion of privatized white ethnic identities by juxtaposing two narratives that construct competing meanings of an "ethnic community." The popular ethnographies I examine here indict a common past, immigrant patriarchy, but they are at odds with each other regarding the kinds of community belonging that they endorse.

Specifically, I analyze the writings of Helen Papanikolas and Constance Callinicos to scrutinize how each constructs the past upon which she acts and to chart their respective visions of community and the place of usable pasts in it. I reflect on Papanikolas's practice of storytelling as a site that discursively actualizes an ethnic collective centered on historical memory. I contrast this intervention with Callinicos's *American Aphrodite: Becoming Female in Greek America* (1990). A counternarrative to the hegemony of ethnicity as success, this latter text reclaims vernacular culture for women. It constructs ethnicity as a uniformly oppressive traditional community, envisioning the materialization of women's liberation through a gendered performance of the past in an exclusively all-female space. Reading these projects against each other illuminates ethnicity as a site of radical polyphony, in which each voice struggles to produce its own vision of community "in relation to the critical political priorities" of its author (Martin and Mohanty 1986, 210). Taken together, they counter the ethnic amnesia and ahistorical, celebratory heritage narrative underwritten by the documentary *The Greek Americans.*

Whither the Ethnic Community?

How do assimilation and the current emphasis on ethnicity as voluntary affiliation reconfigure an ethnic community? At the outset, this is the wrong question to ask. It presupposes an already existing entity, the ethnic community, one that conjures up images of actual or metaphorical face-to-face, close-knit, and mutually interdependent social relations. In this representation, common in the popular imagination, ethnic people possess a community readily defined as a constellation of identifiable attributes. In this manner, as I showed in my discussion of *The Greek Americans,* knowledge about a community can be regulated, and authority to represent its interests is vested in ethnic spokesmen or in politicians.

But the social and material basis of community is far from fixed; changes in its composition and in the nature of its social and economic relations and boundaries can transform an aggregate of coethnics, often dramatically. Furthermore, community is an ideological construct whose meanings vary across social constituencies. For the second generation, immigrant communities of the past stood for desirable ties, solidarity, and satisfying human interaction but also for undesirable remnants of parochial, even primitive, behavior. For outsiders, on the other hand, immigrant neighborhoods commonly represented insularity, vice, and social, sanitary and cultural threats to the nation. What is more, the meaning of community has changed historically. Contemporary "ethnic community" events, such as festivals in gentrified neighborhoods, evoke positive images cast in the language of civic responsibility: volunteerism, caring, mutual support, openness, and inclusion. Micaela di Leonardo (1984) attributes the new positive twist in the meaning of the term—its "virtue and necessity" (133)—to "a number of converging sources: the white ethnic renaissance, the gentrification of inner cities by young white professionals, the intensification of grassroots organizing efforts by former student activists turned 'community activists'" (ibid.). For highly dispersed, suburbanized populations, community represents something totally removed from the close-knit immigrant neighborhood so entrenched in the popular imagination. This new conceptualization, she continues, "leads to a nonmaterial, a conceptual, definition: we are no longer talking about small settlements, about limited groups of people who see one another daily over a lifetime. We mean instead that *someone* perceives 'togetherness' in a social network, or group of networks or even a social category, and thus labels the individuals in that network or category as a community" (ibid.).

If community is a social construct, my task is to examine what scholars and ethnics mean when they refer to or evoke its image. When Chrysie Constantakos (1990), for example, points to the dramatic transformation currently under way among Greek Orthodox communities—a historically enduring yet dynamic form of ethnic and religious organization in the Greek world—she assumes a specific idea of community.[1] Her initial point of reference is the immigrant community, which she posits as a bastion of obligatory membership and ethnic culture that determines collective identity. She then proceeds to contrast this immigrant Gemeinschaft with the transformed ethnic community, an entity in which belonging becomes a matter of individual choice. Drawing from her personal memories as well as from the work of Robert Bellah et al. (1985), she argues that "collective [Greek American] identity is progressively being replaced by private personal identities, and the 'community of memories' becomes gradually a blending of 'community' and 'lifestyle enclave' in favor of the latter" (115).[2] Individual participation in community activities rests on voluntary association and not on obligation sanctioned by the ethnic culture. As a result, the social life and memory that is embedded within the collective becomes fragmented and individualized.

Constantakos's mapping of Greek America's transition from mechanical to organic solidarity resonates with ethnographic research that indicates the transformation of white ethnic communities into collectives actualized on the basis of choice, rational calculation, and thin commitment, as well as the concomitant disintegration of their authority to determine ethnicity (Bakalian 1993). This configuration reveals the weakening of the collective as a community of memory, a dramatic manifestation of which is evident in Papanikolas's grim realization during her lecture circuit across Greek Orthodox communities in the United States. Having dedicated her life to chronicling immigrant histories, the popular ethnographer kept discovering, to her dismay, the depth of her ethnic audience's historical amnesia. Confronted by popular forgetting, she was astonished and "struck by how little Greek Americans and their children knew about the experience of their parents and grandparents and the culture that they brought with them" (2002, xi).[3]

Although historical memory is in fact receding in Greek America, the ethnoreligious community has not been fractured to the point of total privatization. The heritage discourse and the operation of a corporate Greek Orthodoxy continue to produce collective participation, which is embedded within institutional life. Practices of common religion and of partaking in church-based secular events and organizations produce collective local, national, ethnic, and transnational memory. Annual Greek-language school celebrations, for instance, reenact the narrative of Greek independence from the Ottoman Empire. Commemorative albums recount community history. Museums and cultural centers are established to preserve heritage, archives are produced, and oral history projects are initiated. Local communities participate in national commemorative rituals, such as Veterans Day, paying tribute to its members who died in America's wars. Plaques and ceremonies honor past parish council presidents, financial donors, and members who have distinguished themselves in civic and professional life. Scholarships reward students for academic excellence. National and local newspapers, popular magazines, newsletters, and brochures regularly refer to "the community" and reflect on its future. At the national level, institutions still employ the language of community to refer to a residentially dispersed and heterogeneous entity that is projected around a shared vision of ethnoreligious belonging. Within specific localities, this entity is actualized through individual participation in common parish activities that "bind them through history" (Constantakos 1990, 107) into a community of remembrance that "look[s] to both the past and the future" (107).

Of course, Greek Orthodox communities in the United States neither exercise total control over the social imagination of their members nor represent the communitarian ideal of a moral way of life that is largely constituted by its past.[4] Communities are never unproblematic sites of collective belonging, but are politicized aggregates that negotiate boundaries of inclusion and exclusion. It is not, therefore, wholly correct to conceptualize white ethnic communities through a past in which immigrant communities functioned as traditional bastions of a shared way of life, as all-encompassing repositories of memory. Although social pressures to conform to a cultural and moral norm certainly were not absent, the immigrant community also functioned as a stage for dramatic—often fierce—political, cultural, and social debates. Sociologists and anthropologists report that these communities have been defined by class, intracultural and intergenerational conflicts and internal strife over morality and values, making it impossible to project homogeneity onto these entities (Constantakos 1987; Karpathakis 1994; Roudometof and Karpathakis 2002). In the most polarized cases, institutional splitting has occurred, or dissenting individuals have simply walked away. It is not unusual, however, for the institution to continue to function as a single unit while accommodating internal conflict. Local Greek Orthodox communities, though fractured, nevertheless continue to command fierce allegiance from diverse publics as a site providing spiritual nourishment, a channel of social and economic support, and an institutional venue to promote Greek cultural interests.

Neither homogeneous nor harmonious, a Greek Orthodox community is also an entity of partial attachment. Actualized around a host of practices—the church, meetings of organizations, the festival, the classroom, the social dance, the choir—the community forms only one sphere of interaction among a multitude. Not unlike the Jewish *minyan,* Artemis Leontis (1997) writes, sites of Greek Orthodox assembly "operate for some Greeks, for some of the time, for some activities or aspects of social life, and only in some ways" (88). This partiality, therefore, helps us conceptualize the local community as a porous terrain of multiple sites. At the same time, limiting the mapping of Greek America to sites associated with the institutional space of Greek Orthodoxy is to draw too narrow a boundary. One must consider secular community-making practices, such as attending an ethnic museum event or a university course on Greek American ethnicity. Furthermore, partiality discourages the understanding of community members in relation to ethnicity alone and encourages analysis of their place in relation to alternative cultural affiliations. Therefore, the notion of wholeness— of a well-demarcated domain—that the term community commonly evokes is inadequate here for anyone wishing to illuminate the complex contours of white ethnicity.

With increasing frequency, critics analyze the cultural production of ethnicity in specific textual and institutional sites—a theater troupe, a festival, a museum exhibit, an autobiography—to explain the construction of identity, community, and belonging in concrete narratives and practices (Kondo 2001). Within these specific contexts, ethnicity escapes reduction to a single monolithic entity. Leontis (1997), for example, complicates the notion of an ethnic community by evoking "the image of net-work" to visualize "the interconnected threads of communication, associations, and institutions that comprise Greek America" (92). Clearing a fertile conceptual territory for scholars of Greek America in particular and for scholars of ethnicity in general, the rich explication is worth quoting in full:

> Net-work suggests that we not look for a continuous, well-circumscribed
> plane in America densely occupied by Greeks and their offspring. In-
> stead we should think of the different locations where Greek interests
> coincide or collide. We should consider nodes of activity—some inter-
> connected, some isolated, some few and far between. We should study
> transformations in institutions that have emerged to promote those
> interests: professional associations; newspapers, magazines; political
> lobbies; literature societies; festivals that reproduce a "Greek experi-
> ence" of recreation and dining; language schools; parades. (93)

If ethnicity conceived as network does not arise naturally but always is created through cultural work, what kinds of practices bring about specific interconnections among its "nodes of activity" or pull other links apart? Specific interventions may strengthen existing connections or even multiply their numbers. The disconnection of a single node may affect the rest of the field. And one seemingly innocuous change may reach even the most remote and isolated of nodes. In the process, the introduction of change may be resisted in some sites and embraced in others, with unforeseen implications.

The metaphor of the network encourages one to address ethnicity in terms of *positioned,* site-specific cultural production, shifting the conceptual terrain of ethnicity into the plural: from singular ethnicity to ethnicities, from a usable past to usable pasts. In this reconfiguration, ethnicity can no longer be perceived as a totalizing cultural resource that is generationally depleted until drained, its cracked sediments mirroring the dissolution of ethnic coherence and collective expression. Instead, the task becomes to analyze how different kinds of ethnic pasts are produced across the network, in distinct nodes, and by situated subjects with different stakes and varying institutional positions. It is necessary to trace the contours through which these social interconnections will be seen through their historical depth and where they converge or diverge in time and space. Thus white ethnicity can be analyzed through an examination of the kinds of ethnicities that are produced in specific nodes—a festival, a university classroom, a PBS documentary, a Hollywood film, a popular ethnography—among others. The challenge is how to chart the complex contours of their temporal and spatial relationships, paying attention to how the effects of specific nodes of production ripple through the wider terrain of cultural, ethnic, and racial relations.

But from what location does one decide to enter this expansive field of multiple passages, and what are the politics of deciding on one specific point of departure and not another? A reflection on the gendered past of Greek America offers the contour that will initiate the exploration of those nodes and contours that illuminate the differential constitution of community through the production of usable ethnic pasts.

The Gendered Past

The past is punctuated by gaps and silences when it comes to the experiences of Greek immigrant women. Scarce in the archival record and underrepresented in scholarship, women's perspectives are now being rehabilitated by academics, memoirists, autobiographers, popular ethnographers, and historians. But still this scarcity generates frustration and critique. Phyllis Chock, a pioneer in the professional anthropological study of Greek American women, expresses her disappointment over the treatment of women as "subsidiary actors" in ethnic canonical histories, which she charges with harboring a masculine bias (1990, 150). Likewise, Leontis (1997, 104) expresses her dismay over the scant representation of Greek America in academic discussions, including discussions of gender. In this context, popular ethnography functions as a crucial venue for circulating knowledge about women and thus restores their public visibility.[5]

Papanikolas and Callinicos, the two ethnographers whose narratives on community making I examine in this chapter, weave similar accounts of the past as a domain of gender inequality. Both arrive at the same caustic conclusion—that immigrant culture devalued women—agreeing that Greek patriarchy severely limited women's lives. Outlined below in the broadest contours, their narratives map polarized social landscapes defined by male cultures of domination and the oppression of women. Aspiring to Americanization, yet committed to preserving embattled ethnicity, male Greek America maintained a gendered duality between the sphere of community and family, seen as the bastion of ethnic reproduction, and the public domain of enterprise, understood as a zone of male assimilation. In this emerging order, the control of women's sexuality was ethnicized, as women were projected as biological and cultural custodians of the Greek ethnos in migrancy. The acute pressure to marry within the group and the resolute opposition to women's education sustained the idea of the community as a fortress that had to be defended against the leveling effect of externally imposed assimilation. Seen as the last bulwark of ethnic defense, the female body came under surveillance, and its movement in the spaces of America—the neighborhood, the university, the prom, the date, the sleepover—was severely curtailed.

In Papanikolas's and Callinicos's accounts, Greek patriarchy was translocated to the United States. Migration transplanted practices that sanctioned male-induced controls of women's desires and activities, commonly enacted in terms of surveillance of women's movement in space. Anthropologists of rural Greece have documented the significance of gender-based spatial organization as a means to effect such restrictions. They have mapped the public sphere of traditional Greek villages as a closely monitored and gender-segregated domain that organizes both movement and the range of permissible activities. The spaces allocated to women—the home and visits to relatives, the church, and the cemetery—constitute a regulative social universe designed not only to reinforce their traditional obligations as mothers and nurturers of immediate kin as well as domestic, social, and unofficial ritual caretakers but also to police their sexuality. For in a gendered order that construed women as "morally weak, easily deceived, incapable of sustained and intelligent resistance to the advances of men, and, therefore, potentially the root of all evil" (du Boulay 1986,140), the physical and symbolic separation of men and women acted as a sexual deterrent. Women were placed under the protection of men to whose authority they had always to succumb, at least in public appearance. In a peasant world that zealously guarded scarce material and symbolic resources—of which prestige and honor, as well as women's productive and reproductive labor have long been integral elements— the subjugation of female sexuality acquired paramount significance. It ensured the protection of family and male honor, *filotimo,* a traditional Greek value predicated on strict conformity to public morality. Always threatened by women's perceived vulnerability to sexual access, the preservation of familial honor justified spatial surveillance, if not confinement. The material and symbolic stakes were high. Conformity accrued the symbolic capital of social prestige and its concomitant material rewards. Women's sexual transgressions were punished with social ridicule and ostracism, mechanisms of social control that Michael Cacoyannis so dramatically captured in his internationally acclaimed, Golden Globe–winning film *Girl in Black* (1956, Hermes Film). As a result, women were subjected to emotional abuse, social devaluation, even physical violence.

These gendered cartographies are consistent with the manner in which feminist anthropologists have theorized the inscription of women's domination in social space. Shirley Ardener (1981) has described how hierarchical relationships, such as those between men and women, can be thought of as "'social maps', which are frequently . . . realized on 'the ground' by the placing of individuals in space" (13). Ardener speaks about the operation of powerful ground rules to delimit women in space. Such ground rules were applied with particular urgency under conditions of migrancy, when immigrant fathers intensified their efforts to constrain the field of social interaction for their daughters. In the pioneering days of the predominantly male world of Greek migrants, the absence of the communal surveillance that had enforced traditional gender ideologies in the village rendered the domestic sphere a crucial site for the continued domination of women in the New World. For instance, Papanikolas describes how a charismatic folk healer turned into an autocratic tyrant when it came to enforcing traditional codes of honor: "When her oldest daughters entered their teen years, the young Greek laborers coming home from the mill saw fit to pass Magherou's house, hoping for a glimpse of them. Their father painted the window gray, so that the young men could not look in and his daughters could not look out" (1989, 22). The possibility of breaking away from old regimes of control through migrancy was canceled by the enforcement of patriarchal ideologies through new means of spatial confinement. The patriarch redrew the borders of vision to create a place of confinement and thereby negated the possibility of imagining a future beyond the boundaries of the immigrant household. In this case, the spatial ordering of gender relations in the Old World was transplanted into the New, imprisoning the American-born in an impermeable domesticity. Immigrant traditions demarcated the domain of vision, literally and metaphorically.[6]

Sexuality is itself a space that could be colonized, fixing women within male-circumscribed social margins. Traditional moral values, such as modesty, functioned as essential ethnic boundaries that set the ideals of Greek womanhood apart from nonimmigrant America. Following the logic of oppositional identity, American gender relations, and often the whole society, were represented as a unified space and subsequently demonized as immoral and corrupt. The conditions to oppress the daughters of the immigrants were set by this cultural template, crisscrossed by Greek patriarchy as well as Greek and American nationalisms.

In this retelling of women's pasts, I have provisionally reproduced the space of Greek America in terms of a gender binary with one pole centered on an introverted, female-centered domain of ethnic preservation and the other defined by an outward-oriented, controlling male sphere. This is to dramatize how the dialectic patriarchy-nationalism failed immigrant women. In the social imagination of the American-born generation, the admonition to preserve Greek language and custom represented an incomprehensible defense of peasant culture. Seen as authoritative, oppressively parochial, and stifling, the vernacular world of the immigrants stood as the antipode of American modernity. Documented in autobiographies, analyzed in social sciences, described in literature, and dramatized in films like the popular blockbuster *My Big Fat Greek Wedding,* the gendered process of intergenerational transmission reads as a list of prohibitions deployed to contain the new generation of women within the insular world of tradition. A "cult of domesticity," as sociologist Alice Scourby (2003, 36) has aptly put it, immigrant patriarchy generated a structure of deeply felt resentment, as evocatively voiced by the character Effie in Helen Papanikolas's short story "The First Meeting of the Group":

> "Oh, don't give me that! It's the same old crap! Women don't know anything. Men do. That's how we were raised. We'd have to listen to those puffed-up peasants who made a little money in America with their damn speeches about the Greek language and customs, and we were always put down. The boys got to do anything they wanted,

but we had to be nice and demure." Effie mimicked the last words, pursing her little mouth primly. "I had to press my brothers' pants and shine their shoes before they went out on dates." (1993, 174)

Unlike the professional folklorists in Greece who sanitized the folk for middle-class consumption from a distance, socially mobile Greek Americans experienced the vernacular intimately, as an experiential, lived-in understanding of ethnicity. Caught in the complex interface of multiple and often clashing cultural worlds, second-generation women became outspoken critics of folk custom. But they neither discarded this past wholesale nor adopted a singular perspective toward it. A close analysis of two popular ethnographies illuminates this point.

Gendered Spaces of Immigrant Pasts and Ethnic Ambivalence

Autobiography offers a glimpse of the complex process associated with the making of ethnicity, the place of the past in the lives of the daughters of the immigrants, and the relationship of the second generation to the culture of the first. In the passage that follows, Papanikolas takes an acerbic look at the patriarchal immigrant world and worldview. She focuses on a routine event in immigrant communities at the time, the speech extolling immigrant virtues and exhorting ethnic preservation. Her reminiscence brings attention to the fact that the reproduction of tradition was contested within Greek America.

> Again we had to listen to pompous men tell us to keep up the Greek customs and ideals and to our mothers' exhortations to be *semni,* "modest." Hysteria lay just beneath our skin, waiting. During one meeting Kolokithas—"Squash"—short, red-faced, went to the bathroom at the back of the hall. The long rush of urine hitting the toilet bowl came back as clearly as if he were in the middle of the room. Strangled giggles from us girls, our hands clamped over our mouths, shuffling about in our chairs in a futile attempt to hide brought hundreds of parental eyes to glare at us and moments later at returning Squash. With a serious look on his round face, he pulled down his vest in a business like manner, took his seat, and folded his arms across his chest, his head cocked, to resume hearing the importance of keeping up the customs and culture of the fatherland. (1987, 45–46)

Subversively satirical, the passage situates intergenerational differences on a collision course. The making of immigrant daughters into ethnic women takes place within the gendered symbolic order of the community. On the one hand, the public function of advocating ethnic reproduction fell on the men, who, according to tradition, should monopolize political offices. Even the sight of a woman "discussing politics," for instance, made Papanikolas's father, Yorgis, glower (18). Consequently, it was "pompous fathers [who] came [to Greek-language schools] to pontificate in village dialects about the catastrophe that would befall us [children] if the Greek language died out in America" (17). On the other hand, tradition placed paramount responsibility on mothers as the domestic guardians of the moral order. Part of the cultural complex of honor, *dropi* (shame) requires public conformity to traditional ideals of modesty. It is a mechanism of social control through which the collective safeguards its norms by punishing those who transgress its moral boundaries. Ostracizing noncon-formists, it brings shame on the individual—and the family of the individual—who breaches collective expectations of propriety. Dropi becomes a crucial instrument for cultural reproduction. In the context related by Papanikolas, dropi, embodied as modesty, habituates the daughters of the immigrants to the larger patriarchal order. As "the future mothers of the race" (44), women were socialized to embody the traditional order; bodily constraint in social conduct demarcates control of sexuality to discipline ethnic preservation.

Still, the gendered order of the event is breached. Papanikolas uses the language of hysteria to convey the deep anxiety experienced by individuals subjected to an authoritative reproduction of their domination. The daughters of immigrants are vigilant subjects, prone to subvert the imposed patriarchal discipline. Their outburst of laughter disrupts the solemnity of the ritual event, bringing attention to the irony of a situation in which peasants act as guardians of national culture. If cleanliness, order, and decorum stand for civilization, dirt and disorder represent what the Enlightenment has construed as the opposite of culture: nature. Culture and nature are seen as conceptually antithetical, the former defined in the absence of the latter; this is why the presence of natural elements in the domain of culture could be perceived as a threatening intrusion, an anomaly. Natural—that is, "uncultured" behavior—intrudes on the ritual event designed to extol immigrant culture and whose very orderly decorum signifies civilized behavior. Crude and undisciplined, Squash's release of a biological need undermines the civility of the event. Squash lacks the control to avert the intrusion of nature into culture, and the attentive guardian of Greek custom becomes a bearer of natural, uncivilized behavior. Disorder lurks beneath the semblance of order. Through their act of spotting this pollution and bringing it to public attention, the daughters of the immigrants hold a mirror to the community, pointing out the symbolic distance between its claim to civilization and culturally unbecoming behavior. The immigrants, in fact, represent the folk, who cannot embody civilization and therefore cannot inhabit the American nation. The experiential proximity of the second generation to the immigrant folk, on the one hand, and to American modernity, on the other, precludes the idealization of the former.

But if the immigrants are an embarrassing counterpoint to modernity, the folk Gemeinschaft also represents social intimacy and aesthetic richness. Participation in this environment brings about a deeply satisfying sensory overload, according to Papanikolas:

> How joyous when the warm yeasty scent of baking bread filled the air and mothers called us to eat slices of warm bread slathered with butter. . . .
>
> The beginning of school and the ritual making of wine and tomato paste in Greek Town would for years mean autumn to me. . . . Mothers carried out buckets full of tomato skins, which were immediately pounced on by a mass of droning, iridescent blue-green flies. All the while the mothers called to each other over wire fences, mostly about their children. Folk cures for fevers, for the dread *pounta*—pneumonia—and croup, judicious advice on who was best for dispelling the evil eye. (1995a, 9)

Yet the gendered household economy stands for primitivism as well. "Although visiting Greek Town was usually satisfying," Papanikolas writes (1987), "I did not want to live there in the houses with their lean-tos, sheds, washhouses, and where mothers . . . wrung the necks of the chickens . . . chopped off the heads of rabbits and skinned them in a flash. I was always eager to return to my silent house" (21). The proximity of immigrants to nature is a source of the author's personal alienation from the folk, and brings about a distancing effect, an intense desire to flee. The reliance of the immigrant economy on the domestic processing of animals places the courtyard at a distance from civilization, dissolving the boundaries between culture and nature. In their killing of animals, women interface with nature in the way of the primitive. In contrast, the author's own home stands as a tranquil haven for individual reflection, where privacy shields her from what she perceives as folk primitivism.

The folk are antithetical to modernity, and the author's realization of this fact requires a flight away from the traditional community. If, for example, modernity controls the physiology of the human body and elevates hygiene as a cultural ideal, tradition is oblivious to it. If modernity praises the self-determining individual, tradition determines the behavior of the folk collective. In this respect, the folk Gemeinschaft demarcates a fundamental alterity, a place of a different order, alien to modernity: "[In Greek school], sitting next to girls whom I avoided in American school, whose armpits smelled, who believed in the evil eye and *all* village superstitions, who had been embroidering dish towels for their trousseaus since they were six, I fantasized about the passenger train that I would someday board to be carried through the rock mountain gates into the canyon beyond and away, away" (1987, 44, emphasis added). What disturbs the author here is the failure of the folk to function as agents, their total conformity to the symbolic order of the immigrant village. In this scenario, the folk are situated outside history because they are not involved in its making. They are situated outside American modernity, as well, because its markers—progress, rationality, hygiene—leave the immigrants and their children unaffected. A conceptual dichotomy arises between the immigrant folk, who are seen as passive bearers of tradition, and ethnic Americans, who are portrayed as agents of change. Cultural stasis fixes the immigrant in a fundamentally different temporal order, that of Old World traditionality. Therefore, immigrant spaces—the language school or the ethnic neighborhood—are places where the prevailing rules of social conduct do not correspond with those of modernity. They function as cultural and temporal heterotopias alien to the ethnic subject, whose imperative becomes to establish a conceptual and spatial distance. In this respect, Papanikolas's (misplaced) insistence on representing the folk Gemeinschaft as wholly vanished (Anagnostou 2008a) can be read as an allegorical announcement of the arrival of Greek America in American modernity.

Inertia and passivity make the folk objects of tradition. As a total way of life, folklore shapes subjects who "[f]ollow the profound command of culture" (Papanikolas 1984, 30), as in the following telling passage: "[American miners] stayed away from the mines when they had premonitions and bad dreams . . . . The Cretans were not so encumbered. Whether they had bad dreams or not and even if the sense of doom was inside them, they reported for their shifts because Fate could not be cheated; one's fate was determined at birth" (Papanikolas 1971, 73). A normative duality between American and Greek subjects is posited here, as the former act upon experience while the latter fatalistically submit to the dictates of tradition. Such an opposition erroneously cancels agency among the Greek folk.

Understood in this manner, folk immigrant status meant exclusion from whiteness, as the latter was associated with the rational self-governance that was the quintessential political principle of white citizenship. But securing a distance from immigrant "folkness" did not guarantee racial inclusion in American modernity. In the shifting racial boundaries of the early twentieth century, immigrant working-class activism could result in racial demotion for the entire ethnic collective. While socioeconomic mobility earned the Papanikolas family respectability and inclusion in whiteness, for example, Helen was denied access to the white section of her segregated public school because Greek immigrants had gone on strike. The hard-earned privileges of whiteness were taken away as the state activated mechanisms of social control. Indignant that her own claim to Americanness was rejected, Papanikolas cast a critical glance at the nativist ideology that imposed second-class citizenship on the American-born children of the immigrants. At the same time, as a child, Papanikolas internalized an aversion toward immigrant difference. "Cretan children played by themselves, ran, chased, shouted in their dialect," she writes, "angering me that they spoke Greek on the school grounds" (1987, 14). An institution designed to function as an apparatus of 100 percent Americanism at the time, the school represents an assimilationist national space, setting up the second generation, at least partly, to sanction assimilation.

But if immigrants represent a crude way of life and undesirable difference, they also stand for heroism. If the Gemeinschaft partially repels, a performance that celebrates the national past or folk past generates a deep sense of ethnic recognition and belonging. Reminiscing about growing up Greek in Helper, Utah, Papanikolas (1995a, 11) lets out the national passion (for Greece) that stirred her heart: "How can it be explained that although I disliked Greek school so much, when I stood on the church basement stage and acted my part in the epic dramas of the Greeks fighting their overlord Turks, I felt a stirring of love for those hard, resilient people of my heritage?" Significantly, the subject is perplexed by the power that ethnic identification exerts upon her. As Michael Fischer (1986) aptly puts it, ethnicity "is often something quite puzzling to the individual, something over which he or she lacks control" (195). The stage reenactment of the Greek war of independence against Ottoman Turkey—a staple of celebrations among school children in Greek America—produces ethnic identification. The commemoration of the nation's heroic past—expressed as sacrifice and valiance in folk songs, popular imagery and school sketches—generates deep ethnic sentiments that connect the individual with the Greek nation. Ethnicity here is embodied in social practices that habituate the children of immigrants into the symbolic order of ethnic nationalism and the passions it stirs. The resulting attachment is experienced as a deep but puzzling psychic force that expresses itself beyond individual determination or choice. According to Fischer, it manifests itself as a "compulsion of an 'id-like' force . . . [the Freudian] it-ness of experience." It is expressed as a "recognition of something about one's essential being . . . [that] seems to stem from outside one's immediate consciousness and control, and yet requires an effort of self-definition" (196–97).[7]

Making Community through Historical Remembering

The experience of the immigrant peasant Gemeinschaft engendered a profound ambivalence in Papanikolas's sense of belonging. If the vernacular offered the comfort of primordial connectivity, a profoundly satisfying experience, it also shackled individuals, particularly women. Associated with restraint and fulfillment of obligations, vernacular culture both repelled and attracted the ethnic self. How did Papanikolas position herself vis-à-vis this past? Her life story exemplifies a trajectory away from ancestral ties and obligations. Her pursuit of a life as a novelist, writer, folklorist, and historian emphatically marks a departure from the immigrant generation that commonly discouraged female education while encouraging male mobility through business or lucrative professions.[8] This challenging of gendered limitations underlines Papanikolas's determination to shatter the grip of tradition, illuminating the importance she assigned to agency as an ethic for living. But she never turned her back on the ethnic collective that grew out of that past, returning to it from the novel position of a vested chronicler and storyteller: a scribe of the past. The commitment to document and the act of writing about the immigrant experience offered Papanikolas a place of dwelling, a center hospitable to ambivalence and cultural betweenness. This location enabled her to recognize the importance of ancestral ties and immigrant values but did not require a total identification with the past that harbored them, in fact providing an occasion to critique Greek American ethnicity, as I will discuss in the next chapter. But writing was never an activity wholly disengaged from the intended audience of coethnics. Papanikolas invested in creating a community based on historical remembering not solely through storytelling but also through "practices of commitment"—that is, active participation in the community through "patterns of loyalty and obligation that keep the community alive" (Bellah et al. 1985, 154). As a storyteller of collective experience, as a public intellectual and cultural activist, she strove to nurture a community of historical remembrance.

Sustaining communities of belonging becomes the key concept here. An homage paid to Papanikolas in a 2003 special issue of the *Journal of the Hellenic Diaspora* illuminates her devotion, generosity, and talent in establishing dense interpersonal ties with a diversity of constituencies, including coethnics, scholars, and public-sector researchers. Long-term participation in ethnic preservation projects and a vast record of public lectures testify to her resolute determination in collective engagement. It is through these "practices of commitment" that she sought to counter the wave of amnesia that looms over Greek America, often pleading with her interlocutors not to lose sight of how the past shapes the present and linking a multitude of diverse constituencies through a shared historical consciousness. As Leontis (2003) observes in her contribution to that issue, community served as a "compass point" in Papanikolas's life through her "art of telling" (21). "Like the time-tested art of storytelling in villages, Papanikolas's stories resonate with community because they produce a sense of being-in-community even as they expose its weakest points" (24) she writes. Prominently profiled in the mass media and popular press, this art of storytelling links various contours making up Greek America into a self-conscious community. Thus, there is justification to recognize her posthumously published novel, her literary farewell, as a "writer's last statement to her audience, and to her *community*" (Frangos 2006, 22, emphasis added).

The function of narratives as a means of producing community reveals an otherwise not readily discernible contour that connects the past and the present or, more precisely, produces a usable past in the present. After having theorized ethnicity as network, Leontis (2003) revisits the concept of ethnic community, this time drawing from her own personal memories and readings to provide us once again with a lead to unravel this skein. She explains how the significance of storytelling that in the past worked to enable a specific brand of community—an inclusive, heterogeneous collective that resists disintegration even when powerful conflicting interests force it apart—carries over in the present:

> Papanikolas has always been keen on mastering a storytelling tradition that was alive for as long as her parents were with her, stories that remained alive in her memory and in the memories of her readers. If my own memories do not deceive me, I think it is right to say that storytelling and its less esteemed relative, gossip, as practiced in Greek villages, did not veer far from its function in Papanikolas's writing. In the more oral, rural, peasant culture of Romiosini that Papanikolas's ancestors brought with them, storytelling was a way of mending community life made threadbare by too much proximity, too few resources, too many clashing interests. (23)

This fragment of memoir asserts the *collective* importance of storytelling—both oral and written—and its integrative function, dovetailing nicely with the memories of another scholar who is also biographically connected with Greek

America, Chrysie Constantakos (1990). Reflecting on the social significance of life story as a device for intergenerational transmission, she, too, testifies to the ubiquity of storytelling in her immigrant family, noting its importance in bridging generational differences. Elders narrating life stories maintain and strengthen interpersonal relations, she proposes, contributing to the making of communities of various scales based on the production of shared memories.

Leontis's passage illuminates how lived memory among the immigrant progeny mediates the way in which the popular ethnographer produces community. This rendition interfaces immigrant orality in the past with ethnic writing in the present, both seen to perform an identical function: maintain a sense of community as centrifugal forces of discord or competition pull it toward dissolution. Storytelling creates contexts to sustain a community of always potentially dissenting and conflicting interests. Once again, as my reading of Papanikolas's corpus shows (2008a), the folk past—expressed as storytelling to mediate conflict—is far from vanished; an author steeped in the genre of oral storytelling morphs it into fiction. The contours of this past resolutely keep encroaching on the present.

As a scribe of the past, Papanikolas thickens the nexus of connections within the contours of Greek America, making ethnicity a matter of reflection in a multitude of sites: the ethnic press and popular media, the academic book and journal article, the community museum and the archive, the academy, and formal and informal networks of sociability. Her narratives about success and failure, cooperation and conflict, betrayal and loyalty, ethnic rage and joy, activism and complacency, mutual care and narcissism, heroism and exploitation, sameness and change, indictment of ethnic racism, and affirmation of ethnic values have disseminated images of Greek ethnicity deeply and widely throughout the contours of the network. Her prolific output left its imprint on multiple nodes producing ethnicity in the United Sates. Through her writings on the working class, women, and Greek American consent to whiteness, ethnic audiences are brought to grapple with internal diversity and "dangerous memories" of intra-ethnic exploitation and racism (Bellah et al. 1985, 153) and are encouraged to reflect on how the past informs the meaning of Greek America at the dawn of the twenty-first century. The popular ethnographer actively wove her own vision of ethnicity-as-collective centered on historical memory and the production of usable pasts. She was resolute in maintaining the value of the past to inform the making of identity and belonging in the present, a dimension that I will examine closely in the next chapter, particularly as it pertains to ethnic whiteness.

Papanikolas translated a profound personal ambivalence toward ethnicity into an activist immersion in community politics. Making both intracommunity differences and ethnic self-critique central to her work, she nevertheless created contexts or built on available venues—book readings, teaching, public lectures, preservation sites—to sustain all sorts of collectives, each constituted around her deeply felt need to remember historically. If she entwined herself with various communities—researchers, archivists, teachers, students, and academics—she also centered Greek America as a collective that could be realized as a meaningful entity of coethnics deliberating over the differences and the conflicts that inflected the community.

Documenting an Oppressed Collective

Popular ethnographer Constance Callinicos, in contrast, turned to intracommunity conflicts for the basis of a fundamentally alternative politics of gendered ethnic belonging. Her *American Aphrodite* (1990) documents the specificity of women's experiences from a feminist perspective. It represents the Greek America of early twentieth-century peasants and their descendants as an oppressive patriarchy that women indict and from which they desperately seek to escape. Callinicos's position diverges drastically from that of Papanikolas. She proposes that for women oppressed by patriarchy, community can be constituted only in all-female spaces, away from male structures of domination. Gendered separation, she argues, enables women to liberate themselves from reigning patriarchy and collectively to rehabilitate the ethnic past on their own terms. In this polemical work, ethnicity is inflected by profound, incommensurable gender differences. Callinicos's ethnography advances a bitter cultural critique, turning intraethnic gender inequalities into the basis for a radical politics of difference.

American Aphrodite defies easy classification in any genre. In part a fragmentary biography of the author's grandmother, it also includes a brief portrait of her mother as well as a rich autobiographical component. The book builds on an oral history project, which consists of the author's interviews with a total of 111 women across three generations. It gives voice to the "picture bride" generation of the 1920s and 1930s and to the daughters and granddaughters of that cohort. The sample does not include post–World War II immigrant women, as the author makes clear. For her research, Callinicos scoured the country between 1978 and 1982, seeking to interview women who had grown up in various places in the United States but who shared the social background of early twentieth-century rural Greece. Separated by geography but connected through an "almost identical upbringing," these three generations of women "were acculturated," she distressedly points out, "as Greek peasant girls, first, last and always" (29). It was the transplanted Greek village in America, the *horio,* that defined their existence.

Inspired by second-wave feminism, Callinicos's work bridges the personal and the social and seeks to expose the mechanisms of women's oppression and to bring about social change. Drawing on ethnographic studies of women, the text displays anthropology's and women's studies' shared concern with the cultural constitution of gender and folklore's interest in the reworking of tradition. It simultaneously participates in and contributes to discussions about women's liberation from patriarchal control, the reconfiguring of immigrant and ethnic identities, and the making of alternative, all-women's spaces for performing the feminist reclamation of tradition. In her preface to Callinicos's book, Aphrodite Clamar celebrates its research agenda:

> Greek American women have been without a voice since the first Greek immigrants arrived here as wives, mothers, sisters and daughters. . . . But because we had no voice, no one cared to acknowledge the phenomenon that we represented—Greek American women, possessed of a particular culture, living a special way of life, surrounded by a special set of circumstances. . . .
>
> Now, . . . Constance Callinicos has helped us find our voice—and now it is there for all to heed. No longer are we mute; no longer anonymous; no longer absent. We are here. (*Eimaste edw.*) Attention must be paid to us. (1990, 9–10)

These passages situate Callinicos's popular ethnography within a tradition of women's studies in which the documentation of women's personal experiences becomes a feminist instrument for personal and collective empowerment. Like oral history for feminist purposes in the 1970s, the collection and circulation of interviews with women are seen as practices that build women's solidarity and challenge power hierarchies. Barbara Kirshenblatt-Gimblett has pointed out that in such work

> folklorists and oral historians affirmed the solidarity of ordinary women by stressing the commonalities in women's experiences in the oral histories they collected. . . . By affirming the right of any woman to interview any other women, whether or not the interviewer was professionally trained, they challenged the academic hierarchy and its authoritarian monopoly on history. Women doing oral history was to be an inclusive, broadly based, and empowering process by, for, and about women. (1989, 137)

Both as an autobiographical testimony of gender oppression and as an angry ethnographic indictment of women's collective victimization, *American Aphrodite* advances its own politics of empowerment and imagines new kinds of performative spaces in which to subvert patriarchal traditions.

The Folk Past: Patriarchy Frozen in Time

In its autobiographical dimension, *American Aphrodite* works as a narrative of personal transformation. It reconfigures the oppressed and traumatized self of a granddaughter of immigrants through self-imposed exile from the immigrant culture. The flight away from oppressive patriarchy becomes a condition necessary for catharsis and for the refashioning of an individual who seeks to reclaim her ethnic identity on her own terms. In its attention to conditions of exile, displacement, and rupture and to the processes enabling relocation, reclamation, and resynthesis, the book brings the past into a creative yet polemical dialogue with the present. The autobiographical element is of particular significance here because it furnishes a textual space for the self to reflect on the conditions of its refashioning (Seyhan 1996). Postmodern culture revels in the consciousness that identity is no longer a fixed, singular entity but a dynamic multiplicity of components. From such a position, Callinicos turns to autobiography first to underscore the overwhelming constitutive function of immigrant patriarchal traditions in her life and subsequently to advocate for her own vision of the place of the past among women in Greek America. In recalling her early socialization in the "world of Greek village women" in America (110), she evokes her immersion in a rich folklore. Callinicos remembers specific proverbs, dances, and songs; she discusses folk beliefs; she appreciatively recollects listening to enthralling tales. In this reminiscence, the immigrant folk past comes alive as a valued practice by the American-born granddaughter:

> My grandmother's childhood was spent in the shadow of the oracle at Delphi (she came from Roumeli), but she knew nothing of Olympian gods and goddesses. Nor was she conversant with names like Homer, Ulysses, Sappho, Socrates and Aristotle. She chanted by memory long prayers and hymns learned in her village church, sang endless strophic folk songs which she taught to me during my own childhood with her. She told me long and fascinating stories about her life in Greece, interesting as any I could have read in Aesop or Grimm. (22)

"In the shadow" of the ancient past! Classical Greek culture—so ideologically vital in the politics of both nineteenth-century Greek nation building and the assimilation into the nation of business-owning Greek immigrants in the 1920s—lies physically near yet culturally distant from the world of the folk immigrant-to-be in the early twentieth century. As Richard Dorson (1978a, 45) aptly writes, "Olympus beckoned invitingly across the centuries, and modern Greek folklorists strove to connect their peasant tales with the classic myths." Yet the point of reference for Callinicos's grandmother is the complex configuration of vernacular practices and beliefs. Valued here as much as classic works of ancient Greece or seminal texts of German ethnology, it captures the imagination of the young author. The oral performance of this culture connects the immigrant grandmother with the ethnic granddaughter. It presents a moment of socialization into ethnicity and shared social intimacy: "She will sing for me. I will sing with her, and she will teach me yet another folk song, one more story about love, death, or heroism" (42). The granddaughter pleads for a repetition of a storytelling performance: "Yaya [grandmother], sing me the song. Sing me the one about the lady, *yaya,* the one in the window" (41). The grandmother obliges, recounting yet again the boldness of a young male villager aggressively interrupting a public celebration in his pursuit of a mate:

> Make way, move over
> So that I might pass;
> Make way! So I
> Won't disturb your dance.
>
> Make way! I will sell
> Will sell the goats,
> Make way! So I can
> Buy you a pair of earrings
> . . .
> Can it be, can it really be
> I saw you at your window?
> Can it be, can it really be
> I saw you at your window? (38)

The song points to the tension between agonistic male exuberance and conformity to community norms. Decisive and aggressive, the male asserts his own performative space within the community, both figuratively and metaphorically. He brings public attention to his ability and determination to win the heart of the woman he desires. Potentially threatening and disruptive, the male seems willing to respect the social order insofar as the community defers to his interests. He is, in fact, of the community, but he is also distanced from it as a *person* who performs his masculine desire. Here we witness "a poetics of social interaction" that celebrates the competitive male self, his self-regard (eghoismos) "announc[ing] his personal excellence" (Herzfeld 1985, 11).

Space and desire are gendered in this song. The male occupies the center of the public stage; his presence is unambiguous. In contrast, the presence of the woman he desires is fleeting. While the male flaunts his desire in public, the female is elusive and silent, confined within the protective domain of domesticity. The audience of the song can imagine her only as a shadow at the window, a boundary between the private and public domains. In the sexual economy of the village, her sexuality is shielded from public view, regulated and surveilled. The song reproduces a dichotomy noted by anthropologists in traditional Greek villages between the public space as the realm of male agonistic sociability and the private domain of the home as the natural place for women.[9]

As a little girl, Callinicos was "fascinated . . . [and] would listen" (111) to the lore. As an adult, she launches a bitter critique of folklore as a form of patriarchal control. She indicts folk culture as a site where women are denied agency and the power of self-affirmation. She is admonished not to nurture ambitions because "attempts to expand horizons would bring bad luck . . . , set a curse upon her family, [and] cast her out into the tempest (*thiella*), where she would be doomed to be blown about for eternity by the Winds of Chance, set upon mercilessly by evil spirits" (ibid.). Likewise, folk practices discipline female sexuality: little boys are applauded for dancing exuberantly; for the author, modesty is encouraged: "[My grandmother] takes my small hand in hers. 'Here, sweet girl. Watch me. Do as I do. Step lightly, modestly. Listen to the music. Always delicately and modestly. Never kick the feet up off the ground. Too much like a man that way. This is a woman's dance. A little lift of the skirt, a modest woman's way. Never too much'" (43). Here, a moment of intergenerational intimacy and cultural transmission functions as a gendered moment that reproduces the ideology of female modesty. As Jane Cowan (1990) observes, teaching dancing in this manner transmits the embodiment of a sexual economy of shame—a central value in the traditional Greek code of honor—through a central social practice in Greek society.[10] If "dancing is more than knowing the steps [but] involves both social knowledge and power" (xii), the female body is disciplined to perform the gendered order of dominated sensuality. Or, to use Paul Connerton's (1989, 71) framework, this training represents a practice of transmission that engraves collective memory into "bodily social memory." It habituates the individual ethnic body to patriarchal hegemony.

In Callinicos's representation of her family—and elsewhere—immigration transplants the patriarchy that oppresses women through generations. In this account, the Greek village has been transported to the New World and is reproduced within the immigrant household intact, as if in a hermetically sealed time capsule. The grandmother submits to archaic cultural dictates that as-sign women the function of cultural bearers of ethnic patriarchy under condi-tions of migrancy:

> In fact, my grandmother *did* live in the village, even though her body was here in America. She raised her daughters in the village of her birth, teaching them to raise *us*, her granddaughters, in the village of her birth. . . . I wonder now, sometimes, what that power [she pos-sessed] would have meant to us had she been willing or able to use her influence in a positive way, encouraging us, cheering us on into full and productive lives outside the Greek ghetto mentality, boundaries set by her Greek Village in America. (23)

In her autobiographical reminiscence, Callinicos portrays her immigrant family as a static, closed system, its boundaries a totalized patriarchal cultural geography. It represents an instance of Greek immigrant noncontemporaneity.[11] Her ethnographic analysis of women's personal narratives extends this suffocat-ing landscape to encompass the totality of the social sector of Greek America that her book explores.

The Politics of Women's Voices

Callinicos appears to cast a wide net in developing her oral history project. She features at length the perspectives of women whose memories reach as deep as the first years of Greek immigration in the early 1900s; she also interviews the daughters of those immigrant women as well as their granddaughters, like herself far removed from the circumstances of early twentieth-century immi-gration. In *American Aphrodite,* the author's narrative voice shares ethnographic authority with the women's personal testimonies to point to women as victims of recurring verbal, psychological, and physical abuse. In their accounts, women deploy metaphors of incarceration, confinement, and asphyxiation to under-score the pressure to conform to gender expectations in Greek America.[12] They recount male-induced controls that seek to regulate women's sexuality, stifle their educational aspirations, and crush their personal and emotional develop-ment. A thread in the narratives documents instances of abuse leading to emo-tional suffering and even psychological pathologies. The interview setting serves as a forum in which women speak out to map the devastating effects of patri-archy in Greek America. They indict patriarchy as they point out its power to make women themselves (their mothers) the guardians of oppressive traditions. Through Callinicos's authorial mediation, the women make public a painfully real aspect of the Greek American experience.

Early in her introduction, Callinicos reflects on her narrative as a site of knowledge production. "*American Aphrodite* is one, and *only one* writer's attempt to document and illuminate the complexity of female life among us" (18), she writes, recognizing the partiality of her account as well as the heterogeneity of women's experiences. In expressing her "fervent hope" (ibid.) for additional writings on women's lives in Greek America, she advocates a particular politics of location premised on the plurality of women's subjectivities. There can be "no 'one, true and orthodox' definition of Greek American woman" (17–18) she remarks, as she envisions a future of open-ended possibilities: "At bottom, the rules must be our own, the decisions highly personal, the core of this issue being the questions of 'Who decides? Who defines for me what I am or am not? What part of the "ime" [being] which is Greek will I choose for myself? What part shall I discard when (and if) it threatens my very life? And, most important, which people shall I choose to be a part of my world after I have defined it for myself?'" (18). As a feminist who interrogates hegemonic, male-centered definitions of women, Callinicos envisions the making of ethnic selves in terms of personal choice, multiplicity, and individual agency. In place of the power of (male) culture to generate the meaning of gendered ethnicity, she views women as authors of their own subjectivities. The individual is assigned the power to overcome the past and to invent herself anew in a reflective conversation with layers of her own ethnic biography.

Yet Callinicos's sensitivity to diversity evaporates when she assumes the position of an authoritative translator of the ethnic past. In contrast to her stated commitment to pluralism, she portrays Greek American women of early twentieth-century rural backgrounds as an undifferentiated and oppressed collective. Once she identifies the operation of patriarchy in Greek America, she proceeds to homogenize that culture as patriarchal, representing all the men who inhabit this social field as a yet another uniform collective. The interview material becomes a tool to legitimize this totalizing claim. The voices of her ethnographic interlocutors generously share textual space with the author to produce a monophonic account of the past. Women are construed in terms of the singular enunciation "the Greek woman," the male-controlled "Good Greek Girl" (25).[13] Alternative male subjectivities, such the one recovered by Steve Frangos (2005), are cancelled. Like the containment of ethnicity in the documentary *The Greek Americans,* the erasure of difference here becomes possible through a "synecdochic fallacy" (di Leonardo 1998) by which the sample is taken to represent the whole. Operating under the rubric of a shared rural culture, Callinicos fails to take into account that crossing boundaries between various cultural worlds has long been an integral component of rural Greek life and its histories of immigration. In chapter 1, I quoted historical anthropologist Thomas Gallant's observation (2001) that "[t]he view of the Greek village as isolated in space and frozen in time . . . at best is misleading and at worst inaccurate" (97). In view of new evidence, an example of which I will discuss in chapter 5, we should also start rethinking the Greek American family as a highly heterogeneous and contested social unit, not the uniform gender prison that Callinicos portrays it to be. Social change and the transformation of subjectivities through cultural contact and histories of immigration are silenced in her account. Conveniently ignoring ethnographic and historical nuances, Callinicos founds her argument on a number of rhetorical strategies to establish her reconstruction of the ethnic past as *the* inviolate truth.

Callinicos's ethnographic authority depends on the exclusion of male perspectives from the account. Women's experience is presented as a domain of knowledge whose articulation and access is restricted solely to women. As a woman researcher and collector of voices, Callinicos arrogates to herself the authority to represent female Greek America. She writes, "What I sensed from these women was that there was a perception of the world that could never be given a voice by any but us: females telling about being female" (14). Here, resort to a gendered insider status narrows the legitimate sources of ethnographic knowledge. She also excludes alternative perspectives when she naturalizes patriarchy as a total fact. Her claim that she employs no methodology but instead relies on a wide range of random social interaction makes the case that women's oppression can be retrieved as a transparent truth. In failing to engage with its own hermeneutics, her account does double violence in its representation. While Callinicos claims to give voice to women, she mutes alternative perspectives. As she collectivizes women's subjugation, she denies them agency in the past. She represents immigrants as frozen in the past, colonized by patriarchy, and functioning as its guardians. She portrays them with a flattening uniformity, as passive patriarchal perpetrators. Her failure to acknowledge the partiality of women's oppression—though it was a devastating experience for many women—and her insistence instead on its totality constitute the core of Callinicos's ethnographic poetics and feminist politics.

In fashioning an oppressed collectivity that indicts patriarchal structures, Callinicos aligns herself with the feminist practice of "consciousness-raising" popular in post-1960s American feminism. As Susan Rogers suggests, "'consciousness-raising' [entailed] an institutionalized process by which neophyte feminists learned first, that they are subordinated, and second how and in what forms this subordination occurs" (1978, 138).[14] This strategy, as Chris Weedon (1987) observes, allowed women to interpret their problems not as personal failing but "as a result of socially produced structures" (85). In this respect, *American Aphrodite*'s totalization of the subjugation of women dramatically underscores the urgency to mobilize female victims of patriarchy into a politically conscious collective.[15]

With the advent of poststructuralism and the deconstructive turn in anthropology, we can no longer think of ethnographic representations as transparent facts. Ethnographic texts circulate ideologically loaded interpretations of reality that compete to assert their own truths and to contest the truths of others in a field of power relations. Their social potency rests on convincing the body politic and, in turn, on mobilizing collectivities on their behalf. The making of a public record of women's past (but also present) victimization becomes crucial for the making of an activist collectivity that seeks to liberate itself from cultural oppression. As Ana Maria Alonso (1992) argues, social memory is crucial "to the symbolic constitution of social groups and social identities" (408). Not unlike nation building, memories offer shared sentiments of solidarities and "create felt fraternities" (410) that may inspire social action and effect social change. Along these lines, Callinicos's account constitutes a nation of women around the sign of the oppressed, marginalized, muted woman. Here, the imagining of a gendered nation rests on the making of oppressed victims and on the powerfully shared emotions that such representations incite. Mobilizing women's resistance around the singular symbol of the oppressed "ethnic woman," she encourages women to imagine alternative ways of embodying tradition: to form all-female collectivities to reclaim and to perform ethnicity outside patriarchy.

Reclaiming the Vernacular and the Making of Community

American Aphrodite participates in the feminist project of "chang[ing] the tradition that has silenced and marginalized" women (Greene and Kahn 1985, 1). The book aligns itself with feminist predecessors that challenged patriarchy by bringing to consciousness its mechanisms of oppression. Knowledge of domination and its causes "was seen as an essential first step to political awareness and to the mobilization of women to effect reasoned political, social and personal change" (Rogers 1978, 138). For a number of feminists, including Callinicos, this emancipation starts at the level of the body. If patriarchy demands that women control their bodies, their challenge entails an assault on the everyday and ritual habits that produce modest, meek, reserved bodily behavior. It involves resituating embodied practice or—once again, in Connerton's terms—challenging hegemony through the confrontation of its naturalized site, "bodily social memory." To this effect, Callinicos turns to a hegemonic practice that disciplines female bodies, folk dance.[16] Seeking to reclaim ethnicity instead of thoroughly rejecting it, she assigns women the agency to rehabilitate the past under conditions of their own making.

An intimate social gathering of women—which the author calls *panegyri* (a community's celebration)—creates the context to resituate ethnic expressive culture. It is a private event in which women of various sexual orientations, ages, and ethnicities meet to celebrate the birthday of Callinicos's sister, establishing an all-female space in which to socialize outside the structures of male domination: "We fantasize a gathering, a huge coming-together of Greek women, old and young, who travel to a meeting ground to join hands, embrace, dance and sing our grandmothers' songs, feel the beauty of our Greek womanculture free of the Greek man's glare, or his leer, not to speak of his rigid expectations of us as his servant" (1990, 285).[17] Here, women seek to distance themselves from male domination through an alternative gender economy, a separate all-female space. In this manner, Callinicos attaches herself to a specific strategy in the history of the feminist movement. As Anna Enke (2003) observes, creating women's spaces, such as all-female coffeehouses, health clinics, communes, and schools, was an integral component of grassroots women's liberation groups in the 1960s and 1970s. These collectives, some of which were active well into the 1980s, nurtured sociability as well as political activism. They valued protest and prized women's self-expression outside male controls. Citing Verta Taylor and Leila Rupp (1993), Enke (2003) approaches these spaces as sites of "temporally and spatially limited separatism" (637). They were often endorsed as a necessary strategy to step outside "sexist social arrangements." It was thought that "only in gaining complete autonomy from men, and in simultaneously denying men the ability to treat women as objects, servants, and second-class citizens" would women be able to overcome patriarchy (ibid.).

How is it possible for Callinicos to desire a flight away from folk gender oppression and to long for a collectivity centered on a vernacular expression, dance, that reproduces hierarchical gender ideologies? The patriarchal admonitions of her grandmother rise in high pitch against her desire to actualize an unencumbered collective in which women "join hands, embrace, dance and sing our grandmothers' songs": "[W]e hear in our heads the sound of *yaya*'s voice. She is shaking her bony finger at us, exhorting us to modest behavior. Not too high, women never kick their feet so high. A shame for us to leap into the air. Only the man dances like that. Here, like this. Move the body in small motions, watch not to lift up your head. And your eyes. Always keep your eyes to the ground, like modest women" (1990, 288). Folk dance habituates women's bodies into modesty. It entails a cultural practice through which performers embody and reproduce ideologies of gender. In her ethnographic analysis of what she calls "dance events," anthropologist Jane Cowan (1990, 4) calls attention to the multiple and contested meanings associated with dancing. She observes that traditional folk dances script different body postures for the dance leader. For males, exuberant body movement communicates much-lauded cultural competence. Women, in contrast, are expected to exhibit bodily restraint and measured movement.

If women's domination takes place through the control of their bodies under a system of patriarchy (B. Turner 1984, 3), the quest for women's liberation requires a new politics of the body. In the dance event of the panegyri, dance itself becomes the medium of this reconfiguration, as women violate the gender-specific rules of Greek folk dances by performing dancing postures traditionally reserved for men. With "the hypnotic melodies of the clarinet" and the "incessant beating of the drum" (Callinicos 1990, 288) as the sensory background, the leader of the folk circle dance appropriates male behavior and creates an emerging kind of imagery: that of a woman dancer who, in leaping with "her billowing skirts swirling at her ankles," (ibid.) kicking up her legs, and shouting, regenders male performative competence. It is "through traditional and popular culture, [that] women find methods and opportunities to express individuality and voice their own as well as their group's concerns," thereby resisting domination (Greenhill and Tye 1997, 171–72). And as Barbara Le Blanc (1997) puts it, "More than entertainment, and more than just an aesthetic form, dance embodies some aspects of social practice and denies others, exacts restraint upon the dancer's body but also at times frees it, and formalizes movements that skew as well as mirror social forms" (101). The new embodiment through dance celebrates the production of "undisciplined women" (Greenhill and Tye 1997) who assault tradition as they appropriate it for their own purposes.[18]

This transgression of gender boundaries disrupts the unreflective reproduction of the past. In fact, it introduces a radical rupture in the complex historical development of Greek folk dances. As Gillian Bottomley (1992) shows, the meaning and performative contexts of folk dances have undergone profound changes in Greece and among Greeks abroad. Initially associated with village- and region-specific expressive culture, they have become highly stylized spectacles of national identity, tourist displays of traditional authenticity, and an integral part of urban youth entertainment. In the context of pluralistic democracies, Greek folk dances function as key sites for ethnic socialization, the performance of identity, and the memory of national and regional origins. Yet in the face of such transmutations, their gendered order has remained largely intact in ethnic festivals, arguably the most visible displays of Greek traditional culture in the United States. In outward-oriented displays of ethnicity through dance, the past generally continues to script the conventions of the gendered embodiment of male exuberance and female restraint.

Framed as an all-female, socially intimate, and culturally subversive dance event, the panegyri dramatically contrasts the commodified and popular church-centered Greek festivals in the United States.[19] In the private space of the pan-egyri, women are able to challenge the immigrant past that naturalizes gender ideologies in the practice of dance. Callinicos brings to consciousness the idea that ethnicity is not innocuous, although it may be generally and unreflectively accepted as such. Her aim is to redefine folk dancing from a widely accepted naturalized expression of ethnicity to a source of gender subordination. Like Bottomley (1992), who posited that "second-generation immigrants" are particularly positioned to "understand and resist [naturalized] forms of domination" (133), Callinicos occupies a social niche that enables her to render the immigrant and ethnic habitus visible and, therefore, subject to change. As a gendered ethnic subject located between the immigrant culture and the feminist movement, she draws upon feminist language to identify, to make sense of, and to confront traditional forms of gender oppression, seeking to reclaim the value of ethnicity for those women who have been subjected to the violence of ethnic patriarchy. The poetics of the panegyri enable Callinicos to make a case for the value of Greek culture for those who have been injured (Papajohn 1999) by Greek ethnicity. All-female and inclusive, the dance event creates a site of change, reclaiming expressive culture for women: "The culture has now, and always will belong to us, Greek women" (Callinicos 1990, 289). In this capacity, it functions as a vital link with the past, creating a utopian gender collective in which the boundaries of the past and the present collapse. It represents a moment when women relatives of all generations are imaginatively brought to join the circle dance and to achieve cathartic communion through laughter generated by the power of subversion. "Dancing with us our mothers, our aunts, or girl cousins, our *yayas,* their dead *yayas* . . . [they are now] free to dance, free to kick up their legs, stomp, shout, sway, sweat, and laugh. Loud, deep, raucous, hysterical, joyous laughter" (ibid.).

What does all this tell us about white ethnicity? The construct of an all-female collective around the reinvention of folk expressive culture rewrites the "white ethnic community" as it was represented in the 1970s in two interrelated counts. Callinicos preserves the portrayal of that community as unjustly oppressed and morally superior to the oppressor, though this time it is the male ethnics that perpetrate the violence of domination. The notion of white ethnicity as closely knit and claiming "a unique and valuable cultural heritage" (di Leonardo 1994, 182) is reserved for Greek women only. This representation takes place in counterdistinction to the Greek ethnic community, which is construed as primitive, Oriental, and therefore nonwhite. In other words, Callinicos recasts the narrative of white ethnicity along gender lines, declaring women to be its rightful guardians. The idealized white ethnics of the 1970s serve here as a template for the actualization of a genuine all-female community around the ephemeral dance event. Callinicos's construction sheds the negative pole of the immigrant Gemeinschaft—backward, parochial, and authoritative—to embrace its positive counterpole—close-knit, intimate, and mutually caring.

At the same time, this ethnic dance event does not claim exclusivity. It encompasses women from diverse sexual orientations as well as ethnic and racial backgrounds, realizing itself as a multiethnic collective through shared participation in ethnic expressive culture. Community here is created within a space defined at the intersection of gender exclusivity, on the one hand, and ethnic openness and fluidity, on the other. It can be thought as a kind of border zone that draws rigid gender boundaries while it simultaneously calls for the collapse of class, ethnic, racial, national, generational, and sexual boundaries within its demarcated space. In this kind of "terrain[,] opposition is not only reactive but also creative and affirmative," producing an alternative space for the making of nonuniform, novel collectivities (Lavie and Swedenburg 2001, 13). Interestingly, it is still gendered white ethnicity that serves, at least in part, as the cultural basis of this interethnic and interracial community. Reconfigured to eliminate oppressive aspects from the immigrant past, the white ethnic community continues to exercise its powerful grip in the continuing ethnicization of American society. Once again, as in the film *My Big Fat Greek Wedding*, Callinicos's brand of gendered white ethnicity "represent[s] the golden historical mean between the . . . primitiveness of Gemeinschaft and the . . . modernity of Gesellschaft" (di Leonardo 1994, 176–77).

From the position of an insider, Callinicos produces a thick description of practices and perspectives that constitute what Japanese folklorist Yanagita Kunio calls the "invisible culture" (quoted in Toelken 1990, 15) of private sociability.

Shielded from public view, alternative performances of identity are brought to the attention of outsiders only through the offices of an intermediary and produce a gendered ethnic counternarrative. In this function, the account intervenes to resituate histories of enforced silences into testimonies of oppression but also reveals cultural creativity and subversive potential of a marginalized social entity. Providing a space for collective redemption, it gives voice to alternative subjectivities otherwise muted or excluded from hegemonic regimes of cultural representation. But unlike Papanikolas's community-centered practice of commitment, *American Aphrodite* provides no location for the reader to imagine a politics of difference outside the ephemeral gendered social gathering that she endorses. It offers no position for those who wish to initiate social change from within the "ethnic community."

In juxtaposition to Veras's *The Greek Americans,* Callinicos's *American Aphrodite* endorses the understanding of ethnicity as a contested social terrain. A polemical ethnography, it antagonizes the representation of the Greek as the model ethnic, foregrounding the occasions when Greek ethnicity historically failed women. In remembering the failures, the book provides an alternative script for ethnic success, one based on the capacity to exercise agency, resist oppressive social structures, imagine alternative ways to embrace ethnicity, and venture beyond the alleged insularity of the ethnic culture.

But in spite of its celebration of difference, the ethnography reduces ethnicity to an undifferentiated, monolithic whole. It portrays male Greek America of early twentieth-century rural background as the eternal nonwhite folk, Oriental at its core. Orientalist metaphors abound to establish its non-Western foreignness. The ethnic family is uniformly depicted as a pathological harem; the women are insulated within the "ghetto philosophy" (30), "cover[ing] themselves with the veil" (ibid.). The account disdainfully devalues the vernacular through an unabashedly Orientalist discourse. If *The Greek Americans* asserts that immigration selected the Occidental dimension in Greek heritage, *American Aphrodite* denies this development. Both claims stand as a reminder of the power of Western hegemony to constitute Greek identity, this time in the context of Greek America. Stigmatizing the immigrant vernacular as inferior and Oriental means consenting to the Orientalist discourse that construed Greek peasants as degenerate primitives, outside American whiteness.

Herein then lies the analytical utility of examining ethnicity in specific sites, by situated authors, in terms of its poetics and politics, and in history and discourse. It helps interrogate representations of white ethnicity as a single knowable entity, a reduction underwriting all sorts of exclusions. Furthermore, it illuminates those ideological contours that fracture an ethnic domain and those sites in which competing communities are actualized through varying appropriations of the past. Crucially, such processes of community making counter the view of white ethnicity as an aggregate of private identities. Popular ethnographies do not reproduce ethnic collectives as a mirror image of immigrant culture, but seek to materialize new ways of imagining collective expressions of ethnicity.

This attention to the politics and poetics of ethnic self-representation in relation to history and discourse will continue to serve as compass in the next chapter in order, yet again, to resist totalizing claims about ethnic whiteness. My aim will be to identify narratives that dismantle ethnic whiteness, without losing sight of the admittedly thick contour of ethnic race talk. My interest lies in mapping how ethnicity is disarticulated from whiteness and rearticulated into an emergent ethos of interracial solidarity.

CHAPTER FOUR

Interrogating Ethnic Whiteness, Building Interracial Solidarity

Popular Ethnography as Cultural Critique

She pulls off her shoe and takes out the three pennies. The
gray head of Mr. Yacobowski looms up over the counter. He
urges his eyes out of his thoughts to encounter her. Blue
eyes. Blear-dropped. Slowly, like Indian summer moving
imperceptibly toward fall, he looks toward her. Somewhere
between retina and object, between vision and view, his eyes
draw back, hesitate, and hover. At some fixed point in time
and space he senses that he need not waste the effort of a
glance. He does not see her, because for him there is nothing
to see. How can a fifty-two-year-old white immigrant store-
keeper with the taste of potatoes and beer in his mouth, his
mind honed on the doe-eyed Virgin Mary, his sensibilities
blunted by a permanent awareness of loss, see a little black
girl? Nothing in his life even suggested that the feat was
possible, not to say desirable or necessary.

—Toni Morrison, *The Bluest Eye*

[An] honest [community of memory] . . . will remember
stories not only of suffering received but of suffering
inflicted—dangerous memories, for they call the
community to alter ancient evils.

—Robert N. Bellah et al., *Habits of the Heart*

[L]ike any other individuals on this earth they [Greek
Americans] have qualities but also shortcomings and they
have met not only success, but failure.

—Stephanos Zotos, *Hellenic Presence in America*

ONE DOMINANT CONTOUR of ethnic self-representation turns complex human beings into the celebrated model white ethnics. This chapter goes beyond this self-congratulatory caricaturing to showcase popular ethnographies that venture into dangerous memories and negative self-portrayals of ethnicity. The texts discussed here counter the discourse of ethnic perfection by centering on ethnic flaws. Unlike certain anthropologists who are reluctant to disclose sensitive self-knowledge to the public, these ethnographers adopt a different posture. They expose hidden secrets, openly display failures—racial prejudice by white ethnics, immigrant xenophobia, apathy toward the plight of others—and criticize what they perceive as social defects. In doing so, they debunk the mythology of success through a virulent ethnic self-critique and contribute in this manner to a Greek American academic and literary counterdiscourse. If critical self-examination "means showing our 'dirty linen' or stepping on very sensitive toes, so be it," academic Harry Psomiades (1987, 100) writes, joining Helen Papanikolas, among others, in rupturing Greek America's "shame-culture and fear of revealing secrets" (Karageorge 2000, 85).[1] My analysis closely follows how and to what end popular ethnographers deploy their critique, attending to how their narratives generate usable pasts that contest ethnicity's complicity to whiteness.

In an essay seething with a profound sense of racial injustice, Nobel laureate and distinguished humanities professor Toni Morrison (1994a) encourages her readers to reflect on the ubiquity of race in structuring inequality in the United States. The conclusion of Elia Kazan's film *America, America,* "the story of a young Greek's fierce determination to immigrate to America" (97), serves as her point of departure. In it, the "new immigrant . . . fresh from Ellis Island" is granted a job as a shoe shiner at Grand Central Terminal. Noting this act of generous inclusion, where American workplaces open their doors to immigrant newcomers, Morrison draws attention to a contrasting act of exclusion. As if tempted by the success of the Greek, "a young black man, also a shoe shiner . . . enters and tries to solicit a customer. He is run off the screen—'Get out of here! We're doing business here!'—and silently disappears" (ibid.). This sequence of welcoming acceptance on the one hand and contemptuous dismissal on the other represents for Morrison a larger historical process through which immigrants are incorporated into the dominant social structure at the expense of the blacks.

Stavros Topouzoglou, the immigrant character in Elia Kazan's novel *America America,* enters the United States as an indentured servant. But historical patterns of immigrant consent to whiteness validate Morrison's position that immigrant opportunity is created "on the backs of blacks," launching the newcomers on the path of mobility while "pressing African Americans to the lowest level

of the racial hierarchy" (1994a, 97). As in the example I discussed in the introduction regarding segregated Greek bars in Detroit, immigrant acceptance and
inclusion was a matter of passively acquiescing to existing racial hierarchies. For
Morrison, this stance functions as a rite of passage that transforms immigrants
into newly minted whites. "This interloper into Stavros's workplace is crucial
in the mix of signs that make up the movie's happy-ending immigrant story,"
she argues: "[A] job, a straw hat, an infectious smile—and a scorned black. It is
the act of racial contempt that transforms this charming Greek into an entitled
white. Without it, Stavros's future as an American is not at all assured" (ibid.).

The historical consent of white ethnics to what Morrison calls race talk—expressed as the acceptance of segregation and the overall exclusion and belittling
of racial minorities—provides ammunition for a research agenda that increasingly dismisses European ethnicities as ideologies in the service of antiminority
politics. Intellectuals narrating the plight of oppressed groups and advocating
their rights are not willing to forgive European immigrants who opted for the
privileges of whiteness. How can they abstain from this critique when the white
immigrant gaze, as shown in Morrison's (1994b) passage prefacing this chapter,
embodies the kind of everyday racism that denies recognition of black humanity, fixing the racial other as a nobody in an abject state of nonsubjectivity (see
Weedon 2004, 7–8)? Therefore, scholars who dissect the privileges of whiteness launch a devastating critique of European ethnics. Though justifiable, this
critique forgets to take into account progressive racial locations that emanate
from within white ethnicity. It misses the opportunity to recover agendas that
could create bridges linking interracial and interethnic constituencies through
relations of solidarity. The purpose of this chapter, therefore, is to challenge
the uniform indictment of white ethnics as mouthpieces of race talk while at
the same time *not* denying their historical complicity in reproducing race-based
hierarchies. It does so by identifying two examples of popular ethnographers
who critique white ethnicity and by unraveling the implications of interrogating
the making of whiteness internally.

These two ethnographic critiques originate from within Greek America: an
indictment of racial prejudice by author Harry Mark Petrakis and an accusation
of white ethnics for immigrant intolerance and apathy toward the disfranchised
by Helen Papanikolas. My discussion offers a departure point from which to
reflect on the sensitive issue of ethnic self-critique and to identify the making
of those usable pasts about race relations that could serve as a blueprint for the
future of white ethnicity. But I proceed cautiously. While I agree with the necessity of these critiques, I challenge assumptions that reduce white ethnicity to a

monolithic collective of oppression. For this purpose, I once again analyze the texts not only to identify the interests that they serve but also to confront the totalizing truths they claim. I begin by reflecting on what is at stake when ethnographers reveal to the public secret ethnic knowledge and on the challenges that the ethnic self-critique presents to my own reading of it.

Ethnicity, Knowledge, Power

Writing about the Pomo Indians, of whose community he is a member, ethnographer Greg Sarris (2001) wonders about the implications of making knowledge about his community public. A reflexive anxiety punctuates his account: "What am I doing writing about the Bole Maru [Dream Dance cult]?" he asks. "What am I doing telling this story?" (35). These questions arise against the backdrop of a historical consciousness that knowledge about vulnerable groups functions as an instrument of power. Memories of the appropriation of insider information for the purpose of political or cultural domination serve as a compass for ethnographic practice. The anthropologist opts for partiality, a rhetoric that is consistent with historical patterns of intercultural communication in his community's cross-cultural encounters. "We know then what to say and what not to say. We shift and adjust our behavior, our responses" (28). It follows that negative self-representation raises the critical ire of those most likely to be affected by it. "Woe to us on that day of reckoning!" exclaims Israeli scholar Gershom Scholem about Philip Roth's novel *Portnoy's Complaint,* voicing the fear that "the Jews, not the [Jewish American] author, would pay the price for 'Portnoy'" (Acocella 2004, 96). Here, a novel critical of the Jews and written by a Jewish American raises consternation over the power of representation to inflame transnational anti-Semitism. In generating this kind of rage, Roth shares the company of Greek American Harry Mark Petrakis, an author who crams Greektown, USA, with "sacrificing parents" but also "with windbags, adulterers, [and] errant offspring" (Moskos 1990, 102). "Although Petrakis has received literary awards and recognition," Charles Moskos notes, "his writings have also raised the ire of some touchy Greek Americans who felt they were maligned as a group. In this sense, portions of Petrakis's ethnic audience have reacted similarly as have Irish Americans to James T. Farrell, Jewish Americans to Phillip Roth, or Italian Americans to Mario Puzo" (ibid.). One should not, of course, render these literary representations as atypical, as deviations from the "quiet, peace-loving, issue-avoiding, church-attending, PTA-member Greeks" (Dallas-Damis 1982, 221), since the claim of atypicality neutralizes intragroup differences and contributes to the discourse of ethnic normalization. At the same time, one must proceed cautiously in navigating those contours of ethnicity that challenge ethnic ideals.

This sensitivity springs from a historical consciousness that the practice of representing Others functions within power/knowledge. In this Foucauldian formulation, knowledge about Others is always subject to appropriation by regimes of power/knowledge—the legal system, discourse on immigration, administrative policies, employment agencies, real estate practices, or the other mundane micropractices of everyday life—with unforeseen effects on vulnerable collectivities. Historical precedents demonstrate that specific interpretations of Others can contribute to the making of new contexts for political and social action or inaction. Yilmaz Guney's cinematic representation of the Kurdish issue in Turkey and his realist documentation of the tragic consequences of adherence to the honor code, for instance, rid at least one viewer of the film "of any desire ever" to visit the place (Kinzer 1999). It is said that former president Bill Clinton was convinced of the necessity of NATO intervention in Kosovo after reading in Kaplan's *Balkan Ghosts* about the allegedly primordial (thus socially irresolvable) causes of ethnic conflict in the Balkans. Last but not least, the mockery and ridicule in the U.S. mass media that portrayed Greeks as eternally incompetent Orientals seriously compromised foreign attendance at the 2004 summer Olympics in Athens. Only when that image was challenged by the facts did the poison-pen media turn to profuse apologies to the Greek people "for defamation of character" (Killion 2004). Words and images entangle Others in webs of representations whose impact on social life, from travel to military action, can be nothing other than unmistakably real.

If knowledge about historically vulnerable people can become an instrument of domination, control, and scorn, then minorities may come to regulate the knowledge that they are willing to share with outsiders, ensuring some degree of power over their own representation. This explains why minorities are so vigilant about the public presentation of themselves and why scholars who represent them have become so attuned to the politics of representation. Conscious of the implications that images and texts may have on identifiable people, many scholars, intellectuals, and popular ethnographers exhibit heightened reflexivity—to the extent possible, given the unintended consequences of representation—in how they write and what they write about Self and Other. This is because ethnicity, as "an ideologically accented culture," to appropriate José Limón's (1991, 115) wonderfully apt phrase, can be turned into a force of cultural domination or, alternatively, a site for mobilizing resistance to it.[2] As he reminds us, the production of ethnic meanings about a people—who these people are and how this knowledge is put to service for various interests—comes about as a result of "ideological battle[s]" (117). When colonial anthropology, for example, represented the working-class Mexican Americans (*mexicanos*) of southern Texas in flattened, unflattering stereotypes—lazy, passive, and inferior—it was furnishing symbolic resources in the literal and metaphorical warfare that was being waged at the time for domination of the region. Alternatively, it was Américo Paredes, a "native" anthropologist, who in the 1950s sought to "reverse the tide" of enduring colonialist anthropology. He critiqued domination and turned to a corpus of epic ballads to represent those allegedly lazy and passive mexicanos in terms of their heroic resistance against domination. How we come to know an ethnic collective is always a function of contested representations, a politics of knowledge. The ethnic is not a transparent figure, but a real human being tagged with a signifying label. In the current idiom, ethnicity is constructed, and this construction acquires its potency at the intersection of power and ideology. In S. Encel's (1981) much misunderstood phrase, "[T]here are no ethnics, 'only ways of seeing people as ethnics'" (quoted in Bottomley 1992, 61).

Display and Concealment in Greek America

The encounter between Richard Dorson and his ethnographic interlocutors, noted in chapter 1, allows a glimpse into the politics of display and concealment in Greek society. Michael Herzfeld (1987) has shown that the rhetorical manipulation of what is said and what is left unsaid in Greece is consciously scripted in relation to context and intended audiences. Hence arises the historical incongruity, as he argues, between "self-knowledge and self-display" (95). This tension acquires a particular potency when the presentation of the national Self is at stake. Images and texts produced by Greek insiders and intended for consumption by non-Greek outsiders are scripted to conform to an idealized, positive representation of Self. Partial representation hides cultural flaws from the public view; self-criticism and admission of imperfections are reserved for internal consumption. Understood as *disemia,* this rhetorical manipulation commonly manifests itself in relation to two crucial poles of Greek identity, "*a polarity between two ideal types*" (113, emphasis in original): the positive Hellenic model, which centers Greek identity on the idealized classical past, and the Romeic model, which points to corruption by foreign, Oriental intrusions and a lived experience of social and moral flaws.

The politics of self-display is particularly prominent in Greek America, enhancing its symbolic capital in the multicultural agora while sacrificing internal variability. The celebrationist model sanctions this containment because it produces and extols the ideal ethnic in conformity with national expectations of proper Otherness, but this unity comes at the expense of ambiguities, contradictions, social failures, and intragroup differences. In stripping ethnics of their complexities, it molds multifaceted human beings into one-dimensional positive stereotypes in the service of ethnic interests. The narrative of model white ethnicity is paradigmatic in this regard. Interestingly, a similar reductionism, this time a negative one, operates from the opposite end of the spectrum of conversations on race and ethnicity, when academics and intellectuals who speak and act on behalf of the racially disfranchised uniformly indict white ethnics, obliterating internal heterogeneity. But the construction of ethnics as benign, morally impeccable subjects or, alternatively, as historical perpetrators of racial domination forgets to take into account a *self-critical* stance that interrogates ethnics from within for their social and political failures. But even this critical position becomes fraught with homogenizing tendencies when, for instance, it is cast in absolute terms that erase meaningful intraethnic diversity. But for the purpose of this discussion, it is the openly self-critical posture that obviously troubles the operation of the disemic model of identity in Greek America.

The disruption of triumphalist, self-congratulatory white ethnicity acquires particular poignancy in the wider context of unequal power relations. I draw my inspiration here from the work of Dimitris Tziovas (1994b), who, in sketching a preliminary genealogy of Greek identity as duality, appropriately situates Greek disemia in this framework (see also Caraveli 1983). He invites scholars to examine Greek identity as syncretic and therefore multifaceted, not contextually dual. I focus on the justifiable complaint that disemia reproduces global asymmetries between proper Westerners, understood as model Occidentals, and improper partial Orientals, construed as the corrupted periphery. According to Tziovas, disemia reproduces this hierarchy when it constructs Greeks as situational Orientals and part-time Occidentals in relation to a West uniformly construed as rational, disciplined, and orderly. This model works ideologically in its capacity to obfuscate Western corruption, abuse, and moral and social flaws while pointing out these same weaknesses as signs of Greek society's political and social immaturity.

In the context of Greek ethnicity in the West, this hierarchy reduces the multidimensionality of Greek identities that Tziovas's critique aims to recover. As chapter 2 made clear, assimilation through the model of Occidental perfection contains ethnic complexity within what could be called "cookie-cutter ethnicity." What adds ironic poignancy to this state of affairs is the fact that ethnic hagiographies aspire to a national ideal increasingly tainted by exposés of rampant corporate and political corruption in the United States. In this political economy, the realities of national imperfection add value to model ethnics who emerge as the embodiment of national virtue. It is particularly noteworthy then, that popular ethnographers springing from Greek America confront Greek disemia and the ideology of the model ethnic, posing a new set of critical challenges on self-representation and opening new possibilities for imagining alternative ethnic locations.

Ethnicity as Self-Critique

In "A Tale of Color," Harry Mark Petrakis (2001–2) reports a narrative told repeatedly by his mother, Stella Petrakis, in family settings. Immersed in the richness of the Greek immigrant storytelling tradition, which he often acknowledges in his writings, Petrakis is attuned to and evocatively captures an inherent dimension of the genre, its variability: "When I knew the story by heart," he writes, "my mother continued filling in the shadows and dreams" (40). An eyewitness of the narrated events, his mother kept enriching the details of the narrative with each retelling. Turned into text, this life story focuses on a single harrowing truth: the pervasiveness of racism in the 1950s America and its devastating effects on the lives of individuals.[3]

The plot of the story resonates with the anthropological method of the extended case. Developed by the Manchester school of social anthropology, the extended case situates the actions of individuals within specific, unfolding social events and presents them in a narrative form. The reader follows the actions of the subjects in their settings in parallel with an accompanying anthropological analysis of the narrative. In similar fashion, "A Tale of Color" exposes its readers to a series of incidents in which a biracial couple, a Greek immigrant woman and an African American man, traverse racially polarized Chicago. Along the way, the narrator interprets the events for the audience and comments on the nature of social relations under the prevailing structure of racism.

The story chronicles painful experiences of immigration and racial discrimination. For Sofia, the female protagonist, immigration entails cultural dislocation and the startling experience of American-style racism. She met her husband Denzel when he was stationed in Greece as a member of the U.S. military. Denzel, once again a civilian, returns to a familiar social world of rigid racial divisions. Searching for work and stability, the couple temporarily inhabits diverse social zones, each time ostracized by neighbors unforgiving of racial border crossing. Their transgression of cultural norms is socially penalized through a series of spatial exclusions. Their interracial marriage, a border zone embodying difference, stands as an aberration in spaces sustaining homogeneity. Shunned by the Greek Orthodox parish on Chicago's South Side, Sofia and Denzel are also denied entry into the all-white neighborhoods of the residentially segregated city. During their stay in an ethnically segregated working-class neighborhood they are subjected to the "virulent fury" (42) of racism and flee in the face of violent intimidation. Turning to the security of Denzel's family in the city's South Side black community, they confront intolerance there, as well. Their temporary sanctuary on the far West Side of the city "in a polyglot neighborhood where poverty outweighed prejudice" (44) is terminated by their penury and the illness of their baby. Marginalized, poor, and alienated from familiar cultural worlds, the couple is brought to the verge of collapse. Sofia is given sanctuary by a middle-class Greek family in the suburbs, and Denzel moves into a YMCA dormitory. Their new residential arrangement mirrors that of the racially divided city and accelerates their eventual separation. Their experience of racial ostracism culminates when Sofia and her baby relocate to her natal village in Greece, while Denzel remains in Chicago and becomes lost in the anonymity of the city.

It is useful to read "A Tale of Color" against anthropologist Victor Turner's use of the extended case in order to fully explore issues of critical concern in my work: the social uses of the immigrant past, ethnicity, and the politics and poetics of popular ethnography. The narrative is structured as a series of events patterned after the phases that Turner (1980) posited as universal characteristics of what he called "social dramas." He saw social life as a series of events, each a process defined by four stages: rupture in social relations, crisis, redressive action that leads either to reintegration and a return to the status quo or to recognition of the schism and social transformation. Read in this manner, "A Tale of Color" draws attention to the manner in which individuals interact within the social structure of race relations. In the story, the interracial union between Sofia and Denzel represents a breach of a cultural norm and brings about the crisis, manifested as ostracism. In this process, a number of competing structural principles vie to redress the process of exclusion. Denzel's kinship ties temporarily prevail against racism, but they eventually wilt under its full force. The potential for interracial working-class solidarity cannot be realized because of ethnic racism. And the efforts of Petrakis's mother to support these individuals are rebuffed by the immigrant/ethnic community. Immigrant property owners become complicit in racial exclusion by refusing to rent their suburban properties to the couple. In this account, racial prejudice becomes the overarching structural principle, displacing the redressive efforts aimed at the social integration of the couple. In 1950s Chicago, the couple is contained in a state of perpetual liminality, as "outcasts, suspended between two worlds, neither of which would accept them" (42).

From the struggles within this ideologically accented terrain, the author's mother emerges as a moral force and agent for change. Stella Petrakis is praised in Greek America as a legendary Chicago civic activist and self-sacrificing philanthropist, her life guided by "the Christian principles of faith, love and hope" (Thomopoulos 2000, 19). Throughout the story, her narrative persona acts as a tradition bearer committed to religious ideals. With "a reputation as a rebel . . . [who] might even have taken a certain pride in defying community norms" (Petrakis 2001–2, 41), she feels compelled to help the couple, "not in the name of civil rights but because she thought it was the moral and compassionate thing to do" (40). Here, a religious immigrant heritage based on the universal ethic of love antagonizes the enduring local tradition of racial segregation. Under conditions of migrancy, the past is recontextualized in relation to dominant structures in the host society and becomes meaningful in the everyday struggle against racial exclusion. As a guardian of this tradition, the narrative persona of Stella Petrakis takes the immigrant/ethnic community to task. "Remember what it was like when the first Greek immigrants came to this country!" she sternly reminded parish members a number of times. "We fought prejudice against our people then! Now we should not forget those struggles. If we cannot accept these young people for who they are, we have no right to call ourselves Christians!" (42).

The use of the past in the passage establishes connections between a historical experience of discrimination and a religious tradition in order to rescue a core value of the latter, compassion toward the disfranchised. The reported speech of Stella Petrakis turns to the authority of a historical precedent of collective exclusion and a shared ethnoreligious heritage to oppose a dominant structure, racism. These references to the past "imbue history with power" (Largey 2000, 241) to reclaim traditional values and in turn shape a progressive present. Here, tradition is *emergent*. Its meaning is created in a specific context, when the immigrant past is enlisted to oppose racial oppression. It is, in fact, *rearticulated,* as the Christian principle of universal love becomes a usable past in the service of antiracist struggle.[4] Together, religion and the memory of nativist persecution of immigrants serve as a defensive bulwark against racism. The strategy fails, however, as one individual's Herculean ethopolitical commitment sinks under the weight of prejudice. The social transformation of race relations does not take place.

Entering a community minefield—the dark past—Petrakis brings to public consciousness a Greek American counternarrative.[5] His story establishes racial prejudice as a total fact, challenging the ideology of the American dream. The topoi of this ideology—America as an egalitarian land of opportunity, socioeconomic mobility as a dividend of hard work—are undermined by the devastating toll that racism exacts from individuals. The narrator traces the experiences of the couple through a series of oppositions. It is significant that the narrator first situates the couple in what can be described as a preimmigration cultural Eden. In Sofia's natal village, the pair enjoys the blessing of the family and interracial solidarity between the villagers and the "black soldiers [who] had fought with Greek partisans and were regarded as friends and allies" (Petrakis 2001–2, 40). Through this juxtaposition, the story dramatically underscores the fact that Greek America has internalized the host nation's ideology of whiteness and, as a result, has experienced a moral fall in America. In this respect, "A Tale of Color" undermines the hegemonic narrative of America as a redemptive place where Greek Americans have realized a state of cultural and moral excellence.

The narrative undertakes an ideological reversal of the classic stories of immigrant transformation, what Werner Sollors (1986) calls "narratives of conversion" (31). In this genre, the passage from immigrant to American is associated with a profound sense of renewal, an obliteration of the former, Old World self. This kind of cultural transformation is perceived as a deeply felt conversion experience, a liberating rebirth. Immigrants express a radical sense of self-reconfiguration and of pleasures felt anew in the experience of their disembedding from traditional structures and participation in modernity (Giddens 1991). For the narrator of "A Tale of Color," however, the reverse process is true. The story is told as an indictment, a demythologization of the American dream. Individual agency, so valorized in the ideology of immigrant success, is severely constrained by a social structure imbued with racism. In the case of Denzel, hard work does not translate into socioeconomic mobility. The coveted middle-class status in the land of opportunity is reserved for those who comfortably inhabit the space of whiteness and reproduce its ideology. Far from emancipating immigrants, modernity incarcerates them through an ideology of racial hierarchies. As subjects who consent to racial contempt, immigrants are alienated from the humane aspects of social relations embedded in traditional forms, a condition that results in collective ethopolitical failure.

The Limits of Ethnicity as Cultural Critique: A Tale of Caution

"A Tale of Color" is written in the tradition of anthropology as cultural critique. The author unearths a story from the ethnographic margins and places it at the center of public attention, contributing a new layer to the palimpsest of critical writings on racism. The fact that the author sees racism as a relevant contemporary issue adds to the moral vindication of its telling. "In these days," he opens the essay, "when reasonable men and women accept the fairness of civil rights . . . [the story] is still timely today because marriage between the races continues to evoke hostility and even hatred" (2001–2, 40). Petrakis is a vested critic. In speaking out against racial bigotry, he builds on his immigrant family's tradition of commitment to defend diversity. Elsewhere, he has translated the deep appreciation his father felt for his acceptance in America—a "miracle," as he used to refer to it—into a plea for generalized ethical responsibility for ethnic and postethnic America (Petrakis 1999). As the beneficiaries of America's magnanimity, the "sons and daughters of immigrants, grandsons and granddaughters of immigrants," he pleads, "must renew and fulfill" the vision of America as a genuine sanctuary of difference (10). Petrakis envisions the postimmigrant generations as guardians and agents of an uncompromising ethos of pluralism.[6]

Petrakis brings to Greek America a long and venerable anthropological tradition of liberal sympathy for the downtrodden and the dispossessed. As a discipline committed to documenting the richness of humanity, anthropology takes pride in its social relevance as a medium of inclusion as well as political advocacy. Committed anthropologists historically have injected a moral vision for social justice and human dignity into their scholarly projects, to lash against the exploitation and plight of the subjects they study—the poor, immigrants, racial minorities, indigenous peoples. It was an anthropologist, Franz Boas, who fought on behalf of the despised early twentieth-century immigrants the ideological battle against the scientific racism then pervasive in several Ivy League institutions.

Anthropological advocacy combines a concern for the dissemination of marginalized perspectives with criticism of systems of domination. Reflexive ethnography generously accords textual space to subjects whose voices have been excluded from mainstream regimes of power/knowledge, identifies exploitative structures, and engages in political activism to influence social policies. In this tradition of a deeply felt solidarity with the exploited, anthropologists take pride. It enables them to reach beyond the privileges and relative material comfort of the academy and to identify with the poor and the maligned.

My own decision to showcase this internal critique of racism is in alignment with the tradition of anthropology as cultural critique. I see my metaethnographic task in the same manner in which George Marcus and Michael Fischer (1986) envisioned the multiple functions of critical anthropology: to critique dominant ideologies, to "expose and recast both habitual ways of thought as well as the conventional social-science ways of representing them" (153). The basic principle of anthropology as cultural critique builds on a "strategy of juxtaposition." The critical task is to "make the reader conscious of difference" (117) by disrupting common sense and challenging established ways of thinking—in short, by defamiliarizing what an audience takes for granted. To make this juxtaposition possible, the ethnographer assumes an intermediary critical function and scans the ethnographic field in search of counternarratives. Through this method, "the challenge of serious criticism" becomes "to bring the insights gained on the periphery back to the center to raise havoc with our settled ways of thinking and conceptualization" (138). This periphery may be a non-Western society or perhaps a subculture at the margins of the ethnographer's own society. As an example of the latter case, Marcus and Fischer comment on the work of Paul Willis, who showcases "the social criticisms and observations of the working class itself" (132):

> By representing their [working-class people's] critique of society, the ethnographer makes the cultural criticism more authentic: it is no longer the critique of the detached intellectual; rather it is the critique by the subject unearthed through ethnographic engagement. The importance of ethnography is that there are potentially many such critiques, and it is for the cultural critic to discover them, represent them, indicate their provenance or incidence, and explore their insight and meaning. These, after all, are the sources of diversity in the cultural arena. (132–33)

I wish to point out here that anthropology so conceived offers an attractive, albeit problematic, method for the metaethnography of ethnicity. Its value lies in underscoring the importance of the metaethnographer as a consciously critical reader and writer, one who is sensitive to the plurality of voices in the social field. Its criticism of hegemony and its politics of inclusiveness are its great contributions. Yet in my reading of "A Tale of Color," I would like to interrogate one central assumption of anthropology as cultural critique, namely that it is unproblematic to critique a dominant ethnicity.

Scholars and writers seem to enjoy a certain sense of moral vindication when they lash out against and attempt to undermine power structures and hegemonic social forces (the corporate world, the middle class, the racially privileged). But this all-encompassing critique rests on the problematic assumption that these categories are transparent, already-known entities, the same assumption that underlies Petrakis's text. I wish to nuance his representation of Chicago's Greek America of the past. In doing so, I draw inspiration from anthropology's reflexivity on crucial questions at the heart of the discipline's raison d'être: the

dissemination of knowledge about a people. There are certain moral and political implications when ethnographers represent Others—and no guarantees that
seemingly innocuous ethnographies produced today will not serve to legitimize
policies of oppression tomorrow. Ethnographic knowledge, however sympathetically represented, can be appropriated in the service of hostile centers of power.
To represent ethnicity is a daunting task when one, in a flash, can cite numerous
historical cases in which ethnicity has functioned as a tool of state-sponsored
oppression. When a Western anthropologist assumes the now venerated ethnographic position of criticizing ethnic oppression, the violation of human rights of
minorities, and exploitation in the workplace in a society politically vulnerable
in the larger geopolitical configurations of power, more than a journal article
or monograph is at stake. In a global arena in which the boundaries between
anthropologists and the people they describe have become increasingly porous, anthropology's ethical and political accountability has been raised with
particular urgency. In anthropology's hall of mirrors, how can an ethnographer
look an anthropological subject in the eye with the lurking consciousness of a
potential—no matter how well meaning the ethnographer intends to be—of
contributing to processes of symbolic or social domination?

In view of anthropology's function in the ideological ratification of systems
of exploitation, such as colonialism, issues associated with the representation of
Others have been articulated with particular force by vested critics, diaspora
and postcolonial intellectuals, bicultural anthropologists, and feminists. The
volume of their battle cry only matched the value of the stakes involved. For
postcolonial critics who are of many places—the Western academy, the West,
the non-West—their position of power to represent Others sparks a critical
examination of self-positioning and a passionate plea for ethically and politically
responsible criticism:

> Western theoreticians—especially those "Third-World-born" critics
> residing in the West—who speak for the need of liberating the "Third
> World" from the West's economic and political power—need to be much
> more cautious in their claims, lest they unwittingly and unintentionally
> themselves become neocolonizers who exploit the cultural capital of
> the colonized in a process in which those voices are appropriated for re-
> investment in those "banks of the West" that currently offer the highest
> rate of return to speculators in trendy academic markets. For one who
> lives in the West and speaks from the center about marginal cultures,
> it is extremely difficult and problematic to represent the Other. As one

such critic myself, I have felt the need to constantly ask myself, "Who are we?" "Whose voice is it when we speak?" "Are we also the beneficiaries of the very system we are decrying?" One needs to persistently ask the question "does my study mean anything to people back at home?" Clearly these are ponderous questions with no easy answers, or perhaps no answer at all. But responsible criticism needs to ask them, and one cannot but lament that one does not find them more foregrounded in the exciting and stimulating studies that have been produced in the West in recent years. (Chen 1995, 17–18)

An acute sensitivity to matters of representation pervades the analyses of anthropologists with multiple cultural affiliations, feminist ethnographers, and cultural critics who are only partially anchored in hegemonic centers of power, such as the American academy. For those critics, questions of positioning, audience, and accountability are inseparable from their own specific locations. How does one write for the Other, when the Self is part of the Other? The stakes in this kind of politics of representation are particularly high for feminists and bicultural anthropologists, who have been at the forefront of academic battles over issues of representation (Abu-Lughod 1991). Impressed with the stark realization that anthropological knowledge can have unintended consequences on human populations, anthropologists anxiously have contemplated a set of pressing questions over their authority to represent Others.

But why invest in critical reflexivity, one might object, over the cultural representation of a benign ethnicity like Greek America? Even if the ascription "Greek" meant a nonwhite minority in early twentieth-century America, Greek America's "racial odyssey" (Jacobson 1998, 3) has now entered a new historical phase. Enjoying high rates of assimilation and socioeconomic success, secure in the social and political establishment, middle-class Greek America to a large extent now finds itself comfortably entrenched in privilege. Its social spaces—the suburbs—are located worlds apart from the zones of poverty and racial stigma inhabited by racial minorities. "It is currently chic to be Greek," observed scholar John Petropulos as early as 1977 (27). Why then exhibit critical sensitivity vis-à-vis an ethnicity that persistently flirts with the centers of power and, through its narrative of model white ethnicity, is complicit to the oppression of racial minorities?

Even to raise this objection assumes the existence of a binary between a stable center and fixed margins. This assumption no longer holds true in view of developments in critical theory that expose neat binaries as instruments of domination. Although centers do exert real power, they are far from immutable. If specific sets of differences lay claim to a center of power, difference, as Smaro Kamboureli (1996) notes, "is always a matter of intensity, and is weighed differently in given historical moments. Its meanings are variable, shifting, even provisional" (3). An ethnic position, no matter how steeped in power its center it might be, could always be appropriated in a manner disadvantageous to its own interests. This is the case because ethnic categories refer to historically contingent marked collectivities subject to negative resignification. Ethnicity is "a consciousness of kind," in Gillian Bottomley's (1992) lucid definition, "constructed and reconstituted in relation to specific political and economic circumstances" (57). Following this formulation, assimilated ethnics in positions of power can turn into devalued minorities as the meanings attached to their ethnic group change, depending on political conditions, geopolitical interests, national security, changing demographics, or shifting of centers of power. Ethnicization may work well in the sites of celebratory multiculturalism, but it can function as a structural constraint in the competition for social capital. Greek America, a collectivity that invests heavily in the ideology of the model American citizen, has learned this lesson the hard way. As poet and writer Yiorgos Chouliaras (1997) observes, "Greeks are treated as losers on both ends of multiculturalism." On the one hand, the attack on Eurocentrism pierces their ethnic pride, assaulting the Greek classical past "as 'oppressive' and 'racist'" (345). "This intellectual climate has encouraged, for example, negative reviews of a recent major Greek antiquities exhibition in the U.S. by such publications as the *New York Times, Time* magazine, and the *New York Review of Books*" (ibid.). On the other hand, Greeks "rarely find any relief from opponents of multiculturalism who disassociate modern-day Greeks from their illustrious ancestors and generally treat contemporary Greek culture as rightfully marginalized" (ibid.). Scorned as cultural oppressors, they still harbor the sensibility of the culturally oppressed, a predicament that once again testifies to the reductive power of certain discourses to marginalize white ethnicities.

Furthermore, Greek Americans discovered that they can always be subjected to the power of the dominant society and redefined as "foreign," despite their claims to the contrary. Hearing country music celebrities in support of George H. W. Bush in the 1988 presidential election campaign making "fun of Dukakis's name as unpronounceable and, by implication, foreign" (Alba 1990, 365n9) brought home to Greek Americans the understanding that when the stakes are high, there is only a thin line separating acceptance from ridicule.

At this point, I wish to destabilize the generalized truth of "A Tale of Color," namely its representation of Chicago's Greek America as a collective uniformly hostile to interracial unions. In other words, I must continue writing against culture, against the notion of Greek America as a homogeneous entity (Abu-Lughod 1991). I insist on demonstrating the partiality of "A Tale of Color" because it may mask alternative histories of positive acceptance, collaboration, and solidarity between Greek Americans and people of color. To "dislodge the grounds from which persons and groups securely represent others" and themselves (Clifford 1986a, 22) is a necessary step toward disrupting statements that claim access to total truths. I am interested in destabilizing their authority—not to cancel their truth, but to displace it as one (partial) truth among others. The value of such a reading arises from its function as a precaution against the *effortless* appropriation of knowledge about ethnicity from regimes of power/knowledge hostile to this ethnicity. Therefore, I undertake a close reading of Petrakis's narrative to show how its indictment of an *entire* people rests on rhetoric, not on total knowledge of the collective.

"A Tale of Color" reproduces the assumptions of professional modernist ethnography in which ethnographic authority is established through textual devices of persuasion. Its rhetorical power lies in its function as an eyewitness account. The flesh-and-blood author, Petrakis, assumes a narrative authorial persona who reports his mother's oral testimony. The narrator both documents her reported speech and comments on it, as well. The rhetorical effects of this narrative strategy are twofold. In his capacity as the recorder of the story, the flesh-and-blood author turns himself into a chronicler of historical events that "might not even earn a footnote in the long sorrowful chronicle of racial intolerance and hate" (2001–2, 46). At the same time, the narrator—not unlike an ethnographer who rhetorically capitalizes on his presence in a culture to construct his authority—authenticates the truth of the story by closely adhering to the reported narrative of personal experience. As a self-appointed "patron [who] . . . vowed to help them in any way she could," Stella Petrakis has fully experienced the social drama (41). Her status as an eyewitness lends authority to the truth of the narrative. It attaches rhetorical force to the experience and to the vested indictment of racism.

But one should keep in mind that the story generalizes the extent of racism in Chicago's various communities on the basis of a single eyewitness testimony. In that sense, it functions as a monoglossic narrative, merely reporting a single interpretation of the events. The reader follows Stella's cameralike point of view and is exposed to her reading of the intentions and wishes of the various protagonists. There is no way of knowing, however, how other social actors felt about and interpreted the series of events. In making a claim to a generalizing truth, the narrative disregards alternative interpretations and practices of race relations among Chicago's Greeks. Its truth, as James Clifford would have it, is partial; its politics and poetics, intertwined. A generalized truth adds rhetorical weight to a cultural critique that indicts an entire community.

To acknowledge partiality is not to deny the political economy associated with ethnic whiteness in America. "A Tale of Color" is a textual rendering of a wider cultural phenomenon with objective correlates: the white flight to the suburbs; the passive acceptance of racial segregation among immigrant business owners in Detroit (Georgakas 2006); the racial biases of the GI Bill, what Karen Brodkin (1998) boldly calls affirmative action for whites; and the racism of the European ethnics who forcefully opposed racial integration in the 1950s and the 1960s, defending and consolidating in this manner their tenuous hold on whiteness (Sugrue 1996, 241).

Yet one must not allow objective patterns to hide internal variability. Although Petrakis's purpose is noble—an uncompromising critique of racism—his narrative ultimately homogenizes the racial geography of midcentury Chicago. It generates a normalizing discourse that sidesteps alternative points of resistance, interracial solidarity, and alliances. In fixing Chicago's Greek America as racist, it cancels heterogeneity and bypasses the possibility of unearthing regional Greek American antiracism at the time. In this respect, its progressive politics is susceptible to counterproductive readings. Conscious of these implications, my reflexive reading of "A Tale of Color" in terms of its textual poetics and politics resists its appropriation as a mirror of *the* Greek American stance on race relations.

Rehabilitating the Vernacular: An Allegorical Thread in a Realist Ethnography

Helen Papanikolas's work escapes the dualist trap of depicting ethnics as either saints or villains. An ethnohistorian who valued empirical evidence above all else and passionately strove to document and disseminate it, she did not shy away from making public what she considered the flaws of the Greek vernacular. At the core of her research lies an ethnographic realism obstinately demanding the accurate representation of the available evidence. "She insisted on presenting the facts no matter how unpleasant," Theony Condos (2005) remarks, reporting the historian's self-assessment: "I'm a realist. I don't write fantasy." Against this epistemological background, the code of vendetta, lying, cunning, and the patriarchal oppression of women—all of which she includes as integral to the immigrant culture, and all of which are fiercely opposed as morally and socially offensive by many Greek Americans—share textual space with positively valued aspects of the vernacular.

This inclusion of both positive and negative aspects is evident in the last book published during her lifetime, *An Amulet of Greek Earth*. Rich in examples of the aesthetic and social value of immigrant folklore, the book pieces together diverse elements of a scattered and understudied archival record. The work represents the culmination of a five-decade-long career dedicated to the painstaking collection of ethnographic material and to long-term archival research. It integrates the author's historical and folkloric work, a considerable portion of which is already available in the author's published corpus, consisting mostly of scholarly articles and essays.

Characterized by interpretive contradictions, a collage of incommensurable epistemologies, and obvious scholarly omissions, the book presents an analytical challenge. In some respects, it approximates but does not equal or surpass the author's earlier carefully researched and meticulously crafted work. Published when Papanikolas was well into her eighties, it stands as a synthesis of a life's work, the writing accelerated perhaps by the pressure of aging and illness. But in an era when professional ethnographies written by celebrated anthropologists such as Margaret Mead and Margerie Shostak are demythologized for holding grave fallacies, I resist the scholarly impulse to hold accountable this popular ethnography for its limitations. I take my lead from Dan Georgakas (2004), who, in his review of *An Amulet*, anticipates and seeks to preempt academic quibbles:

> Academics will rightly complain that episodic accounts do not con-stitute a formal argument. They can assert that a particular custom presented as Greek may actually be regional. They will be able to list numerous exceptions to every generalization. . . . What are we to make of a section on the Greek press that only presents three newspapers? . . . Such reservations about *An Amulet* make the error of wanting a collec-tive narrative to conform to the needs of a formal history, an encyclo-pedia, or a theoretical essay. Papanikolas is not attempting a definitive and detailed account of the experiences of the Greeks in America. . . . Instead, her goal is to impart the feel, sound, and flavor of the culture that the Greeks brought to America and how it fared. (112)

How then does one read this work? My reading identifies in the text an allegori-cal thread that rehabilitates the immigrant vernacular as a usable past in order to build interracial solidarity. James Clifford (1986b) offers the insight that eth-nographies do not merely "describe real cultural events"; they also, simultane-ously, "make additional, moral, ideological, and even cosmological statements" (98). "Inescapably allegorical," ethnographic texts produce—intentionally or unintentionally—definitions of what is meaningful in life (99).

This reading enables me to connect *An Amulet* with a wider concern evident in Papanikolas's corpus, namely the relationship between privileged white ethnics and stigmatized racial minorities. A passage from her early writings helps trace a contour that animates this interest. She writes, "The Cretans and Roumeliots greatly prized leventia, that zest for life, that quickness to act regardless of danger, that gaiety and generosity of possessions and self, the championing of the less strong" (Papanikolas 1971, 62–63). The gendered noun that designates regional affiliation (Roumeliots, for males) leads one to surmise that the author refers to male immigrants and their posture of danger-defiance, an ethos that anthropologist Michael Herzfeld (1985) has discussed as "poetics of manhood," about which I will have more to say in the next chapter. But Papanikolas also documents the centrality of the ethic of empathy toward the poor and the vulnerable among pioneer Greek immigrant women (Anagnostou 2004–5). Here I argue that this component of the past—"the championing of the less strong"—informs Papanikolas's function as an intellectual committed to the cause of the disfranchised. It is deployed as a usable past to articulate a new political purpose for Greek America while promoting a related agenda of white ethnic–racial minority relations. Not unlike Stella Petrakis, who rearticulates Greek Orthodoxy to combat racism, Papanikolas rearticulates this element of the immigrant vernacular to confront whiteness. To recognize the allegorical operation of ethnographies, as Clifford (1986b) suggests, is to acknowledge "the political and ethical dimensions of ethnographic writing" (120), "to take responsibility," that is, "for our systematic construction of others and of ourselves through others" (121).

Beyond Display and Concealment: Humanizing Immigrants

An Amulet represents the ultimate contribution to the author's project of rehabilitating the immigrant past. True to her dual commitment to objective history and to the recovery of usable ethnic pasts, the work evokes a wide range of Greek American folk and popular culture, to subsequently call on audiences to appreciate the aesthetic and social value of the vernacular, while also acknowledging its moral imperfections. "Romiosini was a noble culture and also one of secrecy, shame, and blame-throwing, both in battle and ordinary life" (2002, 48–49). Reclaiming its value as the foundational origin of Greek America, she writes: "[T]he Romiosini culture that the Greeks brought with them was remarkable. If people did not know it, they could not value its uniqueness, could not understand why we Greek Americans are who we are today" (xi–xii). And, once again, "I want them [Greek Americans] to be aware that they have this [Romiosini] treasure. They should keep it" (quoted in Condos 2005).

But in attempting to recover Romiosini, Papanikolas revisits a treacherous past. She enters a potential gender minefield, for instance, when she advocates its wholesale preservation, a position that will likely generate an incredulous resistance among women. Take, for example, those who made it their life's task to flee from its onerous patriarchal grip. We are reminded of what actress and author Olympia Dukakis said in a passage quoted earlier: "It was impossible to stay within the Greek culture because I recognized that there was something controlling about it, something limiting and oppressive, and I felt that my options were being closed down" (Karageorge 2004, 28). Ethnicity limited women's lives—literally and metaphorically demarcated their domain of vision—as Callinicos's trenchant critique demonstrates.

Fully aware of the restrictive power of ethnic patriarchy—and herself ambivalent about the immigrant past—Papanikolas navigates this territory cautiously. She makes no apparent effort to strip this past of what many may perceive as cultural flaws. But she seeks to counter forgetting with the explicit aim of sustaining a community of memory, along the lines discussed in the previous chapter. The value of immigrant Romiosini lies in founding an enduring ethnoreligious institution, a praise reserved for the closing thoughts of the book: "The children of immigrants . . . remember those fathers and mothers who tried valiantly to preserve their culture. The survival and strength of Greek Orthodoxy in America is justification for the great effort they made for that vibrant, unique culture" (282). Greek Orthodoxy owns a historical debt to the immigrant past.

But the act of remembering works on yet another level, that of national inclusion. All histories of immigrant experiences possess something "memorable, each with a certain beauty among the harsh early difficulties" (2002, xii). They "should be made known to those who followed," she writes. "Otherwise they will be lost, never to communicate the humanity of these early immigrants who helped build America" (xii). Narratives about the past are not to be merely appraised for their historical value but must be recognized for their aesthetic, social, and national significance. In this respect, Papanikolas sets out to answer the urgent question that film director Elia Kazan raised, but never answered. If "we are all IMMIGRANTS . . . that we all came here LOOKING FOR SOMETHING," he emphatically cried out, "[w]hat is the responsibility of the dream to the dreamers?" (Kazan, quoted in Georgakas 2005, 15). What is the responsibility of America to immigrants? And, as Harry Mark Petrakis (1999) puts the question, what is the vision that American ethnics—the descendants of the immigrants—"must renew and fulfill" (10) in relation to the well-being of America's cultural, racial, and religious minorities?

The humanization of immigrants and their nationalization as economic agents works on two related semantic levels. First, the political import of viewing immigrants as humans lies in its antiracist implications. Historically, the perception of the newcomers as inferior appears in tandem with their dehumanization. Working-class status, in particular, has historically fed images of ethnic and racial Others as less than human in literature, theater, and popular culture. In Eugene O'Neill's *The Hairy Ape,* for example, "the ethnic stokers are objectified by association with their shovels, which force them into the bent posture of pre- or sub-human life forms" (B. Smith 1995, 24). Second, the notion of nonnative labor as foundational to national progress firmly inscribes immigrants into the nation. An enduring narrative of immigration posits manual labor as a sign of national inclusion, as testimony that "more Americanism [lies] in the horny hand of an immigrant who dug our subways, laid out our railroads . . . than possibly you might find in the well-educated, native born citizen" (Dubroff, quoted in Urciuoli 1998, 183). This narrative functions ideologically to safeguard the nation's acceptance of cultural and racial newcomers. The representation of immigrants as humans and as a national asset seeks to redirect the discourse on immigration from one of ambivalence and xenophobia to one of inclusion. The allegorical thread of Papanikolas's work is consistent with the view of ethnography as "a hierarchical structure of powerful stories that translate, encounter, and recontextualize other powerful stories" (Clifford 1986b, 121).

To "communicate the humanity" of the immigrants! The rendering of the immigrant past in terms of social merits and flaws moves beyond the politics of display and concealment. It escapes the reification of Romiosini and its subsequent and convenient appropriation as an eternal, transcendental national quality. Moving beyond idealization and reification, Papanikolas extends the plea to approach immigrants as both flawed and heroic, imperfect and valiant, stymied by harsh circumstances and undaunted. Immigrants must be viewed as *anthropoi,* Papanikolas invitingly proposes. The term *anthropos,* in the Greek sense of the word, captures the notion that human beings are inescapably creatures of fault, capable of lofty achievement *and* petty defect. It is human to transgress norms, to enter banned moral territories, to subvert ideals. This applies when individuals challenge prohibited boundaries: "The Greeks were human after all, and songs testify to yearnings for forbidden love between Christians and Jews, between Moslems and Greeks" (9). Humanity is also in full display when people resort to lying, cunning, and casting of blame as adaptive tools for survival.[7]

In humanizing immigrants, Papanikolas opens up an alternative location for Greek America. Notorious for affixing a single meaning to diverse populations, ethnic labels are often manipulated to signify uniform moral collectives wrapped around the illusion of perfection. The image of the model ethnic represents precisely this sort of production: the ethnic as a mirror of an imaginary national impeccability. Veiling the socially flawed terrain of nationality and ethnicity, the integration of the ethnic into the nation becomes viable here through the shared illusion of a national myth, that of social innocence. But another field of commonality becomes imaginable once the nation's Others are recognized as the nation's fellow humans. In her insistence on representing immigrants as humans in her ethnographic and literary work, Papanikolas finds herself in the good company of writers such as Zadie Smith and Saul Bellow, who have grappled in the same vein with the vexed issue of representing racial and ethnic Others. As Joan Acocella (2005, 101) poignantly observes, "Smith, with her predecessors, could help do for blacks what Saul Bellow, fifty years ago, did for Jews; that is, make them normal subjects for the novel, no longer people who have a sign over their heads saying 'Jew' or 'Black' but regular people, with the same privilege of texture—of self-contradiction and error, and thus a tragic force— as white people" (101). This location dismantles the prison that keeps ethnics as historical hostages of a discourse that equates individual character with nation and biology: a flawed individual equated with an essential flaw of the ethnic collective. An alternative perspective presents itself, one that seeks to account for success and failure in terms of both common humanity and political economy. A Greek immigrant who sacrificed his life to secure a home but failed to realize his yearning—who failed to achieve the American dream—represents a tragic individual. The story about this person must be told—profound frustration, social injustices, limitations, and all. It must not be hidden as something inimical to collective ethnic success. It is to those excluded from privilege that Papanikolas insists on directing the public gaze. Drawing from the immigrant vernacular a particular usable past—the championing of the less strong—she sets out to articulate a politics of empathy and interracial solidarity. This immigrant ethos must serve as the guiding principle of the nation's racial politics, Papanikolas argues, and the vision that white ethnics "must renew and fulfill."

Recognizing the Humanity of Racialized Others

To avoid the reductive trap of portraying white ethnicity as uniformly antiminority, one must consider the internal spaces within ethnic whiteness that promote a counterpolitics. Papanikolas, for one, has spoken and stood up on behalf of immigrants and racial minorities. A passionate plea to respect despised Others appears repeatedly in her interviews and speeches. Not unlike Harry

Mark Petrakis, she has broached the subject of racism in public, interrogating white ethnics for their anti-immigrant views. Safeguarding the humanity of minorities and preserving historical memories of their experiences become the cornerstones of her assault on public hostility or apathy toward the plight of the despised and the poor. Her introduction to a popular book featuring photographs of Utah's ethnic and racial populations exemplifies this position. In it, she draws from her ethnographic authority to invite audiences to gaze at nonwhite faces through the lens of history. Through this mediation, she imparts historical knowledge to the viewers as she instructs them how to find meaning in the act of looking at racial images: "We see in several pictures of those who had been young during the first quarter of this century a serenity that belies the miseries and anxieties they had known as aliens in a culture with roots in New England Puritanism" (Papanikolas 1988, xix). Visual realism obscures historical realities. In a manner echoing her aesthetic mode of locating the true meaning of the immigrants' internal lives (see Anagnostou 2008b), the folklorist declares her ability to uncover underlying truths. Her reading of photographs discovers hidden meanings as it situates personal biographies in history. Photographs of racial Others serve as a pretext to educate viewers through the narration of history.

> In some faces, as in the Japanese newspaper publisher in her early nineties, we sense the unconscious self-worth of one who has doggedly persisted toward an altruistic goal. Restrictive immigration laws, ethnic ghettos, relegation to balcony seats in theaters, the Ku Klux Klan marches and cross burnings of the early 1920s, the anti-immigrant hysteria of the First and the forced relocation of the Second World Wars are old memories to her now. (1988, xix–xx)

Papanikolas's poetics centers our gaze on a racially charged object, the body. Historically, discourses on race have used the body as a site to constitute powerful aesthetic, social, moral, and political hierarchies. As Richard Dyer (1997) comments, the white body in the West has functioned as the norm against which nonwhiteness was evaluated. The racialization of skull and body size, posture and skin complexion, nose shape and hair texture turns human populations into subjects whose worth is measured by the proximity of the racialized body to the ideals of whiteness. In racism, the bodies of racial Others are made a source of abhorrence, a sign of irreducible inferiority or even subhuman failure. Justified by racism, discourses of colonialism and slavery marked nonwhite bodies as a source for dirt, pollution, inferiority, disease, sexual lust, and criminality.

The legitimation of racism rests on the production of a specific kind of knowledge about non-Western bodies. Rather than censoring talk about what it considers threatening and polluting, racism thrives in the production of perceived truths that construe certain populations as racial and inferior. As Sara Ahmed (2002) notes, drawing from Michel Foucault, racism relies on the process of making bodies known through a set of images and statements. Becoming objects of knowledge, bodies in racist discourse are known and seen in particular ways so that they can be accordingly regulated. Knowledge produced by science and institutions that legitimized the subjugation of people of color contributed to a discourse where non-Western bodies were invested with negative meanings, generating feelings of hate, fear, and disgust. Thus, racist representations of the body carry serious material and social effects. Denial of access to resources, spatial exclusion, and sexual sanctions all contribute to produce, maintain, and ensure asymmetrical difference. As David Theo Goldberg observes, "The bodies of others . . . are human bodies that, because of their differences, are forced to work, alienated from their labor product, disenfranchised, or restricted in their right of social entry and mobility" (1993, 54). The devaluing of the bodies of Others by racist representations is part of a larger process of social classification, which relegates specific populations to the bottom of powerfully ingrained hierarchies.[8]

If ethnic and racial bodies measure distance from whiteness, Papanikolas inscribes them instead as sites of common humanity. She interprets photographs of bodies in relation to history, exposing traumatic experiences in a way that generates compassion. Photographs, then, aid in the production of social memory; they invite the telling of stories about the past in which the personal and the collective intertwine. This, for example, is how she introduces an individual who lost his father in the 1924 Castle Gate explosion, a disastrous mining accident that cost numerous lives: "We see in the chiseled face and mellow eyes of an immigrant son the symbol of a generation of children who learned early that beyond their ethnic 'towns,' their people were not only aliens in a new country, but also in a religious environment in which they were 'gentiles'" (1988, xx). Historical knowledge becomes necessary for photographs to function as collective storehouses of memories and to generate empathy. Papanikolas maintains that knowing the social forces that have shaped the personal biographies of the "now aged immigrants, Indians, blacks, and their children" (xxii) in history will result in heightened interclass and interracial understanding. In this manner, she invests hope in the transforming function of education: that the "influence [of the book] will reach beyond each group's ethnicity to enlighten the public with the history and humanity of people vaguely known" (ibid.).[9]

But bridging the class and racial divide in American society necessitates acknowledgment of not only immigrant moral imperfection but also the flaws of the nation's own citizens. The invitation to recognize the humanity of Others through photographs comes hand in hand with a critique of the wider, more socially and economically comfortable public that in its apathy and complacency fails to recognize that histories of oppression have resulted in racial marginalization. This is a flaw that Papanikolas wishes to correct.

A Yearning for Empathy, a Plea for Interracial Solidarity

The hope for racial equality rests on the capacity of individuals to transcend their specific class and racial locations and to understand the experience of poverty and racial marginalization. In a commencement speech that she delivered in 1984 at the University of Utah, Papanikolas addressed her young audience of college graduates in a manner intended to evoke a shared historical experience of marginalization. "As I look at you graduates," she said, "I recognize in your faces, full-blown in some, slight in others, the ethnic people of your past. Among you sit men and women whose sorrowing ancestors were summarily sent to federal reservations when settlers arrived" (1995b, 241). These remarks ethnicize faces and then proceed to recall memories about the past. Citing the specific grievances of each and every persecuted group, the speaker creates a common identity for her listeners around the experience of exclusion, albeit differential. Although she does acknowledge the varying magnitude and duration of discrimination as between southeastern European immigrants and racial minorities, Papanikolas appropriates this shared experience for her own purposes, to connect organically with minority students in her audience and to build solidarity among diverse constituencies. Empathy, as an affective connection among human beings, is a crucial element that can bring about interracial identification. She generates this connection through a two-step process: by recalling an example of her own betweenness while growing up in Utah and by illuminating the experience of internal exile as the defining feature of a minority subject.

> Memory reminds me that as a child of immigrants I was uncertain, even though I was born in Utah, that I was an American. When schoolmates taunted us immigrant children to "go back where you came from," we answered with anger and impotence, so unsure were we of our birthrights. . . . Those well-fed and comfortable in their identities find it difficult to understand the souls of Indian, black, Mexican, and Southeast Asian children. These children are forever immigrants, even

those whose ancestors were born in this land. How easy to speak of bootstraps and of education available to all and condemn dropouts and the young unemployed. (1995b, 244–45)

This passage is dense in its implications, as it performs a variety of functions. By invoking the memory of growing up Greek American, she aims to generate identification among those who experience identity as internal exile, that is, among those who have been of the nation but have been classified as national outsiders. The personal narrative recalls the experience of the Greek second generation in the 1920s and 1930s as one of racial betweenness and national dislocation—in fact, one of abjection from the national imaginary. This ethnic cohort witnessed the exclusion, both violent and symbolic, of immigrants, minorities, and political dissidents. Exclusion in the past drives Papanikolas's interest in building interracial constituencies in the present. She wants Greek Americans, in particular, and white ethnics, in general, to remember this heritage—to make it the center of their identity—as a means of forming interracial solidarities.

In her speech, one can hear echoes of the politics and poetics of black scholar, intellectual, and political activist W. E. B. Du Bois. The notion of "double consciousness" that Du Bois developed in his *Souls of Black Folk* (1903) pointed to black America's experience of the interplay between national identity and racial domination. The power of this work, as Paul Gilroy points out, "is still felt in the special resonance which the term 'soul' continues to enjoy in modern black political discourse and cultural axiology" (1993, 126–27). In referring to the *souls* of those who historically have been thought of as less than American, Papanikolas's speech deploys a politics grounded in Du Bois's vision of interracial solidarity, while expanding it to include the children of European immigrants as America's internal Others. Du Bois wrote in *Dusk of Dawn* (1940): "The badge of colour [is] relatively unimportant save as a badge; the real essence of this kinship is its social heritage of slavery; the discrimination and insult; and this heritage binds together not simply the children of Africa, but extends through yellow Asia and into the South Seas" (117). The heritage of intimidation among white ethnics resonates with (but is not identical to) the unprecedented heritage of "discrimination and insult" inflicted on people of color. Still, for Papanikolas, the shared heritage of exclusion and fear creates a position from which to disassociate assimilated ethnics from whiteness. If whiteness exiles racial Others from full inclusion in the nation, this common heritage furnishes the conditions to create interracial solidarities. In this respect, it can be said that this position recalls but modifies the concept of "new ethnicities" proposed by Stuart Hall (1988). Hall engages in an identity politics different from the one discussed here, since he proposes the formation of interethnic alliances among minorities on the basis of a shared experience of racism and discrimination. But the underlying principle of his formulation is useful for my purposes. He calls for the disassociation of racial identity from ethnicity, proposing the signifier "black" as a unified social category based on shared histories of marginalization, not on common cultural, linguistic, or physical characteristics. Following this thread, Papanikolas calls for a white ethnic position that while it recognizes the vastly dissimilar experiences of racism between European immigrants and racial Others, it supports "black" coalitions; it does not antagonize them.

This interest is expressed against the background of a painful awareness—shared by the speaker and her minority listeners—that ancestry still may determine authentic national belonging. Native birth does not guarantee the status of an insider. Though of the nation, the children of immigrants and minorities bear the effects of their parents' foreign ancestry. The historical equivalence between whiteness and genuine national belonging still lingers, Papanikolas maintains, condemning nonwhite American citizens to psychological and emotional estrangement. The contradiction between the democratic promise of universal inclusion and the historical use of ancestry (descent) as a criterion for true national membership remains unresolved. Though recognized as equal national subjects in the law, racial minorities still possess the quality of the alien in the popular imagination. Construed in this manner, they experience the perpetual double consciousness of being simultaneously insiders and outsiders of the racialized nation.

As David Leiwei Li (1998) observes, for instance, although market multiculturalism and the civil rights movement "pronounced the death of the explicit legal exclusion of the Asian . . . , it did not herald a birth of full Asian American inclusion" (6). Drawing from the psychoanalytic work of Julia Kristeva, Li frames the Asian American as an abject subject, who experiences the tension between enjoying legal rights yet being denied full national inclusion, what he renders as "the part of ourselves that we willfully discard" (ibid.). This is "a unique form of contemporary oppression," he states, "that is executed not as brutal state tyranny, but as an underground, unconscious, yet structural 'immobilization' and 'reduction' of a group" (7).

White ethnics are largely spared this oppression, a privilege that unequivocally conveys the disappearance of those conditions that forced the children of southeastern European immigrants, like Papanikolas, into internal exile.[10] Subjected to forced assimilation—notoriously racialized as a "white massacre" (Bakalian 1993, 2)—they were coerced into sacrificing distinctiveness in exchange for acceptance. Papanikolas writes of how the "grandchildren of those first immigrants, whose names were either shortened arbitrarily by official in Ellis Island, by judges awarding them citizenship, or by themselves in frustration at the reactions of 'true' Americans, are at home in America and at the same time proud of their roots" (1995b, 247). Now, "[s]econd-generation Italians who had been ashamed as children to admit they ate spaghetti opened pasta restaurants" (ibid.). Devoid of stigma, middle-class white ethnics now occupy the territory of "those well-fed and comfortable" in the class and racial divide. According to Papanikolas, the forgetting of what it means to be at a distance from the normative center places the descendants of formerly despised immigrants in this privileged position. Elsewhere, she makes clear her dismay at this amnesia (2000): "When people become secure they are careless about other people. A good example is the Mexican immigration. . . . They are poor, they are in the same position the early immigrants we've been speaking about. I hear children of immigrants voice derogatory terms about newer immigrants." Ethnics are on trial here for embracing whiteness and, in doing so, betraying in practice the venerable national creed of universal inclusion. They have failed to translate their own historical experience of marginalization into a progressive usable past. In this regard, the question posed by Michael Novak (1971) almost thirty years ago still must be raised with urgency: "How much . . . we [the PIGS] learned in America by being made conscious of our olive skin, brawny backs, accents, names, and cultural quirks is not plain to us" (61).

Aligning herself with a liberal tradition of American democracy, the popular ethnographer interrogates the white ethnics' inability to translate their own historical experience of oppression into a politics of empathy toward those who are currently the Others of whiteness.[11] Papanikolas holds ethnics accountable for failing to turn their own histories of exclusion into a usable past in service of egalitarian inclusion. This critique puts on trial the bootstrap ideology and the ideology of the model ethnicity that it legitimizes. It charges that ethnic success is stained by a double historical failure: a failure to empathize with vulnerable populations, as I noted, and a failure to comprehend class stagnation in terms of injustices inherent in the political economy, not of cultural merit.

Papanikolas posits a dramatic interracial and interclass divide to raise a crucial question that pierces the heart of the epistemological and critical project of the humanities and the social sciences: Is it possible to transcend radical difference and to understand Others? If so, how, and to what end? Exposing a gap in the capacity of those comfortably entrenched in the middle class to comprehend the dispossessed, the speech affirms but also moves beyond a politics of empathy. She delivers a fundamentally optimistic message inspired by secular humanism. She places faith in the universal value of education as a means of bridging opposing class and racial worlds. Although she wishes to maintain cultural differences, she proposes that a shared ethos of caring and political activism on behalf of the nonprivileged will ultimately minimize social divides.

If George Veras advances the interests of the Greek American middle class, Helen Papanikolas is a custodian of an ethical and political sensibility that sides with the cause of the maligned and the poor. Her public advocacy, which promotes the interests of these constituencies, articulates a vision of progress. To make social mobility universal, she proposes a program of action based on the dialectic between group belonging and universal inclusion. The sight of diverse humanity brought together as a collective around a common goal, education, affords the speaker an opportunity to build on the notion of difference and commonality. African Americans, American Indians, Chinese, Greeks, Italians, Japanese, Jews, Mexicans, and South Slavs may be separated by specific, though intersecting, histories, but they are also brought together in the common aspiration for education, meaningful life, and mobility. A rite of passage that marks mobility, the graduation ceremony, becomes a venue for Papanikolas to articulate the allegorical message embedded in her ethnography. Mobility should not translate into the forgetting of a painful past, and mobility must not result in a society further polarized along class and racial lines—the well-fed and the helplessly impoverished. This requires sustained educational policies, an ethic of interracial solidarity, cultural critique, and the dismantling of everyday and institutional racism.

As an intellectual who speaks on behalf of the disfranchised, Papanikolas enters a volatile cultural field defined by contested explanations of differential ethnic mobility and proposals to alleviate race-based poverty. In broad contours, her programmatic speech offers as a solution an education-centered political and social activism that encompasses both institutional and everyday life. She boldly joins the fray of multicultural politics in education when she explicitly sides in favor of bilingual programs; on the other hand, ever mindful of stereotypes and sensitive not to offend, she cautiously navigates what she sees as the cultural flaws of unnamed ethnicities. "Other parents come from a cultural background that is highly permissive towards children," she points out. "They must be taught the worth of education" (1995b, 246). But she avoids the traps of culturalism when she posits both structural factors and cultural elements as forces causing poverty. Within this framework, she coaxes the graduates to assume the double duty of supporting universal education and committing to their own ethnic institutions. Consistently with her emphasis on remembering, and with a firm grasp on how one's positioning vis-à-vis the immigrant past may affect the ethnic future, she cautions against forgetting how the past has shaped the present of minority students, now at the threshold of the professional middle class.

> On your way to reaching your highest potential, may you not forget your people. They need you. Colleges founded with the sweat and blood of black educators are struggling to survive today because their graduates are not supporting them financially. Ethnic students who actively work for their rights during college days often lose interest in scholarship programs for those climbing up behind them. Often in their quest for material goods and what they perceive as social acceptance, they turn from their culture. (1995b, 246)

A component of philosophical humanism defines the scholarly and intellectual work of Papanikolas. Unmistakably, she frames her subject in a vocabulary of equality, empathy, respect, progress, care, autonomy: the individual who is capable of acting alone to advance the social good. Praised for her commitment to the values of "dignity and freedom, . . . equality and hope" (241, editors' note) she has also organized her analysis of the immigrant experience and interethnic relations through an ethic of empathy (see Anagnostou 2004–5). One may argue that herein lies the relevance of Papanikolas's narrative of progress and her critique of intractable class and social arrogance. To speak about these issues through the idiom of humanism—as she consistently did in a variety of public forums, such as scholarly writing, documentaries, interviews, and speeches—means to maximize public access and in turn to shape people's views on controversial social issues. Of course, the turn to humanism, as Abu-Lughod (1991) observes, risks the endorsement of a system of thought notable for its shortcomings, particularly its limited ability "to understand how we as subjects are constructed in discourses attached to power (158).

Yet pressing issues of academic social relevance leads Abu-Lughod to cautiously embrace what she calls "tactical humanism":

> Because humanism continues to be, in the West, the language of human equality with the most moral force, we cannot abandon it yet, if only as a convention of writing. In advocating new forms of writing—pastiche, dialogue, collage, and so forth—that break up narrative, subject

identities, and identifications, antihumanists ask their readers to adopt sophisticated reading strategies along with social critique. Can anthropologists ask this? Already, complaints about boredom and resistance to being jarred have been leveled against experimental ethnographies. Humanism is a language with more speakers (and readers), even if it, too, is a local language rather than the universal one it pretends to be. To have an effect on people, perhaps we still need to speak this language, but to speak it knowing its limitations. (ibid.)[12]

The preoccupation with remembering, so prevalent in Papanikolas's work, may "produce an aftertaste, a feeling of discontent" in some quarters, as Artemis Leontis (2003, 24) points out. "Is that all?" she asks in her critical appraisal of the popular ethnographer's work. "Papanikolas's fiction and non-fiction raises a serious question: are we [Greek Americans] a presence in this country only through remembering? The flip side of this: what will we have *after* we remember?" (ibid.). Concern is raised about a disconnection between memory, the present, and cultural becoming.

My analysis of Papanikolas's approach to remembering as a way of mobilizing usable pasts inevitably guides the reframing of these questions. In her work, the connection between the past and the present emphasizes the *inalienable* relationship between the object of memory and the subject of recall. What and how one remembers will shape one's worldview and agency. Folklorists who reflect on the relevance of the past have captured this entanglement. According to Pat Mullen (1992, 2), folklore is not "the study of the past but rather the study of present situations informed by the past." Therefore, Papanikolas's work poignantly confronts the questions I raised in the introduction of this book. Ethnic pasts do become a useful contemporary compass. They ratify specific modes of being in the present, and they articulate particular ethical visions of becoming in the future. In other words, memory performs contemporary cultural work. Acknowledging this interconnectivity between the past and the present inevitably requires, as I have shown, a fine-toothed combing of texts and practices to discover how the remembering of immigrant pasts gives shape to and directs contours of cultural becoming for white ethnicity today. I will be returning to these questions throughout the rest of the book.

Papanikolas made it her life's work to document conflict and exploitation, violent uprooting and gender oppression. Her attention to how the past affects individuals testifies to her profound care for human well-being. A social realist, she avoided the compromise of idealizing the immigrant past. But while she worked to reconstruct history faithfully, she also invested in the making of usable ethnic pasts. One may not share her faith in liberal education as the most effective politics to bring about a wholesale structural change to improve the lives of the impoverished. But the moral and political force of her public presence as an advocate of racial minorities is unmistakable. Scholars who ignore her political and ethical vision to unmake whiteness from within the space of white ethnicity do so at their own peril. The profound manner in which the past shaped her personal identity as well as her politics of interracial solidarity complicates the view of white ethnicity as surface identity, a topic to which I now turn.

CHAPTER FIVE

Ethnicity as Choice?

Roots and Identity as a Narrative Project

How far is the person free to affirm or deny the constitutive
components of identity? If all or most is fixed, what is the
possibility of choice; if all or most is chosen, what is the
possibility of constituting a certain identity?

The further more complicated question is: how much
choice does the political agent have in the construction of their
own story as against the effects of contingency or chance as
well as the limitations of given characteristics?

——Maureen Whitebrook, *Identity, Narrative, and Politics*

[I]dentity is the product of historical contestation, a response
to oppression or part of organizing to retain or regain power
or privilege, essentially the emotive component of political
action——or inaction.

——Micaela di Leonardo, "White Ethnicities, Identity
Politics, and Baby Bear's Chair"

INDIVIDUALS CONNECT ON many levels with personal, familial, regional, and
immigrant pasts to claim an ethnic identity. The discourse on roots, in particular,
guides the quest of fashioning an identity out of the past, in fact requiring that
a meaningful identity is shaped out of what necessarily becomes a usable past.
Roots orient individuals researching family biography and engage them with
ancestral cultures and histories of immigration. In this sense, they entangle individuals with a number of options (the kinds of pasts one explores and the manner in which one explores them, for example) and social determinations (the
social probing to search for roots in the first place and deeply embedded cultural
attachments that may privilege the exploration of certain pasts and marginalize
others). Therefore, narratives detailing the quest for roots offer themselves as

convenient sites for exploring an individual's complex entanglement with agency and the determining forces of history and culture. In other words, they help us understand the degree to which the element of choice influences the assignment of meaning to the past and the extent to which social discourses interfere with, or even override, the element of choice in the process of constructing an identity. But, why, after all, should one feel compelled to assess the place of choice and determination in the making of identities?

The importance of choice for white ethnicity has been most systematically addressed by symbolic ethnicity, an influential strand within sociology. The leading commentators on this issue, sociologists Herbert Gans and Mary Waters, conceive of white ethnicity as a pool of available cultural resources (ethnic traditions, family customs and lore, consumer culture, and the media) from which individuals voluntarily draw to create personally enriching identities and temporarily connect themselves with larger collectivities. In this respect, the chosen traditions serve as usable pasts that enmesh individuals in webs of meaningful connections: they provide a feeling of uniqueness, a venue for connectedness, and a forum for socially legitimate creative expression. Their function is seen in sociopsychological terms. "Symbolic ethnicity fulfills this particular American need to be 'from somewhere,'" Waters (1990, 150) writes. It mediates "a dilemma that has deep roots in American culture," namely the tension between individual uniqueness and social conformity. The capacity to sustain, temporarily, a sense of ethnic belonging counteracts what is perceived as modernity's deadening uniformity and anomie.

Symbolic ethnicity privileges the autonomous subject who exercises free will, reason, and knowledge to choose among available "ethnic options" (Waters, 1990). Though social circumstances may influence specific choices, the individual operates as a sovereign subject who acts rationally upon ethnic identification. The subject surveys the benefits that accrue from the adoption of a specific identity (social prestige, personal relevance) to rationalize the choice. Nowhere is this emphasis on sovereignty and control more apparent than in the contextual manipulation of identity to maximize social prestige and personal fulfillment for the individual choosing to adopt an ethnicity. Understood in this manner, symbolic ethnicity offers a new angle to approach identity: the polar opposite of ethnicity as determiner of behavior. "Symbolic Armenianness is voluntary, rational, and situational, in contrast to the traditional Armenianness of the immigrant generation, which is ascribed, unconscious, and compulsive," Bakalian (1993, 6) writes, drawing a rigid dichotomy between immigrant ethnicity and the model of American white ethnic identities unencumbered by history, culture, and the unconscious.

But it is precisely because it stresses this disembeddedness that symbolic ethnicity fails to give due attention to the vastly complex process of identity formation.[1] By approaching the human subject as a rational free agent, this paradigm cannot possibly account for how social discourses and history come into play in the fashioning of identities. Therefore, it becomes crucial to reflect upon the kinds of identities that symbolic ethnicity conceptualizes: shallow, readily multiplying, easy to maintain and to discard. What is at stake when identities are seen as the epitome of postmodern fluidity? I raise this question because the way in which one conceptualizes identity is inevitably associated with the way in which one understands and acts on social life. "Who we understand ourselves to be will have consequences for how we experience and understand the world," Paula Moya writes (2000, 8). "Our conceptions of who we are as social beings (our identities) influence—and in turn are influenced by—our understandings of how our society is structured and what are particular experiences in that society are likely to be" (ibid.).

This realization raises a crucial question: Where can one secure an ethnic location from which to act meaningfully and *assume responsibility* for that action in an increasingly shifting and unstable social field? Is it possible, as Calvin Schrag (1997) notes, that "the postmodern counteractant of celebrating plurality, incompleteness, and difference may well be an overreaction that leaves us with a subject too thin to bear the responsibilities of its narrative involvements" (27–28)? And as Maureen Whitebrook (2001) asks poignantly, "if all or most is chosen, what is the possibility of constituting a certain identity?" (68). In view of the social implications associated with claiming an identity, it is imperative to acknowledge identity construction as a vastly complex process and to analyze it in depth.

I undertake the task of carefully attending to the construction of ethnic identity in the remainder of this book. Seeking to correct the excess of sovereignty that symbolic ethnicity grants to the choosing subject in the making of identity, I take on a close reading of a popular ethnography, Michael Kalafatas's *The Bellstone: The Greek Sponge Divers of the Aegean—One American's Journey Home* (2003), which also functions as a narrative site of identity construction. I explore how discourse, history, and power relations embed the author in enduring identities and how, in turn, these identities perform all kinds of cultural work: organize one's sense of place in the world; reverse relations of domination; suggest ways to connect individuals with collectivities; and advance a vision of society inspired by specific usable pasts. These outcomes I show, may come about as the effects of individual agency or as the result of historical and cultural determinations.

To invoke Louis Althusser's oft-quoted example for my purposes, an individual may be constituted as an ethnic subject by responding to the language that hails it to identify with a position ("A Greek is one who speaks Greek"). The subject recognizes the call as being addressed to it, bringing about a process of identification whereby the individual subjects itself to the power of enunciation and becomes the agent of the ideology in question. But it must be emphasized that this process of interpellation is not total. The subject may also resist the power of discourse by counteroffering a reinterpretation of the specific hail ("A Greek is one who feels Greek even though he does not speak Greek"), producing an alternative subject position. Thus, interpretive agency (the multiplication of meaning attached to a single referent, in this case the definition of "Greek") is the key concept here because it brings about a proliferation of diverse identity positions (choices) and therefore a range of affiliations and commitments. But crucially, the choosing "I" "is always already socially located," as Linda Martín Alcoff (2000, 341) puts it succinctly. Identity is the product of discursive experience already at work and the complex negotiations surrounding the powerful identifications that this experience exerts on individuals, not the product of the sovereign, knowing subject who simply rationalizes available options and constraints.[2]

Thus, if we wish to illuminate additional contours of white ethnic identity, we must examine contextually, patiently, and in depth how identity is constituted, practiced, and negotiated within specific social locations. To be sure, my reading in this chapter traces one specific narrative contour, aiming not to offer an example of representative identity construction but to illuminate how deeply carved, thickly textured, and multidimensional a single identity can be. Here, I neither furnish statistics to refute the conclusions of symbolic ethnicity nor examine identity construction in relation to symbolic ethnicity's analytical locus, an individual with multiple ethnic ancestries. Instead, the emphasis on the detailed analysis of a specific identity narrative seeks to focus attention on identity formation and in turn to counter the one-sided privilege that symbolic ethnicity accords to choice. I demonstrate the complexity of identity making, a process glossed over by symbolic ethnicity, and I show how identity is articulated at the intersection of individual agency *and* powerful cultural determinations. Critics may dismiss this as an exceptional and statistically insignificant case study at their own peril. Attentive readers will identify throughout this book numerous examples wherein identity cannot by any stretch of the imagination be viewed as merely an ethnic option among second-generation Greek Americans.[3]

Identity as Narrative

Narratives on identity tell stories about how individuals understand themselves and how they respond to categories ascribed to them by others. Identities, according to Stuart Hall (1996a, 4), are "constituted within, not outside representation." As symbolic constructions, they emerge when vested individuals narrate "popular historical account[s] of who they are, [and] where they came from" (Hall 1996b, 131). And as Ien Ang (2000, 1) notes, identity becomes "the way we represent and narrativize ourselves to ourselves and to others." Identities articulate a definition of who one is at the intersection of various positions—class, gender, race, ethnicity—and in relation to historical struggles over cultural ownership, specific biographies, and the social valuation of group belonging. In this capacity, they are invested with the potential to shape the way in which audiences understand and act upon the world. For all these reasons, identity narratives serve as key sites for examining the complex contours of white ethnicity and its relevance. Identity narratives raise and probe the questions: How is identity generated? How and why does identity change through time? What is the role of the past in enabling certain identities? How do individuals negotiate dominant understandings of identity in specific times and places? How do individuals anchor themselves in ethnicity, and for what purpose? What is the social outcome of centering action on specific understandings of ethnicity? Narrative constructions of identity bring forth the processual dimension of identity formation, enabling expansive mappings of its contours.

I am keenly aware that the analysis of narrative identity requires a fundamental acknowledgment of the operation of choice in the making of identity. As Whitebrook (2001) recognizes, "In the case of narrative identity, an element of the choice involved is the choice of what to tell and what not to tell. Stories are constructed; narrative identity does not record or register each and every fact, but rather presents a picture, a selective description 'drawn from life'—in most senses than one" (72). Herein lies the challenge: simultaneously to confirm that reflexivity constitutes an indispensable element in the fashioning of ethnicity and to demonstrate that the identities so configured are highly mediated by history and culture and, furthermore, sustain enduring commitments that bear their imprint in social life.

The Bellstone, the aforementioned popular ethnography, encapsulates this dual function. The gaps and silences about the narrator's past dramatically bring to the fore the authorial choice to exercise control on the telling of his life story. Uncertain of how the ethnic past shaped the narrator's youth, the reader witnesses the narrator's early flight away from ethnicity and into the fold of the dominant culture. Resolutely resisting the obligation to learn Greek, the authorial persona opts to disembed himself from determining ethnic structures. Instead, the narrator, "so desirous of being an American" (2), subjects himself to Americanization, claiming an identity that features prominently in the subtitle of the book, *One American's Journey Home*. In this sense, the narrator tells a quintessential American story of assimilation as consent. Highlighting choice and agency, the narrative simultaneously acknowledges that the drive for crafting an ethnic identity emerges in response to contingency. Gripped by a moment of discovering family heritage—a poem titled "Winter Dream," written by a grandfather—the narrator embarks on a journey to the ancestral place to discover his roots and to tell the story of ethnic and familial pasts. In fact, the past encapsulates the narrating subject in its webs. "As I retell this story," the author writes, "my grandfather's poem . . . [guides] me to some rapturous place beneath the sea, I know not where" (4). A literary artifact from the past propels the subject to travel, practice ethnography, and construct ethnic identity through narrative.

Triggered by contingency, the making of identity becomes an act of purposeful reflexivity. Identity is achieved. It represents a process of becoming. It cannot be thought of as taken for granted, ascribed. Once again, Whitebrook (2001) captures the point that agency is inevitably implicated in the project of crafting an identity as a reflexive telling, not as an already scripted narrative. "[T]he acceptance of contingency can free the person to address their identity by re-reading—and thence re-telling—the narrative of their life," she writes (101). The author, then, enters the discursive field of Greek ethnicity reflexively. In achieving an identity, as I will show, agency is enlisted to resist, for example, national narratives representing the identity of Greeks living abroad. What is more, the narration highlights how identity changes throughout the life cycle, placing emphasis on openness and becoming. At the same time, however, the meaning of identity is heavily mediated by history and culture. Histories of discrimination and ethnic counternarratives as well as forces of assimilation and memories of cultural domination and violence shape the meanings attached to identity. In addition, cultural constructs, such as family inheritance, lineage, ethnic prestige, and practices of naming, anchor the making of a stable identity. In this narrative construction, we cannot possibly represent the subject as a largely autonomous agent who surveys the field of available options and negotiates constraints to rationalize the fashioning of an ethnic self. What we do witness at work in this popular ethnography is the constitutive capacity of history, discourse, and culture to produce multifaceted, deeply textured identities. Because it approaches identity as a rationally selected source of meaning, symbolic ethnicity offers a model inadequate to account for how identity is produced at the thick intersection between agency and historical and cultural determinacy. It analytically suppresses how the "I" that engages in the act of interpreting ethnic options is always already constituted in specific ethnic locations through the operation of discourse.

Pilgrimage and Identity as a Narrative Project

It is most unlikely that the reader of *The Bellstone* will fail to register the earnest tone of the author's quest for ancestral roots. The seriousness is established unequivocally at the outset of the book. Quoting Paul Theroux, the author declares himself "a passionate pilgrim" (2). Described as a "remarkable personal odyssey" (ibid.), the search for roots and family origins took Kalafatas from his home in suburban Boston to numerous places associated with the history of Greek sponge diving across the globe. The odyssey, which includes travel to the author's ancestral Aegean island of Symi and to Greek communities in the United States and Australia, is indeed vested with pilgrimage-like qualities: resolute faith in the significance of the journey, singularity of purpose, determination in its pursuit, and a sense of awed self-fulfillment in the actual experience of the places and cultures of destination. Significantly, if pilgrimage marks a progression toward "transformation—perhaps of both the self and society" (Frey 1998, 219), the popular ethnography does work, as I will argue, toward achieving a new identity and charting a direction for social change.[4]

But the quest represents more than pilgrimage; the anthropological practice and methods on which Kalafatas (2003) relies to tell his story qualify the experience as a transnational popular ethnography. Motivated by a poem written in Greek by his paternal grandfather in 1903 and translated by award-winning poet and translator Olga Broumas in a "brilliant rendering" (283) into English in the 1990s, the author sets out to grapple with the historical past. "I wanted to ask," he emphatically pronounces, "what I desperately wanted to know: Why had so many divers died or been paralyzed [in the Dodecanese Islands around the turn of the nineteenth century] long after knowledge of proper deep-diving techniques had become widely available?" (3). The pilgrimage is "undertaken out of felt necessity" (Driver 1998, 42) to answer a historical question. In this ethnography-pilgrimage, the historical intersects with the personal. "And most of all, I wanted to know," Kalafatas continues, "why my grandfather, who had taken up pen against the powers-that-be, uttered as his last words: 'They have killed me'" (3). Animated by twin familial and historical purposes, the ethnographic research–pilgrimage results in *The Bellstone,* a popular ethnography that anthropologist David Sutton calls "an unusual work of scholarship and a deeply personal book" (2003, 294).

Interweaving anthropology, ethnography, fiction, folklore, poetry, family biography, autobiography, biological science, religious studies, psychology, and oral history, *The Bellstone* offers a fascinating account about roots and routes, origins and migration, ethnic identity and cross-cultural contact, the relation between literature and memory, and the popularization of professional anthropology. It is also guided by the explicit concern to assign meaning to now largely extinct practices such as sponge diving. In this making of usable pasts, the author invests more than the passion and faith of a pilgrim; he earnestly undertakes an ambitious learning project, immersing himself in the humanities as well as the biological and the social sciences.

Throughout the book, Kalafatas, a former Brandeis University admissions officer and a son of Greek immigrants, demonstrates the end result of this scholarly expedition. Fluent in the language of the ethnography and folklore of Greece, widely read in history and literature, and competent as a creative writer, he produces a multifaceted and gracefully written narrative. His work produces diverse knowledge. It documents the social history of a vanished traditional occupation, identifying changes wrought in it by modernization. It represents histories of immigration by appropriating insights from professional anthropology. It illuminates how the past can be brought into a dialogue with the present through anthropology and literature. And it offers a site to reflect on how a personally vested excavation of regional history and family ancestry shapes the making of ethnic identity. Given this multiplicity, the interpretive challenge becomes how to pull the various narrative threads of this work together and how to illuminate their interrelationship. True to the aim of the chapter, I focus on how these multiple threads intertwine to produce identity.

This focus on identity is not merely the result of my research interests. It also springs from the author's view of himself as a *pilgrim,* a self-ascription that inescapably frames any examination of his work in terms of identity. This connection becomes inevitable because, as sociologist Zygmunt Bauman (1996) insightfully observes, to define one's life in terms of pilgrimage means to link it inextricably with a project of identity building. This relation is warranted because to lead a life in the manner of the pilgrim means to commit oneself—systematically, persistently, consistently, and uncompromisingly—to the realization of a concrete goal, to center oneself on achieving a tangible aim. This investment rises out of necessity, as Bauman reminds us, in response to a world that is experienced as alienating and devoid of meaning. This is precisely why the configuration of life as pilgrimage promises to capture meaning that renders the experience fulfilling at the end of the journey. "Destination, the set purpose of life's pilgrimage," Bauman characteristically writes, "gives form to the formless, makes a whole out of the fragmentary, lends continuity to the episodic" (22). It is this commitment to achieve a meaningful experience, this project of "bringing in" (ibid.) meaning in one's life that ties the notion of life as pilgrimage with identity. The sought-after meaning comes to define the pilgrim, attaching an identity to his quest. If pilgrimage is "a way of becoming which is realized in performance" (Russell 2004, 233), *The Bellstone* represents a performative site that narrates the achieving of the ethnographer-pilgrim's identity.

It would be wrong to assume here that the text represents a parochial expression of a modern—that is, stable and fixed—identity only later to dismiss it as an exception. On the contrary, what makes it an ideal site to complicate the notion of symbolic ethnicity is the fact that it maps the author's multiple and shifting identities. In fact, one may argue, following Susan Stanford Friedman (1998), that its narrative poetics is driven by a series of intercultural encounters that reconfigure identity in various times and places. The text accommodates numerous self-ascribed identities for the author: American, American Hellene, Bostonian with Irish upbringing, ethnic Greek, and diaspora Greek. While the narrative remains silent about the narrator's acknowledged attachment to Irish Boston—one more instance in which the author exercises his authority not to tell—it still illuminates the complexity of white ethnicity as a layered set of multiple identities. The pilgrimage sets in motion the narration of identity negotiated but also constituted at the intersection of a person's biography, history, family, regional and ethnic origins.

The Discourse on Ethnic Roots and Identity as Sameness

Ethnicity thrives on the vocabulary of roots, tradition, ancestry, memory, and descent. Such language frames the quest for ancestral origin, heritage, and family lineage. It encourages individuals to probe into a specific past to discover or recover a sense of themselves—Where do I come from? Who were my ancestors?—that is embedded in a distant time and, often, a faraway place. To trace origins means to visit a past, an experience that creates feelings of deep belonging. It entails establishing cultural and biological links, the raw material out of which ethnic identity is commonly made. It also means connecting individuals with social entities larger than the self, such as a family or an ethnic collective. In this capacity, the search for origins is said to compensate for modernity's signal psychological and social ill, alienation. Harry Mark Petrakis underscores this perceived dichotomy when he remarks, "When you are born in a city like Chicago, where there are no roots, you need that sense of a past and a heritage that gives your life its ritual and its meaning" (quoted in Tsine 2005, 3). Here, ethnic belonging is privileged as an antidote to modern rootlessness and anomie in urban America.

As Marshall Berman (1982) contends, it was in the 1970s, through the culture of personal memory and roots that modern societies "seemed to have learned that ethnic identity . . . was essential to the depth and fullness of self that modern life opens up and promises to all" (333). Or, as Bauman (1996) would have it, roots in modernity become the purpose of life as pilgrimage precisely because it is a world devoid of meaning that "commands life to be lived as pilgrimage" (22).

Anchoring ethnic identities to a past promotes practices of self-discovery and institution building. The post-1960s proliferation of interest in the exploration of roots in the United States testifies to this productive dimension. The advent of affordable air travel encouraged journeys to the ancestral homeland. Ethnic communities mobilized to establish heritage museums and to display tradition in festivals and parades. Universities, often enticed by generous financial contributions from immigrant communities, were convinced of the value of teaching previously unexamined ethnic histories and cultures. Interest in tracing family genealogies grew. Films, documentaries, and books, most famously the award-winning novel *Roots* by Alex Haley (1976), explored origins and ancestry.[5] These developments announced a dramatic reorientation in how American society saw itself. Early twentieth-century assimilationist politics had demanded that immigrants abandon their ancestral ties—seen as biological and cultural pollution by nativists—to achieve full social integration. Attachment to the past was a political threat, one that destabilized national cohesion. The American theme of affiliation as consent required the total forgetting of ethnicity. But the civil rights era brought about the recognition of ethnic roots, origins, and hyphenation as a legitimate component of national identity. To be an American meant to be from somewhere, a place of belonging that individuals were encouraged to explore. No longer was ethnicity seen as antithetical to Americanness. In fact, being from somewhere was celebrated as a quintessential element of *American* identity, lending credence to the rhetoric of America as a nation of immigrants. Of course, the valorization of white ethnic roots did not spring up naturally as an inevitable culmination of the modern thirst to connect with the past. As I mention in chapter 2, it occurred at a moment when political battles over cultural rights and interethnic strife over the distribution of resources elevated picturesque white ethnicity into a desirable sign of national openness.

The nexus of practices associated with roots brings about at least two distinct modes of thinking about identity. On the one hand, it may represent identity as a timeless group essence, immune to historical change. This view usually goes along with the notion that biology, landscape, and environment determine the character of a people in a nation. Analyzing the politics of creating Italian identities abroad, Anne-Marie Fortier documents the ubiquity of this perspective. Defining a collective that resides outside the ancestral homeland in relation to the "land of origins," she writes, brings identity "into contact with geographically and genealogically coded 'origins,' thus transforming it into a pseudo-biological property of human life" (1998, 210). In other words, blood and environment are seen as key determinants of an ethnic identity that remains constant in diaspora. In Fortier's case, this model serves the interests of the ancestral nation-state that seeks to consolidate the political and emotional allegiance of diasporic populations around the notion of a seamless national essence.

Environmental determinism makes its presence felt in *The Bellstone*. The text is interspersed with references to identity springing from a nationalized landscape, the Aegean Sea. The significance of the sea, about which I will say more later, lies in its capacity to elicit an irresistible desire among those regional populations that border it by calling islanders and coastal people to become part of it, to traverse it. The sea continues to draw these populations beyond their immediate environment, into the diaspora. It determines immigrant spatial movement, as it did for the author's father, whose decision to settle in Tarpon Springs, a city whose sponge industry is historically connected with Greek immigrants from the Dodecanese, represented the desire "to return to the Dodecanese, to find his way back to the people of the seaways and slipways" (160). "My father was answering the Greek mariner's call, the siren call of the sea, the call to origin" (ibid.), the author declares. In the narrative, the allure of the sea represents a timeless national property, an eternal substance of Greek national character. In portraying immigrant divers as "our eternal Odysseus" (129), the author links past and present around the archetypal seafarer, Odysseus. The desire to sail away becomes a defining feature of a regional identity rooted in Greek antiquity.

The portrayal of immigrants as scions of Odysseus makes *The Bellstone* part of a long history of Greek self-representations that define national character as a function of seafaring. As Ioanna Laliotou (2004) shows in the context of early twentieth-century transatlantic emigration from Greece, journalists, historians, and intellectuals sought to make sense of the emigration fever at the time by designating seafaring as a timeless component of Greek character. Emigration was explained in terms of innate national attributes—"the inherent desire to migrate (*philapódimon*) and the innate ability to adapt culturally" (65)—and in this manner, was grafted onto the broader contours of Greek national history. This narrative extended the diachronic horizons of Hellenism deep into antiquity by making references to the archetype, Odysseus, as well as to histories of ancient Greek colonies, linking this past with the contemporary desire to migrate. The parallels between the expression of this discourse by academic historian Konstantinos Amantos in 1923 and by Michael Kalafatas in 2003 are remarkable:

> The Aegean Sea gave Hellenism a certain orientation . . . the easiness of transportation through the sea resulted in the dispersion and final disappearance of millions of Greeks . . . . Although Hellenism came from the North, when it encountered the calmness of the Aegean Sea, it was so seduced by it, that it followed its direction blindly. (Amantos, quoted in Laliotou, 65)

> Risk aside—or because of it—the Greeks found diving in the Gulf [of Mexico] rapturous, even irresistible. A siren voice once again called Odysseus to a dangerous destiny. Always Mother Sea has been the Great Seductress of Greek mariners: they become all-forgetting in her presence. Mother Sea whispers into the "unwaxed ears" of the Aegean divers, *"Forget the risk . . . Your mother calls you to the Deep . . . Come to me, Come to me."* (Kalafatas, 148, emphasis in the original)

Evidently the portrayal of the Greek immigrants as scions of Odysseus irresistibly pulled by the sea builds on enduring constructions of Greek national character. Here, historical discourse *determines* the representation of Greek identity in terms of an immutable essence.[6]

Identity as Difference in Diaspora

But the discourse of roots does not inevitably reproduce identity as sameness. This is a crucial point because the model of identity as national character conveniently suppresses examination of those social and political forces that shape the cultural content and symbolic boundaries of ethnicity. For example, it cannot account for the changes in expression and labels of self-ascription of a single ethnic collective through time and across space. Instead, as research on how cultural minorities mobilize around roots has shown, the search for origins often moves beyond geoenvironmental and biological determinism, introducing alternative definitions of belonging. This is the second mode of thinking about identity.

The Bellstone aptly illustrates this point when its author discovers a new set of meanings associated with the debate over the definition of a "Greek." Invited to speak at the symposium "Symiots of the Diaspora" during the 1998 Symi Festivals, he recounts a moment of epiphany when a public forum on Greek people abroad produced two competing models of diasporic identity. The telling of the event is somewhat sketchy, though its message appears unambiguous. It juxtaposes a state-sponsored position on the Greek diaspora, as enunciated by George Papandreou, the Greek foreign minister at the time, with a popular narrative on the meaning of Greek identity abroad. The author contrasted Papandreou's "vision of [global] Hellenism as a galaxy, with Greece just a somewhat larger star in that galaxy" (221) with his own alternative understanding: "But for me, 'epiphany' came later, when an effervescent twenty-year-old student, Alexandros Baralis, a second-generation Symiakos from Marseilles, rose to say, to huge applause, '*If you feel Greek, you are Greek!*' That includes a third-generation Symiakos like me, living near Boston, and, of course, philhellenes everywhere" (ibid.). Diasporic narratives of belonging, as Andrea Klimt and Stephen Lubkemann (2002, 149) note, frame "a particular line of argumentation, not a distinct shared set of beliefs about the self." They add, "[D]iasporic discourses frame terms of argument rather than terms of definition" (ibid.) wherein "particular types of social connections and disconnections" (147) are articulated and contested. From this perspective, the author's recollection articulates a grassroots sentiment—a "transnationalism from below" (Guarnizo and Smith 1998, 6)—to differentiate itself from the state-imposed definition of who could count as a Greek. Further, it resists the hegemonic view of the Greek diaspora in relation to a center, by proposing a counterimagining of the diasporic body politic, one that disconnects identity from descent and territory. Its line of argumentation therefore seeks to redefine the boundaries of Greek identity.

The language of identity as feeling competes with the ideology of identity as descent. It shifts the terms defining "Greek diaspora," providing an alternative to the ascription *omogenia* (of the same race)—a term widely used by state representatives as well sectors of the ethnic media—to refer to Greek populations outside Greece. Disengaging identity from biology and geography, it proposes identity as cultural affinity. In this context, a grassroots counterconsensus emerges across a heterogeneous group of individuals who share the diasporic experience and define it in their own terms.[7]

This redrawing of boundaries further expands the definition of Greek identity by blurring the differentiation between Greeks abroad and philhellenes. The bold proposition of aligning the two social categories formulates a new imaginary of an emerging global Greek identity and refutes the normative criteria of ethnic inclusion (ancestry and cultural markers of belonging, such as language) that often position diasporas as organic parts of the nation. The notion of the diaspora as an extension of the nation—and therefore as a singular entity—is disrupted and subsequently reimagined as an inclusive, open-ended

collective with unspecified coordinates. The emerging social category that includes diasporic Greeks and philhellenes on the same conceptual plane proposes
a new global Greek identity, which, being disassociated from ethnic descent and
an encompassing shared culture, is imagined in terms of a subjectively experienced cultural connectivity.

So reconfigured, global Hellenism turns into an expansive terrain that includes
highly diverse multiethnic populations whose sole commonality lies in differential affect toward and selective affiliation with aspects of that terrain. This terrain
accommodates as legitimate any claim underscoring cultural attachment, from
an appreciation of Greek learning, to a resonance with Greek music or support
of a Greek political cause. Such a flexible formulation dismantles deeply embedded hierarchies that privilege nativity and ethnicity (understood as descent) as
prerequisites to accessing an authentic Greek identity. This reconfiguration calls
for an appropriation of Paul Gilroy's (1993) emphasis on the usefulness of the
diaspora concept. I paraphrase a passage in order to shift attention away from
his analytical block of "racial commonality" and toward a commonality based on
affect and action. He writes, "The worth of the diaspora concept is in its attempt
to specify differentiation and identity," diversity and similarities, "in a way that
enables one to think about the issue" of commonality "outside of constricting
binary frameworks—especially those that counterpose essentialism and pluralism" (120). The narrative of identity as feeling shatters hierarchies; it finds no
resonance in the view of "Greece [as] just a somewhat larger star in that galaxy"
and puts into question the claim that Greece is the center of Hellenism.

The retelling of the moment of epiphany adds yet another layer in the author's
constellation of regional, national, and diasporic identities. We find ourselves here
in a terrain of multiple identities. The author's identification as a (white) American does not infringe on the operation of alternative ethnic identifications and,
in fact, enables it (see Waters 1990). What is more, receptivity to the notion of
identity as feeling to newly define a subject in diaspora validates a strand in social theory that sees identities as malleable and changing through an individual's
life cycle. In other words, identities are understood as a dynamic and open-
ended process—indeed, as I mentioned earlier, always in the making, "always [a]
project, not [a] settled accomplishment" (Calhoun 1994, 23). Or as Stuart Hall
(1994) insists, identity "is a matter of 'becoming' as well as of 'being'" (394).[8]

Individuals reinvent themselves within their lifetime. If, as a young person,
Kalafatas turned away from his family's stories about the immigrant past, as an
adult, he turns ethnic roots into the compass of his identity. The exploration
of the past becomes crucial in the cultural production of ethnicity because it

sparks identity renewal and reinvigoration. Stuart Hall's (1993) observation about individuals who "are obliged to inhabit at least two identities" (361–62) is particularly apt here. As an open-ended process, he writes, identity "moves into the future through a symbolic detour through the past," enabling subjects "to *produce themselves anew and differently*" (362).

Symbolic ethnicity celebrates the author's embrace of a reformulated Greek identity as paradigmatic of individual choice. Here is a newly circulated script of belonging that the author appropriates as a fundamental component of self-definition. Principally, symbolic ethnicity isolates those factors that constrain but also make this choice available: the author's Greek ancestry; his biographical connection with the experience of Greek diaspora, not that of the Greek nation-state; the lack of fluency in the Greek language—the author did not speak Greek earlier, but took it up in earnest upon embarking for the pilgrimage to the ancestral home. Undoubtedly, the author does exercise a measure of agency when he intersubjectively shares the enlargement of the conceptual boundaries of Greek identity. But symbolic ethnicity neglects to address how identity may be deeply embedded in—and occasionally determined by—culture and history and, as we shall see, how this identification underwrites commitment to ethnicity.

This disregard elides the larger question of how the ethnic past enters into the process of identity formation. It ignores how historical layers of meaning may play an instrumental role in shaping identity. A reflection by scholar William Connolly (2002) captures the limitations of identity as choice. Identity "is deep in its contingency," he maintains, because "happenstances of genetics, family life, historically specific traditions, personal anxieties, demands, and aspirations, surprising events (the death of a parent, the intrusion of a war) all enter into its composition and give shape to the porous universals that mark me as human" (119). Identity is deep, then, in the manner in which history, ethnicity, and family relations intervene to produce it. In order to shed light on this aspect of identity making in *The Bellstone*, it is necessary, therefore, to take a detour and to situate the poem "Winter Dream" and the poet, the author's paternal grandfather, historically, connecting the literary artifact and its producer with histories of immigration, discrimination, the struggle for recognition, and resistance to modernity. Placing the poem in history will illuminate how the past functions to inform continuities and discontinuities with the performance of ethnic identity in the present.

The Poem in History

Our people destroyed
    by its [the diving suit's] ways,

honor and pride are lost,
    self-interest glories in their place.
There are no ethics, arrogance rules,
    pouring out of those Helmets.
The diving bosses are the cause
    of this barbaric shamelessness.

      (Metrophanes Kalafatas, quoted in Kalafatas 2003, 230)

In 1863, "the Industrial Revolution arrived in the Dodecanese islands" in the form of the deep-sea diving suit (Kalafatas 2003, 12). In contrast to traditional naked diving—"the first technique" as the composer of the poem, Metrophanes Kalafatas, calls it—the new technology enabled divers "to see, to remain underwater—it seemed—indefinitely, and to descend to previously unobtainable depths" (13). Most important for the ensuing economic race for the world markets, the new technology "increased the diver's productivity by a hundredfold" (ibid.). Although present-day oral accounts emphasize the initial resistance to "giv[ing] up their proud, beautiful, and ancient craft of naked diving" (ibid.), the use of the "first technique" declined dramatically. The economic benefits secured by the new technologies of sponge fishing sustained an ethos of rational calculation that outweighed any attachment to the customary technique. The dominance of the new technology stood for the triumph of modernity over tradition.

    The introduction of the deep-sea diving suit to the predominantly Greek-speaking islands brought the region, then under Ottoman control, into a close orbit of the capitalist world market. The social and economic networks already connecting these sponge-producing islands with regional centers grew denser and wider. By dramatically intensifying material production, the new technology transformed Symi, the poet's birthplace, into a global economic center. The island was already a crucial node in the empire's communication system. Michael Kalafatas writes: "Turks called Symi *Symbekir,* 'the island of the lightning fast boats,' and they placed Symi in charge of the postal service at sea for the entire Ottoman world" (21). With "an ever-increasing demand and increased sponge yield that came with the *skafandra* [diving suits]," this regional significance was superseded by a global one. "Symiot and Kalymnian merchants," the author observes, "had established an international network with representatives in London, Paris, Bordeaux, Trieste, St. Petersburg, New York, and other cities that organized the world market" (24). These newly founded international ties were not an isolated phenomenon sparked by the microeconomic significance of the region. Instead they were part of a larger reshaping of the Ottoman economy through policies and bilateral conventions designed to increase trade between the empire and Europe. The "Anglo-Turkish commercial convention in 1838," for example, ended century-old restrictive controls that had privileged guild monopolies, favoring instead market competitiveness (Augustinos 1992, 79).

For islands with traditions in the sea-sponge trade, participation in the world market brought about a profound social and economic restructuring. The traditional guilds, designed to monopolize sponge production and to ensure a relatively egalitarian distribution of resources, were brought to their knees by the relentless competition favored by the free market. Merchant captains who owned the means of production, the boats, were the primary beneficiaries, capable of "earn[ing] an entire fortune" in a single season (Kalafatas 2003, 23). The author's research on that era reveals the astonishing opulence and cosmopolitanism of the islands: "By 1900 land values in Pothia, the port city of Kalymnos, rivaled those of the great cities of Western Europe" (ibid.). "It was the era of the great Symiot houses—beautiful neoclassical homes built with designers from Venice, furnishings from Paris, and grand marble staircases cut from distant Carrara" (ibid.). It was also an era of great demographic explosion, economic prosperity, and bustling commercial activity. The influx of immigrants resulted in a threefold increase in the population of Symi—from eight thousand to more than twenty-two thousand—between 1850 and 1912. Profits trickled down to divers, who could earn two and a half times more than they could in other jobs. "The sea seemed an inexhaustible gold mine, and the divers shared in the bounty" (ibid.). Indeed, "it was the Golden Age of sponge fishing" (ibid.).

Moreover, as Nicholas Doumanis (1997) notes, the incorporation of the islands into the capitalist world economy placed a social and economic premium on education. The promise of social mobility through "new employment opportunities in commerce, the bureaucracy, and the professions" (92) brought the locals into immediate contact with modernity through an increasingly nationalized educational system. "The Greeks of the Ottoman Empire profited greatly from modernization," Doumanis suggests. "[B]y the end of the nineteenth century, Dodecanesians of all classes were according more and more importance to literacy and learning, as almost every Dodecanesian village had an established primary school" (93). Valued as a symbol of secular modernity, literary societies sprouted throughout the Greek-speaking Ottoman world and flourished in the islands. As Roger Kasperson notes, "Educational and cultural achievements, voluntary theaters and intellectual organizations, and local community government were most fully developed on the islands of Symi and Kalymnos" (quoted in D. Sutton 1998, 17).

From a peripheral though vital Ottoman province, Symi was transformed almost overnight into a cosmopolitan metropolis. Its population exploded, its cultural life flourished, its standard of living skyrocketed. The islands seemed to turn the promise of the Enlightenment into material reality. Technological progress, economic prosperity, and cultural sophistication legitimized the project of modernity, embraced simultaneously by secular intellectuals and international capitalists, though for different reasons.

But the introduction of Western capitalism into the region also brought social and economic upheaval. Imported secularism and the emerging hierarchies devastated the moral fabric of the traditional basis of social organization, the local community. Self-reliant, inward-looking, and rigidly regulated by a council of elders and priests, these communities had acted as "agents of social continuity by accumulating and retaining the customs and traditions around which the public and private life of the local group revolved" (Augustinos 1992, 41). "In the interests of the community," the all-male village council—the *dimogerontia*—oversaw "all manners of activity . . . including regulating the harvesting and the care of the livestock, providing public services including education, health and indigent care, maintaining communication with the outside world, and even setting regulations for proper behavior" (47).

Modernization resulted in a violent collision between the outward-looking, ever-expanding world of Western capitalism and the customary ethos in the island, destabilizing in the process the cardinal principles of the latter. The traditional guilds that organized sponge production and trade and ensured their relatively egalitarian ethos were dismantled in the face of free-market competition. Profit-driven practices of diving assaulted long-venerated traditions—such as the burial of the dead—and resulted in devastating environmental depletion and human loss.

Metrophanes Kalafatas's poem "Winter Dream" is a response to this violent collision between modernity and tradition. Thrilled by rumors of the legal abolition of the diving gear by the sultan, the poet raises his voice as an authoritative defender of the traditional order. Through its advocacy for the political goal of abolishing the use of the deep-sea diving suit in the sponge-producing islands in the Aegean Sea, the poem participates in the symbolic and material struggles developed around the modernization of the region's core economy, natural sponge production. The poem represents an instance of cultural politics aimed at influencing the course of a historical process set in motion almost forty years earlier. Originally written to inspire local political activism in the 1900s, the poem also inspires Kalafatas's pilgrimage to his roots. The analysis of the poetics and politics of this quest will illuminate how history intervenes to inform the making of the author's identity today.

Immigrant Histories as Roots: Anthropology and the Poetics of Self

Michael Kalafatas interprets the poem and the historical events to which it responded through a learned conversation with anthropologists specializing in Greece. Systematic references to and reflections upon ethnographic work on ritual lamentation, gender identity, dreaming, popular uprising, and regional resistance to capitalist intrusion are ubiquitous in *The Bellstone*, shaping its interpretive framework. Such an extensive intellectual debt is given due acknowledgment: "There is a tribe of anthropologists (I love terms of venery), to whom I owe special thanks for 'shining light in dark places'" (284). The author credits this tribe for his understanding of the *semasia* (significance) of ancestral roots.

A key passage in *The Bellstone* alerts the reader to the importance of ethnography in shaping the author's understanding of the past. To make sense of why divers willingly risked their lives during sponge diving and why his grandfather wrote "Winter Dream," the author displays his anthropological learning when he expertly concludes, "I think of how my grandfather's poem was *all words about actions* and how the diver's daring was *all actions about words:* both were poetically proclaiming, '*I am good at being a man.*' Both constituted, in [anthropologist Michael] Herzfeld's locution, 'a poetics of the self'" (82). The excerpt juxtaposes two fundamentally different cultural practices, writing poetry and diving for sponges, and despite their apparent disparity, points out their real commonality. The focus lies not on what the poet or the diver does, but on *how* each performs his respective craft. They are similar in the sense that each is practiced in a way that brings social distinction, as I will explain momentarily, to the practitioner. What poetry and diving share is an agonistic ethos defined by competitive performative excellence.

Anthropology here inescapably contributes to the authorial quest to make sense of the past. Concepts such as "poetics of the self" and the related concept of "agonistic ethos" mediate the interpretation of the diver's and the poet's being "good at being a man." It was ethnographer John Peristiany (1966) who brought attention to the centrality of agonistic behavior in the Greek-speaking world. This male-centered ethos ostensibly values fierce opposition to anything that threatens *isotimia*, that is, the "right to be treated as a person entitled to equal esteem" (188). But an agonistic worldview should not be seen as a reaction *against* social forces that render a person less than equal to—that is, inferior to—someone else. Instead, it inherently entails a cultural attachment of value to social action aspiring to exceed community norms. Recognized by the community in terms of performative excellence and rewarding its practitioners with social distinction, this ethos is inherently public. The following commentary by Herzfeld illustrates how this ideal is put into practice in a highland village in Crete:

> [I]n ... [local] idiom, there is less focus on "being a good man" than on "being good at being a man"—a stance that stresses performative excellence. . . . Actions that occur at a conventional pace are not noticeable: everyone works hard, most adult males dance elegantly enough, any shepherd can steal a sheep on some occasion or other. What counts is . . . effective movement. . . . The work must be done with flair; the dance executed with new embellishments . . . and the [animal] theft must be performed in such a manner that it serves immediate notice on the victim of the perpetrator's skill: as he is good at stealing, so, too, he will be good at being your enemy or your ally—so choose! (1985, 16)

Closely following this conceptual framework, Michael Kalafatas similarly concludes that divers were good at being men by stealing a moment from death. This defiance in the face of death constitutes a pivotal element in the author's excavation of his roots as usable past. As we will see momentarily, the ethos of risk-taking becomes the centerpiece of his charting of ethnic and intergenerational identity. In what follows, I will untangle the various narrative threads that build on the poetics of self to construct ethnic identity in the diaspora and to establish an intellectual link between the poet of "Winter Dream" and the author of *The Bellstone,* grandfather and grandson.

Ethnocentrism, Distinction, and Histories of Oppression

Michael Kalafatas's preoccupation with establishing ethnic distinction is startling in its unabashed ethnocentrism. References to the cultural superiority of early twentieth-century Greek immigrants, the preeminence of Greek language, the social and economic accomplishments of Greek Americans, and the magnificence of ethnic ancestry abound in the book. Laden with pride in ethnicity, the narrative participates in the celebratory yet competitive discourse of multiculturalism. "Among ethnic groups in the United States, Greeks stand first in educational attainment and second in income," the author intones (149), revisiting in this manner the common topos of Greek America as success (see Anagnostou 2003). This ideology of model ethnicity is rooted in discourses of the past that marked immigrants as probationary Americans. The extolling of ethnic success in the present echoes the burden of social Darwinism in the past, which demanded that immigrants demonstrate their fitness to American modernity through a performance of social and economic success. The text reverses historical domination. If immigrants in the past were deemed racially and culturally inferior, *The Bellstone* transgresses the axiom of cultural relativism to declare the ethnic superiority of the Greeks.

This politics of representation pierces the heart of an early twentieth-century discourse in American modernity that violated the immigrant quest for equal esteem (isotimia). By stigmatizing southeastern European immigrants, including the Greeks, as intellectually inferior and racially unfit to partake equally in the rights and privileges of a modern democracy, nativism placed the burden of inclusion on the immigrants. The academy and popular culture as well as the media and public opinion saw immigrants as alien entities and, ultimately, a grave biological and civilizational threat to the national body. Subjected to symbolic and physical violence, immigrants were coerced into abandoning their traditions and severing their Old World ties. Their humanity denied, they came face-to-face with everyday practices of denigrating exclusion. Olympia Dukakis exposes this wound when "she remembers being tied to a tree with socks stuffed in her mouth and seeing her aunts being pelted with stones, all because they were Greek" (Apessos 2003, 12).

In its representation of immigrant histories from an ethnic point of view, *The Bellstone* challenges contemporary audiences. Coerced into a position of inferiority, Greek America engaged in a historical struggle to demonstrate its isotimia with the nation. Its recitation of its success and cultural virtues in the present registers the degree to which it has internalized the discourse that rendered it inferior in the past. Kalafatas takes the ubiquitous narrative of ethnic success a crucial step further. He declares that, all along, Greek immigrants were outperforming their hosts in all sorts of social, cultural, and political domains. They built, for example, interracial relations of economic equality with African American crews working alongside Greeks on sponge production. They functioned, therefore, as the guardians of American ideal of equality, while native whites relegated black people to second-class citizenship under the racist regime of Jim Crow. More American than the Americans themselves, Greeks not only confronted whiteness but also possessed a superior culture. The author argues that it was the poetics of manhood and its corollary, the ethos of performative excellence that allowed Dodecanese sponge fishermen to outperform their occupational competitors in the Gulf of Mexico.

Similarly, Kalafatas pronounces the linguistic eminence of Greek. He cites the Greek origins of English words with a frequency sufficient to spark exasperation in an otherwise sympathetic reviewer. "At times the anecdote is reduced to etymology," anthropologist David Sutton (2003, 296) writes, "with Kalafatas displaying a lexical imperialism reminiscent of the father in *My Big Fat Greek Wedding.*" A manifesto of linguistic chauvinism is foisted upon the reader, as if to compensate for histories of linguistic subjugation. "Returning home from Holy Trinity Church on 'Big Friday' night," Constance Constant (2005) recollects, "Chicago streetcars were again filled with Greek conversation, softly spoken, so we wouldn't be called 'greenhorns,' 'God damn Greeks,' or worse" (267).

The Bellstone rewrites immigration by reversing early twentieth-century racial hierarchies and by recasting inequalities in terms of culture. Against the backdrop of histories of ethnic oppression, it reclaims a positive immigrant identity based on social excellence. But the text leaves intact the principal assumptions of the discourse that it seeks to subvert, deploying a politics of representation that is likely to infuriate readers by its ethnocentrism. Far from being a socially innocuous exercise in nostalgic memory, the search for roots in this instance carries the sting of the loaded politics of reversing cultural and ethnic hierarchies, a politics also embraced by racial minorities. As Paul Gilroy (1993) notes, in Afrocentric narratives, "Blacks [also] become dominant by virtue of either biology or culture; whites are allocated a subordinate role" (191). In the Greek case, we witness the public visibility of a historically suppressed narrative of immigrant ethnocentrism[9] in the context of renewed competitive constructions of racial and ethnic hierarchies, which pose whiteness as superior to undesired ethnicity among certain populations (see Perry 2001).

Continuities in Regional and Family Identity: Names as Distinction

The Bellstone not only creates a noted ethnic pedigree but also establishes a distinguished regional and family lineage. The author's fascination with heredity and "pride of origin" (168) draws from a racialized discourse that links appearance, intelligence, and character. An old British Naval Intelligence report that depicts Symians and Kalymnians as "exceptionally vigorous, intelligent stocks, curiously different in build and temperament" (168) feeds the author's propensity to claim prestigious ancient genealogies. By explaining the physiology of square-cut shoulders—a feature that he, his sons, and relatives in Symi share—as a genetic adaptation to deep-sea diving, Kalafatas treats it as a marker of regional identity. The author appropriates the idea of regional physiological typologies as a collective biological inheritance for his own purposes: to insert himself and his family into a narrative that links personal physical appearance with royal ancestral pedigrees. "As I read the report of British Naval Intelligence," he confesses,

"I could only think, in a delirium of self-flattery, of king Nereus of Symi whom Homer called, 'second in handsomeness only to the great Achilles'" (169).[10]

The regional, familial, and personal are brought together through a common genealogy by which the author lays claim to an aristocratic lineage. This reveals a genealogical thinking whose compass centers on distinction. Of paramount importance in this mode of thinking is the ultimate embeddedness of the person in a prominent ethnic ancestry. The poet is imagined as the intermediary link connecting aristocratic origins deep in the classical past with the diasporic present: "Dead at thirty-eight, he remains forever young; his hair pitch-dark like that of my sons, John and Daniel. In his silhouette I see the famed cut of the Symiot: square shoulders, strong jaw, and face of grace sculpted by noble forebears. He looks like King Nereus. His poetic eyes are set on the razor-sharp horizon" (277). The narrative endows the author with a distinguished pedigree based on family name—a marker of patrilineal identity in Greece—and physique.

How does the author represent the poet of "Winter Dream"? And what kind of family identity does this representation establish? Biographical information about the poet is fragmented, pieced together through figments of authorial imagination as well as through ethnohistoric facts. We gain a glimpse of his life and cultural proclivities through a letter contrived by the author of *The Bellstone.* Imagined as the final farewell of the poet's widow on her deathbed, the letter does more than to reflect on Metrophanes's personal character and the cultural milieu in which his life was embedded. It displays the author's literary skills but also, more importantly for my purposes here, his ethnographic grasp of the significance of Greek naming customs and their relation to family and cultural memory.

The "purloined letter," as the author styles it, situates the poet in relation to coexisting social worlds of early twentieth-century Greek-speaking world under the Ottoman Empire: secular modernity and a deeply ethnoreligious worldview. Expected by his family "to become a priest and a Church leader" (224), after a brief sojourn in the seminary on the island of Patmos the poet defected to the world of classical education and literature. Seduced by the pull of secular learning, "The Power of the Word," he joined the ranks of a particular social class, what Nicholas Doumanis (1997) identifies as the *morfomenoi* (educated). "He became a teacher, school principal and poet. He loved the writers of antiquity and of the Cretan renaissance, like Vitzentzos Kornaros" (Kalafatas 2003, 225). An avid sailor whose love for poetry earned him the sobriquet "poetry-in-sail," he must have felt at home in the harbors of the Dodecanese Islands: "Poetry was so loved in the Aegean that it was sold there on the streets of the islands" (ibid.).

The epistolary confession of the poet's wife further probes this poetic universe. A person who enjoyed reminiscing about the folk dancing and traditional costumes of her village, Anastasia also "loved to learn." How fortunate she was to have united with the learned Metrophanes: "Two souls, one heart" (224)! "Your grandfather," Anastasia is purported to have written, "pulled back a curtain, and there I saw a world I never knew of books and poems and passion." He, a man of a politically and socially prominent Symiot family, and she, a village girl, "were wed for eternity by . . . love and by the power of The Word" (ibid.). Here, the boundaries of the urban-rural divide become porous through marriage. Anastasia's simultaneous appreciation of vernacular and literary cultures points to a creative cross-fertilization. Far from being isolated, the world of the villages is connected with both local and extralocal cultural circuits in the fin-de-siècle Dodecanese society.

The letter places the poet at the center of his community's moral universe. With "an intractable hatred toward self-gain . . . he dressed the naked, ministered to the ill, took in the foreigners and gave them blessing" (223). Lavishly praising his philanthropy, compassion, faith, self-sacrifice, and love for *patridha,* the place of his birth, it portrays the poet as a man of distinction and the embodiment of the ethos of the traditional community.

The author of *The Bellstone* continues the legacy of familial distinction though a virtuoso anthropological performance. For, through the inventive sketching of the poet's ethical portrait, the fictional letter becomes a display of Michael Kalafatas's anthropological expertise. It demonstrates the author's grasp of the value of names in Greek society and their significance as venues of intergenerational continuity. That the letter is addressed to the grandson—and elder brother of the author—Metrophanes is not fortuitous. As one who shares the poet's first name, the addressee becomes a crucial emotional link in remembering the deceased poet. In fact, because his name evokes memories of the deceased poet, he became a cherished child for Anastasia who "fussed so over" him (225). The "affective dimension" associated with traditional naming practices rests in the capacity of names to perpetuate familial memories. To hear the name of a deceased relative being spoken again is thought to resurrect that person, a powerful commemorative act (D. Sutton 1998, 184). As anthropologists of Greece observe, such naming practices work to ensure continuity between past and present. Named after his paternal grandfather, as custom dictates for firstborn sons, Metrophanes brings immediate "ancestors back to life" (Vernier, quoted in D. Sutton 1998, 183). Memories of an eponymous ancestor become a valued cultural property: "When you are older, you will read this letter and know the glory of the name you carry" (Kalafatas 2003, 223), the poet's wife instructs her beloved grandson. The inherited name generates ancestral memory.

But this commemorative practice extends beyond individuals, attaching distinction to the family name itself. Written as an encomium to the poet, the letter ensures intergenerational preservation of a familial legacy. Names are associated with a family's social standing and prestige. "The metaphoric connection of name and honor," David Sutton writes, "link[s] those people who live in the present to the past of the family or lineage" (1998, 183). Read in this light, the letter contributes to the making of a distinguished family heritage. Once situated in relation to Greek naming practices, the imagined letter turns into a culturally embedded commemorative act.[11]

As badges of distinction, names and physical appearances retain their value insofar as they circulate in communities sharing cultural norms. But their passage from one symbolic system to another may bring about dramatic semantic shifts. The symbolic assault on immigrant names is a potent historical example. But even in the present, ethnic names may be problematic, as they mark foreign status. Kalafatas writes humorously, yet bitterly, in this regard:

> By conservative estimate I have spelled my name 25,000 times. . . . [T]he receptionist in my office, when asked to spell my name, would say, "Kalafatas: All the vowels are A's, and it's 'K' as in kiss, 'l' as in love, 'f' as in fudge, 't' as in toffee, and 's' as in sugar." Somehow I never spelled it that way. In America the subtext of spelling an "ethnic" name is the act of an outsider trying to *spell* his way in. So it was a joy to arrive on Rhodes and Symi where the name brought instant recognition, if not fame. As a child I had listened, time and again, to my father say that the Kalafatas family was "one of the oldest, most aristocratic families in the Dodecanese islands." This from my father the leftist. (*Irony,* too, is a Greek word.) I lived in America, however, and knew the name was no advantage. (192–93)

Ethnic names function as symbolic markers of difference. Assaulted by assimilation and monolingualism, they come to communicate foreignness. This is why resistance to the anglicization of one's name, particularly prior to the advent of multiculturalism, is perceived as an act of cultural defiance and confers ethnic pride within the community. Actress Olympia Dukakis, for instance, "[d]ue in part to all of the ethnic tensions and her pride in her Greek heritage, . . . chose not to change her name. 'It was a big issue early on,' she explained, adding that she was often told that she was 'too ethnic' for a part, just by virtue of her name alone" (Apessos 2003, 12).[12] And the following comment by George Stephanopoulos, former senior advisor to President Bill Clinton and current ABC correspondent, further brings this point home: "Every time I went on TV or was in the newspaper, you would see that long name underneath, Stephanopoulos, you know, and people come up to me all the time and say, 'I'm so glad you didn't change your name. I'm so glad you made them learn how to spell your name'" (quoted in *The Greek Americans* 1998).

In what follows, I will show that *The Bellstone* restores the distinction of an ethnic family name in diaspora. If the signifier "Kalafatas" carries no advantage in the anglophone world, if it in fact presents a cumbersome inconvenience, it is reframed as a mark of distinction. It is imbued with prestige through the author's pursuit of performative excellence centered on agonistic engagement with the discourse of professional anthropology. Once again, the narrative identity of the author cannot possibly be understood only in terms of choice. Instead, it is embedded in cultural practices linked with a transnational past— the poetics of manhood—historical relations of domination, and the discourse of anthropology.

Discontinuous Continuities: Performative Excellence in Shifting Contexts

Pointing to the extinction of collective immigrant culture, the author duly explains the decline of sponge diving, an occupational tradition, as the result of a dramatic intergenerational rupture. "The poetics of manhood can cross an ocean, but in a land of plenty it has trouble crossing the generations," he attests. "The deep-water diver no longer exists in Tarpon Springs" (146). The poetics of manhood is disrupted because the material and cultural conditions that sustained risk-taking, death-defying behavior among immigrants no longer exist to entice similar feats among their offspring. Intergenerational continuity is interrupted as "the younger generation opted out for more reliable and safer occupations . . . head[ing] off to college" (149). At first glance, the "poetics of manhood" appears to have vanished, part of an irrelevant past, a "foreign country" in Greek America. Yet a careful analysis of the narrative shows otherwise. The arguments advanced in *The Bellstone* constitute in themselves the performative excellence demanded by the agonistic ethos of the poetics of manhood. In this sense, the book itself is a link between the past and the present; it demonstrates that the poetics of manhood is still central to the author's identity, albeit in the context of anthropology and in relation to a different interpretive community.

Interspersed with a vast number of literary references, *The Bellstone* makes a claim that the author remains true to his family's intellectual genealogy. Like his grandfather, he is a morfomenos, an educated person. The evidence of authorial erudition is overwhelmingly conspicuous. Kalafatas richly draws from the Greek and Western literary canon, adding a new cultural dimension to what is primarily an ethnohistoric commentary. Thick with quotations—from Constantine Cavafy and George Seferis to Mark Twain and Marcel Proust—the text unmistakably manifests its author's cultural literacy. The consumption of literature and professional ethnography—let alone their critical appraisal—serves as a social marker of distinction. The sophisticated interpretation of poetry, dexterous quoting of literary sources, and conversance with academic anthropology demonstrate the author's possession of a specific form of knowledge, what Pierre Bourdieu (1984) calls cultural capital. In performing his critical appreciation of high culture, his interpretive facility with texts not ordinarily accessible to a lay audience, Kalafatas establishes intergenerational continuity within a distinguished family lineage.

But this display of learning is undertaken through a specific cultural angle. *The Bellstone* performs knowledge in a mode that resonates with the agonistic spirit of the poetics of manhood: the goal of any action is to outdo one's adversary, to defeat one's rival in a contest of performative excellence in the task at hand. The popular ethnographer undertakes a similar performance in relation to the field of cultural anthropology. Intellectually indebted to this academic discipline, he strives to outperform it, to prove in fact that his brand of ethnography offers an account superior to that espoused by his professional kindred. It is crucial here to note that the text accomplishes this act agonistically, adhering to the Greek cultural logic of the competitive poetics of self. It performs its superiority by appropriating rules set by the profession, namely the importance that interpretive anthropology places on the worldview of the people whose social life it seeks to elucidate. Known as the emic approach, this orientation privileges local explanations of phenomena, elevating them to a status of theoretical insight. It is no wonder, then, that the popular anthropologist organizes his ethnography around an emic explanation: "Of my list of possible causes for the high casualty rates, Nikolaos [a local diver] said, '*Ola, ola,*' all contributed" (92).

The popular ethnographer surveys the field of a professional debate to expose and contest its limitations. "I have learned that a Great Divide exists among anthropologists," he observes. "On one side are those who hold a 'materialistic' view in explaining social phenomena. . . . [On the other side are] [t]hose who hold the 'ideational' view believ[ing] that the ideas harbored by a culture cause people to act the way they do" (76). But this presents a narrow perspective, he asserts. Inserting himself in the debate, Kalafatas advances his own interpretation, which he claims as a superior form of truth. "Why does an admission officer get mixed up in an ideological debate among anthropologists? Because I want to understand why the divers took the risks they did" (ibid.). "Like the Colossus of Rhodes, with his legs straddling Mandraki harbor, I straddle the Great Divide: I believe both positions hold truth" (ibid.).

The popular ethnographer straddles this great divide by subsuming evidence from fiction and poetry, anthropological theory, ethnography and history, classical and modern sources. This dexterous intertwining of genres results in a multifaceted, eclectic text that best approximates the bold innovations of experimental ethnography. This textual performance across genres and disciplines is, therefore, more than an impressive display of erudition. Kalafatas undertakes his own poetics of manhood, turning it into a culturally specific textual performance by which he seeks to outdo his professional interlocutors.

In the Greek context, Michael Herzfeld (1987) foregrounds the potential of the poetics of manhood to reverse relations of domination. He notes that ethnographic subjects—whether peasants or illiterate mayors—take pride in acts of agonistic excellence as a means of outfoxing educated outsiders or state representatives and so deflecting "[t]he very embarrassment of subordination" (103). The popular ethnographer's agonistic engagement with a dominant social discourse, such as anthropology, reconfigures this performative dimension of Greek identity in the context of international relations of power. To achieve international distinction, the example of Kalafatas implies, one must thoroughly understand the codes of one's own adversaries and competitively surpass them. To put it differently, ethnic prestige in diaspora may require competence in one's own culture, but it necessitates the *performance of assimilation* in the host society.[13]

For a Greek American beyond the immigrant generation, the agonistic ethos of competitive excellence presents a discontinuous continuity. No longer deployed face-to-face in the context of a community, it is now expressed in relation to nonethnic social entities, such as professional anthropology. The context of its appraisal and evaluation has shifted from the competitive sociability of the male coffeehouse to the equally competitive realm of knowledge production. But the textual performance of the poetics of manhood also establishes a continuous link between the author of *The Bellstone* and the poet of "Winter Dream." As a demonstration of cultural capital, the book confers distinction on its author, weaving in this manner an intellectual affinity with the poet. And if the poet risked his life through literature, his grandson puts his authorial reputation on the line by defiantly producing an experimental popular ethnography that challenges professional anthropology. What is more, *The Bellstone*'s bold ethnocentrism carries the risk of alienating the author from his immediate social circles in the university community and elsewhere.

The Bellstone is more than a tribute to a distinguished ancestor, more than an act of remembrance. Instead, the text establishes an identity for the author through culturally embedded practices. The values associated with family inheritance, social distinction, kinship, naming systems, and the performance of excellence function as usable pasts through which to achieve identity. My analysis shows that identity in this narrative construction is a matter of both being and becoming. If the element of selective reflexivity is not absent from the performance of white ethnicity, neither is the lack of cultural and historical resources that fix identity as a predetermined entity. I have shown how preexisting ideologies of biological inheritance, histories of domination, and cultural scripts of remembering provide the meanings for constructing a stable and relatively coherent identity. Social discourses, therefore, mediate and occasionally determine the making of ethnic identity.

The very process of achieving this narrative identity illustrates the vast investment that may underwrite the formation of white ethnic identities. A line in Jean-Paul Sartre's philosophical thinking about the interrelationship between the past and the present helps frame this making of identity as investment. "One does not possess one's past as one possesses a thing one can hold in one's hand, inspecting every side of it," Sartre wrote. "[I]n order to possess it I must bind it to existence by a project" (quoted in Hufford et al. 1987, 41). "[A]t its very source," he observed, the past "is bound to a certain present and to a certain future, to both of which it belongs" (Sartre 1956, 110). *The Bellstone* animates a specific ethnic past through the project of tracing ancestral roots in the manner of the pilgrim. In the process, it weaves a contemporary authorial identity via the discourse of roots. And it does so copiously, achieving an identity through immense material and symbolic expenditure.

Bauman's view of pilgrimage as identity provides the framework for the argument that white ethnicity matters. *The Bellstone* places faith in a stable meaning residing in the ancestral past. The quest for ethnic roots centers identity as a project in the making that demands an enormous effort for its narrative representation. To capture the seriousness of this commitment, pause for a moment to reflect on the time and energy, effort and dedication, skill and determination, knowledge and imagination, and material and symbolic resources that were invested in the fieldwork and research that led to *The Bellstone*. Think of the labor that went into the writing of the book! The narrator's quest for meaning that is anchored in ancestral roots represents an approach to identity making encountered more often in modernity than in postmodernity.

Rather than representing a readily discarded, shallow identity, *The Bellstone* exemplifies the making of identity in terms of an arduous process, a crafting of a deeply felt attachment. This kind of narrative construction foregrounds the notion of identity as a process that entails struggle and investment, a process that can best be viewed as a "project" in Sartrean terms—that is, identity in the making (Calhoun 1994, 23). Following Bauman (1996), one can safely claim that the text represents a site where identity is *"built at will,* but built *systematically,* floor by floor and brick by brick"* (23, emphasis in the original). We may, of course, as Gayatri Spivak (1992) points out, "learn identity letter by letter," in an indispensable recognition of the power of language to constitute subjects (790). Narratives construct identity letter by letter, word by word. Kalafatas's building of identity in this manner imbues *The Bellstone* with particular critical poignancy because the project unfolds during a moment when the social conditions that sustain the ethos of the pilgrim are disintegrating. Putting it differently, the text is of particular intellectual interest because it embodies an approach to identity that is receding from public consciousness. What used to be a prevailing way of life in modern society, the manner of the pilgrim, is hardly sustainable and may even be thought of as under threat of extinction in postmodern conditions. The postmodern world of fleetingly superficial and readily discarded identities cannot be "hospitable to the pilgrims any more" (Bauman 1996, 23).

Is *The Bellstone* the last gasp before the projected total white ethnic surrender to fleetingly playful identities? I offer no predictions, for I view identity as a contingent historical process and therefore impossible to chart through predictive social science. Who among those who predicted the twilight of ethnicity almost twenty-five years ago could have foreseen that a white ethnic in the present would construe identity as pilgrimage? As I have pointed out, my analysis of a single text in this chapter is meant to showcase the complexities associated with the making of personal identity and the constitutive function of history and culture in this process. My discussion also advances the argument that white ethnic identity still matters and that its achievement requires deep social and emotional investment. Obviously my study is in no position to assess the degree to which identity as lifestyle has taken hold in Greek America. But neither is symbolic ethnicity authorized to represent white ethnicity as a depthless performance of ethnicity construed exclusively as a bundle of options.

What my analysis does demonstrate is that in postmodernity, the construction of fixed and stable identities coexists with flexible accommodation of change and agency—and that the past does offer a vital resource for the making of ethnic identity. To further explore the power of the past to nurture an ethic of obligation and duty, I turn next to how the poem "Winter Dream" traveled across space and time and how its meaning was transformed in relation to the cultural geographies framing its circulation. This analytical shift from roots to routes will enable me to interrogate yet another blind spot of symbolic ethnicity, namely how history and power make available certain expressions of ethnicity while silencing or marginalizing others. It will also make it possible to illuminate yet another contour, the changing uses of ethnic pasts through history and their centrality to making or unmaking whiteness in Greek America.

CHAPTER SIX

Redirecting Ethnic Options

Historical Routes of Heritage

[A] good theory of identity does more than simply celebrate
or dismiss the various uses of identity—rather, it enables
cultural critics to explain where and why identities are
problematic and where and why they are empowering.

—Paula Moya, *Reclaiming Identity*

Marked by its European origins, modern black political
culture has always been more interested in the relationship
of identity to roots and rootedness than in seeing identity
as a process of movement and mediation that is more
appropriately approached via the homonym routes.

—Paul Gilroy, *The Black Atlantic*

As a consequence of this process [of political intimidation],
Greek America developed a kind of amnesia. It forgot its
own turbulent history in America. Illusions grew: that
the transition from impoverished immigrant to affluent
American had been relatively brief and painless, that
America had always loved its Greeks.

—Dan Georgakas, "The Greeks in America"

IN WHAT WAYS did history mediate the encounter between the immigrants and
the dominant society? And how have social discourses in the past shaped the available contours of white ethnicity today? Symbolic ethnicity brackets the crucial
questions of how specific immigrant cultural forms interacted with host structures and how some of them came to be recognized as available ethnic resources
in the present while others were suppressed, silenced, or even eradicated. This

inattention to processes of exclusion conveniently leaves out questions of cultural domination and political oppression in the historical encounter between the dominant society and immigrant cultures. In fact, the theory's reluctance to acknowledge the operation of power in the constitution of immigrant subjectivities renders it ideologically suspect. What are we to make of the shocking assertion that "American ethnics have always been characterized by freedom of ethnic expression" (Gans 1979, 13), for example, when overwhelming evidence demonstrates how nativism brutally oppressed the "new immigrants" in the United States in the years after World War I? In this instance, the concept of "choice" mystifies the process, allowing ubiquitous social practices and policies responsible for cultural and economic marginalization to escape interrogation.

An alternative landscape becomes visible, however, once "ethnic options" are examined as a specific mode of cultural production embedded in history; inevitably, this perspective casts light on ethnicity as a domain defined by exclusion and inclusion. It demonstrates how expressions of roots that we take for granted today—dance, ethnic cuisine, and the revitalization of language—came about, not naturally but as the result of a power struggle. It explains, for example, why Greek dancing was performed indoors, behind drawn blinds, as a precaution against nativist hostility in 1930s rural America (according to recollections of elders I have interviewed) and how it has now turned, arguably, into a popular "choice" among the youth for performing Greek ethnicity. A historical investigation also explains why certain immigrant practices and political activities ceased to capture the social imagination of white ethnics. It illuminates the manner in which what was considered a viable course of action in the past has been relegated to the cultural margins in the present. I must therefore supplement my discussion of identity and roots with an examination of "identity as a process of movement and mediation" (Gilroy 1993, 19) across space and time, that is, in terms of routes. In adopting this approach, I intend to show that history mediates, if not determines, the making of usable ethnic pasts. To correct the partiality that symbolic ethnicity accords to the present, I maintain that *history* makes itself *present* in white ethnicity, albeit in a radically transformed manner.

I initiate this historical inquiry by examining how a specific literary artifact is imbued with meaning as it travels through space and time. Scholars have already noted that inquiring into how material culture travels and attending to the effects of that travel make for a powerful research approach, one that, interestingly, also organizes *The Bellstone*. As David Sutton (2003, 295) comments in his review of the book, "'Follow the object,' is the injunction of many in current anthropology and cultural studies, and Kalafatas responds to this call, following sponges through their natural and social contexts." In telling his family story, however, Kalafatas also follows another kind of cultural artifact, a poem. In what can be seen as a prelude to his nostalgia for a primordial past, he writes:

> Long ago, in a more innocent time, before the arrival of the deep-diving equipment, young men in pursuit of sponges would descend to the bottom of the sea on just a single breath of air, using as a weight and rudder a beautiful, flat, marble diving stone. On the island of Symi where my grandfather was born, it was called "bellstone," after its shape. As I retell this story, my grandfather's poem is *my* bellstone, guiding me to some rapturous place beneath the sea, I know not where. (2003, 4)

Rooted in struggles against material and cultural domination, the poem is entangled with complex histories of immigration, ethnicity, and travel. Initially composed to heighten local consciousness about modernity's assault on the moral principles of a traditional community, it was declared a diasporic nationalist political manifesto by the poet's immigrant sons, who took the initiative to publish it. Deployed primarily in the service of regional and international political causes early in the twentieth century, it is read by the author of *The Bellstone* as a redemptive allegory. Composed in Greek in 1903 to address local and, later, diasporic populations, the poem was translated into English in the 1990s, reaching beyond its first intended audiences. In what follows, I will identify the specific discourses that rerouted the significance of the poem and will talk about the conditions that made the poem—a cultural artifact of the preimmigrant past—relevant to any given historical present.

Specifically, I will discuss the meanings that the poem generated, first in the Dodecanese Islands at the time of its composition and later in the United States, where it was first transported as the "sole heritage" of the poet's immigrant sons (Tsine 2004). I will dwell, in particular, on the significance that the author of *The Bellstone* attaches to it in the 1990s when he followed its story back to the Dodecanese, identifying the kinds of social and political visions that it sustained. I will also address how its meanings changed over time, raising the following questions: What do these histories of travel across space and through time tell us about white ethnicity? And what happens to literature as it moves away from the place of its production?

The key word here is *routes* in its relationship to *roots*. The analytical utility of the term lies in the attention that it brings to what happens when cultural artifacts and ideas are transported to new places and there interact with new discourses. Approaching ethnicity through routes instead of roots offers many advantages. If the quest for roots often reinforces fixed and ahistorical identities, a consideration of routes highlights the changing contours of identity in relation to specific histories. If roots privilege the circumscribed cultural geography of some fixed point of origin, routes chart identities in relation to multiple locations. If roots seek authenticity, routes illuminate cross-cultural fertilizations. Routes call attention to the kinds of meanings that are generated when cultures travel across national or regional borders and interact with other systems of meaning elsewhere. Attending to routes demonstrates that meanings associated with a locality are constituted through these interactions, rather than inherently residing in a supposedly authentic original. As James Clifford (1997, 3) characteristically puts it, "Cultural centers, discrete regions and territories, do not exist prior to contacts, but are sustained through them, appropriating and disciplining the restless movements of people and things."

I have already shown in the previous chapter how the clash between tradition and capitalist modernity altered the social universe of the Dodecanese Islands, and I have touched upon how, in turn, literature was deployed to address a social crisis. Now it is time to examine in more detail the political significance of "Winter Dream" at the time of its composition and subsequently ask in what ways the meaning of the poem was reconfigured during its temporal and spatial travels in the United States. My task becomes to identify how the poem is incorporated into political ideologies, cultural movements, and social discourses in the United States in two discrete historical moments: interwar assimilationist America and turn-of-the-twentieth-century multicultural America. My interest lies in investigating how these circulations of a literary artifact produce meaning for roots and how pasts are turned into meaningful presents in a hegemonic cultural center like the United States. But before proceeding with an investigation of the poem's multiple routes, I must reflect critically upon two specific points: the poem's return to its place of origins and its availability to English-speaking audiences.

Literary Heritage: National Jewel or Placed Literature?

As the poem circulated on the island of Symi and later in the United States, a series of commentaries have framed it in aesthetic and national terms. When writer Irene Voyatzi-Haralambi introduced the poem to audiences at the Symi Arts Festival in 1996, she drew attention to its beauty: "The poem is like an old jewel buried in the sand. And now the time has come for it to be an ornament in the spirits and hearts of the people" (quoted in Kalafatas 2003). Similarly, Olga Broumas, the award-winning Greek-born poet depicts the poem as "deeply beautiful; in fact, . . . [a] national treasure of Greece" (quoted in Kalafatas 2003, 2). Not unlike an archaeological treasure, this popular poem, which adheres to the traditional poetic form of rhymed fifteen-syllable meter, belongs to the nation and its literary canon.

When Broumas uses the language of monumentality, she participates, perhaps unwittingly, in the archaeological model of understanding tradition. According to this perspective, the folk provide irrefutable evidence of the presence of the past in the present. They testify to the uninterrupted, linear continuity of the nation embedded in vernacular culture. Traceable to German romanticism and, particularly, to the philosopher Johann Gottfried von Herder, this monumental approach to folklore proved particularly useful in the context of nation building. As Michael Herzfeld (1986a) argues, the discipline of folklore in Greece was instrumental in validating both national identity and the "cultural status [of the Greeks] as Europeans" (11). The lore of the folk stood as "monuments of words," a national treasure of "verbal archaeology" (100) that furnished evidence to counteract European skepticism or outright hostility toward the idea of Greek continuity. The folk were the living specimen, so to speak, who embodied a living tradition traced to the glorious Greek ancient past.

What do we lose sight of when we approach "Winter Dream" as a beautiful artifact of national heritage? In his analysis of state and folkloric appropriation of *poietáridhes,* composers of traditional written narrative poetry in Cyprus, George Syrimis (1998) interrogates this kind of aesthetic nationalism. He charges that the paradigm of folklore as a mirror of a seamless national identity compromises the modernity of tradition. It removes poetry from the context of its production and, as a result, reduces its complexity. The idea of folk poetry as a diachronic mirror of the nation ignores the conditions that frame its creation and perfor-mance. In this manner, the model demonstrates "a total lack of consideration of modern folk poetry in and of itself" (211). Syrimis objects to the use of the ideo-logically laden vocabulary of "monuments of word" and "treasuring" to interpret this poetry because, as he puts it, "both phrases suggest a certain containment of modern folk poetry and a macabre, lifeless, yet still precious ventriloquism of the ancient dead" (ibid.). The nationalization of the folk objectifies and ossifies an ever-changing "malleable and innovative" tradition (218).

Similarly, to speak of "Winter Dream" as a national treasure is to neutralize the political import of the poem as an instrument in the service of class struggle. In pitting Greek and international capitalists against the exploited Greek folk, the poem at one time disrupted the ideology of national coherence. It fractured the imagined solidarity of the nation along deep class divisions. Neither can a static aesthetic-national reading of the poem account for its changing social and political uses through time. It is necessary, therefore, to set aside the aesthetic interpretation in order to create a generous space in which to read the poem in terms of the cultural and political work that it performed in any given context. Such an interpretive framework directs attention to the diverse constituencies that appropriated literature both at home and in the diaspora. This focus opens a space in which to reflect on the diasporic routes of ethnicity, a topic that is not always at the forefront of whiteness studies. In this terrain, we find advocates for social justice, *paideia* (learning), and a heritage of opposition to economic exploitation.[1]

At the same time, the poem's investment in shaping the moral and political fabric of a locality invites reading of it as "placed literature" (Ball 2002)—literature that shapes the social imagination of a place. It raises interpretive questions, such as "Who defines the place?" "For what purpose?" and "What is at stake once a place is imagined in one specific manner at the expense of another?"

But I am also interested in what happens once a placed literary text is transported elsewhere through emigration. I wish to address the social imagination that the poem sustained during its travels and the kinds of political action that it generated. I would like to ask how the immigrant sons of the poet used the poem and how the poem shapes the worldview of the grandson today. This reading brings into focus the interplay of continuities and discontinuities in diachronic deployments of the poem. It illuminates both roots—which signify stability, identity, continuity, and commitment to a locality—and its homonym, routes— a concept suggesting change, movement, and discontinuity. I analyze the cultural politics of the poem in three distinct times and places. The first will take us to Ottoman Symi, when the poet composed the poem. The second will transport us to the first two decades of the twentieth century in America, when the sons of the poet became entangled in labor unrest and leftist unionism as well as diaspora politics. The third will anchor us in the present, as Michael Kalafatas's popular ethnography of travel reroutes the significance of "Winter Dream," the placed literature of the past, for contemporary audiences. A particular contour meanders throughout this discussion, one that takes us across national geographies and through radically different historical periods: the way in which usable ethnic pasts make or unmake whiteness in the United States. I try not to lose sight of this contour, though necessary turns in the discussion may render it occasionally invisible or leave it faint in the background. All this is framed by the central question that I raise in this chapter, namely, how a historical analysis of the social construction of ethnic pasts interrogates the ideology of white ethnic options.

Poetry and the Political Function of Intellectuals

As I have already pointed out in the previous chapter, the poem became entangled in wider cultural battles over the orientation of Greek society in the face of imported modernization. The clash between local indigenous structures and state-sponsored Western institutions generated a volatile political and cultural climate that rippled through Greek society for most of the nineteenth and well into the twentieth century. The specific nature of the conflicts varied from place to place because of the fragmented and uneven manifestation of capitalism in the region.

A wave of Greek national concerns washed through the region that included Ottoman Symi at the start of the twentieth century. A number of urgent questions confronted intellectuals, including the place of Byzantine Orthodox heritage in a nation priding itself on the prestigious secular origins of ancient Greece and the place of the vernacular in a state modeling itself after the West. They also had to consider whether to discard local custom in order to imitate Western mores and how to regard the cultural significance of the traditional community in a modern nation-state. These questions were played out dramatically in the Dodecanese Islands, where capitalism and ethnic nationalism had begun to intrude. Secular humanist institutions, such as literary societies and libraries, were spreading, posing a fundamental challenge to church authority. Greek modernity also pervaded these Ottoman provinces in the form of a state-sponsored nationalism, which used primary education as an apparatus to socialize subjects into the nation. The secular curriculum of these schools also posed a challenge to ecclesiastical authority. Furthermore, the aggressive encroachment of capital was incorporating the islands into world markets, assaulting the largely egalitarian social structure of local societies. All in all, the new, imported social order was posing a fundamental challenge to localities that once had organized themselves on the basis of faith and custom. "Winter Dream" intervened in this struggle between modernity and tradition to regulate the direction of cultural change in the area. It opposed the intrusion of capitalism, seeing in it a major threat to the moral fabric of the ethnoreligious, premodern community.[2]

The linguistic register of the poem and the purposes for which it was written testify to the dense, cross-cultural circulation of ideas and practices in the region. "Winter Dream" was composed in katharevousa, a consciously archaizing and somewhat artificially constructed variety of Greek based in part on the Greek vernacular but "purified" of foreign loan words and "enriched" with material (both grammatical and lexical) from the ancient Greek language. This was the language officially sponsored by the Greek state at the time, and its use here reveals overwhelming reach of the state in these parts of the Ottoman Greek Orthodox world.[3] By using the language of the educational apparatus, the poet, a school principal, was participating in the project of Greek modernity: to inculcate national consciousness among generations of Greek-speaking Ottoman subjects. But insofar as the poet was aiming to enlist wider audiences in his anticapitalist cause through a high linguistic register, his politics reflected the paradox of purism. As Gregory Jusdanis (1991) notes, "The elevation of extremely formal and ornate writing as the national verse seems to have contradicted purism's pedagogical project" (69-70).[4] Furthermore, the poet's reliance on a popular aesthetic—the poetic form of rhymed fifteen-syllable meter—and the simultaneous use of a high linguistic register testifies to the era's "linguistic and literary anarchy" that fed "an eclecticism unrivaled in Greek history" (76).

More important for my discussion here is the poet's use of poetry for the purpose of bringing about cultural change. This action aligned him with social practices in Greek society at the time, when literature was put at the service of "the ideological battles of the day" (112). Unlike the aesthetic understanding of literature, in which a novel or a poem is evaluated for its literary merits alone, literature in Greece, as Jusdanis argues, functioned as a venue for writers and critics to promote their own version of national identity. Literature here becomes an integral part of a specific political project. In this vein, the school principal turned to poetry as a forum to advance his biting critique of capitalism and to offer his own political vision for the island.

Already implicated in Greek modernity, the poet sought to shape the identity of the region. "Winter Dream" advocated the legal abolition of the deep-sea diving suit by the Ottoman authorities and favored a return to naked diving, the traditional technique for sponge harvesting. This demand for a return to a simpler technology was accompanied by a plea for the reinstatement of the precapitalist order. In the poem, Symi functions as a personified female narrator under duress. She laments the destruction of the island's social, moral, and economic fabric, as she praises its customary ethos as an egalitarian universe that ensures the common good:

> I have professors, doctors, drugs,
>   and pharmacists who make them,
> a library and schools and girls
>   in girl-schools with their teachers.
> So all poor parents educate their children without cost,

and can be healed back from disease,
medicine being free.
I'm grateful to my offspring, I,
    their mother and their country,
who treat each other with such grace.

(Metrophanes Kalafatas, quoted in Kalafatas 2003, 235–36)

The poet endows Symi with a voice that lavishly praises the island's past as a self-sufficient, virtuous community rooted in an ethic of public welfare. It juxtaposes this past with the Westernized present of the 1900s to create a sharp opposition between the two. The island—construed as homeland—is praised for its natural beauty, morality, customs, and Orthodox heritage. It is recalled as an authentic past defined by egalitarian social relations, harmonious collaboration, philanthropy, and an ethic of compassion and care.[5] In contrast, the poem posits unregulated Western modernization as a grave threat to the entire fabric of the pre-Western community. Capitalism feeds individualism and greed, which assault the egalitarian core of village social structure and corrupt local morality. It destroys the relatively egalitarian sponge-diving guilds. It leads to irreverence toward tradition. By framing modernization in this manner, the poet launches a politics of nostalgia centered on a critique of capitalism and Western modernity.[6]

But the poem moves beyond a mere critique of capitalism: it prescribes a two-step mode of political action. First, it surveys the devastating impact of Westernization on the local community, which exalts the values of the folk, and then juxtaposes their ethos with an externally imposed disruption of their community's fabric. In this manner, it designates the locality's inhabitants as the guardians of its moral principles. This populist agenda sanctions the will to return to the order of the past but also works as a mechanism of social control. In recalling memories of a historical precedent in which a violent grassroots popular uprising failed to ban the deep-sea diving suit, the poem works as a programmatic statement of the conditions under which the community must address the crisis. It raises and answers the question of who will mediate, and on what terms, the return to the ideal community. The intellectuals are appointed to negotiate local matters with powerful outside political forces. To this effect, the poem commemorates a leftist intellectual, Lithuanian-born Karl Vasilievich Flegel, who took up residence on the island of Kalymnos in 1892 and dedicated his life to international activism on behalf of the divers' cause. It praises Flegel as a local hero, recognizing him as a "masterful benefactor":

Blessed more than once he reached our shores,
studied and learned our torments. And was so moved by the machine's criminal
miserable results, he undertook himself the task
to practice good and undo harm.

(41)

By making Mother Symi the speaking subject, "Winter Dream" works rhetorically to legitimize the poet's politics. It is the patridha, which possesses moral authority, that prescribes the conditions for a return to the precapitalist local ethos. The voice of the homeland—the logos of the topos, to draw upon Artemis Leontis (1995)—entreats a return to the past that endows the place with its traditional identity. By sanctioning *political* forms of intervention, the poem charts the future of the place in modernity. Localities must rely on intellectuals and political activists who operate within, not outside, the power structures of transnational capitalism. In the turbulent contact zones that resulted from the collision of capitalism and local structures of meaning, the poem functions as placed literature that seeks, via an antimodernist discourse on roots and authenticity, to return to an idealized past. In modernity, as David Lowenthal (1985) and others have pointed out, nostalgia springs up in response to alienation and the apocalyptic sense of an imminent loss of tradition. Nostalgia compensates for the profound disruption of customary practices and community life. A powerful myth in industrial society attaches currency to an idealized notion of a tightly knit and humanly satisfying community of the past, though in reality the village community is often plagued by factionalism, oppression of women, and ostracism of those who fail to conform to social norms.

Rerouting Political Activism I: Equality and Labor Struggle

On its first transnational route, "Winter Dream" was once again deployed on behalf of the ancestral homeland. Privately published in the original Greek by the immigrant sons of the poet in 1919, the poem was seen as a tool in the service of diaspora politics that advocated the union of the Dodecanese Islands with Greece. Specifically, it was presented as an ethnographic document intended to influence public opinion regarding the political struggles between Greece and Italy and to tilt the balance in favor of the former. Its stated purpose was "to acquaint the public with the [Greek] life and customs of our island," now "that the name of Dodecanese is universally known for its freedom fight against the Italians," and to serve "as eternal memorial to its composer's soul" (quoted in

Kalafatas 2003, 191). The paradox of the universal appeal expressed in a national language aside, the publication of "Winter Dream" under these conditions exemplifies the view of literature as an indispensable component in political struggles, this time on behalf of Greek national causes. The poem steadfastly continued its function as placed literature, this time serving the interests of the Dodecanesian diaspora that sought to inscribe the region within the nation.[7]

The poem's uses multiplied in transnational circulation. In addition to functioning as a nationalist tool, it nurtured the political imagination of the poet's sons, driving family continuity in the diaspora. It becomes difficult to establish *directly* the poem's function as an intergenerational pledge to political ideals; the author's commentary in this regard is sparse. But a certain political sensibility links the poet and his sons, one glimpsed through Michael Kalafatas's (2003) confessional reminiscence of growing up in a family preoccupied with the political: "When I was a child, my father never told me children's stories; instead he would tell me stories from Greek political history. . . . I learned the word 'plebiscite' at age seven. I was the only child at my elementary school who knew the word" (190n). The author's socialization into the world and words of politics stands for more than an instance of political education in a family setting. In a wider narrative context, it represents the intergenerational transmission of a specific mode of political consciousness that centers on combating social injustice. Tracing it to what the author defines as the leftist politics of the poet, Michael Kalafatas values this kind of consciousness as a family inheritance and an intergenerational link. Though marginalized in the text—often relegated to footnotes—the commentary on the political activism of Nikitas Kalafatas, the author's father, is important because it provides valuable insights into how a political ethos travels and is practiced in diaspora.

A graduate of the naval engineering college in Greece, Nikitas Kalafatas nurtured a class consciousness that resonated with the anticapitalist politics of "Winter Dream." Below, I provide selected key narrative passages that outline a partial political portrait of a multifaceted and politically engaged individual:

> My grandfather's left-wing politics, and my father's left-wing politics. They were all part of a certain tradition of progressive Dodecanese politics, whether homegrown or not. (43)

> My father survived, but he would never forget his ties to the Dodecanese or his love and hope for the common people. In the late 1920s, he served as president of the Greek Educational League in Chicago, an organization that appeared on the Attorney General's list

of Communist-front organizations. . . . My father spoke on the same platform with William Z. Foster and Earl Browder, presidents of the American Communist party; and in 1927 he led the Greek contingent, when ethnic groups and leftists put a hundred thousand people on the streets to march on behalf of Sacco and Vanzetti.

A love for social justice was handed down from the poet Metrophanes to his son Nikitas; a dream deferred. (135n)

The political import of "Winter Dream" did not exhaust itself as a critique of capitalist encroachment in a specific region. Its vision of an egalitarian society nurtured the political imagination of the poet's immigrant son, who took a position against the profound injustices inflicted upon immigrant laborers and native-born workers by turn-of-the-century industrial capitalism in America. Writing about what arguably may be labeled the darkest era for immigrants from southeastern Europe, social historian Matthew Frye Jacobson effectively captures the torturous "superexploitation of nonwhites and immigrants" (2000, 72). "The overall response to immigrant labor in the United States," he writes,

> was fiercely double-edged: if immigration made possible the emergence of the United States as a major—ultimately *the* major—industrial power, so did "the immigrant," as a charged cultural icon, come to symbolize the ugliest features of corporate capitalism amid rapid industrialization—its exploitative wages, its inhuman hours, its physical dangers, its degradations—and ironically, so did the immigrant become a scapegoat for those very excesses of capital. (72–73)

Widespread exploitative practices in hiring, supervising, compensating, and housing workers were coupled with racial denigration. "Though foreign workers in some real sense actually *constituted* 'American labor,' they were despised, repulsed, and plotted against politically by congeries of organized groups who recognized the name as applying only to themselves, not to this invasion of degraded foreigners" (87).

Confronted by the abuses of industrial capitalism, the poet's son, Nikitas, translated the anticapitalist critique of "Winter Dream" into political activism on behalf of the working poor and the racially despised. Siding with the communist Left in the 1920s was a defiant posture, one that testified to the new immigrant's uncompromising commitment to the ideals of class and racial equality.[8] Such political activism engendered social and political risks. In the aftermath of the Palmer Raids, when state-sponsored witch hunts relentlessly persecuted and summarily deported suspected radicals, the Communist Party remained underground through most of the 1920s, coalescing again only in the later years of that decade (Karpozilos 2004).[9]

The leftist political vision of an egalitarian society and its principles of working-class unity and interracial solidarity must have provided an attractive forum to develop the social ideals expounded in "Winter Dream." After the decline of the anarcho-leftist Industrial Workers of the World, which had pioneered a "multi-national, multiracial unionism" and therefore had approximated most closely the Marxist ideals of interracial solidarity (Roediger 2005, 83), the newly founded Communist Party in America (1919) provided the best alternative for immigrant political activism free of racial bias.[10] The Communist Party sought to transcend racial differences in the name of working-class solidarity. This approach stood in contrast to that of the powerful American Federation of Labor—tainted with a long history of racism and exclusion of immigrants—and that of the Socialist Party, which "as a whole never did entirely abandon a nativist rhetoric and logic" (Jacobson 2000, 87). "[T]he dream of American equality came true to the Left Wing," Theodore Draper (1957) points out, "where they were received without prejudice and given a means of political expression" (34).

Did the risk-laden activism of the poet's son in radical politics provide a forum for the culturally constituted performance of competitive excellence? Did labor struggle furnish the context wherein the new immigrant could not only articulate his class consciousness but also perform the poetics of manhood in America? This is a tempting hypothesis because the immigrants' commitment to radical politics was associated with surplus social value. Labor leaders, for example, praised the militancy and "the heroism of new immigrants" as a manly outperformance of native-born unionists and, in the context of Louisiana labor politics, as an honorable act that "put southern whites to shame" (Roediger 2005, 85). Similarly, participation in the broad international coalition that lobbied the American government on behalf of Nicola Sacco and Bartolomeo Vanzetti, two Italian radical immigrants arrested for the 1919 and 1920 bombings on Wall Street and executed in 1927, carried heavy risks. As Michael Miller Topp (1996, 140) notes, the "deaths [of Sacco and Vanzetti] showed . . . how dangerous how life-threatening it had become to be an immigrant radical in the United States." Did direct confrontation with the forces that crucified justice, to paraphrase Roberta Feuerlicht (1977), provide Nikitas Kalafatas with a political stage on which to perform his poetics of manhood, to steal an hour from death?[11]

The narrative in *The Bellstone* offers no definitive answer. But one conclusion seems inescapable. Advocating immigrant isotimia (in the form of egalitarian

industrial unionism) the communist Left could accommodate the culturally specific agonistic ethos of male honor, providing a space for class and ethnic identity to coexist, not to exclude each other. In this respect, "Winter Dream" was
reconfigured as placed literature vis-à-vis the host society. Its ecumenicity—as
a critique of capitalism—and its particularity—as a culturally embedded ethos
of isotimia—converged, seeking to influence the political direction of what was
to become the immigrant's new home. In this transnational route, the poem's
universal vision of equality grew roots, albeit tenuous ones, in American political modernity.

Bringing the past into the present through the egalitarian ethos of "Winter
Dream" resulted in a double exile for Nikitas Kalafatas. He was ostracized from
full national belonging and must have been banished from whiteness as well. As
a foreigner who was politically active in redressing the appalling injustices associated with industrial capitalism, he was scapegoated and conveniently placed
outside the boundaries of proper Americanism. As Jacobson (2000) writes,
"Throughout this period, defining radicalism as inherently 'un-American' and
pinning it exclusively on foreigners became the common sleight of hand by
which Americans disowned the social conditions that capitalism had spawned
and which radicalism was meant to address" (90). At the same time, expulsion
from the nation meant nonwhiteness. As early as 1919, and in response to growing radicalism, the state introduced the War Plans White Initiative, a contingency
plan designed to neutralize anticipated African American and new immigrant
insurrections (Roediger 2005, 143). The name of the plan aptly suggests the
historical conflation of radicalism and nonwhiteness, a connection that also extended to Native American resistance to colonization and later immigrant labor
unrest. This racialization served as a state strategy to suppress immigrant resistance to capitalist abuses. In Minnesota, for example, "where immigrant miners
lived near Indians, the charge that Finnish labor radicals culturally resembled
and consorted with the 'countless savages bent on slaughter, rapine and plun-
der' circulated freely" (63–64). Contrasting the "red Finns" (a term punning on
both leftist political orientation and a comparison to Indians) with "the churchly
'white Finns'" (64), licensed savage police repression. Political radicalism, in this
context, meant exile from whiteness.

Rerouting Political Activism II: State Oppression as "A Heritage of Fear"

The state-sponsored political persecution that was inflicted upon reform-minded
immigrants lingered well beyond the 1920s and was revived as generalized
ethnic surveillance when the United States entered World War II in December

1941. Treating most European ethnic groups from Nazi-occupied countries as a political risk, the Roosevelt administration launched a program to monitor these national minorities under the auspices of the infamous Office of Strategic Services (OSS), the predecessor of the CIA. War-related developments presented a new dynamic for Greek America. On the one hand, the glorification of Greece's valiant resistance to Mussolini by the American press generated intense ethnic pride. On the other hand, Greek America's precarious position as an American ethnic minority necessitated conspicuous public acts of political allegiance to the state.[12] Peter Zervakis (1998–99) captures this tension when he writes, "Greek-Americans, who got used to being spied on by their American neighbors, colleagues, and close friends, tried passionately to demonstrate that their commitment to America did not suffer because of their Greek ethnic pride" (218). Public allegiance was expressed at the grassroots level when "[t]housands of Greek-Americans joined the U.S. army" and institutionally when the Greek Orthodox church held rogation services for President Roosevelt throughout the country. Mobilized under "the parole 'America comes first,'" AHEPA was allowed to sell war bonds valued half a billion dollars for the U.S.," becoming the only "ethnic organization . . . granted this privilege" (219).

But what about those ethnics who were labeled hostile aliens? The personal reminiscence of college professor Marianthe Karanikas (2001–2) about her family's political oppression between 1942 and 1956 offers a glimpse into the human dramas that marked the experience of leftist-leaning ethnic intellectuals from the era of the OSS well into the era of McCarthy.[13] Bitterly recalling her father's scrutiny by the FBI, a fourteen-year-long investigation that eventually forced the family into hiding, Karanikas documents how labor activism in the past became a haunting reminder of state power in the present. Her brief portrait of her father, scholar Alexander Karanikas, introduces the multifaceted dimensions of his political and cultural activism (see Georgakas 1994). A son of Greek immigrants, college professor, poet, author, prolabor commentator, antifascist activist, and politician who ran for Congress as a Progressive Party candidate in New Hampshire in 1948, Karanikas came under FBI scrutiny when he declared his intention to serve the United States as an officer. His daughter's account (2001–2) relates that during a political witch hunt, patriotism alone cannot deter state intrusion into the lives of political idealists. Referring to the investigation, she writes, "They wanted names, any names, long names, short names, names to chant, to make recant, names to haunt on a dry December night. My father was polite, they noted, and very patriotic. But he laughed when they asked for names. The people he knew from the old days acted with the most noble intentions. And so the file reported that the subject saw no reason to name people who wanted to help the world" (232).

This confessional narrative sheds more light on the unevenness of post–World War II inclusion of politicized Greeks in whiteness. Investigated for "alleged un-American activities," Alexander Karanikas, "held treacherous views such as 'equal rights for Negroes.' Of course he was considered a communist" (232). As John Noakes (2003) argues, the FBI under J. Edgar Hoover "racialized its investigation of subversiveness in the early Cold War period" (728). It linked political and social advocacy for "equal citizenship rights for black Americans" with communist-inspired attempts "to subvert the American way of life" (745). Criticism of American racism at the time was branded un-American, and it represented national outsiderhood in both political and racial terms. Holding the nation accountable for failing to meet its ideals of equality stood for communism and nonwhiteness—because whiteness, at that time, was equivalent to the political and racial status quo. Expanded political surveillance sought to constrain representations of race in institutional powerhouses such as the Hollywood film industry, but it also targeted populations not considered fully American. "While considered generally content, blacks, immigrants, the working class, and other 'unsophisticated' populations were understood as having only a fragile commitment to American values and traditions and therefore as vulnerable to the seductive, if false promises of radicals" (730).

Alexander Karanikas, an activist who would be admired today for his progressive views on race relations, was subjected to multiple layers of exclusion: national, ethnic, and racial. Construed in the manner I outlined above, his politics earned him the stigma of being a traitor, a title pinned on him by "[t]he publisher of the largest newspaper" in his native New Hampshire (Karanikas, 2001–2, 233). The Cold War demonization of political and social progressives not only marked Karanikas as a national outsider but also distanced him from ethnic whiteness by labeling him a communist. At the outset of the Cold War, leftist politics stood at odds with the dominant political (re)orientation of ethnic communities. As labor historian Dan Georgakas (1991) notes, the transnational politics of the period transformed the relationship between secular ethnic organizations and the community on the one hand, and Greek American communists on the other hand. During rubber strikes led by Greek communist organizers in Akron, Ohio, for example, both Greek churches in the town "opened their doors to the strikers and fully supported the union" (107). In contrast, during the Greek Civil War in 1940s, "[a]s all Greek-American organizations not in the CP [Communist Party] orbit enthusiastically supported the [anticommunist]

American policy in Greece, any vocal dissenters faced immediate ostracism from the community" (Georgakas 1994, 23). Political shifts in AHEPA, "the largest and most influential Greek fraternal order" at the time (10), also erected barriers to communist membership. In the 1930s, Greek radicals had cooperated tactically with AHEPA's leadership—mostly New Deal liberals—to project a united front in response to "distress over the Great Depression" (Georgakas 1991, 104) and the fascist ascendancy in Greece. Dropping its militancy in the 1930s, the American Communist Party "abandoned its previous policy of emphasizing class differences in favor of a popular-front approach" (104–5) that aimed not at a revolution "but [at] a trade union movement" (105).

But the adoption of the Truman Doctrine, which officially pledged American political and military support to keep Greece outside the communist orbit, caused "an overwhelming majority of organized Greek-Americans" to distance themselves from Greek communists (Zervakis 1998–99, 236). By shifting their "traditional prewar liberalism to political conservatism, supporting the Greek king and lobbying for Greek national interests as loyal anticommunist Americans in the emerging East-West confrontation" (236), Greek America could reconcile its ethnic interests with political Americanism. In 1947, in a change of membership policy that dramatized these developments, AHEPA "introduce[d] McCarthyism into its own ranks . . . check[ing] all new applicants for membership in their organization for any possible subversive activities. Future members of AHEPA were to be free of any communist background" (ibid.).

Those who refused to realign themselves paid the consequences in racial, class, and national terms. Being branded as un-American and ostracized from middle-class white ethnic respectability underlined a larger expulsion from whiteness. The advocacy of Karanikas's father for racial equality—his "treacherous views such as 'equal rights for Negroes'"—was punished for its failure to conform to whiteness. A family legacy of stigmatization—the author's mother was "[c]onsidered black as a child, [and] a traitor in her youth" (239)—brings about a consciousness of dual displacement from dominant national and racial centers.

The experience that scarred this family will resonate with those Greek Americans whose own family histories are connected with leftist activism. A climate of intimidating surveillance smothered former leftists, as political radical Demosthenes Nicas testified in an interview with Dan Georgakas (1991): "With the advent of McCarthyism in the 1950s, the FBI was at [the Nicas family's] door every week. Neighbors and friends were consistently told they were subversives. Demosthenes Nicas was harassed, blacklisted, and threatened with deportation"

(109). Those who operated outside the boundaries of proper political Ameri-canness shared a historical experience of intimidation. "[My father] returned to Cambridge, Massachusetts," Michael Kalafatas (2003) lets out, "joined General Electric, and built jet engines; and like his father, he fought for social justice, the FBI tap, tap, tapping at our door because of his advocacy of the UE as the union-of-choice at General Electric" (161).

"McCarthyism and the Cold War closed the era of the Communist Left, wiping out not only its memory but the memory of its predecessors" (Georgakas 1994, 28). But it was not merely leftists or socialists who were vigorously persecuted. Any political voice dissenting from American policy toward Greece during and after the Greek Civil War, a bloody conflict between British- and later American-supported government forces and the military branch of the Greek communist party, was silenced. As Georgakas (1987b) observes, "The intensity of federal pressure was partly due to the Greek Civil War and was a kind of preemptive first strike to clear the ground for a compliant pro-NATO Greek America" (67). This juncture of domestic and international politics stifled Greek America's tradition of critical dissent. Scholar L. S. Stavrianos and journalist Constantine Poulos, both of whom openly opposed U.S. policy in Greece, were harassed, denied promotions, and faced systematic opposition from academic and commercial presses to the publication of their work. The ethnic press remained silent in the face of these abuses. "[A]nxious not to be tainted with charges of Communist sympathies, [it] strove to be identified with American foreign policy" (Georga-kas 1987a, 11). Those not blacklisted were expelled. As Steve Frangos (1996) reports, "During the 1950s untold numbers of Greeks were deported. Whether believed to be labor leaders, socialists, communists, or otherwise 'undesirable,' thousands of Greeks were held at Ellis Island before they were sent back to Greece. A number of oversize coffee table books on the history of Ellis Island prominently show graffiti, written in Greek, by these unfortunate individuals" (14). In some respects, these "expressions of protest and pain have become part of the physical heritage of Greeks in the U.S." (ibid.). But whatever traces of memory survived, the political onslaught served as a cautionary tale about the extent to which democracy could accommodate social critique or political radicalism. Even in the late 1980s, when the McCarran-Walter Act was still in effect, scholars were cautious not "to name individuals or organizations cur-rently active in Greek affairs with direct links to the left of the 1940s" (Geor-gakas 1987b, 66). It should come as no surprise then that a trenchant critique of American capitalism was published in the *Journal of the Hellenic Diaspora* only under the protective blanket of anonymity (P. T. and G. A. 1975).[14]

A legacy of horror still haunts the psyche of individuals touched by this dark era of American history. The travails of Marianthe Karanikas's family bequeathed to her a "heritage of fear" (233) that resurfaced when she was warned of local Ku Klux Klan activism while interviewing for a college teaching position in the Ozarks. Personal memories of ethnic persecution in the past unfolded a sense of menace that enveloped her. Her testimony underlines the "primary experience . . . of fear and of vulnerability" that terrorized, through various degrees of violence and intensity, all those who were subjected to political repression and the vicious nationalism of whiteness (Jameson 1988, 70). It gives voice to "the experience of fear in all its radicality, which cuts across class and gender to the point of touching the bourgeois . . . is surely the very 'moment of truth' of ghetto life itself, . . . : the helplessness of the village community before the perpetual and unpredictable imminence of the lynching or the pogrom, the race riot" (ibid.). Burdened by this history of hounding, Marianthe Karanikas found refuge in the imagination, in the desire to exist in a nonlinguistic domain. In order to preclude the possibility of bigotry, she longed for a domain devoid of ethnic labels. Fracturing the alleged comfort of assimilated white ethnics, her narrative renders ethnicity a nonoption. What attributes mark the author as a stranger to rural Arkansas? What profound terror demands an act of self-effacement and the yearning for a postethnic location? The narrative commentary is sparse in this regard. But by foregrounding ethnic vulnerability in some parts of the United States, it provides a context for a provisional nod of recognition to Veras's politics of positive ethnic stereotyping. And it must serve as a powerful reminder that the analysis of white ethnicity must be examined in relation to specific localities, distinct regional contexts, and particular family histories.

Rerouting Political Activism III: Equality and the Antimodernist Yearning

The Bellstone engages with "Winter Dream" on several interpretive levels. Drawing on the work of anthropologist Michael Taussing, Kalafatas discusses the poem politically as a local indictment of capitalism. Not unlike those workers described by Taussing, whose belief system linked capitalism's profit motive with the devil, the poet connects the capitalist reorientation of the sponge industry with imagery of the Adversary. In the poem, capitalists are portrayed as "the devil's legions" (118) and "the new technology [as] 'Satan's Machine' and the 'Tool of the Devil'" (119). For the author of *The Bellstone* and the grandson of the poet, the poem also sustains intergenerational memory of a family's commitment to social justice. In fact, the narrator appoints himself the guardian of his grandfather's vision for social equality, a self-designated "legatee of [family] dreams" (160), whose original political intent was to deliver to society "a dream deferred," the dream of social justice. In this case, a literary text is turned into an intergenerational heritage that connects the poet's anticapitalist politics in the early 1900s with his sons' leftist politics in the 1920s and, in turn, with the author's yearning for equality in 2000. In its travels, "Winter Dream" is redefined as family inheritance rooted in a tradition of generational commitment to speaking up publicly to advocate for equality.

Kalafatas finds sustenance in this vision in yet another poem, this one drawn from the canon of Greek literary modernism. Written by the Nobel laureate George Seferis (1900–1971), the poem "Mythistorema" inspires the legatee of "Winter Dream":

> I woke with this marble head in my hands;
> it exhausts my elbows and I don't know where to put it
> down.
> It was falling into the dream
> as I was coming out of the
> dream
> so our life became one and it will be very difficult for it
> to separate again.
>
> (quoted in Kalafatas 2003, 160)

For Seferis, a poet who was preoccupied with memory, the Greek classical past—metaphorically evoked through the image of a broken statue—constitutes a ponderous burden and an inestimable national heritage that the poetic narrator simply cannot let go. Because it is represented as fragment, the past resists total recovery though forced integration with the present. The desired synthesis becomes possible only in a mythical time, when the boundaries between dream and reality collapse. The poem links the authorial self and the nation, as Martha Klironomos (2002) argues, pointing to the incompleteness and instability of memory and underlining the futility of the effort to fully access the past. At the same time, its modernist poetics effect national continuity through "an integrated vision between past and present" (229) when the poetic persona fuses with the material sign of the classical legacy.

Kalafatas's reading of Seferis dispenses with the aesthetic quest for diachronic national unity to extract, instead, the notion of a family's past as an invaluable political heritage that cannot simply be let go. This interpretation configures "Winter Dream" as a repository of memory that underwrites a political and moral imperative. It requires an individual's determination to act upon historical memory: "Or might dreams unfulfilled in one generation be transmuted through the alchemy of time and family and be left to the next generation; left for a son and a grandson wandering around with a marble head in his hands, trying to find a place to put it down? Left for a grandson to tell a story of children dying in the sea and the need for us all to be outraged at injustice" (Kalafatas 2003, 161). Poetry serves as a resource to link generations to a specific set of duties: the obligation to preserve historical memory through the act of retelling. In the family legacy so construed, memory narratives are invested with the power to constitute a politically active collective. To identify how this kind of body politic can be realized, Kalafatas draws from the reservoir of classical learning. Quoting the Greek historian Thucydides, he writes that it is "left for us to realize . . . that 'Justice will not come to Athens until those who are not injured are as indignant as those who are injured'" (ibid.). What we witness in this instance is an attempt to use classical heritage to amplify a usable past construed out of a family's histories of activism. Memories of the past become usable for Kalafatas only insofar as they sustain the political ethos of countering social injustice.

Kalafatas sees the premodern community as a usable past that charts for the American public a path toward realizing the vision of social equality. Like the professional anthropologist who returns home to share gems of native wisdom with Western audiences, the author as pilgrim-fieldworker views his harvest of ethnographic meaning as a precious gift to his readers. Specifically, he becomes a herald of good news to that sector of the public craving personal enrichment, spiritual renewal, inner peace, and harmony through the teachings of primitive wisdom. To this readership, the ancient technique of breath-holding diving is offered as a moral lesson and a promise. The popular ethnographer associates its practice—chiefly among the sponge divers of the Aegean, but also among Japanese pearl gatherers—as "a method of living" that embodies the virtues of the folk community: piety and social equality. The technique represents an authentic form of life worth rescuing from oblivion and worth circulating as a usable past today. The premodern method of naked diving is extracted as an "ethnographic pastoral" (Clifford 1986b, 110), as a meaningful foundation on which to anchor contemporary morality. The acquisition of the values that it embodies becomes the prerequisite for the moral redemption of contemporary selves. These values offer themselves as the tools necessary to bring about spiritual rebirth and to fulfill the alleged human need to connect with a primordial, authentic self.

Building on evolutionary theories of the aquatic origins of humanity, the author posits the sea as the irresistible primordial home. "The sea draws us still; it is the beckoning mother," he writes. "We want to return from whence we came. And some of us do" (96). As the origin of humanity, the "Mother Sea" represents a place of harmony and peace, an unspoiled refuge from urban cacophony and environmental degradation. Kalafatas draws from the experience of individuals, such as California-based oral surgeon Terry Maas, who still practice breath-holding diving: "In quiet cadences—almost religious in tone—Maas speaks of leaving behind the noise, intensity, and smog of Southern California and slipping below the surface into a watery world literally unchanged over thousands of years. He descends noiselessly, patiently waiting for curious 'fellow fish' to come to him" (103).

But communion with the Mother Sea and blissful interspecies coexistence are not readily accessible. They come at a cost, demanding moral and spiritual cleansing. The folk past here serves as a prescriptive compass for achieving spiritual harmony. The "nobility and serenity" (115) of the naked divers and the values they purportedly embody—goodness, faith, and humility—are offered as a model for contemporary life. Following these moral guidelines guarantees access to authentic experience. Drawing from psychologist Carl Jung, for whom "water is our unconscious—our feminine side, the deep that lies beneath us all" (ibid.), the author posits the sea as the metaphorical destiny where humanity is able to come face to face with its primordial self. The following two passages unequivocally advance the author's evangelical message for humanity:

> In the end breath-hold diving is a kind of art form, requiring the diver to be in a meditative state, alert and utterly relaxed, when returning to Mother Sea. Jacques Mayol used yoga and the naked diver his piety to attain that state. Piety put the naked diver in right relationship with his God, with his *syndrophi,* his comrades, and with Mother Sea. . . . "What does God require of us?" Micah asks, but "to do justly, to love tenderly, and to walk humbly with one's God." (114–15)

* * *

> What resonates about this story for all, Greek and non-Greek, is not only the primordial wish to return to the sea, to our watery birth, but the wish we all have to return to ourselves, to the watery deep of our unconscious, and to know the gifts kept there for us. We wish to return to the first technique. (115)

Herein lies the meaning promised at the pilgrim's destination. Acting as a quasi-religious figure, the pilgrim-anthropologist delivers the redemptive message: the moral life of the premodern folk provides the compass for contemporary spiritual life. As the "first technique" guided the naked diver "through life's uncertain journey," a return to it promises to anchor the Western self to its primordial authenticity (ibid.). Reflective anthropologists have not missed the religious overtones of this sort of ethnographic claim. "Fieldwork . . . takes on the aura of a religious pilgrimage; . . . The returning anthropologist is often regarded, and may regard herself, as having gained charisma—and, like a prophetic figure, as having the right, with or without furnishing empirical evidence, to proffer new behavioral commandments" (di Leonardo 1998, 31).

By establishing the primitive as the venue for redemption, Kalafatas joins an enduring thread of bourgeois thought in the West, ethnological antimodernism. In this mode of thinking, the idealized folk community and its overarching symbol, the "noble savage," posit both a superior alternative to corrupt modernity and a resource for grappling with the social and psychological malaise of modernity. Reflecting on contemporary fascination with the tribal and the exotic in American society, anthropologist Michaela di Leonardo (1998) poignantly adds a historical dimension to ethnological antimodernism. The current fixation on "escap[ing] from the contemporary West through refuge in the 'timeless' exotic, evokes as well earlier elites' widespread sense of inauthenticity, futility, 'experiencing life at a remove'" (2). She goes on to identify the significance of ethnological antimodernism in contemporary debates about racism, the women's movement, and the environmental crisis, pointing to its centrality to "the American 'crisis of meaning,' including the role of religion and irrational experience in a secular, rationalist state, and concern over social inequality" (32). Cultural critic Seng-mei Ma (2000) reinforces the function of this brand of antimodernism in advanced capitalism. As individuals become increasingly alienated, she observes, "the 'Western' self feels drained, in need of recharging or healing in a spiritual sense, for which purpose the 'primitive' Third World cultures are deployed" (112).

What is more, according to David Lowenthal (1989), "[i]n America, 'ecological' and egalitarian principles sanctify left-wing nostalgia" (28). *The Bellstone,* then, inscribes a heritage of leftist politics in the nostalgic discourse of antimodernism. It exhibits remarkable affinities with New Age spirituality, one of the cultural pillars of ethnological antimodernism. Like its New Age counterparts, it borrows from a wealth of disparate cultural traditions, mixing diverse elements to convey a message about spiritual healing. Sources from religion and science, psychology and spirituality, anthropology and vernacular culture are cited and absorbed to serve narrative aims. The reader will note Christian teachings, both Catholic and Greek Orthodox, as well as biological explanations of origins as components of this eclectic pastiche. The metaphysical notions of a cyclical return to primordial origin coexist with Christian temporal linearity, promising a future egalitarian society. The politics of environmental activism is expressed side by side with the thirst for self-gratification. Liberal multicultural-ism, with its preoccupation with ethnic roots and ancestry, accommodates, as I will show below, universal calls for human redemption. In fact, the notion of Mother Sea reinscribes a commonplace topos of New Age literature, the im-portance of native wisdom to reconnect with Mother Earth, and in doing so, it reproduces its distaste for the modern. Consider, for example, the astonishing similarity of Michael Kalafatas's underlying message to that of Lynn Andrews, a popular New Age spiritualist. The former certainly echoes the latter, who adds a racialized hue to the narrative of personal redemption. "My work has to do with becoming a bridge between the primal mind and white consciousness," she writes. "[W]e as a people . . . have lost our sense of Mother Earth and Nature" (quoted in di Leonardo 1998, 37).[15]

The Bellstone also reproduces the principal assumptions of early folklore scholarship. This kind of folklore sought to document preindustrial remnants of authentic folk life in isolated rural pockets; its practitioners regarded industrial-ization as a major rupture between peasants and their presumably authentic links with nature. As Richard Dorson (1978a) notes, "In the older theory of folklore, Mother Earth and the peasant and pastoral life cradled the seasonal rituals and traditional culture that folklorists studied, not only in oral but also in physical forms" (32).

In its all-absorbing capacity to create a pastiche of multiple cultural sources, The Bellstone does not fail to tap into the Western hegemonic discourse that posits Hellenism as the origin of Western civilization. Under the rubric of its New Age sensibility, the quest for ethnic (Greek) roots, the making of national (American) identity, and ancient Hellas as the topos of Western origins are all conflated into a single primordial human urge for a return to its alleged aquatic origins. "Like salmon—perhaps like us all—the Greeks try furiously to swim their way back to origin. Perhaps Greeks and Americans are more spirit-twins than we think. The last lines of The Great Gatsby speak of time and of the watery journey of our collective unconscious: 'So we beat on, boats against the current, borne back ceaselessly into the past'" (160, emphasis added). The Mother Sea exercises its pull irrespective of nationality. Unavoidably, the particular is turned into the univer-sal, as all humanity is thought to direct itself toward a collective unconscious. This ecumenicity allows the author's ideas to transcend cultural differences and enables the author to return to a common topos in Greek American discourse, the identity of American and Greek origins, this time located in the primordial past. But the interchangeability of national (American) and ethnic (Greek) identity compromises the social distinction that springs from the possession of golden ancestral origins. Not prepared to concede his prestigious pedigree, Kalafatas revisits the issue in the epilogue of the book and conjures a way out of this quandary. The solution lies in an ecumenical particularism expressed in a series of crucial passages, beginning with the extension of acknowledgments to a host of beloved friends:

> These four men of Dodecanese origin love sponges: the touch of sponges, the feel of sponges, the fetching of sponges, the smell of the sea in sponges, the aroma of Sponge Rooms filled to the rafters with sponges, the scent in heir nostrils and on their clothes, the scent of Mother Sea all around them, the scent of origin. That scent has borne them back ceaselessly into their Hellenic past—across the seaways, back beyond Byzantium, back to the forty-seven ships the Dodecanese sent to Troy. It has brought them to Eleni, to Helen, to the face that launched a thousand ships. It has brought them face-to-face with Sweet Mother Greece. (285–86)

The universal place of human redemption, Mother Sea, is ethnicized; it becomes Hellenic. Sweet Mother Greece stands for a diachronic transcendental topos where Greeks and non-Greeks, mariners and nonmariners are bound to return for spiritual nourishment. The New Age discourse spiritualizes Western Hellenism. Following up on the previous thought, the author appreciatively and suggestively cites commonplace references linking secular Western Hellenism with the notion of ancient Greece as civilizational origin: "Walter Jaeger wrote, 'We must always return to Greece because it fulfills some needs of our own life . . . . Other nations made gods, kings, spirits. The Greeks alone made men.' In the end we all return to Greece, and easily so because, as Shelley said in his *Preface to Hellas* in 1821: 'We are all Greek'" (286).

The author appropriates this discourse to produce what I call "New Age Hellenism." By conflating the spiritual with the cultural, New Age Hellenism poses as the Occidental counterpart to what critic Sheng-mei Ma calls "'an alternative' Orientalism or New Age ethnicity" (2000, 111). Ma identifies this discourse in the fiction of Amy Tan, claiming that the novelist's "ethnicizing the primitive contributes significantly to her success among white, middle-class, 'mainstream' readers living in the climate of New Age" (113). Similarly, *The Bellstone*'s ethnological antimodernism explains its broad, popular appeal and commercial success. As reported by journalist Zoe Tsine (2004), the author's own account illuminates this point: "[The author] said that despite its Greek storyline, the book's underlying message has resonated unexpectedly with his non-Greek readers. 'The subtitle, *One American's Journey Home* is the part all Americans are connected to because all Americans have a deep profound longing for a lost past,' he told the Herald newspaper." The book resonates with a nonethnic readership precisely because it taps into a deeply embedded disposition within the space of American whiteness. Its emphasis on authentic origins buried in a primordial human past aligns it with historical "narratives of modern American selfhood [that] always, finally, hook into some notion of *Ur*-human nature based on a vision of primitive/past life" (di Leonardo 1998, 32).

Gendered Routes of Nostalgia

Before I discuss the implications of the poem's routes for symbolic ethnicity, I must pause and address yet one more way in which "Winter Dream" is resignified in its circulation in *The Bellstone,* almost a century after its initial composition—the way nostalgia for the premodern represents a vested collectivity, such as women. A gender politics is inextricably attached to the original poem in that the object of the poem's nostalgia, patridha's customary ethos, is profoundly patriarchal. In a fascinating historical exploration of the social universe of Ottoman Greek Orthodox "traditional communities," Gerasimos Augustinos (1992) illuminates the power of male elders to discipline women's public conduct. One such set of regulations, drawn up by community leaders in the town of Sinasos, shows how the welfare of patridha was intimately connected with gender-specific prohibitions: "Women are to refrain from wearing excessive amounts of gold jewelry and clothes of bright colors" (51). "Women are forbidden to go to the fort" (52). "Women are not to sit on the front stoop in the evening" (ibid.). Not unlike the immigrant patriarch who sought to confine his daughters within the home (see chapter 3), male elders in the patridha appeared determined to circumscribe the boundaries of women's public presence for the sake of moral order. One could anticipate here a harsh critique of the poet's nostalgia from the women whose anguished voices Constance Callinicos brought forth to public attention.

Although *The Bellstone* reproduces the longing of "Winter Dream" for a premodern past, it departs significantly from the poem's original politics of nostalgia. This rupture can be explained through the cultural work of the ironic streak that runs throughout *The Bellstone*. It can be said that in his longing for the patriarchal past, while at the same time undercutting it and rewriting it as nonpatriarchal, Michael Kalafatas works with a nostalgia of "an ironized order," as Linda Hutcheon puts it (1998, 8). "From a postmodern point of view," she writes, "the knowingness of this kind of irony may be not so much a defense against the power of nostalgia as the way in which nostalgia is made palatable today: invoked but, at the same time, undercut, put into perspective, seen for exactly what it is—a comment on the present as much as on the past" (ibid.).

If the poet's desire to return to the past seems unburdened, as I have already pointed out, by a concern with gender-specific forms of domination, this is not so for the poet's grandson, the author of *The Bellstone*. Michael Kalafatas's account represents women as social agents, not as passive spectators. In fact, it seeks to reconfigure how his readership, including Greek Americans, imagines gender in the Greek context. An intertextual reference to the documentary *The Greek Americans* points to ethnic discomfort with traditional gender roles—a discomfort, that is, with an Orientalist stereotype—to expand the way in which womanhood is imagined in Greek society.

> In 1999 the Public Broadcasting System in the United States produced a television special on the Greek-Americans, showing highly accomplished, second-generation, Greek-American men and women nervously chuckling over the power of the *nikokyra,* the woman of the house, in the old-country households in which they were raised. Normally it is an interior power—found within the confines of the home—but periodically it surges into the public spaces, as happened in the Dodecanese. (62)

The popular ethnographer acknowledges what Ernestine Friedl (1986, 42) has identified in Greek rural society as the male "appearance of prestige" and "the realities of power" and then moves on to challenge international stereotypes of Greek gender relations. If "[o]utside of Greece, Greek women are perceived as traditional and deferential to the men," his account casts womanhood in terms of heroic defiance, expressive sexuality, emotive power, and political engagement. In the hierarchical vein discussed in the previous chapter, the author draws from Edmund Keely's *Inventing Paradise* to portray Greek women as "less inhibited than most Anglo-Saxon women in expressing emotions, 'sexual and otherwise'" (62). It is beyond the scope of this discussion to elaborate on the implications of a Greek American male ethnographic narrative that normalizes women as national types and rewrites the image of the domestic nikokyra in terms of ethnically superior sensuality. I would like to bring into focus, however, the appropriation of the image of heroic womanhood by the discourse of ethnological antimodernism. Kalafatas writes, characteristically, "From the deep past, almost as Jungian archetype, flowed empowering stories of the *andreiomeni:*

the female warrior of Greek folk song and legend" (63). Popular ethnography absorbs scholarly knowledge for its own purposes, in this case explicitly from the work of Elizabeth Constantinides (1983). It simultaneously yearns for a past that restricted women and assigns agency to the women of the past. Herein lies its ironic dimension. We witness here a gendered politics of nostalgia that underwrites a primordial poetics of womanhood parallel with but independent of the poetics of manhood that serves as the ethnographic narrative center.

Roots and Routes of Nostalgia

This chapter maps the routes of a poem across space and through time to illustrate how history and power shape the making of usable pasts in the present. Framed in this manner, the travels of "Winter Dream" help identify continuities and discontinuities between the immigrant past and the ethnic present. And situating this literary artifact in specific contexts illustrates how the meaning of ethnicity is *determined* by social discourse at any given historical moment.

Initially composed in reaction to a socioeconomic crisis, the poem resisted the emerging hegemony of capitalist structures, indicting modernization as detrimental to the social ethos of the (idealized) premodern Greek Orthodox community. A virulent cultural critique, "Winter Dream" posited the traditional *patridha* as foundational truth in order to legitimize its advocacy for a return to an autochthonous ethnoreligious order. It was the discourse of antimodernism—circulated widely at that time across the Greek-speaking world—that legitimized its resistance against modernity. By participating in the cultural struggle over the place of the traditional past in modernity, the poem made allowance for some degree of secular humanism and incorporation of modernity into a locality. It envisioned a tightly regulated community selectively participating in modernity and controlling social change through the intermediation of intellectuals. And by advocating poetry as a necessary component of an intellectual's political activism, the poem itself became interwoven with social and political struggles. In the fin-de-siècle Dodecanese, "Winter Dream" functioned as a literary text to political ends.

In one of its migratory routes in the 1920s, the poem was infused with a new political purpose. This time, it was the discourse of ethnic nationalism that effected its reproduction and circulation as a public document in the diaspora. A placed literature initially establishing cultural autochthony, the poem was put into the service of a political movement, nationalism, which posits the identity of place and ethnicity to legitimize its territorial claims. In arguing the case for the Hellenicity of the island, the poem was made to function as a sign of national truth. In the Greek diaspora, art continued to be an integral tool in political struggles, this time serving claims of a region's incorporation into the nation.

The complex vicissitudes of the poem's travels within Greek America are interrupted by textual silences; many questions about the poem as a means for political education remain unanswered in *The Bellstone*. Still, a specific route can be identified with certainty. The message of "Winter Dream" against the injustices of capitalism resonated with leftist politics in the diaspora as practiced by the poet's son. Although the specific manner in which the poem was deployed in modern class struggles remains unclear, there is no doubt that it contributed to a family's political heritage of opposing structures of exploitation. Appropriated by leftist immigrant politics in the diaspora, the placed literature was disassociated from its geographic particularity and assigned a new, universal significance. In this new function, it promoted a version of working-class Americanism that fought against the interests of unbridled capitalism.

The charting of the poem's routes also helps trace yet another contour of white ethnicity, that is, how a brand of ethnic political activism was persecuted by state power. If political radicalism had been the target of the state apparatus in the 1920s, it was haunted by the specter of McCarthyism during the Cold War. State power persecuted not only political radicalism but also the progressive politics of ethnics who opposed racial inequalities, and, by implication, the privileges of whiteness. In this historical struggle, the state demonstrated its effectiveness in realigning ethnic communities with dominant political ideology.

Attending to the routes of the poem illuminates a violent process of ethnic depoliticization, a historical domination driven by state power that crushed ethnic political advocacy on behalf of the disfranchised. From this vantage point, what today seem to be innocuous options for symbolic ethnicity are in fact embedded in tumultuous historical struggles over the terms by which ethnics could be admitted into the nation. Because symbolic ethnicity does not take into account how history and discourse constitute the meaning of ethnicity, it is in no position to explain why certain ethnic options have been accorded public approbation while others have become marginalized or simply nonoptions in the terrain of white ethnicity. Why is there no *political movement* advocating social justice for the poor under the banner of European ethnicities? Why is such an activism not available as an ethnic option? Why does it escape the collective ethnic imagination? Symbolic ethnicity cannot answer these questions because it fails to engage with ethnicity as a historical process of cultural production. But it is precisely the brutal disruption and termination of ethnically inflected political activism for social justice that explains its present public invisibility. Ethnicity as a practice to ameliorate poverty has been channeled into a civic ethos promoting community-based or individually initiated compassion, charity, and philanthropy. Such practices constitute part of the dominant social ethos into which ethnicity was called to assimilate. But no direct demands are made in the name of ethnicity for the state to raise the minimum wage or to promote policies friendly to the working class. The denial of this option is the political price paid for a profound historical compromise. As Jusdanis observes, white ethnics "may parade [their identities] in ethnic festivals [but] must keep them[selves] out of politics" in "exchange for their admittance into the civic public sphere" (2001, 170). They buttress the ideology of America as a culturally inclusive democracy by refraining from confronting inequality and exclusion.

Thus the question whether an ethnic subject should envision the actualization of social justice through the discourse of primitivism or through ethnically marked leftist political activism cannot seriously be posited as an exercise of ethnic options. As competing narratives of social transformation, the former enjoys hegemonic ascendancy, while the latter is delegitimized in the face of its historical defeat. In this regard, *The Bellstone* consents to the hegemony of the postmodern aesthetics of the self—in fact, it assimilates itself to this discourse. Constituting yet another route for "Winter Dream," the popular ethnography brings it before a national audience under conditions of postmodernity. It renders "Winter Dream" the object of the discourses of primitivism, New Age spirituality, and ethnicity as roots, positing the premodern past as a redemptive source of social renewal through personal transformation. By routing the poem through the discursive terrain of postmodernity, the popular ethnography establishes a number of continuities between itself and the heritage artifact that it recirculates. In raising a fervent outcry against environmental deterioration, the disintegration of the social fabric, and dramatic, market-produced class inequalities, it opposes the same forces that "Winter Dream" sought to stem in the first place. Furthermore, both the original poem and its contemporary interpretation are supported by the discourse of antimodernism. They yearn for an identical precapitalist past, which they construe as moral, egalitarian, and just. And in each text, the author attributes to poetry the power to direct social change: to oppose socioeconomic fragmentation and to instill a sense of consensus in achieving social justice.

Yet the poet and the popular ethnographer differ in how they view art as an instrument of change. The former saw poetry as an indispensable tool in the political struggles for social change; he saw art as an integral component in directing public opinion to consent to the authority of intellectuals as the prime movers of social transformation through negotiation with political power. But for the popular ethnographer, literature strives toward an aesthetic transformation removed from politics. "[P]oetry cleanses" (278), the ethnographer writes, placing his faith in literature as an instrument for individual moral uplift. To bring to fruition "the dream for social justice," he endorses private action as *the* locus for change, at the expense of political activism. In this phase of its historical travels, "Winter Dream" is *placed* in relation to dominant discourses that privilege private self-transformation over collective political participation.

The Bellstone, then, embeds ethnic heritage in whiteness, in at least two inter-related ways. First, it unmistakably aligns the ethnic quest for roots with the wider discourse of white evocations of the antimodern, in fact inscribing ethnicity into New Age whiteness. And it further entangles the historically racialized narrative of Greece as the origin of the West with this New Age discourse. In tracing the routes of the poem and its reinscription through time we witness therefore the rewriting of ethnicity from dissent to whiteness in the past to assimilation into New Age whiteness in the present. If the commitment to the political message of the poem kept ethnics banned from whiteness during the Cold War and the nascent civil rights movement, the aesthetic interpretation of the poem in accordance with white antimodernism places ethnics at the center of whiteness today.

The Bellstone's nostalgia announces a profound dissatisfaction with the present. In its indictment of society as unjust, it belongs to the tradition of ethnography as cultural critique. In its disapproval of the present, it makes a plea for public outrage against injustices, though it relies on spiritual transformation to seek social renewal via a return to the premodern past. But this critique refrains from naming the specific causes of inequality in the present and fails to lay out and interrogate in open view those structures that imprison certain classes of people in a cycle of poverty. It remains silent about a political solution to social inequality, instead underwriting the belief that a collective of morally reborn individuals will infuse society with goodness. As anthropologist Vassos Argyrou (1996, 78) notes in his analysis of the symbolic confrontation between working-class traditionalists and bourgeois modernity in Cyprus, any rhetoric that points to the past as a Golden Age filled with generosity and egalitarianism constitutes a compelling but ineffective polemic. Nostalgia is analytically inadequate for understanding the workings and implications of capitalism. To redeem the family's deferred dream, the intergenerational wanderer seems in need of new political spaces for placing the marble head.

White Ethnicity as Cultural Becoming

> [A]ctually identities are about questions of using the
> resources of history, language and culture in the process of
> becoming rather than being: not "who we are" or "where we
> come from," so much as what we might become, how we
> have been represented and how that bears on how we might
> represent ourselves.
>
> —Stuart Hall, "Introduction: Who Needs 'Identity?'"

This work complicates the ways in which ethnicities are commonly represented in academic writing. By addressing how popular ethnography builds on the past to imagine a future for ethnicity, explaining how and why heritage is constructed, and considering the implications of creating specific kinds of identities in the larger context of ethnic and racial politics in the United States, it illuminates the complex contours of white ethnicity. It is my hope that as scholars continue critiquing practices of exclusion among white ethnics, they will pause for a long moment to reflect on the findings of this study instead of continuing to trivialize white ethnicity as a shallow cultural resource or to dismiss it as an ideological weapon in the service of antiminority politics.

In this book, I have sought to take a close look at the process of constructing ethnic identities via the making of usable pasts and, in turn, to explore the power of heritage to make or unmake whiteness. The goal of this examination is to illustrate the often overlooked connection between ethnicity and race talk. Heritage, as it is practiced among European ethnics in the United States, appears to be solely about culture. The vocabulary of race, let alone an explicit language of whiteness, is absent from the heritage sites of American multiculturalism. In festivals, parades, community publications, quests for roots, documentaries, and museum exhibits, it is culture—food, dance, music, community, memorabilia, the arts, and family values—that commands center stage. The framing of heritage as

culture renders invisible the importance of heritage as a tool for making whiteness. Working against this discourse, I have sought to demonstrate that whiteness is
not absent from the making of heritage as culture. Even when it is not mentioned
at all, it is there—present and often pervasive, though not always apparent. Because the discourse on ethnicity does not operate as a self-contained entity but
may ratify racial hierarchies, it is necessary to identify this invisible presence.

The critical enterprise of connecting heritage, ethnicity, and whiteness draws
attention to the political implications inherent in the making of an ethnic identity.
When a collective constructs an identity for itself, it also creates a perspective
on Others. Because ethnicity entails not only the making of the Self but also the
making of Others, showcasing one's own success implicitly points to another's
failure. One's badge of honor becomes another's source of stigma. In an interconnected world, the narratives that people tell about themselves have profound, if
not always readily discernible, effects on how they see Others and, inevitably, on
how Others, in turn, will position themselves in relation to them.

Intended to intervene in specific academic discussions of white ethnicity, my
research foregrounds a number of tensions that run through popular representations of a specific white social field, Greek America. It demonstrates the
heterogeneity of this field, which entails conformity with as well as criticism of
dominant narratives of whiteness, where empathy toward vulnerable groups coexists with apathy and even hostility toward them, and where both amnesia and
the imperative to remember are present. Dominant sites within Greek America
contribute to the making of whiteness while others, perhaps less visible, work
toward its dismantling. White ethnicity, therefore, is itself an ideologically accented social field, and popular ethnography is at the forefront of constructing
competing ethnic meanings. An investment in maintaining relatively stable identities anchored in a collective coexists with a drive to creatively fashion private
identities; the call to remember the past historically clashes with discourses
building on ahistorical renderings of that past; portrayals of community harmony—of utopian Edens—in the present and the past collide with descriptions
of conflict and dissent; idealizations of ethnic success cannot escape the shadow
cast by historical failures; and the search for ethnic options leaves the searcher
no choice but to sift facts and events through the screen of history and culture,
taking into account how choices are mediated, even determined, historically.

My analysis acknowledges the hegemony of an ahistorical, culturalist paradigm
of ethnicity, though it also strongly cautions against overlooking the agonistic
tension at work among opposing ethnic representations. In the context of pervasive ethnicization, Greek America is resorting to the classic model of identity

construction: narratives of origins offer celebratory accounts of a valiant, heroic spirit that endures through the ages to bloom again in the present. Here is a metaphysics of identity patterned after the romantic model of an eternal nation. At the same time, this model is being contested by popular and academic writings that view ethnicity as a historically situated experience. Thus, ethnicity unfolds as an ongoing struggle of cultural becoming, heavily mediated by a hegemonic and idealized narrative that circulates widely in the public sphere.

My intervention demonstrates a sense of urgency felt among certain popular ethnographers—a need to acknowledge the importance of history, to conjure practices and institutions that make a difference in the ways in which American ethnics understand and act upon the world, and to figure out ways to turn the past into a usable resource in the present. One emergent strand of this need is the embracing of a historical consciousness against amnesia: a refusal to forget how a past marked by racial intimidation, gender domination, cultural annihilation, humiliation, and class exploitation can inform progressive politics today. Writers like Helen Papanikolas, Harry Mark Petrakis, Constance Callinicos, and Michael Kalafatas revive these memories against what appears to be a surge of popular forgetting. They relentlessly insist on producing usable pasts, which this work showcases. I have noted, for example, the politics of contesting patriarchy within gendered communities that define themselves against the ideology of ethnic success. I have showed how Greek Orthodoxy served to indict racial exclusion. I have dwelled on the commitment to disseminate an ethic of remembering the devastating consequences of belittling racial Otherness and have brought to the fore the investment in preserving the memory of past injustices as a compass for steering toward interracial solidarity. And I have foregrounded the notion that ethnicity expands through dissent, whereas it shrinks through conformity to received notions.

If the volume of these nonhegemonic voices rises above the comfort level of many, it is because popular ethnographers write with an acute consciousness that they must overpower a loud wave of popular amnesia. They write and speak to audiences entrenched in the comfort zone of middle-class whiteness, audiences that appear unwilling to recognize the social and political causes of poverty and marginalization. The specter hanging over this scene is the political indifference that formerly dominated populations—such as sections of white ethnics and some racial minorities, as well—exhibit toward the plight of the exploited and stigmatized. This prospect becomes even more real if one considers that collectives who have experienced the unspeakable horror of slavery's dehumanization themselves display an inclination to abandon the political sensitivity of identifying with the disfranchised. "Blacks today appear to identify far more readily with the glamorous pharaohs," Paul Gilroy (1993) laments in his fascinating journey into black cultures, "than with the abject plight of those they held in bondage" (207).

My research demonstrates the importance of popular ethnography as a resource to envision specific processes of cultural becoming. Such a vision of renewal is multifaceted. It builds on the ecumenical and humanitarian ethos of Christianity. It insists on the value of reflective self-critique to redirect social action. It finds inspiration in the common experience of stigmatization to advance the forging of interracial alliances to improve the lives of those who most desperately need it. It dares to make visible unflattering pasts and to identify their implications for ethnics and others alike. But do ethnic institutions embrace this social vision? To what extent do they debate, reflect on, question, or disseminate nonhegemonic perspectives, translating the dispersed alternative voices into a fertile public dialogue? Moreover, is this social vision part of everyday practice? The fact that the answers to these questions are not readily available—beyond the well-established practice of ethnic philanthropy and the occasional literary and ethnographic examples—speaks volumes to the absence of a public discourse on this subject among certain white ethnic groups. A hegemonic narrative of celebrationist ethnicity strangles Greek America—and possibly white ethnicity in general—as it marginalizes alternative practices and worldviews and abstains from engaging with ethnicity in terms that will advance a historical understanding of interracial connections, which this dominant narrative often silences. The kind of heritage that ethnic gatekeepers promote will determine to a large extent the cultural direction of this social field, the kinds of alliances it sustains, and the kinds of publics it creates. The stakes, therefore, are high. The critical task for scholars is to reflect on how to place themselves in this process of cultural becoming.

Clearly, intellectuals vested in the ethics and politics of pluralism must engage in new cartographies of white ethnicity. One could start this remapping by moving beyond stale dichotomies of assimilation versus preservation, transnationality versus ethnicity, or symbolic versus real ethnicity. Ethnicity can be imagined in terms of positions wherein the categories of immigrants, ethnics, diasporics, and postethnics, though differentiated by class and cultural fault lines, are no longer distinct and hermetically sealed off from each other. Thinking not in terms of neatly delineated categories, but in terms of permutations and points of convergence, one is bound to discover a trove of surprises, such as well-read immigrant diner owners preoccupied as much with learning as with securing a good life for their families. In my own ethnographic work, I have talked with individuals who appear to be postethnic but who speak of deep affiliation with selective aspects of Greek cultural worlds. I have also elsewhere identified Greek American practices associated with pedagogies and philosophies of life that are connected with family or cultural histories but are ignored by academics because of the lack of an adequate model to accommodate the relevance of these practices in the lives of white ethnics (Anagnostou 2003). Autobiographies record the delicate balances that individuals with multiple backgrounds must negotiate, particularly when it comes to transferring cultural heritage to their children. Anthropologists and critical scholars are becoming attuned to how poverty is lived among white ethnics, how gender is experienced and talked about, and how the two interact. Increasing rates of interfaith, interracial, and interethnic marriages beg for further inquiry into the actualization of new kinds of intercultural zones. Transnational connections abound. Historians speak of Greek Australian immigrants as an active force in marketing the fantasy of the American dream in Australia, and anthropologists have started exploring transnational circuits connecting various Greek worlds. Permutations of this kind point to ethnicity as a multifaceted nexus connected through contours of such density and complexity as to overpower the hegemonic notion of an absolute ethnic culture.

There is promise that the casting of a wider research net will yield hitherto untapped resources—social visions, modes of activism, alternative cultural expressions—that matter in the making of ethnicities today. Therefore, this commentary concludes with a strong plea for further critical scholarship. The urgency is fueled by a number of ongoing developments in popular and institutional culture as well as by what appears to be the growing hegemony of an unimaginative, narrow perspective on what it means to be ethnic in the United States. It is, ironically, during an era of proliferating narratives about ethnicity—a period of almost compulsory ethnicity—that the range of ethnic expressions is shrinking, regulated by discourses that work to contain and constrain expressions of difference. If, indeed, this is the moment to seize and to disseminate visions of ethnicity as part of an ethic of pluralism, it remains for intellectuals, artists, academics, and all sorts of cultural agents to figure out how to identify multiple intersections of ethnicity, postethnicity, race, gender, class, heritage, national belonging, and transnational connections and in turn to communicate their research to diverse publics.

Scholars are faced, therefore, with the challenge of reimagining the contours of white ethnicity in order to excavate practices neglected by academic and popular discourses. The simultaneous operation of globalization, ethnicization, transnational flows of people, and intermingling of cultures shatters the notion of a single ethnic culture. Instead, these multilayered cross-fertilizations demand an examination of ethnicity in relation to, not apart from, various systems of difference. Although scholarship addressing these issues is becoming the norm, it still ignores the ways in which these processes play out within the field of white ethnicity. Scholars entering this domain are bound to encounter a dynamic process involving all sorts of cultural and political intersections. The United States supports multiculturalism, though it simultaneously limits it. At the same time, European states with dense histories of emigration—such as Greece, Ireland, and Italy—systematically cultivate ties with their respective diasporas. At the grassroots level, assimilation is valued for its socioeconomic potential, but it may also be resisted, as parents and communities search for new ways of translating ethnicity to capture the social imagination of the next generation. The growing specialization of academic discourse requires skillful translations that build bridges among various constituencies—ethnic institutions, other ethnicities, the academy, communities, and the general public—without compromising complexity. Scholars are positioned at the forefront of this enterprise, which will require rigor and relentless intellectual vitality, given the multiplicity of the audiences: national, ethnic, postethnic, racial, generational, and transnational, among others. Last but not least, poverty within and across ethnicities must be examined with the dedication and sensitivity that the immense industry of low-paid labor deserves. We must address how the vast investment of resources that goes into sheer survival among those whose social conditions do not enable access to the American dream relates with immigration and white ethnicity.

My study has been deliberately organized to showcase some of these tensions within a distinct space of ethnic whiteness. I believe that the failure to further explore the usable contours of a complex terrain such as white ethnicity will mean that we have lost the intellectual and political courage to look beyond the immediate horizon of our own existence. In the eyes of key popular ethnographers, this professional complacency would be unbearable.

NOTES

Introduction: Why White Ethnicity? Why Ethnic Pasts?

1. K. S. Brown and Yannis Hamilakis's reflections on the notion of "usable pasts" are pertinent here: "[I]f the idea of history is limited to the investigation of 'what really happened' in the past, then it is hard to argue for its relevance or pragmatic utility. If, on the other hand, the historian claims for his or her conclusions about the past some present or future significance, then she or he tacitly surrenders the disinterested status of the discipline" (2003, 1). The idea of a usable past serving contemporary interests is central to various disciplines. Writing in the context of American literary history in 1918, Van Wyck Brooks stated: "Discover, invent a usable past we certainly can, and that is what a vital criticism always does" (169). The idea has deep roots among professional historians in the United States, where history suffers from "low prestige" (Brown and Hamilakis 2003, 1). Since the 1950s, historians have made "[v]arious attempts . . . to grant to responsible history use-value as a 'public good' which might further self-understanding, for individuals and communities" (ibid.). Folklorists have investigated how usable pasts can shape identities at the group level, including ethnicity (Tuleja 1997).

2. Tellingly, the notion of the past as a resource to anchor the future of Greek America figured prominently in the Fourth Annual Conference on the Future of Hellenism in America sponsored by the American Hellenic Institute Foundation, a think tank (see Karageorge 2006). Academics writing on Greek America point to the importance of usable pasts as a resource for cultural survival (Georgakas 2004–5; Triandis, 1987). Psychologist Harry Triandis, for instance, reflects on "how the education of Greek Americans may be structured in order to retain desirable elements and suppress the undesirable ones" (1987, 19).

3. This work of fiction reconfigures traditional masculine competitiveness and the immigrant code of the Cretan vendetta—a customary system that locks generations of families in a vicious cycle of honor crimes—into an ethos of ethnic community harmony in the host society, which is reconfigured as home (Anagnostu 1993–94). This cover photograph may function in this context as a sign of what anthropologist Renaldo Rosaldo (1993) calls "imperialist nostalgia" (68), a sentiment "revolv[ing] around a paradox: A person kills somebody, and then mourns the victim. In more attenuated form, someone deliberately alters a form of life, and then regrets that things have not remained as they were prior to the intervention" (69–70). The photograph may be interpreted as an "innocent yearning" (70) for a bygone past defined by competitive masculinity, albeit in a novel that itself seeks to dismantle it—to banish it from Greek America.

4. An image of gun-holding Cretan males in full traditional regalia is also featured on the cover of an ethnography on Cretan identity, Michael Herzfeld's *Poetics of Manhood* (1985). Exoticism may have served anthropology well in the past, but it has become contested by politically vulnerable populations seeking greater control over self-representation.

5. Helen Papanikolas saw the accurate reconstruction of the past as the primary responsibility of a historian. This conviction served to answer her detractors. When confronted by the aforementioned dissenter, she reportedly "blinked with astonishment, as she always does when such a question emerges, and said 'but that is what they did. That was the custom'" (Smart 2005, 119).

6. Anthony Smith (1999) has written voluminously about the importance of the past in the making of ethnicity.

7. As David Sutton (1998) cautions, "heritage" and "tradition" are to be understood not as a priori classifications, but as contingent social categories whose uses and meanings must be examined in the specific contexts in which they are deployed. He points out that "even within cultures, the past comes in many different containers bearing differing labels, from 'history' to 'tradition,' from 'custom' to 'heritage.'" The "different valences [of] these categories" and the distinct cultural work that they perform are often erased when analysts who implicitly "share many of these categories" impose them on local ethnographic realities (3).

8. John Kerry, the Democratic Party's candidate for the U.S presidency in 2004, for instance, positioned Greek Americans within the orbit of proper American ethnics: "The Greek values of family, hard work, education, civic engagement and love of country are American values" (quoted in "Kerry Addresses the Greek American Community," *National Herald,* October 9–10, 2004, 9).

9. The literature on whiteness is too voluminous to fully cite here. The combined scholarship of Matthew Frye Jacobson (1998), David Roediger (2005), and Karen Brodkin (1998) is indispensable in understanding how the legal system, everyday practices, federal policies, intellectual activism, and political mobilization contributed in turning early twentieth-century southeastern European immigrants and their descendants into whites. The underlying concept guiding all these studies follows, implicitly or explicitly, Michael Omi and Howard Winant's (1986) breakthrough notion of "racial formation." This concept "[e]mphasizes the social nature of race, the absence of any essential racial characteristics, the historical flexibility of racial meanings and categories, the conflictual character of race at both the 'micro-' and 'macro-social' levels, and the irreducible political aspect of racial dynamic" (4). It "refer[s] to the process by which social, economic and political forces determine the content and importance of racial categories, and by which they are in turn shaped by racial meanings" (61). Race, of course, is not biologically real but socially constructed, so the terms "race" and "racial" as used in this book refer to racializing social processes and must always be read in quotation marks. It is useful to distinguish here between popular classifications of race and self-ascribed racial identity. Brodkin (1998) uses the term "ethnoracial assignment" to define the former:

"[P]opularly held classifications and their deployment by those with national power to make them matter ethnoracially, politically, and socially to the individuals classified" (1). This assignment does not necessarily explain how an individual views herself, though self-ascription is, of course, expressed "within the context of ethnoracial assignment" (3). For instance, a dark-skinned individual of mixed African and German descent will have difficulty in passing for white within the ethnoracial system of the United States. On the other hand, white ethnicity affords one the option of manipulating ethnic identities (Waters 1990). Jacobson (1998) captures the politics of the disjuncture that could take place between ethnoracial whiteness and a white ethnic's refutation of it: "The notion that Jews . . . [or] Greeks . . . are not *really* white has become suddenly appealing in a setting where whiteness has wrongly become associated with unfair *dis*advantage" (280). Maintaining a distance from whiteness may function in a number of ways in a volatile racial environment that interrogates whiteness as complicity in racial domination. It may serve as a way to disassociate oneself from racial guilt; to evade confronting historical accountability; or to position oneself to access resources available exclusively to ethnics. I should mention that a book directly relevant to my work, Matthew Frye Jacobson's *Roots Too: White Ethnic Revival in Post-Civil Rights America* (2006), was published when this manuscript was at its very last stages of completion, too late for me to seriously incorporate it in my discussion.

10. Whiteness may be practiced as exclusion, as was evident when members of the Artemis Club—a Greek women's student organization formed at Hunter College in the 1930s—shunned a "very dark-skinned" woman of partly African parentage (Georgakas 1991, 107). It is also practiced as conformity to the aesthetics of whiteness. The ideal of female whiteness, for example, carries high currency among middle-class and lower-middle-class Greek immigrant women in New York City. The use of cosmetics by these women to whiten their appearances participates in this ideology; "achieving whiteness" in this manner becomes "a strategic move" to enhance social prestige in the hierarchical racial order (Karpathakis 2003, 30). Ethnics participate, then, in the "reemergence of 'thinking white,'" particularly in a city where white visitors experience its nonwhite population as threatening and "dangerous darker alien masses" in counterdistinction to suburban white America, which is perceived as safe (Bendersky 1995, 136). The practice of whiteness has not been uniform in Greek America. Greek immigrants occasionally resisted whiteness both in private and in public. "In 1973, when Coleman Young, the city's first black mayor, was elected, he noted that thirty years earlier, the only white restaurants in Detroit of any quality that would serve blacks were in Greek town" (Georgakas 2006, 265). And in Tarpon Springs, where "white Floridians did not allow blacks on sponge boats, Greeks employed them as needed, and under the very same terms which applied to Greeks," demonstrating a "democratic ethos" that "infuriated the Ku Klux Klan" (Georgakas 1987a, 47). Similarly, "research on Gary, Indiana shows examples of positive Black-Greek associations. [Though] [i]n Houston, such interracial contacts were not pronounced as Greek Americans quickly learned Jim Crow"

(Roediger 2002, 332). The example of rock and roll musician Johnny Otis, a son of Greek immigrants, who "chose the vibrancy of African American life over what he saw as the relative stagnation of white American mass culture … suggest[s] that it was at least possible to become an American, rather than to become a white American" (334).

11. On whiteness as a structural privilege, see the foundational volume edited by Michelle Fine, Lois Weis, Linda C. Powell, and L. Mun Wong (1997). For a clear exposition of how specific federal programs such as the GI Bill propelled white ethnic socioeconomic mobility while blocking opportunities for African Americans, see Karen Brodkin (1998) and Ira Katznelson (2005).

12. Cautioning against this reification, anthropologist John Hartigan (1999) examines everyday sociability as well as interracial and intraracial interactions to problematize the homogeneity of whiteness. In his detailed, context-specific ethnography, he argues that "racial identities are produced and experienced" differently in distinct locations (14).

13. Elsewhere, I analyze the social and economic conditions that enable the proliferation of popular accounts of ethnicity and explain my rationale for translating such a corpus of interdisciplinary works as "popular folklore" (Anagnostou 2006). To accommodate texts that explicitly draw from and seek to intervene in the discourse of anthropology, here I expand the category of "popular folklore" to "popular ethnography."

14. Histories and ethnographies by nonprofessionals often enjoy great commercial and social success in the United States and have been instrumental in shaping the public's understanding of the past and of ethnicity. As Michel-Rolph Trouillot (1995) observes, "Universities and university presses are not the only loci of production of the historical narrative. Books sell even better than coonskin caps at the Alamo gift shop, to which half a dozen titles by amateur historians bring more than $400,000 a year" (20). And as Steven Hoelscher (1998) shows, *Old World Wisconsin* (1944), the work of an amateur ethnographer and historian, "taught the state's residents to appreciate ethnic diversity and difference" (176).

15. There have been signs of change as Greek Americans more frequently attach a premium to the liberal arts, a development evident on both an individual and an institutional level. Harvard-educated journalist Eleni N. Gage, for instance, drew upon her studies of modern Greek folklore to craft her popular ethnography *North of Ithaka: A Journey Home through a Family's Extraordinary Past* (New York: St. Martin's Press, 2004). In addition, "successful Greek American women in business" speak appreciatively of parents who encouraged their pursuit of a liberal arts education (Vorillas 2006, 56).

16. For further discussion of popular ethnography and the analytical management of its interdisciplinarity, see Anagnostou (2006, 393–95).

17. For a discussion of modern Greek studies as an "interventionist, activist, interested field," see Lambropoulos (1990, 83). My work draws inspiration from this programmatic statement, although textual interpretation and methodological reflexivity become important elements in my interventionist tactics.

Chapter 1:The Politics and Poetics of Popular Ethnography

1. I use the term "arbitrary" to stress the fact that I do not claim that these moments represent a definite historical beginning for the processes I discuss. See Hayden White, *Tropics of Discourse: Essays in Cultural Criticism* (Baltimore, MD: Johns Hopkins University Press, 1978), 32.

2. If Richard Dorson and Robert Georges (1964) echoed each other's rhetoric about the survival of folk elements in modernity, professional folklorist Gregory Gizelis (1980) questioned not only the folkness of the immigrants but also the folkness of the preimmigrant past. Citing early and mid-twentieth-century folklore scholarship on the Dodecanese Islands, he reiterated the position that folk genres, particularly the complex folk tale, were no longer "functioning within the Greek cultural environment of the sponge divers and so [were] not even carried to America" (24). Urging readers not to view the Greeks as folk, he made the case for immigrant contemporaneity in the United States: "The fact that the sponge fishers might have heard tales from their grandmothers but not tell them to their children does not differentiate them from other Americans who when youngsters listened to their parents or grandparents narrating folktales at bedtime" (25). Although he challenged folklorization, Gizelis did not abandon the notion of "folk" and "folklore" as distinct categories. Following Dan Ben-Amos's (1972) rethinking of folklore as "artistic communication in small groups," Gizelis's research shifted focus from the search for folk survivals in modernity to the view of folklore as an *emergent* "process of communication" (1980, xxxvi). Approaching folklore as a dynamic process of "transformations that people made so that their folklore could fit into new situations" (25), Gizelis analyzed immigrant narratives as "rhetorical devices of persuasion" (xxxvii) performed for didactic purposes.

3. William Petersen (1997) draws on research assessing the quality of interview responses to indicate that ethnic and racial minorities are more likely to give answers likely to cast them in a favorable light. He writes, "One of the more troublesome characteristics of responses on ethnicity is the 'vanity effect'—the tendency of respondents to answer questions in a way that they think may enhance their status" (24).

4. The Hellenic-Romeic distinction, a model whose implications I will analyze in chapter 4, seeks to crystallize ideological manipulations of modern Greek identity. It points to "the difference between an outward-directed conformity to international expectations about the national image and an inward-looking, self-critical collective appraisal" (Herzfeld 1986a, 20).

5. Dorson (1978a) showed no interest in examining how extratextual discourses intersect with folklore texts. Preoccupied with the methodological viability of collecting urban folklore, he was guided by a research orientation that stressed the efficient gathering of large quantities of data "in a short space of time" (29). In fact, he argued for the efficacy of folkloric research "among varied ethnic and racial groups" in the city. He wrote, "In less than a month it was possible for a folklorist without previous

acquaintances to record from southern blacks, southern whites, Greeks, Serbs, Croats, Romanians, Italians, Poles, Czechs, Slovaks, Mexicans, and Puerto Ricans and to obtain intensely dramatic and moving personal histories and experiences" (ibid.). Nor did he accommodate questions of immigrant history. As Dan Ben-Amos (1989) notes,

> Rather than attempting to reconstruct folklore in immigrant communities, Dorson examined how immigrants adapted to the new fabric of American life. Thus, by focusing on the final stage of the immigration process, on the integration of the newcomers and their offspring into American society, Dorson lacked the perspective that would have allowed him to study folklore in the life and history of an immigrant group. In spite of the fact that he was committed to the cause of folklore, as a historian and as a scholar of American civilization, Dorson inevitably took an elitist and centrist perspective of folklore in America, viewing ethnic and immigrant folklore in terms of its contribution to the total system he had envisioned when he first proposed his "theory for American folklore" in 1959. (57–58)

6. Scholar and educator Eva Catafygiotou Topping (1995) offers a glimpse into the blurring between orality and textuality in Greek America when she recalls proverbs spoken by her immigrant parents, while simultaneously acknowledging her indebtedness to textual sources on the subject. Along similar lines, folklorist Gregory Gizelis (1980, 89) documents specific cases in which immigrants cited proverbs that they had learned through reading. For a discussion of the relationship between orality and textuality in Greece, a relationship that "is not one of rigid opposition, but rather one of intrication and enfolding," see Tziovas (1989, 321).

7. Ironically, Richard Dorson was "wary of any use of folklore outside the academy" (Thatcher 2004, 187), vehemently detesting those popularizers who "employ no theoretical premises and engage in no basic research in the field or in the library" (quoted in Georges 1989, 3). But his ubiquitous folk have been appropriating professional folklore, as I have indicated, for their own politics of ethnic representation.

8. Michael Herzfeld (1987, 107–11) explores the significance of this discourse of beginnings for the making of modern Greek identity, including a commentary on Greek Australia, and Yiorgos Kalogeras (1992) discusses Greek America in relation to this discourse, as well.

9. Populist discourse refers to this heritage as *Romiosíni,* an ideologically charged term of self-ascription posing serious semantic and ethnographic challenges. Artemis Leontis (1995) writes about the linguistic and ideological complexities associated with its meaning: "*Romiosíni* is very nearly impossible to translate into English. It is the nominalized form of the adjective *romiós,* a Greek vernacularization of the adjective *romaios,* 'Roman.' This name attaches itself to the occupants of the Greek peninsula at some unspecified time after the Romans destroyed Corinth (146 BC). *Romiosíni* is a vernacular coinage of the late nineteenth century. It signifies the national-popular body and its Byzantine-Ottoman-Christian popular heritage, the traditions and language of the *Volk*"

(80). For populism, for which it functions as a cardinal sign, Romiosini construes the common people as the vessel of a noble national spirit. But the semantic fluidity of the term in everyday usage has led ethnographers to examine its context-specific meanings. Michael Herzfeld (1987), for instance, observes that "the very notion of Romeic identity is not only context-dependent, but *includes context-dependency as one of its diagnostic traits.* It resists authoritative definition" (121). I pay close attention to the ways Helen Papanikolas uses this term in chapter 4.

10. The argument that American modernity was rooted in Greek civilization was advanced by late nineteenth-century American classicists who sought to defend the necessity of studying classical antiquity in an era that was embracing the view of history as progress. Although the argument had been made earlier in the century that America "could recapitulate the fate of the classical world" (Winterer 2002, 133), the academic study of that past could now be justified because of the unique place of classical antiquity in the larger scheme of linear cultural evolution. As Caroline Winterer (2002) shows, classicists responded to the idea of the "progress of civilizations" by advancing the view that "classical antiquity, medieval Europe, and nineteenth-century Europe and America formed a single civilization united by cultural commonality" (ibid.). In this context, "studying the march of history from Athens to America" was necessary in order to illustrate the "universal laws of progress" (134). It was the "story of progress" that "linked the Greeks and Romans to nineteenth-century Europeans and Americans" (ibid.). The popularity of neoclassical building styles at the time "testified to an enduring association between the classical world and the highest standards of taste and beauty" (143).

11. On the centrifugal dynamic of regionally based identities and antagonisms as a vital issue in Greek political culture at the time, see Tziovas (1994a).

12. Twenty-one million immigrants arrived in the United States between 1881 and 1920, the vast majority of whom originated from southern and eastern Europe (Feagin 1997, 20). According to Charles Moskos (1990, 8), an estimated 450,000 Greeks, most of them males, immigrated to the United States during the "era of mass migration" from 1890 to 1920. This number includes approximately 100,000 Greeks who emigrated from areas outside the Greek state. It is estimated "that about 40 percent of all Greeks admitted to the United States before 1920 went back to their homeland" (Moskos 2002, 41). A caveat is in order concerning my use of the category "Greek immigrants." Undoubtedly, there were significant class and regional differences among Greek immigrant men and women at the time (Papanikolas 1989, 29). I retain the homogenizing category "Greek immigrants," however, because nationality was the official criterion in immigration policies and the object of popular and scientific discourse.

13. Stratis Haviaras's novel *When the Tree Sings* (New York: Simon and Schuster, 1979) builds on the subversive and open-ended characteristics of popular culture. As Yiorgos Kalogeras (1989) shows, the Greek American author constructs "a suprachronic, multi-layered, magical popular culture which strives to survive despite unpropitious circumstances" (33). The narrator cherishes and builds on these elements for the purpose of

social and self-renewal, only to be confronted by state-controlled institutions that seek to contain and standardize them.

14. Given the endemic historical patterns of *seasonal* emigration from the Greek countryside, communities may be thought of as "transnational villages" exposed to and affected by "social remittances"—the ideas, behaviors, and material and social capital that inevitably circulate in transnational fields of communication (Levitt 2001).

15. Literary societies were (and still are) a regular feature of Greek America. For the children of the immigrants who saw folk culture as only partially satisfying, literature offered a venue for expanding cultural horizons. Historian E. D. Karampetsos (2005) writes revealingly that "even the best of Greek folk life isn't enough to constitute an identity or a way of life" (6). "Those who tried to keep alive the world the immigrants created were condemned to live in a world too cramped for their dreams and aspirations. In my case, literature accidentally came to the rescue" (ibid.). He continues, "Between them, Kazantzakis and Berdyaev, took me out of the often narrow village society I grew up in and gave me a sense of the reality and the vast potential of the world my parents came from" (6–7). The place of literature in the Greek immigrant world deserves a study of its own.

Chapter 2: Whither Collective Ethnic Identities?

1. These are patterns that could apply fairly accurately to Greek Americans. With regard to intermarriage, for instance, "[v]ital statistics kept by the Department of Registry indicate that the numbers of inter-Christian marriages conducted in the Greek Orthodox Archdiocese of America (GOA) have steadily increased. Today, nearly two thirds (63%) of all marriages conducted in the GOA are designated inter-Christian. When Greek Orthodox persons marrying outside of the GOA are also considered, intermarriage rates are likely closer to 75 - 80%" (Greek Orthodox Archdiocese of America, *Departments and Ministries,* "Department of Marriage and Family," http://www.goarch.org/en/archdiocese/departments/marriage/ [accessed March 2008]).

2. This transition is often framed in Durkheimian terms. The new configuration of white ethnicity takes the form of organic solidarity, "the social glue that ties a community through rational interdependence," such as ethnic business and professional societies. It has replaced mechanical solidarity, which "nurtures social cohesion on the basis of similarity," an enduring connection based on a shared culture (Bakalian 1993, 249n32).

3. Institutions have contributed to the formation of "Euro-American" as a staple category of American multiculturalism. Euro-Americans were included in the required American Cultures course at the University of California at Berkeley, for example, after "they were declared an ethnicity on a par with other minorities (as in a sense they were, Asians now being the largest campus group)" (Lowenthal 1996, 82). Moreover, Alba would have felt vindicated when the Greek American organizers of the 1992 Greek festival in Campbell, Ohio, identified themselves as European (*The Hellenes: Destined to*

Succeed, written and narrated by Mike Passas, circa 1990). Yet even a cursory glance at the landscape of Greek American cultural production will identify a richness of narratives, from comedy to documentaries, from parades to festivals, from memoirs to poetry, from films to museum exhibits, all producing ethnically specific identities. It appears that the valence of hyphenated ethnic identities deserves closer attention. In his discussion of racial minorities, Michael Omi (1996) readily admits that racial panethnic "consciousness and organization are, to a large extent, contextually and strategically determined" (181). Why will scholars not concede that European American panethnicity is also context-specific and operates alongside enduring narratives of ethnic belonging, at least for some white ethnics?

4. A notable example is Michael Omi (1996), who builds on Alba to situate white identification in the context of racial identity politics. His work attributes this emergent racial articulation to a projected demographic and political sea change wherein whites will be counted in the future as a political and racial minority. "The prospect that whites may not constitute a clear majority or exercise unquestioned racial domination in particular institutional settings has led to a *crisis of white* identity," he writes (181, emphasis in original). A contested political economy organized around race-based allocation of state resources and the stigma attached to whites as the "oppressors of the nation" (183) heighten the formation of white consciousness, a process evident—among other places—in the "balkanization" (179) of college students along racial lines. A racialized political mobilization is enabled, therefore, in relation to the "historically unprecedented" awareness "that white racial identification could be a handicap" (182). A panethnic racial identity emerges among "whites [who] are concerned that their interests as *whites* are not being articulated, advanced, and addressed" (183). For the political implications of a white-centered racial politics in response to the fear of becoming a "new minority" emerging out of a "displaced majority," see D. Warren (1995, 127, 131).

5. The scholarships offered to high school and college students of Greek descent are too numerous to list here. Therefore, I will identify only a small sample. Established in 1992 and described "as the largest Greek [non-university-based] academic scholarship fund in the country" (Daniels 2000, 17), the *Hellenic Times* Scholarship Fund annually awards some $100,000 in scholarships to American students of Hellenic descent. Similarly, the Panhellenic Scholarship Foundation employs ethnic criteria in granting both merit-based and need-based scholarships. Moreover, professional and humanitarian mutual-help societies abound. In addition to hundreds of local community and AHEPA scholarships extended to students of Greek descent, the New York–based Greek Children's Fund provides monetary assistance to Greek and Greek American children undergoing cancer treatment. In addition, the Hellenic American Medical and Dental Society of Southern California regularly awards scholarships to college students of Hellenic background. As a Greek-born graduate student, I personally benefited from ethnic-based scholarships, having received the Frederick E. G. Valergakis Graduate Research Grant offered by the Hellenic University Club of New York. Furthermore,

Greek American entrepreneurs invest in ethnic institutions. The Calamos Foundation, for example, extended a $2 million gift for a new building to host the Hellenic Museum and Cultural Center in Chicago.

6. The assumptions of the behavioralist model of ethnicity lead to the inescapable conclusion that the post-1960s "new ethnicity" was doomed to fail from the outset. Stephen Steinberg (1981) captures this point in his thesis "that the ethnic revival was a 'dying gasp' on the part of [white] ethnic groups . . . [and was] symptomatic of the atrophy of ethnic cultures and the decline of ethnic communities" (51).

7. In her work on Armenian Americans, Anny Bakalian (1993) "call[s] these depositories for heritage preservation 'knowledge banks'" (45). But her analysis still follows the volunteerist model of ethnicity. It rests on the erroneous dichotomy between ethnicity as determined experience and ethnicity as voluntary cultural attachment, missing the point that ethnic connectivity could be involuntary, determined by psychic and cultural forces, and could express itself in reinvented ways that do not reproduce immigrant behavioral patterns. Anthropologist Michael Fischer (1986) has launched a powerful critique of ethnicity as voluntary choice, one that has not been answered by sociologists. "Ethnicity is not something that is simply passed on from generation to generation, taught and learned," he writes. "It is something dynamic, often unsuccessfully repressed or avoided. It can be potent even when not consciously taught" (195). He demonstrates the value of a nonsociological approach to ethnicity, remarking on the particular potency of unconscious processes—notably transference—to motivate an individual's connection with ethnicity. In this respect, ethnicity may not be a matter of visibility—displayed in symbols or expressed in an ethnographic interview—but a powerful force most readily identified textually, in genres such as ethnic autobiography.

8. The government-sponsored Ethnic Heritage Studies Program of 1972, for instance, incorporated the study of ethnic history into America's elementary and secondary education. This political initiative sought to balance recognition of ethnic diversity with patriotism and social harmony (Scourby 1982, 12). For the representation of Greek America in this program, see the Title IX Project of the Chicago Consortium for Inter-Ethnic Curriculum Development, *Ethnic Heritage in America: Curriculum Materials in Elementary School Social Studies on Greeks, Jews, Lithuanians, and Ukrainians* (Chicago: The Project, 1976).

9. Not all white ethnic festivals sprang up in the post–civil rights era. In his place-centered analysis of the history of a Swiss festival in New Glarus, Wisconsin, Steven Hoelscher (1998) shows how antimodernist amateur historians and ethnographers, academics, state policies, local deindustrialization, the local middle class, and ethnic tourism all contributed to the development of the festival during the interwar period.

10. Significantly, it was folklorists working on American immigration and ethnicity who promoted a shift away from the survivalist strain in folklore and toward the cultural politics of authenticity. Confronted by acculturation, the self-conscious manipulation of immigrant folklore, and the appropriation of ethnic knowledge and customs by popular

culture, a number of folklorists shunned the search for authentic or pure forms, focusing instead on the politics of ethnicity, syncretism, revival, invention, and the interrelationship between folk and popular culture. As a result, their analytical preoccupation was not to locate the authentic, but to examine how authenticity was deployed, by whom, and for what purpose (Bendix 1997, 207–10).

11. White ethnicity contributes to the attractiveness of a city as tourist destination. The Greek Festival, the Irish Festival, and the Oktoberfest are standard fixtures of Columbus, Ohio, guidebooks. Also, television commercials advertising Detroit as a cultural destination feature images of the city's Greektown.

12. Arlene Dávila (2001) examines the role of corporations in the making and marketing of panethnic identities. The intersection of commerce and culture is dramatically illustrated in the language of advertising. When the bilingual magazine *Metohos,* which primarily targets Greeks abroad, advertises its subscription plans as a way for buyers to become "shareholders in Hellenism" and to "preserve Hellenism," it highlights the connection between economic and cultural capital.

13. Media interest in producing ethnic representations is not independent of market considerations. For example, George Veras (2002a), points out that the strong interest that PBS expressed in featuring a documentary on Greek Americans was partly a response to the commercial success of *Yanni: Live at the Acropolis* (produced and directed by Veras Communications, Inc.) among the broadcaster's Greek American viewers. He reports that PBS executives identified the Greek ethnicity of supporters by the ending of their names—"as" and "os"—when the Yanni event was broadcast for fundraising purposes.

14. *The Greek Americans* was followed by *The Greek Americans II: Passing the Torch* (1999), which also was produced by Veras and broadcast on PBS. Both programs have been made commercially available as videotapes and offered during PBS fund drives or sold through the network at other times. The commercial version contains footage not shown in the original television program.

15. All unreferenced quotes are from the televised version of the documentary *The Greek Americans,* unless otherwise specified.

16. Numerous histories, autobiographies, family biographies, community publications, and works of juvenile literature organize themselves around the ideology of ethnic success. See, for example, Nicholas Gage's *A Place for Us: A Triumphant Coming of Age in America* (New York: Touchstone, 1989), Charles Moskos's *Greek Americans: Struggles and Success* (New Brunswick, NJ: Transaction, 1990), Alex Spanos's *Sharing the Wealth: My Story* (Washington, DC: Regnery, 2002), Effie Lascarides's *Apollo's Legacy: The Hellenic Torch in America at the Dawn of the New Millennium* (Brookline, MA: Hellenic College Press, 2000), the Greek Orthodox Clergy-Laity Congress's *How Greek-Americans Help Keep It Burning* (Philadelphia: Twenty-third Biennial Clergy-Laity Congress of the Archdiocese of North and South America, 1976), and Tiffany Peterson's *Greek Americans* (Chicago: Heinemann Library, 2004).

17. The majority of the individuals interviewed for *The Greek Americans* belong to the professional class. Presidents and CEOs of corporations are generously represented, as are high-profile artists and politicians. The perspectives of immigrant and ethnic wage earners are marginalized. This is not unlike the Armenian diaspora community, which "maintains its affluent image in American society by distancing itself from the lower-class domestic workers" (Ishkanian 2002, 406). Veras (2002b) has given speeches on the cultural function of Greek American professionals.

18. Veras (2002a) answers the criticism that the documentary was "an 'East Coast' biased program" by pointing to restrictions imposed by a "very limited budget." This reasoning makes even more curious the director's choice to feature Midwest-based Greek American scholars and to leave out New York–based ones.

19. These statements belong, respectively, to George P. Stamas, cochairman of Wilmer, Cutler & Pickering; Dino Anagnost, composer and conductor; and Charles Moskos, sociologist.

20. Veras also emerged as a much-sought-after cultural translator of Greek America (2001, 2002a, 2002b, 2002c). He has enjoyed the attentions of the ethnic press; he is regularly invited as a media and cultural expert to speak to communities, to serve as a master of ceremonies, or to present his work in academic programs (including my own); and he has received wide-ranging honors and awards. It is a measure of his success among prestigious Greek American circles that AHEPA assigned to him the production of the *AHEPA Millennium* video. On the other hand, his documentary has generated criticism for its simplified representation of Greek Americans. Ann Giannotis, the writer, producer, and director of *The Greeks of Southern California through the Century: The Pioneers, 1900–1942,* for example, has been reported as being "anxious to hit a much higher level of seriousness than media fare like the PBS films about Greeks in America" (Georgakas 2002, 110).

21. The documentary represents Greek America through the safe contour of ethnicity as the embodiment of the American dream. In this instance, there is long way to go before public television fulfills the goals of its original mission to "address the needs of un-served and underserved audiences" (Bullert 1997, 198). The poor, the unemployed, the politically persecuted, and the socially marginalized in Greek America will have to wait their turn to be showcased on PBS. For valuable insights on the "battle over documentary film" on PBS and the increasing marginalization of "independent film makers with strong opinions" who promote politically controversial cultural critiques, see Bullert (1997).

22. Occidentalism is organized by complex conceptual and political nuances rather than a set of fixed attributes (Carrier 1995). For the purpose of this essay, the term "occidentalized ethnic Greek" refers to Greek American self-representations in alignment with values central to an American Western identity, such as democracy, individualism, civic responsibility, order, rationality, and discipline.

23. The documentary reproduces an ideology central to the construction of white ethnicity as the ideal balance between stereotypical white austerity and alleged black unruliness. Anthropologist di Leonardo (1994) captures this tension when she writes,

"While WASPs were 'too cold'—bloodless, modern, and unencumbered—and blacks 'too hot'—wild, primitive, and 'over'cumbered—white ethnics were 'just right.' They could and did claim to represent the golden historical mean between the overwhelming ancientness and primitiveness of Gemeinschaft and the etiolated modernity of Gesellschaft" (176–77). The film *My Big Fat Greek Wedding* is exemplary in this respect, as it advocates ethnicity as the golden mean between authoritative immigrant foreignness and overrestrained WASP coldness. At the same time, the documentary participates in yet another ideological construction of white ethnic community. By foregrounding its assimilative ethos and family values, it neglects to address the "historical version of the negative pole—the stolid, backward, crime-ridden, socially immobile ethnic community" (di Leonardo 1994, 179). Now this image "has been superseded in the public mind by the black and brown poor, whose segregation, poverty, and high crime rates are presumed to be self-caused" (ibid.).

24. A network of Greek Orthodox parochial day schools and afternoon schools that offer instruction in Greek language, history, and culture is sponsored by the Greek Orthodox Archdiocese of America, whose Web site (http://www.goarch.org) reports a total "enrollment of approximately 30,000 students." A Commission on Greek Language and Hellenic Culture was formed in 1998, in response to the archdiocese's initiative to assess Greek education in the United States. Despite its stated optimism, the commission's report expressed "discourag[ement] to hear teachers and priests decry the indifference of the great majority of Greek-American parents, who do not send their children to Greek school and who apparently do not believe in the value of Greek language education" (Rassias et al. 1999, 2). Widely publicized in ethnic media, such as the *Greek Orthodox Observer* and *GreeceInPrint,* the report warned of high rates of language loss. It brought about the observation that the Greek language is becoming foreign to Greek America, becoming, in fact, external to it—a "Greek" language to Greek America (as in the saying "It's all Greek to me") (Kolettis 2004, 22). I must add here that ethnic language preservation in public schools is embedded in ideologies of mobility as well as in ethnic and class hierarchies. Moskos reports a case of "acrimonious dispute" that took place in 1972 when a "large majority" of second-generation Greek American residents and "some of the new immigrants" actively opposed the introduction of Greek language classes in an elementary school located in Chicago's new Greek Town. Opponents of bilingual education "argued that the bilingual approach would retard the immigrant child's entry into the American mainstream, that it subjected Greek American pupils to a questionable and unproved teaching methods [. . .] and that it would stigmatize Greek-American youth as being akin to the poverty stricken Spanish-speaking population" (1990, 84). A number of institutional initiatives point to a renewed effort to revitalize the Greek language in the United States. In Delaware, for example, local Greek American organizations such as AHEPA, in collaboration with the Greek government, seek to capitalize on the No Child Left Behind Act and to use federal seed money to support charter schools teaching Greek.

25. Intraethnic fault lines are reported in encyclopedia entries defining (and standardizing) Greek America: "Greeks share the American work ethic and desire for success and are largely perceived as hard-working and family oriented. They are also said to possess a 'Zorba'-like spirit and love for life. However, many Greek Americans perceive the recent Greek immigrants as 'foreign' and often as a source of embarrassment" (Jurgens 1995, 578). Yet one must not overlook institutional initiatives, such as the Archdiocesan Social Health and Welfare Center in Astoria, which was established in 1971 to assist in the acculturation of the post-1960s "second wave" of Greek immigrants (Coumantaros 1982, 194). The often antagonistic, frequently paternalistic, repeatedly hostile, occasionally sympathetic, at intervals collaborative and mutually supportive, and now and then mistrustful webs of relations linking Greek Americans, Greek immigrants, and Greeks in Greece deserve an in-depth study.

26. Heritage need not be produced at the expense of history. A museum exhibit on women's embroideries in Greek America shows how history can be an integral part of heritage production (Leontis 1997). As a heritage project, this exhibit breathes "a second life" into an abandoned past—immigrant women's practice of embroidering—by adding new significance to it. The exhibit appraises the aesthetic value of embroideries as worthy of museum display, while it reconfigures their significance as sites of material culture that generate narratives of immigration and dispersal. At the same time, the paratexts of this temporary exhibit—catalogues and publications in academic and popular journals—embed in history the practice of embroidery and its intergenerational reception. Constructed in this manner, the exhibit—which I have discussed elsewhere as an instance of cultural translation (Anagnostou 2004b)—adds new value to obsolete practices of the past.

27. The second documentary in the series, *The Greek Americans II: Passing the Torch,* which addresses cultural preservation around issues such as interethnic marriage, does venture into critical reflection and includes diverse perspectives. Statements such as "I have been thinking, what are we doing lately?" or the recommendation to "change the educational system, which to some degree is non-existent" challenge the documentary's often self-congratulatory rhetoric. Similarly, remarks such as "You got a drop of Greek blood in you, you are Greek" and "Hellenism is about a state of mind" point to incommensurable understandings of identity. Yet, the above citations are presented without the benefit of an analytical commentary, which results in an awkward pastiche of noncontextualized points of view.

28. "Within ethnic absolutism, the naturalization of culture [that is, culture seen as an inherent property of an ethnic group] diffuses race and racism in ethnic related discourses of differentiation. As 'race' is culturalized, ethnicity is naturalized" (Fortier 1994, 220).

29. For an example of how a working-class Greek immigrant confronts this cultural devaluation, see Harry Mark Petrakis's short story "Pericles on 31st Street" (1978a, 87—100).

Chapter 3: Whose Ethnic Community?

1. In the context of the modern Greek diaspora, Hasiotes (1993) associates the term "community" (*koinóteta*) with collective integration around an ethnoreligious institution (20). In the United States, this finds expression in the parishes administered by the Greek Orthodox Archdiocese of America, which oversees "some 440 churches in the United States" and numerous "activities, such as an orphanage, a home for the aged, a summer camp in Greece for Greek American youth, programs of religious instruction, and Greek Orthodox parochial schools" (Moskos 1990, 68). Elaborating on the boundaries of koinóteta in relation to Greek America, Leontis (1997) writes:

> The idea of a Greek *koinóteta* in America extends beyond the religious community, however, to include other institutions that may meet in church halls. . . . During a good part of this century, Greek immigrants and their offspring have been instituting communities as places of gathering and mechanisms for preserving a certain way of life against the erosion of assimilation. These do not usually stand alone: they are connected to one another through bridges of kinship, friendship, economic, and political interests. (85)

2. A "community of memory," according to Bellah et al. (1985), is "one that does not forget its past" (153) and sustains "a way of life" (154) that "in an important sense" is constituted by that past (153). A "lifestyle enclave" in contrast, refers to ephemeral collectives realized around private pursuits, most often expressed as lifestyles centered on leisure and consumption. Lacking interdependence and shared history, they "are socially, economically, or culturally similar," and, being exclusive to those with alternative lifestyles, they "celebrate the narcissism of similarity" (72). The lifestyle enclave is seen as a matter of choice, which frees the individual from group-imposed commitments and responsibilities. The actualization of lifestyle enclaves—Elvis impersonators, golfers, body building and health enthusiasts, mountain hikers, and stamp collectors—is cast in terms of voluntary and temporary association. Within the realm of ethnicity, lifestyle enclaves may find expression in mutual-interest activities that attract members sharing similar class, social, and cultural interests on the basis of personal determination.

3. Recently, popular and scholarly accounts sustain memories of past discrimination and anti-immigrant violence (Karampetsos 1998; Papanikolas 2002; Scofield 1997). Greek Americans are becoming aware that national unity, as Renan (1990) has it, was "effected by means of brutality" (11). How this amnesia was constituted historically and how both institutional dictates and psychic trauma functioned to suppress intergenerational memories of national brutality is not fully understood. In the best treatment of the subject, Laliotou (2004) sheds light on the role of the early Greek immigrant press in sanctioning this amnesia. The mainstream press largely excluded "[s]tories of antimigrant discrimination, mob riots, lynchings, and violence" and reported others

"as isolated events" (185). Such reporting officially "registered violence and anti-Greek racism as a self-inflicted phenomenon" (ibid.) justifying nativist violence as necessary to punish those who did not assimilate. Recently, a "New Preservation Movement" mobilized in an ad hoc fashion by communities, museums, heritage societies, and popular historians most visibly brings the past into public consciousness (S. Frangos 2004). The ways in which the past is represented in these accounts deserves a book-length study.

4. The view of a community and its past as determining forces is consistent with the tradition of communitarian thought within which Bellah writes. As a philosophy of society that reacts to excessive Western individualism, communitarianism maintains the need for shared and collectively imposed values. It exhibits, therefore, particular "interest in communities . . . [and] historically transmitted values and mores" (Etzioni 2001, 158).

5. Helen Papanikolas (1989), a pathbreaking researcher of Greek American women, attributes the archival silence of immigrant women to the centrality of orality in early twentieth-century immigrant culture. There have been some notable academic attempts to explore the symbolic and material worlds of women in Greek America. Early projects include the interdisciplinary colloquium "Greek and Greek American Women in Voice and Text," organized by Nadia Seremetakis as early as 1989 at New York University. Sponsored by the Alexander S. Onassis Center for Hellenic Studies, this event featured presentations by Olympia Dukakis, readings by poet Olga Broumas and novelist Irini Spanidou, and a performance workshop on women and music. With the exception of several poems by Broumas, colloquium presentations on Greek diaspora women were not included in the ensuing publication (Seremetakis 1993). Scholars who pioneered work on women and gender include Alice Scourby (1984), Vasilike Demos (1989), and Phyllis Chock (1995).

6. For similar views of the domestic sphere as women's physical and symbolic prison, see also Harry Mark Petrakis, whose fiction points to the effects of patriarchy in severely limiting the social imagination of Greek immigrant women. In his short story "The Judgment," for example, he writes of his abused character Katina: "Ignorant of the barest fundamentals of the knowledge in books, she lived in a teeming cupboard of superstition, myth, village theology, memories, fears, rumors, and the gossip of neighbors" (1978b, 285). Spatial enclosure symbolically demarcated the social death of widows, also signified through wearing black. Margaret Alexiou (1984–85) brings to attention a case documented by D. Scavdi: "[Young widows were] shut into their homes behind barred windows and bolted doors to face a life of increasing isolation and dementia" (24).

7. An interview statement reported by Leah Fygetakis (2002) illuminates the experience of ethnicity as a puzzling, deeply felt experience: "Greekness has always been important. I don't know why yet" (318). For yet another ethnographic statement that captures a similar reflection, see Anagnostou (2004c, 269).

8. Yet this should not lead to hasty generalizations. Steve Frangos (2005a) recovers the story of a Greek immigrant father of peasant origins who steadfastly encouraged

the artistic sensibilities of his daughters, the noted muralists and painters Ethel and Jenne Magafan.

9. The bibliography on the subject is too voluminous to cite here; for a relevant pioneering ethnography, see du Boulay (1974).

10. On the relationship between female modesty and sexuality, see Campbell (1964, 277) and du Boulay (1974, 112).

11. The concept of noncontemporaneity, as developed by anthropologist Nadia Seremetakis (1994, 12), fruitfully brings to attention the importance of the immigrant grandmother to effect the circulation of the past into the Greek American present. In the Greek context, her actions, gestures, stories, and artifacts embody a sensory memory and ethos of social exchange that make possible the circulation of noncontemporaneous knowledge and practices devalued by modernity. In Greek America, the immigrant grandmother, the infamous *yaya,* generates ambivalence, being portrayed as both a beloved figure and guardian of valuable knowledge and a relic of an undesired immigrant past.

12. See, for example, the comments by actress and author Olympia Dukakis. "It was impossible to stay within the Greek culture," she confesses in an interview. "I recognized that there was something controlling about it, something limiting and oppressive, and I felt that my options were being closed down" (Karageorge 2004, 28).

13. "The notion of a generic 'woman' functions in feminist thought much the way the notion of generic 'man' has functioned in Western philosophy: it obscures the heterogeneity of women and cuts off examination of the significance of such heterogeneity for feminist theory and political activity" (Spelman, quoted in Yuval-Davis 1994, 408).

14. As Nira Yuval-Davis (1994) notes, consciousness-raising "is a powerful tool . . . . It can empower people, bond them together in a sense of solidarity which is emotional as well as intellectual or political and can also problematize arenas of life and social norms which tend to be 'naturalized' within hegemonic cultures and which were formerly considered to be outside the arena of 'normal politics'" (414).

15. The collectivization of personal testimonies has been employed as a narrative strategy to amplify the public visibility of oppressed populations and to interrogate power structures. As Kay Warren (1997) indicates, collective representations of eyewitness accounts have been used widely in Latin America "to personalize the denunciation of state violence and to demonstrate subaltern resistance" (22).

16. Folk dances constitute a dominant cultural form in Greek America. Taught both formally and informally, they constitute a highly visible expressive form that the ethnic collective performs at festivals and regional dance competitions. A staple of American multiculturalism, folk-dance troupes are regularly invited to high schools and diversity events sponsored by the dominant society. When the Greek American students in the course I teach on Greek America repeatedly insisted on dancing in the classroom in order to "show our culture to the class," they were turning to dance as a tangible performance of ethnic identity.

17. As Aida Hurtado (1996, 75) notes, oppressed and marginalized groups particularly value ritual holidays: "[C]elebrations . . . become central to Chicano men and women in valuing themselves as human beings because of the enormous economic and social constraints they faced as a result of white racism."

18. But in reference to the Australian case, Gillian Bottomley (2005) reports instances of "gender blending" through Greek popular dance that challenge the dual authority of ethnic and gender-dominant expectations: "[T]he young women who dance with energy and agility the traditionally male dances, such as the *zebekiko* ('the eagle's dance') and the masculinist *hasapiko* (which originated from the butchers' guilds in Constantinople), move into forms of 'gender blending' that are widespread among the younger generation of Australians, but mark significant differences from the expectations of their parents. They are, therefore, crossing borders of gender as well as ethnicity."

19. Stigmatized collectives within Greek America create their own festivals as forums for public visibility. The Ionian Society, for example, "a small Boston-area Greek gay and lesbian organization that existed between 1985 to 1990" (Fygetakis 2002, 294), staged its "own miniversion of a Grecian festival" centered on food and dance during the Boston Gay, Lesbian, and Bisexual Pride Day (293).

Chapter 4: Interrogating Ethnic Whiteness, Building Interracial Solidarity

1. Although anthropologists rightly caution against the reification of the so-called honor-shame value system, numerous ethnographic examples point to its potency in Greek America. The following reminiscence by Helen Papanikolas (1995a) about an incident in the early twentieth century nicely captures the ethnicization of shame under conditions of migrancy: "The worst was the reading of the [Greek Orthodox] priest's love letters [printed in Salt Lake City newspapers] extolling . . . [the] anatomy [of his lover]. I dreaded going to school, hoping no one knew I was Greek" (11). The immigrant code of honor dictated that failure to conform to socially authorized expectations could result in ethnic stigmatization and even ostracism.

2. The term "accent," metaphorically understood, functions "as a sign of particularities, of differences that do not become absent or are not rendered silent" (Kamboureli 1996, 1).

3. The narrative approximates what Michael Angrosino (1989, 3) defines as "life story," which he distinguishes from "life history." He defines the former as a narrative that focuses selectively on key events or on a limited number of important social relationships.

4. My use of the term "rearticulation" follows Michael Omi and Howard Winant: "the process of redefinition of political interests and identities, through a process of recombination of familiar ideas and values in hitherto unrecognized ways" (1986, 146). Significantly, the ecumenical language that the Greek Orthodox patriarchate uses to deracialize Greek identity "and define Hellenes as a cultural and religious group that crosses racial boundaries" has offered a space for interracial couples and their families

to claim inclusion within New York City's Greek Orthodox communities (Karpathakis and Roudometof 2004, 285).

5. Attempts to exhibit undesirable pasts have been met with local fury and censorship. Stavros (Steve) Frangos (2004, 14–17), a steadfast popular chronicler of Greek America, reports the intricate negotiations as well as the contradictions that characterize the politics of exhibiting intraethnic labor exploitation in a Greek American community. Adversarial self-criticism as a mode of public engagement becomes increasingly rare in anglophone Greek America. The commentaries and journalism of Peter Pappas (1993) are a notable exception in this regard. In a polemical essay, he criticizes dominant institutions in Greek America, including the church. The *National Herald* occasionally ventures into intracommunity criticism, its commentators taking to task the overseers of the Greek American educational system and the organizers of the Greek Independence Day Parade in New York City, among others. In the Greek-language media, the satirical online newspaper *To Kalami* (http://www.kalami.net) hosts articles poking fun at Greek American leaders and organizations.

6. Petrakis's father was a Greek Orthodox priest who immigrated from Crete to America in 1916. Petrakis documents his father's resolute commitment to progressive racial politics in his autobiographical *Reflections: A Writer's Life, a Writer's Work* (Chicago: Lake View Press, 1983), 82–83.

7. For example, representations of Greek immigrants must be placed in the context of institutional and everyday power relations. The theatrical posture of immigrant friendliness—what has been captured memorably as the "Anatolian Smile" (Georgakas 2005)—is nothing short of a choreography born out of consciousness that the arrogance of the dominant society may turn, at a moment's notice, into racism, exclusion, expulsion, or outright violence. Those who view this staging of self as duplicity (see Callinicos 1990, 64–65) miss the point that this sort of performative politeness constitutes one part of a defensive repertoire, a weapon of the weak among the immigrants and their children. In the context of psychological and cultural colonization, it should not be surprising to answer the contemptuous arrogance of the dominant culture with calculated caution and internally burning resentment.

8. Greeks have been subjected to racist discourse ranking their bodies against the classical ideals of beauty thought inherent in Americanness:

> Thinking of Homer, of Praxiteles and of Phidias, one looks for Helen, for Hermes and for Athene, but the only Helen I saw in Athens was an American girl, married to a member of the cabinet and whose golden hair, blue eyes and classic features made her once the reigning hostess in the city. And it is only in the islands or deep in the country, where the Albanian plain has never reached, that one finds the facial lineaments and the bodily grace which the ancient sculptor has taught the modern world as being common to all Greeks of classic times.
>
> From *National Geographic*, December 1915, quoted in Karampetsos 1998.

9. The response of a middle-aged white visitor to the exhibit Slavery in New York City is consistent with the aim of Papanikolas. Exposure to the horrors of slavery caused her to experience "more empathy and understanding for a black person" (quoted in Lee 2005).

10. Research is needed regarding the experiences of white ethnics who do not visually approximate phenotypical ideals of whiteness.

11. Papanikolas had roots deep in the ethic of empathy. Practiced by her mother, it was also a defining feature of immigrant women's ethos. She linked empathy to Greek Orthodoxy but also recognized it as a component of Protestant Christianity, valuing it as a means to transcend ethnic and racial differences (Anagnostou 2004–5). The ethic of compassion sparks political controversy in the United States. The Republican Party welcomes the privilege it accords to personal or religious action as the engine for social change, most notably through President George W. Bush's politics of "compassionate conservatism." Because this understanding of compassion neglects the role of (governmental) policies and structural measures in alleviating poverty and discrimination, it has raised objections from liberals. Scholar and public intellectual Cornel West attempts to reconcile a politics of transformation based on the compassionate "love ethic" of Christianity with institutional policies that aim to redress class and racial injustices (see R. Cowan 2003).

12. Defining empathy "as identification with and understanding of another's situation, feelings, motives," Pearl Rosenberg (1997) points to the limits of empathetic identification:

> Those of us who teach in conservative environments may view students who express 'true empathy' for other people as noteworthy and admirable. However, even though empathy is an admirable trait and a needed first step in the education of our students around issues of racism, teaching for empathy is not enough. Empathy has its own dangers. It can, I think, create a false sense of involvement. We can be misled. We can think that we have achieved something significant with our students, but we are actually just getting started, or diverted. (83)

Empathy may generate narratives of self-victimization among those privileged by race and class, creating a false sense that all hardships "are the same" and "obscuring the ways that racist domination impacts on the lives of marginalized groups in our society" (ibid.).

Chapter 5: Ethnicity as Choice?

1. I have argued elsewhere that by neglecting to address the cultural production of identity, symbolic ethnicity becomes a component in the wider discourse on choice as a constitutive element of American identity (Anagnostou 2009).

2. My analytical emphasis on identity, instead of subjectivity or identification, is sensitive to the cautious treatment of the concept after deconstruction. "Who needs identity," Stuart Hall asks, (1996a), if the concept promotes sameness, unity, and fixity,

obliterating contradictions and the multiplicity of identities within the self? This deconstructive critique, though, does not abandon working with the concept of identity. Instead, it places it "under erasure," meaning that the concept is "no longer serviceable—'good to think with'—in . . . [its] originary and unreconstructed form" (1). Concepts such as identity "have not been superseded dialectically, and there are no other, entirely different concepts with which to replace them," Hall writes. Therefore, "there is nothing to do but to continue to think with them—albeit now in their detotalized or deconstructed forms, and no longer operating within the paradigm in which they were originally generated" (ibid.).

3. See, for example, the discussion of Marianthe Karanikas's (2001–2) commentary on ethnicity in chapter 6.

4. The language of pilgrimage as a spiritual journey that reconnects the immigrant self with the ancestral past appears frequently in autobiography and family biography. For writer Demetra Vaka Brown (1877–1946), returning to her native "Constantinople is described in terms of a spiritual journey to self-fulfillment" (Arapoglou 2004–5, 98).

5. In the book, Haley claimed to trace his black ancestors—but not the white— through two hundred years of slavery and oppression. The television version was broadcast in January 1977 for eight consecutive nights, attracting an estimated audience of 80 million (Petersen 1997, 29).

6. Even Thomas Lacey (1916), who made a case against the reigning biologism of his era by arguing about the persistence of *social* heredity of the Greeks as an uninterrupted "common type of mind" (9) throughout Greek history, did not escape the biologizing language of a "natural wanderlust." "There is the same 'wanderlust' as of old," he wrote. "Greek emigrants seek let for their energy in every quarter of the globe, from the United States to the Transvaal, carrying Hellenic traditions and preserving and perpetuating them in a marked way" (30). "Economic necessity reinforced the natural 'wanderlust'" (44).

7. For a remarkably similar case pertaining to the Portuguese diaspora, see Noivo (2002, 272).

8. It is instructive to juxtapose here the contrasting view of Greece as a center in the poetic corpus of Andonis Decavalles. Born in Alexandria, Egypt, to Greek parents, Decavalles spent part of his childhood on Siphnos, in the Cyclades Islands, and attended law school in Athens before emigrating to the United States in 1954, where he saw himself in a state of perpetual self-exile. An academic and a poet who insisted on writing in the Greek language to communicate an essential Greek identity, he expressed a longing for "home" in terms of a nostalgia for roots. He found "home" in highly idealized images of Greece, and particularly of Siphnos, which he praised as a "cultural metropolis from where ideals, traditions, religious and folklore customs, myths, and popular stories emanate" (Stefanidou 2002, 11). Like Kalafatas, but serving an entirely different set of aesthetic and political purposes, Decavalles treats cultural heritage "as having

an irresistible and formidable power that can attract people to it, even those in exile" (39). But unlike the popular ethnographer, who constructs identity in terms of multiple attachments, the poet draws rigid boundaries between an idyllic past and a nightmarish present, privileging Greek as his sole cultural and linguistic identity. What we have here are two contrasting subject positions in the diaspora, one centered on a stable identity directed exclusively toward the place of origins and the other framed on numerous identities, which preclude total identification with the ancestral land.

9. As Thomas Lacey observed, the "[Greek] belief in their classical ancestry has begotten a somewhat narrow and intolerant pride of superiority . . . . There is a certain racial arrogance about the Greek when he is brought into coöperation with other peoples" (1916, 34–35).

10. In patrilineal societies, blood is seen as the "physical carrier of male virtue," a logic of trait acquisition commonly appropriated by nationalism (Herzfeld 1997, 37). The belief in Greek golden blood traced back to classical antiquity sustains the ideology of Greek national superiority, which various regions in the country appropriate to support their claims for even deeper ties to antiquity and, thus, even greater social distinction (ibid.). This discourse is ubiquitous in diaspora family narratives on kinship lines extending deep into Greek regional pasts. Here is how Louis Markos (2006), a professor of English at Houston's Baptist University, speaks about his immigrant grandfather Louie (Leonidas) Markos, born in a village adjacent to Sparta: "In the blood of Louie's family there runs two streams. One flows from the Sparta of Lycurgus and Leonidas: simple, tough, manly. The other flows from the Mycenae of the sons of Atreus: elaborate, highly cultured, slightly Asiatic, even effeminate" (94). In the context of Greek history, regional distinction connects with international alliances in the political struggle for ethnic autonomy. As Thomas Lacey pointed out, "When the Cretans sought American sympathy in their attempt to throw off the Moslem yoke they began their appeal in this characteristic way, 'We, the descendants of Minos and of Jupiter'" (1916, 34).

11. Furthermore, as Renée Hirschon (1989) shows, gift-giving among the Greek Orthodox is meant for remembrance. In Greek America, this practice guarantees the institutional memory of family names because scholarships, donations to community organizations, gifts to cultural and civic institutions, and endowed chairs in modern Greek studies programs are commonly named after the donor. When the Condakes family donated $2 million to the Boston Museum of Fine Arts for the creation of a gallery for Greek art, museum director Malcolm Rogers sounded this cultural chord in his acknowledgment of the gift: "With the naming of the Evanthea & Leo Condakes Gallery for Greek Art, the Condakes family name becomes part of the fabric of the Museum of Fine Arts, standing in good company with the foremost benefactors of this institution" (quoted in Kalmoukos 2005).

12. Actress Melina Kanakaredes also reports that pressure to change her last name underlies, in part, her resistance to doing so (M. Frangos 2003).

13. See, for example, Vassos Argyrou (2002), who explicitly draws upon the ethos of agonistic performative excellence to challenge epistemologies central to his own discipline, anthropology.

Chapter 6: Redirecting Ethnic Options

1. Elsewhere, I have cautioned against a sharp analytical differentiation between ethnicity and diaspora (Anagnostou 2003).

2. Such an opposition was common in Western Europe as well. In his review of nineteenth- and early twentieth-century writers in Britain, William Stafford (1989) identifies those social forces that critiqued modernization to defend the superiority of medieval, precommercial economy. Christianity and Christian socialists extolled the medieval order, which they saw as an ideal human community that functioned to satisfy the whole. Roman Catholics lamented the demise of the monasteries, whose philanthropy they contrasted with post-Reformation greed and selfish individualism (37). Similarly, the guild socialist movement in England posited the guild as "the supreme expression of the communitarian ideal of the Middle Ages" (35), whose relative egalitarian ethos it contrasted with the profit-centered "ethos of the merchant" under capitalism (39). This emphasis on Christian institutions and craftsmen's guilds also organizes "Winter Dream." The poet must have been exposed to European socialism through his direct contact, as we will see, with political activist Karl Vasilievich Flegel (Kalafatas 2003). The infusion of Christianity into socialist thought was also a characteristic of early Greek socialism, whose texts were circulated during the last quarter of the nineteenth century through the activism of intellectuals (Noutsos 1990, 104).

3. Invented by diaspora linguist Adamantios Korais, this register pointed to a modern Greek national identity linked to both the classical and the Byzantine past. Adopted as the official language of the newly founded kingdom, it became the language of choice in the state apparatus. It represented a high register whose mastery through education differentiated its users from the illiterate masses, who spoke demotic, a form of vernacular. An instrument of state power, katharevousa conferred distinction on its users, mostly bureaucrats, educators, state officials, and writers. Opposed by demoticism, a cultural movement that advocated the vernacular as the national language, it was defended by the church, which embraced classicizing Greek as part of its religious heritage.

4. This linguistic paradox was evident in yet another case of early twentieth-century antimodernist activism in the islands of the Aegean. Charalambos Pamphylis, an Icarian intellectual and former politician turned utopian political radical, published his newspaper editorials and speeches in katharevousa in the 1920s, advocating a "return to an earlier Golden Age when they [the islanders] lived in cooperative harmony untouched by feudalism and the first stages of capitalism" (Papalas 2005, 140).

5. This representation approximates the "customary ethos" of mid-nineteenth-century Greek Orthodox communities under the Ottoman Empire as described by social historian Gerasimus Augustinos (1992). The local homeland—patridha—represented a

"corporate body . . . that gave meaning to the existence of the individual and the family" (171). Safeguarding its moral principles was inextricably tied to the preservation of traditional identities.

6. This juxtaposition recalls the uses of nostalgia as a means of addressing the disruptive forces of modernization. As Raymond Williams (1973, 35–45) observes, the idealization of the past as a "Golden Age" and lamentation over its loss serve not only as a nostalgic longing for the former but also as a biting critique of the contemporary social order.

7. This political activism was carried out openly in Tarpon Springs, Florida, where immigrants from the Dodecanese held considerable economic and political power because of their high demographics and key position in the local sponge industry. Given the lobbying efforts of this powerful electorate, it comes as no surprise that it was a senator from Florida, Claude Pepper, who in 1944 attempted to introduce, albeit unsuccessfully, "a resolution in support of a Greek annexation of the Italian occupied Dodecanese" (Zervakis 1998–99, 228).

8. The story of the Greek American Left emerged from academic obscurity largely thanks to the pioneering work of labor historian Dan Georgakas, whose publishing initiatives (1987a; 1994) carved a scholarly niche for the topic. A wave of subsequent publications on the Greek American Left (Peck 2000; Karpozilos 2004) has led to a rethinking of Greek American political history. This revisionist scholarship has overturned the central assumption of dominant historiography, namely middle-classness as *the* defining element of Greek America. This impact is felt in the comments of notable military sociologist and ethnic historian Charles Moskos (2002), who acknowledges that his authoritative *Greek Americans: Struggles and Success* "overstates Greek American social history as essentially a process of embourgeoisement" (33). For the critical importance of the Left in Greek America, see the debate between Moskos and Georgakas (1987) in the *Journal of the Hellenic Diaspora* 14, nos. 1–2, 55–77.

9. The Marxist ideal of transcending cultural and racial differences in the name of worker solidarity promotes interracial labor unification and egalitarian unionism. Yet, as David Roediger (2003) observes, the notion "that the common experience of class exploitation unifies workers across racial lines" exists in tension with "[t]he Marxist idea that material interests have structured the exclusionary tendencies of white workers as capitalism has created (and capitalists have exploited) racial divisions among workers" (190). The latter "can be used to argue for the improbability of meaningful interracial unity or to mitigate the record of racism by white workers in their unions" (ibid.). American Marxism deployed contradictory union tactics, and it certainly was not free of racial prejudice. For instance, "the Workingmen's party, the first Marxist political party in the United States, garnered roughly a third of the vote in state elections during the decade [1870s] behind the no-nonsense slogan 'The Chinese Must Go!'" (Jacobson 2000, 79). As Kostis Karpozilos (2004) observes, "The American communists did not have a clear position on the working-class movement for a long period. Two tendencies co-existed: the first calling for 'dual unionism' and the other advocating the necessity of

working in the ranks of the reactionary AFL. . . . [Lenin] justified the latter position, but until then the communists were mainly working within the IWW [Industrial Workers of the World] unions" (52).

10. It was under the auspices of the IWW that historical foes transcended Old World nationalist animosities and united to form a common front: "Greeks and Turks and Armenians . . . marched arm-in-arm in the picket line" (quoted in Karpozilos 2004, 23). Socialized in radical politics through their participation in the IWW, many Greek immigrant communists observed this principle. According to communist labor organizer Demosthenes Nicas, a former IWW member, social relations among the communist rank and file in Lynn, Massachusetts, were characterized by "total egalitarianism" (Georgakas 1991, 103). Everyday relations then sought to re-create a microcosm of an egalitarian society, which "everyone was convinced . . . could be created" (ibid.). What is more, this political ideology meshed with immigrant cultural values. As Georgakas (1994) observes, "Slogans such as 'An injury to one is an injury to all' easily fused with the concept of *filotimo*" (13). On the debate over why early twentieth-century Greek immigrants joined labor strikes, see Peck (1991). In contrast, the Greek immigrant Left in the 1970s and 1980s in New York City "did not create contacts with the American Left or grassroots organizations advocating for social justice issues. Their frame of reference was and remains, Greek politics" (Karpathakis and Roudometof 2004, 273).

11. A broad liberal and leftist international coalition that included the American Civil Liberties Union, the Socialist Party, the Amalgamated Clothing Workers of America, the International Ladies' Garment Workers Union, as well as numerous American intellectuals and artists defended the innocence of the prisoners: "Even the notoriously cautious American Federation of Labor . . . were convinced that Sacco and Vanzetti had been unjustly convicted" (Topp 1996, 141).

12. Praised in Europe and the United States, the Greek counteroffensive against Mussolini's invading army had a significant cultural impact. On December 16, 1940, *Life* magazine featured on its cover page a Greek *evzone* (infantryman), "a member of the elite corps of the Greek army, in traditional costume, and declared on its front page: 'The Amazing Greeks Win Freedom's First Victory'" (Zervakis 1998–99, 218). That was a time "when fustanella-clad Greek soldiers routed Axis forces in Albania and when Londoners enduring the Blitz pinned miniature evzones on their lapels and sang 'Leave Mussel to the Greeks!' The 'garden salad' in American diners was to be renamed the 'Greek salad'!" (Calotychos 2003, 240). Despite Greek Americans' very public support for the Allied forces, the surveillance of ethnics, seen as potentially hostile aliens, never ceased. When the United States entered the war, for example, a company in White Pine County, Nevada, invited those Greek immigrants that "they trusted to identify 'Greeks who hated America,' because they feared sabotage" (Karampetsos 1998, 89).

13. Political persecution cast an intimidating shadow on leftist intellectuals. Targeted by investigative committees, novelists and scholars lived in fear and exercised self-censorship. Herbert G. Gutman, the author of *Work, Culture and Society in Industrializing*

America: Essays in American Working-Class and Social History (New York: Knopf, 1975) and an activist in leftist Yiddish circles, was called to testify before Congress (Buhle and Georgakas 1996, 8). Henry Roth, a son of Jewish immigrants, member of the American Communist Party (he joined in 1934), and celebrated author of *Call It Sleep,* a best-selling novel, reportedly "burned his notebooks, fearing that they contained evidence of his continuing Communism" (Rosen 2005, 78). The representation of ethnicity in film was similarly determined by Cold War politics. For instance, Hollywood left no choice to American novelist and screenwriter Albert Isaac Bezzerides (1908–2007), of Armenian and Greek (Pontic) ancestry, on how to represent the sponge diving community of Tarpon Springs in the film *Beneath the Twelve-Mile Reef* (1953). According to Yiorgos Kalogeras (2004–5), "The ethnic content of this movie was meant to be nonthreatening for mainstream American society that was experiencing a period of widespread social conformity during the early years of the Cold War and during HUAC's [House Committee on Un-American Activities] height of power" (30). Furthermore, it was pressure exerted by HUAC that forced director Jules Dassin out of the country (27). Bezzerides's film career in Hollywood was stalled at that time; his "friendship with the screenwriters and other Hollywood personalities whose names had been blacklisted during the McCarthy era witch hunt, made it hard for him to find work. His own name ended up on Hollywood's unofficial 'Grey List,' which included anyone that was in the least bit friendly with blacklisted actors" (Chriss 2006, 46).

14. The *Journal of the Hellenic Diaspora* has served as a conduit for alternative historiography. Founded in 1974 as a political forum vested in anti-imperialist, pro–Third World, and prominority movements, it prominently covered left-wing artists and intellectuals. It paid tribute to Trotskyist painter Aristodemos Kaldis (Valamvanos 1979) and featured Theodore Stamos, a painter and member of John Reed's Communist Labor Party (Kasdaglis and Pappas 1982). Because the dominant strain of Greek American historiography paid minimal attention to the left, the journal represented a radical intervention in academic politics. As Dan Georgakas (1994) and Kostis Karpozilos (2004) speculate, repressive political conditions may partially explain why influential chroniclers of Greek America—such as J. P. Xenidis, Thomas Burgess, and Theodore Saloutos, among others—demoted, even denied, the significance of immigrant radicalism. Commenting on Saloutos's "standard ethnic history," *The Greeks in the United States,* Georgakas (1994, 8) notes that "the usually dependable" historian "incorrectly and irresponsibly declares, 'Marxism made no appreciable progress among Greek Americans.'" To account for this position by a "professional historian with liberal politics," Georgakas further reflects that "[Saloutos's] occasional notes on labor show no bias. One can only speculate this particular comment is somewhat related to the atmosphere of the Cold War and its impact on ethnic self-image" (30n3). Even Helen Papanikolas, one of the earliest ethnic historians who openly decried the indecency of capitalist excesses, disassociated participation in the working-class movement from leftist class consciousness. Significantly, the explanation of ethnic radicalism in terms of cultural values—as an

answer to honor violation—perpetuates the image of immigrants as folk, denying their place in modernity via willful participation in class struggle.

15. Ethnographic work further documents Greek American narratives employing the language of primordial connectivity with an ancient Greek past (Anagnostou 2004c, 261–67), indicating the continued operation of "New Age Hellenism" in Greek America.

REFERENCES

Abrahams, Roger D., and Susan Kalcik. 1978. "Folklore and Cultural Pluralism." In *Folklore in the Modern World,* ed. Richard Dorson, 223–36. The Hague: Mouton.

Abu-Lughod, Lila. 1991. "Writing against Culture." In *Recapturing Anthropology: Working in the Present,* ed. Richard G. Fox, 137–62. Santa Fe, NM: School of American Research Press.

Acocella, Joan. 2005. "Connections: Race and Relations in Zadie Smith's New Novel." *New Yorker,* October.

————. 2004. "CounterLives: Philip Roth's 'The Plot against America.'" *New Yorker,* September.

Ahmed, Sara. 2002. "Racialized Bodies." In *Real Bodies: A Sociological Introduction,* ed. Mary Evans and Ellie Lee, 46–63. New York: Palgrave.

Akrotirianakis, Stavros Nicholas. 1994. *Byzantium Comes to Southern California: The Los Angeles Greek Community and the Building of Saint Sophia Cathedral.* Minneapolis, MN: Light and Life.

Alba, Richard D. 1990. *Ethnic Identity: The Transformation of White America.* New Haven, CT: Yale University Press.

————. 1985. *Italian Americans: Into the Twilight of Ethnicity.* Englewood Cliffs, NJ: Prentice Hall.

Alcoff, Linda Martín. 2000. "Who's Afraid of Identity Politics?" In *Reclaiming Identity: Realist Theory and the Predicament of Postmodernism,* ed. Paula M. L. Moya and Michael R. Hames-Garcia, 312–44. Los Angeles: University of California Press.

Alex, Angel. 1974. *Greek Story of Canton, Ohio, 1893–1973.* Canton, OH: privately published.

Alexiou, Margaret. 1984–85. "Folklore: An Obituary?" *Byzantine and Modern Greek Studies* 9: 1–28.

Almaguer, Tomas. 1994. *Racial Fault Lines: The Historical Origins of White Supremacy in California.* Berkeley: University of California Press.

Alonso, Ana Maria. 1992. "Gender, Power, and Historical Memory: Discourses of Serrano Resistance." In *Feminists Theorize the Political,* ed. Judith Butler and Joan W. Scott, 404–25. New York: Routledge.

Anagnostou, Yiorgos. 2009. "A Critique of Symbolic Ethnicity: The Ideology of Choice?" *Ethnicities* 9 (1): 94–122.

————. 2008a. "Against Cultural Loss: Immigration, Life History, and the Enduring 'Vernacular.'" In *Hellenisms: Culture, Identity, and Ethnicity from Antiquity to Modernity,* ed. Katerina Zacharia, 355–77. Burlington, VT: Ashgate.

————. 2008b. "Research Frontiers, Academic Margins: Helen Papanikolas and the Authority to Represent the Immigrant Past." *Journal of the Hellenic Diaspora* 34 (1–2): 9–29.

————. 2006. "Metaethnography in the Age of 'Popular Folklore.'" *Journal of American Folklore* 119 (474): 381–412.

————. 2004–5. "Helen Papanikolas as a Humanist: Immigrants, 'Contact Zones,' and Empathy in the American West." *Modern Greek Studies Yearbook* 20–21:147–73.

————. 2004a. "Forget the Past, Remember the Ancestors! Modernity, 'Whiteness,' American Hellenism, and the Politics of Memory in Early Greek America." *Journal of Modern Greek Studies* 21 (1): 25–71.

————. 2004b. "Private Heirlooms, Public Memories: Tradition and Greek America as Translation." *Gramma: A Journal of Theory and Criticism* 12:109–25.

————. 2004c. "'That Imagination Called Hellenism': Connecting Greek Worlds, Past and Present, in Greek America." *Classical Bulletin* 80 (2): 247–81.

————. 2003. "Model Americans, Quintessential Greeks: Ethnic Success and Assimilation in Diaspora." *Diaspora: A Journal of Transnational Studies* 12 (3): 279–327.

Anagnostu, Georgios. 1999. "Negotiating Identity, Connecting through Culture: Hellenism and Neohellenism in Greek America." PhD diss., Ohio State University.

————. 1993–94. "Anthropology and Literature: Crossing Boundaries in a Greek-American Novel." In *Fantasy or Ethnography? Irony and Collusion in Subaltern Representation,* ed. Sabra J. Webber and Margaret R. Lynd, 195–220. Papers in Comparative Studies 8. Columbus, OH: Ohio State University.

Ang, Ien. 2000. "Identity Blues." In *Without Guarantees: In Honour of Stuart Hall,* ed. Paul Gilroy, Lawrence Grossberg, and Angela McRobbie, 1–13. New York: Verso.

Angrosino, Michael V. 1989. *Documents of Interaction: Biography, Autobiography, and Life History in Social Science Perspective.* Monographs in Social Sciences 74. Gainesville: University of Florida Press.

Apessos, Sophia. 2003. "In Quest to Defy Definition, Olympia Dukakis Discovers Herself." *National Herald,* August 23–24.

Arapoglou, Eleftheria. 2004–5. "Vaka Brown: The Historicized Geography / Geographic History of an Immigrant." *Journal of Modern Hellenism* 21–22 (Winter): 83–103.

Archdeacon, Thomas J. 1983. *Becoming American: An Ethnic History.* New York: Free Press.

Ardener, Shirley. 1981. "Ground Rules and Social Maps for Women: An Introduction." In *Women and Space: Ground Rules and Social Maps,* ed. Shirley Ardener, 11–34. London: Croom Helm.

Argyrou, Vassos. 2002. *Anthropology and the Will to Meaning: A Postcolonial Critique.* London: Pluto.

————. 1996. *Tradition and Modernity in the Mediterranean: The Wedding as Symbolic Struggle.* Cambridge: Cambridge University Press.

Augustinos, Gerasimos. 1992. *The Greeks of Asia Minor: Confession, Community, and Ethnicity in the Nineteenth Century.* Kent, OH: Kent State University Press.

Bakalian, Anny P. 1993. *Armenian-Americans: From Being to Feeling Armenian.* New Brunswick, NJ: Transaction Publishers.

Ball, Eric. 2002. "*Where* Are the Folk? The Cretan *Mantinada* as Placed Literature." *Journal of Folklore Research* 39 (2–3): 147–72.

Barrett, James R., and David Roediger. 1997. "Inbetween Peoples: Race, Nationality, and the 'New Immigrant' Working Class." *Journal of American Ethnic History* 16 (3): 3–42.

Bauman, Zygmunt. 1996. "From Pilgrim to Tourist—or a Short History of Identity." In *Questions of Cultural Identity,* ed. Stuart Hall and Paul du Gay, 18–36. London: Sage.

Bazin, Jean. 1999. "Generalized Ethnography." In "Diaspora and Immigration," ed. V. Y. Mudimbe with Sabine Engel. Special issue, *South Atlantic Quarterly* 98 (1–2): 23–33.

Bellah, Robert N., Richard Madsen, William M. Sullivan, Ann Swidler, and Steven M. Tipton. 1985. *Habits of the Heart: Individualism and Commitment in American Life.* New York: Perennial Library.

Ben-Amos, Dan. 1989. "The Historical Folklore of Richard M. Dorson." In "Richard M. Dorson's Views and Works: An Assessment." Special issue, *Journal of Folklore Research* 26 (1): 51–60.

———. 1972. "Toward a Definition of Folklore in Context." In *Toward New Perspectives in Folklore,* ed. Américo Paredes and Richard Bauman, 3–15. Austin: University of Texas Press.

Bendersky, Joseph W. 1995. "The Disappearance of Blonds: Immigration, Race and the Reemergence of 'Thinking White.'" In "Populism." Special issue, *Telos* 2 (104): 135–57.

Bendix, Regina. 1997. *In Search of Authenticity: The Formation of Folklore Studies.* Madison: University of Wisconsin Press.

Bendix, Regina, and Herman Roodenburg. 2000. "Managing Ethnicity: An Introduction." In *Managing Ethnicity: Perspectives from Folklore Studies, History and Anthropology,* ed. Regina Bendix and Herman Roodenburg, ix–xviii. Amsterdam: Het Spinhuis.

Berman, Marshall. 1982. *All That Is Solid Melts into Air: The Experience of Modernity.* New York: Simon and Schuster.

Bottomley, Gillian. 2005. "Negociation, Polyphony and Difference in Greek Australian Creative Practices." *Revue Européenne des Migrations Internationales* 16 (2): 119–30.

———. 1992. *From Another Place: Migration and the Politics of Culture.* Cambridge: Cambridge University Press.

Bourdieu, Pierre. 1984. *Distinction: A Social Critique of the Judgement of Taste.* Trans. Richard Nice. London: Routledge.

Brah, Avtar. 1996. *Cartographies of Diaspora: Contesting Identities.* New York: Routledge.

Brodkin, Karen. 1998. *How Jews Became White Folks and What That Says about Race in America.* New Brunswick, NJ: Rutgers University Press.

Brooks, Wyck Van. 1918. "On Creating a Usable Past." *Dial* 9, April 11, 337–41. Reprinted in *Critics of Culture: Literature and Society in the Early Twentieth Century,* ed. Alan Trachtenberg, 165–71. New York: John Wiley and Sons, 1976.

Brown K. S. and Yannis Hamilakis. 2003. "The Cupboard of the Yesterdays? Critical Perspectives on the Usable Past." In *The Usable Past: Greek Metahistories,* ed. K. S. Brown and Yannis Hamilakis, 1–19. Lanham, MD: Lexington.

Bruner, Edward M. 1994. "Abraham Lincoln as Authentic Reproduction: A Critique of Postmodernism." *American Anthropologist* 96 (2): 397–415.

Buhle, Paul, and Dan Georgakas. 1996. "Introduction." In *The Immigrant Left in the United States,* ed. Paul Buhle and Dan Georgakas, 1–9. Albany: State University of New York Press.

Bullert J. B. 1997. *Public Television: Politics and the Battle over Documentary Film.* New Brunswick, NJ: Rutgers University Press.

Calhoun, Craig. 1994. "Social Theory and the Politics of Identity." In *Social Theory and the Politics of Identity,* ed. Craig Calhoun, 9–36. Oxford: Blackwell.

Callinicos, Constance. 1990. *American Aphrodite: Becoming Female in Greek America.* New York: Pella.

Calotychos, Vangelis. 2003. *Modern Greece: A Cultural Poetics.* Oxford: Berg.

Campbell, J. K. 1964. *Honour, Family, and Patronage: A Study of Institutions and Moral Values in a Greek Mountain Community.* Oxford: Oxford University Press.

Caraveli, Anna. 1985. *Scattered in Foreign Lands: A Greek Village in Baltimore.* Baltimore, MD: Baltimore Museum of Art.

———. 1983. Review of *Ours Once More: Folklore, Ideology, and the Making of Modern Greece,* by Michael Herzfeld. *Journal of American Folklore* 96 (382): 476–78.

Carrier, James G., ed. 1995. *Occidentalism: Images of the West.* Oxford: Clarendon.

Chen, Xiaomei. 1995. *Occidentalism: A Theory of Counter-discourse in Post-Mao China.* New York: Oxford University Press.

Chock, Phyllis Pease. 1995. "'The Self-Made Woman': Gender and the Success Story in Greek-American Family Histories." In *Naturalizing Power: Essays in Feminist Cultural Analysis,* ed. Sylvia Yanagisako and Carol Delaney, 239–55. New York: Routledge.

———. 1990. Review of *Greek Americans: Struggle and Success,* by Charles C. Moskos. *Journal of Modern Greek Studies* 8 (1): 149–51.

———. 1987. "The Irony of Stereotypes: Towards an Anthropology of Ethnicity." *Cultural Anthropology* 2 (3): 347–68.

Chouliaras, Yiorgos. 1997. "Writing in the Diaspora and the Diaspora of Writing." In *Greeks in English-Speaking Countries: Culture, Identity, Politics,* ed. Christos P. Ioannides, 337–46. New Rochelle, NY: Melissa Media Associates.

Chressanthis, James. 1982. *Remembrance of a Journey to the Village.* Film. Greek Orthodox Archdiocese of North and South America. Davkore Company, Mountain View, CA.

Chriss, Dimitri. 2006. "Greek Filmmaker Honors American Legend." *Greek America Magazine,* May–June.

Clark, Mari H. 1983. "Variations on Themes of Male and Female: Reflections on Gender Bias in Fieldwork in Rural Greece." *Women's Studies* 10 (2): 117–33.

Clifford, James. 1997. *Routes: Travel and Translation in the Late Twentieth Century*. Cambridge, MA: Harvard University Press.

———. 1988. *The Predicament of Culture: Twentieth-Century Ethnography, Literature, and Art*. Cambridge, MA: Harvard University Press.

———. 1986a. "Introduction: Partial Truths." In *Writing Culture: The Poetics and Politics of Ethnography*, ed. James Clifford and George E. Marcus, 1–26. Berkeley: University of California Press.

———. 1986b. "On Ethnographic Allegory." In *Writing Culture: The Poetics and Politics of Ethnography*, ed. James Clifford and George E. Marcus, 98–121. Berkeley: University of California Press.

Clifford, James, and George E. Marcus, eds. 1986. *Writing Culture: The Poetics and Politics of Ethnography*. Berkeley: University of California Press.

Clogg, Richard. 1992. *A Concise History of Greece*. New York: Cambridge University Press.

Condos, Theony. 2005. "Helen Papanikolas—1917–2004." In "The Greek American Experience," ed. E. D. Karampetsos. Special issue, *Charioteer: An Annual Review of Modern Greek Culture* 43: n.p.

Connerton, Paul. 1989. *How Societies Remember*. Cambridge: Cambridge University Press.

Connolly, William E. 2002. *Identity / Difference: Democratic Negotiations of Political Paradox*. Expanded ed. Minneapolis: University of Minnesota Press.

Constant, Constance M. 2005. *Austin Lunch: Greek-American Recollections*. River Vale, NJ: Cosmos.

Constantakos, Chrysie M. 1990. "Stories to Live By: The Role of Older Adults in Transmitting Ethnic Heritage." *Journal of Modern Hellenism* 7 (Winter): 107–15.

———. 1987. "The Greek American Subcommunity: Intergroup Conflict." In *Education and Greek Americans: Process and Prospects*, ed. Spyros D. Orfanos, Harry J. Psomiades, and John Spiridakis, 35–71. New York: Pella.

Constantinides, Elizabeth. 1983. "Andreiomeni: The Female Warrior in Greek Folk Songs." *Journal of Modern Greek Studies* 1 (1): 63–72.

Coumantaros, Stella. 1982. "The Greek Orthodox Ladies Philoptochos Society and the Greek American Community." In *The Greek American Community in Transition*, ed. Harry J. Psomiades and Alice Scourby, 191–96. New York: Pella.

Cowan, Jane K. 1990. *Dance and the Body Politic in Northern Greece*. Princeton, NJ: Princeton University Press.

Cowan, Rosemary. 2003. *Cornel West: The Politics of Redemption*. Cambridge: Polity Press.

Dallas-Damis, Athena G. 1982. "The Greek Heritage and Its Impact on the Greek American Writer." In *The Greek American Community in Transition*, ed. Harry J. Psomiades and Alice Scourby, 217–29. New York: Pella.

Daniels, Eleni. 2000. "Hellenic Times Fund Awards $100,000 to Greek-American Students." *GreekAmerican,* May 12.

Dávila, Arlene. 2001. *Latinos, Inc.: The Marketing and Making of a People.* Berkeley: University of California Press.

Dégh, Linda. 1994. *American Folklore and the Mass Media.* Bloomington: Indiana University Press.

Del Negro, Giovanna P. 2004. *The Passeggiata and Popular Culture in an Italian Town: Folklore and the Performance of Modernity.* Montreal: McGill-Queen's University Press.

Demetracopoulou Lee, D. 1936. "Folklore of the Greeks in America." *Folk-Lore* 47 (2): 294–310.

Demos, Vasilike. 1989. "Maintenance and Loss of Traditional Gender Boundaries in Two Greek Orthodox Communities." *Journal of the Hellenic Diaspora* 16 (1–4): 77–93.

——. 1988. "Ethnic Mother-Tongue Maintenance among Greek Orthodox Americans." In "New Perspectives on Language Maintenance and Language Shift II," ed. James R. Dow. Special issue, *International Journal of the Sociology of Language* 69: 59–71.

di Leonardo, Micaela. 1998. *Exotics at Home: Anthropologies, Others, American Modernity.* Chicago: University of Chicago Press.

——. 1994. "White Ethnicities, Identity Politics, and Baby Bear's Chair." *Social Text* 41 (Winter 1994): 165–91.

——. 1984. *The Varieties of Ethnic Experience: Kinship, Class, and Gender among California Italian-Americans.* Ithaca, NY: Cornell University Press.

Dorson, Richard M. 1978a. "Folklore in the Modern World." In *Folklore in the Modern World,* ed. Richard M. Dorson, 3–51. The Hague: Mouton.

——. 1978b. "We All Need the Folk." *Journal of the Folklore Institute* 3 (September–December): 267–69.

——. 1977. *American Folklore.* Chicago: University of Chicago Press.

——. 1968. *The British Folklorists: A History.* London: Routledge and Kegan Paul.

——. 1950. "Folklore and Fake Lore." *American Mercury* 70 (315): 335–43.

Doumanis, Nicholas. 1997. *Myth and Memory in the Mediterranean: Remembering Fascism's Empire.* New York: St. Martin's.

Draper, Theodore. 1957. *The Roots of American Communism.* New York: Viking.

Driver, Tom Faw. 1998. *Liberating Rites: Understanding the Transformative Power of Ritual.* Boulder, CO: Westview.

Du Bois, W. E. B. 1903. *The Souls of Black Folk.* Chicago: A. C. McClurg.

——. 1940. *Dusk of Dawn.* New York: Harcourt, Brace. Repr., Millwood, NY: Kraus-Thomson.

du Boulay, Juliet. 1986. "Women—Images of Their Nature and Destiny in Rural Greece." In *Gender and Power in Rural Greece,* ed. Jill Dubisch, 139–68. Princeton, NJ: Princeton University Press.

——. 1974. *Portrait of a Greek Mountain Village.* Oxford: Clarendon.

Dyer, Richard. 1997. *White.* London: Routledge.

Enke, Anne. 2003. "Smuggling Sex through the Gates: Race, Sexuality, and the Politics of Space in Second Wave Feminism." *American Quarterly* 55 (4): 635–67.

Etzioni, Amitai. 2001 "Communitarianism." In *The Oxford Companion to Politics of the World,* ed. Joel Krieger, 158. 2nd ed. New York: Oxford University Press.

Fairchild, Pratt Henry. 1911. *Greek Immigration to the United States.* New Haven, CT: Yale University Press.

Feagin, Joe R. 1997. "Old Poison in New Bottles: The Deep Roots of Modern Nativism." In *Immigrants Out! The New Nativism and the Anti-immigrant Impulse in the United States,* ed. Juan F. Perea, 13–43. New York: New York University Press.

Feuerlicht, Roberta Strauss. 1977. *Justice Crucified: The Story of Sacco and Vanzetti.* New York: McGraw-Hill.

Fine, Michelle, Lois Weis, Linda C. Powell, and L. Mun Wong, eds. 1997. *Off White: Readings on Race, Power, and Society.* New York: Routledge.

Fischer, Michael M. J. 1986. "Ethnicity and the Post-modern Arts of Memory." In *Writing Culture: The Poetics and Politics of Ethnography,* ed. James Clifford and George Marcus, 194–233. Berkeley: University of California Press.

Fortier, Anne-Marie. 1998. "The Politics of 'Italians Abroad': Nation, Diaspora, and New Geographies of Identity." *Diaspora: A Journal of Transnational Studies* 7 (2): 197–224.

———. 1994. "Ethnicity." *Paragraph* 17 (3): 213–23.

Frangos, Mark. 2003. "Screen and Stage Star True to Heritage." *National Herald,* August 30–31.

Frangos, Stavros. 2004. *Greeks in Michigan.* East Lansing: Michigan State University Press.

Frangos, Steve. 2006. "Rain in the Valley: Helen Papanikolas' Final Farewell." In "Books." Special issue, *National Herald,* May 27.

———. 2005. "The Twined Muses: Ethel and Jenne Magafan." *Journal of the Hellenic Diaspora* 31 (2): 59–94.

———. 2004. "Grassroots Efforts to Preserve Hellenism." *National Herald,* January 17–18.

———. 1996. "Greek American Geography." *GreekAmerican,* July 13.

Frankenberg, Ruth. 1993. *White Women, Race Matters: The Social Construction of Whiteness.* Minneapolis: University of Minnesota Press.

Frey, Nancy Louise. 1998. *Pilgrim Stories: On and Off the Road to Santiago.* Berkeley: University of California Press.

Friedl, Ernestine. 1986. "The Position of Women: Appearance and Reality." In *Gender and Power in Rural Greece,* ed. Jill Dubisch, 42–52. Princeton, NJ: Princeton University Press.

Friedman, Jonathan. 1994. *Cultural Identity and Global Process.* London: Sage.

Friedman, Susan Stanford. 1998. *Mappings: Feminism and the Cultural Geographies of Encounter.* Princeton, NJ: Princeton University Press.

Fygetakis, Leah M. 2002. "Greek American Lesbians: Identity Odysseys of Honorable Good Girls." In *Reading Greek America: Studies in the Experience of Greeks in the United States,* ed. Spyros D. Orfanos, 291–325. New York: Pella.

Gallagher, Charles A. 1996. "White Reconstruction in the University." In *The Social Construction of Race and Ethnicity in the United States,* ed. Joan Ferrante and Prince Brown Jr., 337–54. New York: Longman.

Gallant, Thomas W. 2002. *Experiencing Dominion: Culture, Identity and Power in the British Mediterranean.* Notre Dame, IN: University of Notre Dame Press.

———. 2001. *Modern Greece.* London: Arnold.

Gans, Herbert J. 1988. *Middle American Individualism: The Future of Liberal Democracy.* New York: Free Press.

———. 1979. "Symbolic Ethnicity: The Future of Ethnic Groups and Cultures in America." *Ethnic and Racial Studies* 2 (1): 1–20.

Geertz, Clifford. 1983. *Local Knowledge: Further Essays in Interpretive Anthropology.* New York: Basic Books.

Georgakas, Dan. 2006. *My Detroit: Growing Up Greek and American in Motor City.* New York: Pella.

———. 2005. "The Anatolian Smile of Elia Kazan." In "The Greek American Experience," ed. E. D. Karampetsos. Special issue, *Charioteer: An Annual Review of Modern Greek Culture* 43:11–19.

———. 2004–5. "The Now and Future Greek America: Strategies for Survival." *Journal of Modern Hellenism* 21–22 (Winter): 1–15.

———. 2004. Review of *An Amulet of Greek Earth: Generations of Immigrant Folk Culture,* by Helen Papanikolas. *Journal of Modern Greek Studies* 22 (1): 111–12.

———. 2003a. "Redefining the Terrain." In "An Homage to Helen Papanikolas," ed. Dan Georgakas. Special issue, *Journal of the Hellenic Diaspora* 29 (2): 41–51.

———, ed. 2003b. "An Homage to Helen Papanikolas." Special issue, *Journal of the Hellenic Diaspora* 29 (2).

———. 2002. "Documenting Greek America." *Journal of the Hellenic Diaspora* 28 (2): 107–12.

———. 1994. "Greek-American Radicalism: The Twentieth Century." *Journal of the Hellenic Diaspora* 20 (1): 7–33.

———. 1991. "Demosthenes Nicas: Labor Radical." In *New Directions in Greek American Studies,* ed. Dan Georgakas and Charles C. Moskos, 95–109. New York: Pella.

———. 1987a. "The Greeks in America." *Journal of the Hellenic Diaspora* 14 (1–2): 5–53.

———. 1987b. "Response to Charles C. Moskos." *Journal of the Hellenic Diaspora* 14 (1–2): 63–71.

Georges, Robert A. 1989. "Richard M. Dorson's Conceptual and Methodological Concerns." In "Richard M. Dorson's Views and Works: An Assessment." Special issue, *Journal of Folklore Research* 26 (1): 1–10.

———. 1964. *Greek-American Folk Beliefs and Narratives: Survivals and Living Tradition.* PhD diss., Indiana University. Ann Arbor, MI: University Microfilms.

Giddens, Anthony. 1991. *Modernity and Self-Identity: Self and Society in the Late Modern Age.* Stanford, CA: Stanford University Press.

Gilroy, Paul. 1993. *The Black Atlantic: Modernity and Double Consciousness.* Cambridge, MA: Harvard University Press.

Gizelis, Gregory. 1980. *Narrative Rhetorical Devices of Persuasion in the Greek Community of Philadelphia.* New York: Arno.

Gmelch, George J. 1984. "Baseball Magic." In *Conformity and Conflict: Readings in Cultural Anthropology,* ed. James P. Spradley and David W. McCurdy, 310–16. Boston: Little, Brown.

Goldberg, David Theo. 1993. *Racist Culture: Philosophy and the Politics of Meaning.* Oxford: Blackwell.

Gordon, Avery F., and Christopher Newfield. 1996. "Introduction." In *Mapping Multiculturalism,* ed. Avery F. Gordon and Christoher Newfield, 1–16. Minneapolis: University of Minnesota Press.

The Greek Americans. 1998. Videocassette. Produced by WLIW 21 Public Television & Veras Communications, Inc.

The Greek Americans II: Passing the Torch. 1999. Videocassette. Produced by WLIW 21 Public Television & Veras Communications, Inc.

Greene, Gayle, and Coppélia Kahn. 1985. "Feminist Scholarship and the Social Construction of Woman." In *Making a Difference: Feminist Literary Criticism*, ed. Gayle Greene and Coppélia Kahn, 1–36. London: Methuen.

Greenhill, Pauline, and Diane Tye. 1997. "Women Transform Their Lives and Traditions." In *Undisciplined Women: Tradition and Culture in Canada,* ed. Pauline Greenhill and Diane Tye, 167–72. Montreal: McGill-Queen's University Press.

Guarnizo, Luis Eduardo, and Michael Peter Smith. 1998. "The Locations of Transnationalism." In *Transnationalism from Below*, ed. Michael Peter Smith and Luis Eduardo Guarnizo, 3–34. New Brunswick, NJ: Transaction.

Haley, Alex. 1976. *Roots.* Garden City, NY: Doubleday.

Hall, Stuart. 1996a. "Introduction: Who Needs 'Identity?'" In *Questions of Cultural Identity,* ed. Stuart Hall and Paul du Gay, 1–17. London: Sage.

————. 1996b. "Politics of Identity." In *Culture, Identity and Politics: Ethnic Minorities in Britain,* ed. Terence Ranger, Yunas Samad, and Ossie Stuart, 129–35. Aldershot, UK: Avebury.

————. 1994. "Cultural Identity and Diaspora." In *Colonial Discourse and Post-colonial Theory: A Reader,* ed. Patrick Williams and Laura Chrisman, 392–403. New York: Columbia University Press.

————. 1993. "Culture, Community, Nation." *Cultural Studies* 7 (3): 349–63.

————. 1988. "New Ethnicities." In *Black Film, British Cinema,* ed. L. Appignanesi, 27–31. ICA Documents 7. London: Institute of Contemporary Arts.

Halter, Marilyn. 2000. *Shopping for Identity: The Marketing of Ethnicity.* New York: Schocken Books.

Hartigan, John. 1999. *Racial Situations: Class Predicaments of Whiteness in Detroit.* Princeton, NJ: Princeton University Press.

References

Hasiotes, I. K. 1993. *Episkópisi tis istorías tis neoellinikís diasporás* [Survey of the History of the Neohellenic Diaspora]. Thessaloniki, Greece: Vania.

Herzfeld, Michael. 2004. *The Body Impolitic: Artisans and Artifice in the Global Hierarchy of Value.* Chicago: University of Chicago Press.

———. 1997. *Portrait of a Greek Imagination: An Ethnographic Biography of Andreas Nenedakis.* Chicago: University of Chicago Press.

———. 1995. "Hellenism and Occidentalism: The Permutations of Performance in Greek Bourgeois Identity." In *Occidentalism: Images of the West,* ed. James G. Carrier, 218–33. Oxford: Clarendon.

———. 1987. *Anthropology through the Looking-Glass: Critical Ethnography in the Margins of Europe.* Cambridge: Cambridge University Press.

———. 1986a. *Ours Once More: Folklore, Ideology and the Making of Modern Greece.* New York: Pella.

———. 1986b. "Within and Without: The Category of 'Female' in the Ethnography of Modern Greece." In *Gender and Power in Rural Greece,* ed. Jill Dubisch, 215–33. Princeton, NJ: Princeton University Press.

———. 1985. *The Poetics of Manhood: Contest and Identity in a Cretan Mountain Village.* Princeton, NJ: Princeton University Press.

Hirschon, Renée. 1989. *Heirs of the Greek Catastrophe: The Social Life of Asia Minor Refugees in Piraeus.* Oxford: Clarendon.

Hoelscher, Steven D. 1998. *Heritage on Stage: The Invention of Ethnic Place in America's Little Switzerland.* Madison: University of Wisconsin Press.

Hsu, Ruth Y. 1996. "'Will the Model Minority Please Identify Itself?' American Ethnic Identity and Its Discontents." *Diaspora: A Journal of Transnational Studies* 5 (1): 37–63.

Hufford, Mary, Marjorie Hunt, and Steven Zeitlin. 1987. *The Grand Generation: Memory, Mastery, Legacy.* Washington, DC: Smithsonian Institution.

Hurtado, Aida. 1996. *The Color of Privilege: Three Blasphemies on Race and Feminism.* Ann Arbor: University of Michigan Press.

Hutcheon, Linda, 1998. *Irony, Nostalgia, and the Postmodern.* http://www.library.utoronto.ca/utel/criticism/hutchinp.html (accessed February 9, 2004).

Ishkanian, Armine. 2002. "Mobile Motherhood: Armenian Women's Labor Migration in the Post-Soviet Period." *Diaspora: A Journal of Transnational Studies* 11 (3): 383–415.

Jacobson, Matthew Frye. 2006. *Roots Too: White Ethnic Revival in Post-Civil Rights America.* Cambridge: Harvard University Press.

———. 2000. *Barbarian Virtues: The United States Encounters Foreign Peoples at Home and Abroad, 1876–1917.* New York: Hill and Wang.

———. 1998. *Whiteness of a Different Color: European Immigrants and the Alchemy of Race.* Cambridge, MA: Harvard University Press.

Jameson, Fredric. 1988. "History and Class Consciousness as an 'Unfinished Project.'" *Rethinking Marxism* 1 (1): 49–72.

JanMohamed, Abdul R., and David Lloyd. 1990. "Introduction: Toward a Theory of Minority Discourse: What Is It to Be Done?" In *The Nature and Context of Minority Discourse,* ed. Abdul R. JanMohamed and David Lloyd, 1–16. New York: Oxford University Press.

Jurgens, Jane. 1995. "Greek Americans." *Gale Encyclopedia of Multicultural America.* Vol. 1., ed. Jusy Galens, Ana Sheets, and Robyn V. Young, 578–95. Detroit, MI: Gale Research.

Jusdanis, Gregory. 2001. *The Necessary Nation.* Princeton, NJ: Princeton University Press.

———. 1991. *Belated Modernity and Aesthetic Culture: Inventing National Literature.* Minneapolis: University of Minnesota Press.

Kalafatas, Michael. 2003. *The Bellstone: The Greek Sponge Divers of the Aegean; One American's Journey Home.* Hanover, NH: Brandeis University Press/University Press of New England.

Kalmoukos, Theodore. 2005. "Leo & Eve Condakes Give 2M to Boston Museum." National Herald, July 8. http://www.thenationalherald.com (accessed July 9, 2005).

Kalogeras, Yiorgos. 2004–5. "Albert Isaac Bezzerides: Translating Ethnicity from Fiction to Film." *Journal of Modern Hellenism* 21–22 (Winter): 17–41.

———. 1998. "The 'Other Space' of Greek America." *American Literary History* 10 (4): 702–24.

———. 1992. "Narrating an Ethnic Group." *Journal of the Hellenic Diaspora* 18 (2): 13–34.

———. 1989. "When the Tree Sings: Magic Realism and the Carnivalesque in a Greek-American Narrative." *International Fiction Review* 16 (1): 32–38.

Kamboureli, Smaro. 1996. "Introduction." In *Making a Difference: Canadian Multicultural Literature,* ed. Smaro Kamboureli, 1–16. Toronto: Oxford University Press.

Karageorge, Penelope. 2006. "Double Identity." *Odyssey.* March–April.

———. 2004. "Life as a Greek American." *Odyssey.* January–February.

———. 2000. Review of *The Time of the Little Black Bird,* by Helen Papanikolas. *Journal of the Hellenic Diaspora* 26 (1): 82–86.

Karampetsos, E. D. 2005. Preface to "The Greek American Experience," ed. E. D. Karampetsos. Special issue, *Charioteer: An Annual Review of Modern Greek Culture* 43: 5–8.

———. 1998. "Nativism in Nevada: Greek Immigrants in White Pine County." *Journal of the Hellenic Diaspora* 24 (1): 61–95.

Karanikas, Marianthe. 2001–2. "Searching for Osprey." In "Writing the Greek-American Experience." Double issue, *Mondo Greco* 6–7 (Fall-Spring): 232–39.

Karpathakis, Anna. 2003. "From 'Noikokyra' to 'Lady': Greek Immigrant Women, Assimilation and Race." In "Gender and International Migration: Focus on Greece," ed. Evie Tastsoglou and Laura Maratou-Alipranti. Special issue, *Greek Review of Social Research* 110: 23–53.

————. 1999. "Politics and Immigrant Political Incorporation: The Case of Greek Immigrants in New York City." *International Migration Review* 33 (1): 55–78.

————. 1994. "'Whose Church Is It Anyway?' Greek Immigrants of Astoria, New York, and Their Church." *Journal of the Hellenic Diaspora* 20 (1): 97–122.

Karpathakis, Anna, and Victor Roudometof. 2004. "Changing Racial Conceptualizations: Greek Americans in New York City." In *Race and Ethnicity in New York City,* ed. Jerome Krase and Ray Hutchison, 265–89. Research in Urban Sociology 7. Bingley, UK: JAI Press.

Karpozilos, Kostis. 2004. "Pre-Communist Greek Immigrant Radicalism in the United States." *Journal of the Hellenic Diaspora* 30 (2): 7–56.

Kasdaglis, Marina, and Peter Pappas. 1982. "A Discussion with Theodoros Stamos." *Journal of the Hellenic Diaspora* 9 (4): 45–52.

Katznelson, Ira. 2005. *When Affirmative Action Was White: An Untold History of Racial Inequality in Twentieth-Century America.* New York: W. W. Norton.

Keil, Charles. 1979. "The Concept of the Folk." *Journal of the Folklore Institute* 16 (3): 209–10.

————. 1978. "Who Needs 'The Folk'?" *Journal of the Folklore Institute* 15 (3): 263–65.

Killion, Ann. 2004. "To the People of Greece: We Apologize." *San Jose Mercury News,* August 21.

King, Desmond. 2000. *Making Americans: Immigration, Race, and the Origins of the Diverse Democracy.* Cambridge, MA: Harvard University Press.

Kinzer, Stephen. 1999. "Turkey, Relenting, Shows the Works of a Kurd Patriot." *New York Times,* April 11.

Kirshenblatt-Gimblett, Barbara. 1998. "Folklore's Crisis." *Journal of American Folklore* 111 (441): 281–327.

————. 1995. "Theorizing Heritage." *Ethnomusicology* 39 (3): 367–80.

————. 1991. "Objects of Ethnography." In *Exhibiting Cultures: The Poetics and Politics of Museum Display,* ed. Ivan Karp and Steven D. Lavine, 386–443. Washington, DC: Smithsonian Institution.

————. 1989. "Authoring Lives." *Journal of Folklore Research* 26 (2): 123–49.

Klimt, Andrea, and Stephen Lubkemann. 2002. "Argument across the Portuguese-Speaking World: A Discursive Approach to Diaspora." *Diaspora: A Journal of Transnational Studies* 11 (2): 145–62.

Klironomos, Martha. 2002. "Ancient [Anamnesis], National [Mneme] in the Poetry of Giorgos Seferis." In "Greek Worlds, Ancient and Modern," ed. Gonda Van Steen. Special issue, *Journal of Modern Greek Studies* 20 (2): 215–39.

Kolettis, Helen. 2004. "It's All Greek to Me." *GreekCircle* 4 (2): 22–23.

Kondo, Dorinne. 2001. "The Narrative Production of 'Home,' Community, and Political Identity in Asian American Theater." In *Displacement, Diaspora, and Geographies of Identity,* ed. Smadar Lavie and Ted Swedenburg, 97–117. Durham, NC: Duke University Press.

Kourvetaris, Yorgos A. 1989. "Greek American Professionals and Entrepreneurs." *Journal of the Hellenic Diaspora* 16 (1–4): 105–28.

Krause, Robert. 2006. "Heart Murmurs from Home." Review of *The Night Gardener,* by George Pelecanos. In "Books." Special issue, *National Herald,* December 2.

Lacey, Thomas James. 1916. *A Study of Social Heredity as Illustrated in the Greek People.* New York: E. S. Gorham.

Laliotou, Ioanna. 2004. *Transnational Subjects: Acts of Migration and Cultures of Transnationalism between Greece and America.* Chicago: University of Chicago Press.

Lambropoulos, Vassilis. 1997. "Modern Greek Studies in the Age of Ethnography." *Journal of Modern Greek Studies* 15 (2): 197–208.

———. 1990. "A Didactic Proposal." *Journal of Modern Greek Studies* 8 (1): 81–84.

Largey, Michael. 2000. "Politics on the Pavement: Haitian *Rara* as a Traditionalizing Process." *Journal of American Folklore* 113 (449): 239–54.

Lavie, Smadar, and Ted Swedenburg. 2001. "Introduction: Displacement, Diaspora, and Geographies of Identity." In *Displacement, Diaspora, and Geographies of Identity,* ed. Smadar Lavie and Ted Swedenburg, 1–25. Durham, NC: Duke University Press.

Leber, George J. 1972. *The History of the Order of Ahepa, 1922–1972.* Washington, DC: Order of Ahepa.

Le Blanc, Barbara. 1997. "Changing Places: Dance, Society, and Gender in Cheticamp." In *Undisciplined Women: Tradition and Culture in Canada,* ed. Pauline Greenhill and Diane Tye, 101–12. Montreal: McGill-Queen's University Press.

Lee, Felicia R. 2005. "The Anger and Shock of a City's Slave Past." *New York Times,* November 26, http://www.nytimes.com/2005/11/26/arts/design/26slav.html (accessed November 27, 2005).

Lefkowitz, Mary. 2001. "A Fable for Our Time: The Destructive Legacy of *Black Athena.*" *Times Literary Supplement,* February 2.

Leontis, Artemis. 2003. "'What Will I Have to Remember?' Helen Papanikolas's Art of Telling." In "An Homage to Helen Papanikolas," ed. Dan Georgakas. Special issue, *Journal of the Hellenic Diaspora* 29 (2): 15–26.

———. 1997. "The Intellectual in Greek America." *Journal of the Hellenic Diaspora* 23 (2): 85–109.

———. 1995. *Topographies of Hellenism: Mapping the Homeland.* Ithaca, NY: Cornell University Press.

Levitt, Peggy. 2001. *The Transnational Villagers.* Los Angeles: University of California Press.

Li, David Leiwei. 1998. *Imagining the Nation: Asian American Literature and Cultural Consent.* Stanford, CA: Stanford University Press.

Limón, José E. 1991. "Representation, Ethnicity, and the Precursory Ethnography: Notes of a Native Anthropologist." In *Recapturing Anthropology: Working in the Present,* ed. Richard G. Fox, 115–35. Santa Fe, NM: School of American Research Press.

Lowenthal, David. 1996. *Possessed by the Past: The Heritage Crusade and the Spoils of History.* New York: Free Press.

————. 1989. "Nostalgia Tells It Like It Wasn't." In *The Imagined Past: History and Nostalgia,* ed. Christopher Shaw and Malcolm Chase, 18–32. Manchester: Manchester University Press.

————. 1985. *The Past Is a Foreign Country.* Cambridge: Cambridge University Press.

Ma, Sheng-mei. 2000. *The Deathly Embrace: Orientalism and Asian American Identity.* Minneapolis: University of Minnesota.

Marcus, George E., and Michael M. J. Fischer. 1986. *Anthropology as Cultural Critique: An Experimental Moment in the Human Sciences.* Chicago: University of Chicago Press.

Markos, Louis. 2006. "Grandpa and the Mountain." *Odyssey,* March–April.

Martin, Biddy, and Chandra Talpade Mohanty. 1986. "Feminist Politics: What's Home Got to Do with It?" In *Feminist Studies, Critical Studies,* ed. Teresa de Lauretis, 191–212. Bloomington: Indiana University Press.

McCormick, John S., and John R. Sillito, eds. *A World We Thought We Knew: Readings in Utah History.* Salt Lake City: University of Utah Press.

Michaels, Walter Benn. 1995. *Our America: Nativism, Modernism, and Pluralism.* Durham, NC: Duke University Press.

Morrison, Toni. 1994a. "On the Backs of Blacks." In *Arguing Immigration: The Debate over the Changing Face of America,* ed. Nicolaus Mills, 97–100. New York: Simon and Schuster.

————. 1994b. *The Bluest Eye.* New York: Plume Books.

Moskos, Charles C. 2002. "Greek American Studies." In *Reading Greek America: Studies in the Experience of Greeks in the United States,* ed. Spyros D. Orfanos, 23–62. New York: Pella.

————. 1990. *Greek Americans: Struggle and Success.* New Brunswick, NJ: Transaction.

Moya, Paula M. L. 2000. "Introduction: Reclaiming Identity." In *Reclaiming Identity: Realist Theory and the Predicament of Postmodernism,* ed. Paula M. L. Moya and Michael R. Hames-Garcia, 1–26. Los Angeles: University of California Press.

Mullen, Patrick B. 1992. *Listening to Old Voices: Folklore, Life Histories, and the Elderly.* Urbana: University of Illinois Press.

Newitz, Annalee, and Matt Wray. 1997. "Introduction." In *White Trash: Race and Class in America,* ed. Matt Wray and Annalee Newitz, 1–12. New York: Routledge.

Niarchos, Sophia. 2001. "AHEPA Float Needs Support of Hellenes Everywhere." *GreekAmerican,* July 21–22.

Noakes, John A. 2003. "Racializing Subversion: The FBI and the Depiction of Race in Early Cold War Movies." *Ethnic and Racial Studies* 26 (4): 728–49.

Noivo, Edite. 2002. "Towards a Cartography of Portugueseness: Challenging the Hegemonic Center." *Diaspora: A Journal of Transnational Studies* 11 (2): 255–75.

Noutsos, Panayiotis. 1990. *I sosialistikí sképsi stin Elláda apó to 1875 os to 1974* [Socialist Thought in Greece from 1875 to 1974]. Vol. 1. *Oi sosialistés dianooúmenoi kai i politikí leitourgeía tis próimis koinonikís kritikís (1875–1907)* [Socialist Intellectuals and the Political Function of Early Social Critique (1875–1907)]. Athens: Gnosi.

Novak, Michael. 1971. *The Rise of the Unmeltable Ethnics: Politics and Culture in the Seventies.* New York: Macmillan.

Oates, Joyce Carol. 2007. "Brilliance, Silence, Courage." Review of *Twenty-eight Artists and Two Saints: Essays*, by Joan Acocella. *New York Review of Books*, March 15.

Omi, Michael. 1996. "Racialization in the Post-Civil Rights Era." *Mapping Multiculturalism*, ed. Avery F. Gordon and Christopher Newfield, 178–86. Minneapolis: University of Minnesota Press.

Omi, Michael, and Howard Winant. 1986. *Racial Formation in the United States: From the 1960s to the 1980s.* New York: Routledge.

Orso, Ethelyn G. 1979. *Modern Greek Humor: A Collection of Jokes and Ribald Tales.* Bloomington: Indiana University Press.

Papailias, Penelope. 2005. *Genres of Recollection: Archival Poetics and Modern Greece.* New York: Palgrave Macmillan.

Papajohn, John C. 1999. The Hyphenated American: The Hidden Injuries of Culture. Westport, CT: Greenwood.

Papalas, Anthony J. 2005. *Rebels and Radicals: Icaria, 1600–2000.* Wauconda, IL: Bolchazy-Carducci.

Papanikolas, Helen Z. 2002. *An Amulet of Greek Earth: Generations of Immigrant Folk Culture.* Athens: Swallow Press.

———. 2000. Interview by Ken Verdoia. http://www.kued.org/productions/joehill/early/papanikolas_interview.html (accessed January 5, 2002).

———. 1995a. "Growing up Greek in Helper, Utah," *Forkroads: A Journal of Ethnic American Literature* 1 (2): 5–11.

———. 1995b. "Utah's Ethnic Legacy." In *A World We Thought We Knew: Readings in Utah History,* ed. John S. McCormick and John R. Sillito, 241–48. Salt Lake City: University of Utah Press.

———. 1993. "The First Meeting of the Group." In *Small Bird, Tell Me: Stories of Greek Immigrants in Utah,* 164–76. Athens: Swallow Press.

———. 1989. "Greek Immigrant Women of the Intermountain West." *Journal of the Hellenic Diaspora* 16 (1–4): 17–35.

———. 1988. "Introduction." In *The Other Utahns*, ed. Leslie Kelen and Sandra Fuller, xv-xxii. Salt Lake City: University of Utah Press.

———. 1987. *Emily-George (Aimilía-Geórgios).* Salt Lake City: University of Utah Press.

———. 1984. "Wrestling with Death: Greek Immigrant Funeral Customs in Utah." *Utah Historical Quarterly* 52 (Winter): 29–49.

———. 1971. "Greek Folklore of Carbon County." In *Lore of Faith and Folly,* ed. Thomas E. Cheney, 61–77. Salt Lake City: University of Utah Press.

Papanikolas, Zeese. 2003. "On My Mother." In "An Homage to Helen Papanikolas," ed. Dan Georgakas. Special issue, *Journal of the Hellenic Diaspora* 29 (2): 11–13.

Pappas, Peter. 1993. "The Social Success and Ethnic Failure of Greek America." In *Greeks in English Speaking Countries*, 91–105. Proceedings of the First International

Seminar. Melbourne, March 27–30, 1992. Melbourne, Australia: Hellenic Studies Forum.

Patrinacos, Nicon. 1982. "The Role of the Church in the Evolving Greek American Community." *The Greek Community in Transition,* ed. Harry J. Psomiades and Alice Scourby, 123–36. New York: Pella.

Peck, Gunther. 2000. *Reinventing Free Labor: Padrones and Immigrant Workers in the North American West, 1880–1930.* Cambridge: Cambridge University Press.

———. 1991. "Crisis in the Family: Padrones and Radicals in Utah, 1908–1912." In *New Directions in Greek American Studies,* ed. Dan Georgakas and Charles C. Moskos, 73–93. New York: Pella.

Peristiany, J. G. 1966. "Honour and Shame in a Cypriot Highland Village." In *Honour and Shame: The Values of Mediterranean Society,* ed. J.G. Peristiany, 171–90. Chicago: University of Chicago Press.

Perry, Pamela. 2001. "White Means Never Having to Say You're Ethnic: White Youth and the Construction of 'Cultureless' Identities." *Journal of Contemporary Ethnography* 30 (1): 56–91.

Petersen, William. 1997. *Ethnicity Counts.* New Brunswick, NJ: Transaction.

Petrakis, Harry Mark. 2001–2. "A Tale of Color." In "Writing the Greek-American Experience." Double issue, *Mondo Greco* 6–7 (Fall-Spring): 40–46.

———. 1999. "Ellis Island Memory." In *Tales of the Heart: Dreams and Memories of a Lifetime,* 5–10. Chicago: Ivan R. Dee.

———. 1978a. "Pericles on 31st Street." In *A Petrakis Reader,* 87–100. Garden City, NY: Doubleday.

———. 1978b. "The Judgment." In *A Petrakis Reader,* 278–90. Garden City, NY: Doubleday.

Petropulos, John A. 1977. "1976 MGSA Symposium: Closing Remarks." *Bulletin of the Modern Greek Studies Association* 8 (2): 23–29.

Propp, Vladimir. 1984. *Theory and History of Folklore,* ed. Anatoly Liberman, trans. Ariadna Y. Martin and Richard P. Martin. Minneapolis: University of Minnesota Press.

Psomiades, Harry J. 1987. "Greece and Greek America: The Future of the Greek American Community." In *Education and Greek Americans: Process and Prospects,* ed. Spyros D. Orfanos, Harry J. Psomiades, and John Spiridakis, 91–102. New York: Pella.

P. T. and G. A. 1975. "Immigration: A View from the Greek Cultural Association." *Journal of the Hellenic Diaspora* 2 (2): 35–38.

Rassias, John A., et al. 1999. *The Future of the Greek Language and Culture in the United States: Survival in the Diaspora.* New York: Greek Orthodox Archdiocese of America.

Renan, Ernest. 1990. "What Is a Nation?" In *Nation and Narration,* ed. Homi K. Bhabha, 8–22. London: Routledge.

Roberts, Kenneth L. 1922. *Why Europe Leaves Home.* Indianapolis, IN: Bobbs-Merrill.

Roediger, David R. 2005. *Working toward Whiteness: How America's Immigrants Became White; The Strange Journey from Ellis Island to the Suburbs.* New York: Basic Books.

————. 2003. *Colored White: Transcending the Racial Past.* Berkeley: University of California Press.

————. 2002. "Whiteness and Ethnicity in the History of 'White Ethnics' in the United States." In *Race Critical Theories: Text and Context,* ed. Philomena Essed and David Theo Goldberg, 325–43. Oxford: Blackwell.

Rogers, Susan Carol. 1978. "Woman's Place: A Critical Review of Anthropological Theory." *Comparative Studies in Society and History* 20 (1): 123–62.

Rosaldo, Renato. 1993. *Culture and Truth: The Remaking of Social Analysis.* Boston: Beacon.

Rosen, Jonathan. 2005. "Writer, Interrupted: The Resurrection of Henry Roth." *New Yorker,* August 1.

Rosenberg, Pearl M. 1997. "Underground Discourses: Exploring Whiteness in Teacher Education." In *Off White: Readings on Race, Power, and Society,* ed. Michelle Fine, Lois Weis, Linda C. Powell, and L. Mun Wong, 79–89. New York: Routledge.

Roudometof, Victor, and Anna Karpathakis. 2002. "Greek Americans and Transnationalism: Religion, Class and Community." In *Communities across Borders: New Immigrants and Transnational Cultures,* ed. Paul Kennedy and Victor Roudometof, 41–54. London: Routledge.

Russell, Larry. 2004. "A Long Way toward Compassion." *Text and Performance Quarterly* 24 (3–4): 233–54.

Said, Edward W. 1994. *Culture and Imperialism.* New York: Vintage.

————. 1975. *Beginnings: Intention and Method.* New York: Basic Books.

Saloutos, Theodore. 1964. *The Greeks in the United States.* Cambridge, MA: Harvard University Press.

————. 1956. *They Remember America: The Story of the Repatriated Greek-Americans.* Berkeley: University of California Press.

Sarris, Greg. 2001. "Living with Miracles: The Politics and Poetics of Writing American Indian Resistance and Identity." In *Displacement, Diaspora, and Geographies of Identity,* ed. Smadar Lavie and Ted Swedenburg, 27–40. Durham, NC: Duke University Press.

Sartre, Jean-Paul. 1956. *Being and Nothingness: An Essay on Phenomenological Ontology,* trans. Hazel E. Barnes. New York: Philosophical Library.

Schrag, Calvin O. 1997. *The Self after Postmodernity.* New Haven, CT: Yale University Press.

Scofield, James S. 1997. "Forgotten History: The Klan vs. Americans of Hellenic Heritage in an Era of Hate." *Greek America* 3 (7): 20–21.

Scourby, Alice. 2003. "Gender, Culture, and Communication." In "An Homage to Helen Papanikolas," ed. Dan Georgakas. Special issue, *Journal of the Hellenic Diaspora* 29 (2): 33–40.

————. 1984. *The Greek Americans.* Boston: Twayne.

————. 1982. "The New Ethnicity: Pro and Con." In *The Greek American Community in Transition,* ed. Harry J. Psomiades and Alice Scourby, 11–15. New York: Pella.

Seremetakis, Nadia C. 1994. "The Memory of the Senses: Part I: Marks of the Transitory." In *The Senses Still: Perception and Memory as Material Culture in Modernity,* ed. Nadia C. Seremetakis, 1–18. Boulder, CO: Westview.

———, ed. 1993. *Ritual, Power and the Body: Historical Perspectives on the Representation of Greek Women.* New York: Pella.

Seyhan, Azade. 1996. "Ethnic Selves/Ethnic Signs: Invention of Self, Space, and Genealogy in Immigrant Writing." In *Culture/Contexture: Explorations in Anthropology and Literary Studies,* ed. E. Valentine Daniel and Jeffrey M. Peck, 175–94. Berkeley: University of California Press.

Smart, Nick. 2005. "The Family Business." In "The Greek American Experience," ed. E. D. Karampetsos. Special issue, *Charioteer: An Annual Review of Modern Greek Culture* 43: 115–23.

Smith, Anthony D. 1999. *Myths and Memories of the Nation.* Oxford: Oxford University Press.

Smith, Beverly Bronson. 1995. "The Semiotics of Difference: Representations of Ethnicity and Nativism in Early Twentieth Century American Theater." In *Staging Difference: Cultural Pluralism in American Theater and Drama,* ed. Marc Maufort, 19–29. New York: Peter Lang.

Sollors, Werner. 1986. *Beyond Ethnicity: Consent and Descent in American Culture.* Oxford: Oxford University Press.

Spivak, Gayatri. 1992. "Acting Bits/Identity Talk." *Critical Inquiry* 18 (4): 756–803.

Stafford, William. 1989. "'This Once Happy Country': Nostalgia for Pre-modern Society." In *The Imagined Past: History and Nostalgia,* ed. Christopher Shaw and Malcolm Chase, 33–46. Manchester, UK: Manchester University Press.

Stefanidou, A. 2002. "A Cosmopolitan Exile's Nostos: Modernity, Memory, and Myth in Andonis Decavalles's Poetry." *Journal of the Hellenic Diaspora* 28 (2): 7–55.

Steinberg, Stephen. 1981. *The Ethnic Myth: Race, Ethnicity, and Class in America.* Boston: Beacon.

Steiner, Edward A. 1906. *On the Trail of the Immigrant.* New York: Fleming H. Revell.

Storey, John. 2003. *Inventing Popular Culture: From Folklore to Globalization.* Malden, MA: Blackwell.

Sugrue, Thomas J. 1996. *The Origins of the Urban Crisis: Race and Inequality in Postwar Detroit.* Princeton, NJ: Princeton University Press.

Sutton, David. 2003. Review of *The Bellstone: The Greek Sponge Divers of the Aegean; One American's Journey Home,* by Michael Kalafatas. *Journal of Modern Greek Studies* 21 (2): 294–97.

———. 1998. *Memories Cast in Stone: The Relevance of the Past in Everyday Life.* Oxford: Berg.

Sutton, Susan Buck. 1994. "Settlement Patterns, Settlement Perceptions: Rethinking the Greek Village." In *Beyond the Site: Regional Studies in the Aegean Area,* ed. P. Nick Kardulias, 313–35. Lanham, MD: University Press of America.

Syrimis, George. 1998. "Ideology, Orality and Textuality: The Tradition of the *Poietáridhes* of Cyprus. In *Cyprus and Its People: Nation, Identity, and Experience in an Unimaginable Community, 1955–1997,* ed. Vangelis Calotychos, 205–22. Boulder, CO: Westview.

Takaki, Ronald. 1987a. "Introduction: Different Shores." In *From Different Shores: Perspectives on Race and Ethnicity in America,* ed. Ronald Takaki, 3–9. New York: Oxford University Press.

———. 1987b. "Reflections on Racial Patterns in America." In *From Different Shores: Perspectives on Race and Ethnicity in America,* ed. Ronald Takaki, 26–37. New York: Oxford University Press.

Taylor, Verta, and Leila J. Rupp. 1993. "Women's Culture and Lesbian Feminist Activism: A Reconsideration of Cultural Feminism." *Signs: Journal of Women in Culture and Society* 19 (1): 32–61.

Thatcher, Elaine. 2004. "Public Folklore in Utah." In *Folklore in Utah: A History and Guide to Resources,* ed. David Stanley, 186–203. Logan: Utah State University Press.

Thomopoulos, Elaine Cotsirilos. 2000. "Presbytera Stella Christoulakis Petrakis (1888–1979)." In *Greek-American Pioneer Women of Illinois,* ed. Elaine Cotsirilos Thomopoulos, 19–57. Chicago: Arcadia.

Title IX Project of the Chicago Consortium for Inter-Ethnic Curriculum Development. 1976. *Ethnic Heritage in America: Curriculum Materials in Elementary School Social Studies on Greeks, Jews, Lithuanians, and Ukrainians.* Chicago: Title IX Project of the Chicago Consortium for Inter-Ethnic Curriculum Development.

Toelken, Barre. 1990. "Folklore and Reality in the American West." In *Sense of Place: American Regional Cultures,* ed. Barbara Allen and Thomas J. Schlereth, 14–27. Lexington: University Press of Kentucky.

Tölölyan, Khachig. 1996. "Rethinking Diaspora(s): Stateless Power in the Transnational Moment." *Diaspora: A Journal of Transnational Studies* 5 (1): 3–36.

Topp, Michael Miller. 1996. "The Italian-American Left: Transnationalism and the Quest for Unity." In *The Immigrant Left in the United States,* ed. Paul Buhle and Dan Georgakas, 119–47. Albany: State University of New York Press.

Topping, Eva Catafygiotou. 1995. "Village Wisdom: Greek Proverbs." *Laografia: A Journal of the International Greek Folklore Society* 12 (2): 7–11.

Triandis, Harry C. 1987. "Education of Greek Americans for a Pluralistic Society." In *Education and Greek Americans: Process and Prospects,* ed. Spyros D. Orfanos, Harry J. Psomiades, and John Spiridakis, 19–34. New York: Pella.

Trouillot, Michel-Rolph. 1995. *Silencing the Past: Power and the Production of History.* Boston: Beacon.

Tsine, Zoe. 2005. "Harry Mark Petrakis: Universality of Expression Every Good Writer's Goal." *National Herald,* April 2.

———. 2004. "Diving into His Past, an Author Finds His Future." *National Herald,* June 4. http://www.thenationalherald.com (accessed June 5, 2004).

Tuleja, Tad. 1997. "Introduction: Making Ourselves Up; On the Manipulation of Tradition in Small Groups." In *Usable Pasts: Traditions and Group Expressions in North America,* ed. Tad Tuleja, 1–20. Logan: Utah State University Press.

Turner, Bryan S. 1984. *The Body and Society: Explorations in Social Theory.* New York: Blackwell.

Turner, Victor W. 1980. "Social Dramas and Stories about Them." *Critical Inquiry* 7 (1): 141–68.

Tziovas, Dimitris. 1994a. "Heteroglossia and the Defeat of Regionalism in Greece." In *Kambos,* 95–120. Cambridge Papers in Modern Greek 2. Cambridge: Modern Greek Section, Faculty of Modern and Medieval Languages, Cambridge University.

———. 1994b. "I ditiikí fantasíosi tou Ellinikoú kai i anazítisi tou iperethnikoú" [The "Greek" in the Western Imaginary and the Quest for the Post-national.] In *Éthnos-krátos-ethnikismós* [Nation—State—Nationalism], 339–61. Athens: Etaireía Spoudón Neoellinikoú Politismoú kai Yenikís Paideías.

———. 1989. "Residual Orality and Belated Textuality in Greek Literature and Culture." *Journal of Modern Greek Studies* 7 (2): 321–35.

Urciuoli, Bonnie. 1998. "Acceptable Difference: The Cultural Evolution of the Model Ethnic American Citizen." In *Democracy and Ethnography: Constructing Identities in Multicultural Liberal States,* ed. Carol J. Greenhouse with Roshanak Kheshti, 178–95. Albany: State University of New York Press.

Valamvanos, George. 1979. "A Life-Long Sojourn in the Aegean: A Tribute to Kaldis." *Journal of the Hellenic Diaspora* 6 (2): 89–93.

Vargas, Sylvia R. Lazos. 1998. "Deconstructing Homo[geneous] Americanus: The White Ethnic Immigrant Narrative and Its Exclusionary Effect." *Tulane Law Review* 72 (5): 1493–1596.

Veras, George. 2002a. "Impact of PBS Greek-American Documentaries." Speech, Columbus OH, May 23. Veras Communications, http://www.verastv.com/speech_columbus_may23.htm (accessed January 5, 2004).

———. 2002b. "The Role of Greek-American Professionals in Promoting Hellenism in the United States." Speech, American Hellenic Institute, October. Veras Communications, http://www.verastv.com/speech_role_of_greek.htm (accessed January 5, 2004).

———. 2002c. "The Journey of Being Greek." Speech, Anatolia College, Thessaloniki, Greece, June 29. Veras Communications, http://www.verastv.com/speech_journey_greek.htm (accessed January 5, 2004).

———. 2001. "Media Opportunities for the Athens 2004 Olympics." Speech, October. Veras Communications, http://www.verastv.com/speech_athens2004.htm (accessed January 5, 2004).

Vorillas, Athena. 2006. "In the Company of Women." *Odyssey.* March–April.

Waldinger, Roger. 2003. "Foreigners Transformed: International Migration and the Remaking of a Divided People." *Diaspora: A Journal of Transnational Studies* 12 (2): 247–72.

Walzer, Michael. 1992. *What It Means to Be an American*. New York: Marsilio.

Warnke, Christine M. 1996. "Greek Immigrants in Washington, 1890–1945." In *Urban Odyssey: A Multicultural History of Washington, D.C.,* ed. Francine Curro Cary, 173–89. Washington: Smithsonian Institution.

Warren, Donald I. 1995. "White Americans as a Minority." In "Populism." Special issue, *Telos* 2 (104): 127–34.

Warren, Kay B. 1997. "Narrating Cultural Resurgence: Genre and Self-Representation for Pan-Mayan Writers." In *Auto/Ethnography: Rewriting the Self and the Social*, ed. Deborah E. Reed-Danahay, 21–45. Oxford: Berg.

Waters, Mary. 1990. *Ethnic Options: Choosing Identities in America*. Berkeley: University of California Press.

Weedon, Chris. 2004. *Identity and Culture: Narratives of Difference and Belonging*. New York: Open University Press.

———. 1987. *Feminist Practice and Poststructuralist Theory*. London: Blackwell.

Welz, Gisela. 2000. "The 'Grand Narrative' of Immigration: Managing Ethnicity in a Museum Context." In *Managing Ethnicity: Perspectives from Folklore Studies, History and Anthropology,* ed. Regina Bendix and Herman Roodenburg, 62–75. Amsterdam: Het Spinhuis.

Whitebrook, Maureen. 2001. *Identity, Narrative, and Politics*. London: Routledge.

Williams, Raymond. 1977. *Marxism and Literature*. Oxford: Oxford University Press.

———. 1973. *The Country and the City*. New York: Oxford University Press.

Wilson, William A. 1989. "Richard M. Dorson as Romantic-Nationalist." In "Richard M. Dorson's Views and Works: An Assessment." Special issue, *Journal of Folklore Research* 26 (1): 35–42.

Winterer, Caroline. 2002. *The Culture of Classicism: Ancient Greece and Rome in American Intellectual Life, 1870–1910*. Baltimore: Johns Hopkins University Press.

Wood, Robert E. 1998. "Tourist Ethnicity: A Brief Itinerary." *Ethnic and Racial Studies* 21 (2): 218–41.

Yuval-Davis, Nira. 1994. "Identity Politics and Women's Ethnicity." In *Identity Politics and Women: Cultural Reassertions and Feminisms in International Perspective,* ed. Valentine M. Moghadam, 408–24. Boulder, CO: Westview.

Zervakis, Peter A. 1998–99. "The Greek Diaspora in the United States and American Involvement in Greece after World War II." *Modern Greek Studies Yearbook* 14–15: 213–40.

Zotos, Stephanos. 1976. *Hellenic Presence in America*. Wheaton, IL: Pilgrimage.

INDEX

Abu-Lughod, Lila, 30, 143, 145, 159–60
African Americans: and acceptable difference,
    9; in *America, America* (Kazan), 130–31;
    conflict with Greek Americans, 93;
    education and historical remembering, 158;
    and G.I. Bill, 234n11; Greek American
    solidarity with, 155–58, 182–83, 208–9,
    233–34n10; and interracial empathy, 153,
    250n9; marriage with Greek Americans,
    136–38; and model minorities, 91. *See also*
    interracial marriage; interracial solidarity;
    race talk; racism
AHEPA, 53–55, 94, 207, 209, 239n5, 242n20,
    243n24
Alba, Richard, 15, 63–68, 72–73, 75, 144, 238n3
Alexiou, Margaret, 38, 40, 44–45, 246n6
American Aphrodite (Callinicos), 97, 114–28
American Hellenic Institute Foundation, 231n2
American Hellenic Progressive Association. *See*
    AHEPA
Amulet of Greek Earth, An (Papanikolas), 4, 146–51
Argyrou, Vassos, 223, 253n13
Armenian Americans: and Cold War political
    persecution, 256n13; and economic success,
    242n17; ethnicity among American-born, 87;
    identity as obligation, 95; and PBS Heritage
    Specials Series, 75; solidarity with Greek and
    Turkish immigrants, 255n10; and symbolic
    ethnicity, 163
Asian Americans: as abject subjects, 156;
    education and historical remembering, 158
assimilation: as condition for distinction, 189;
    into ethnicity, 86; ethnicization as, 67–68,
    83–86; into whiteness, 53, 68, 216, 223
Augustinos, Gerasimos, 178–79, 218, 253n5

Bakalian, Anny, 66, 67, 81, 99, 157, 163, 238n2,
    240n7
Ball, Eric, 198
Bauman, Zygmunt, 169–70, 190–91
Bazin, Jean, 77
Bellah, Robert, 99, 111, 113, 245n2
Bellstone, The (Kalafatas), 164, 166, 168–69, 172,
    187–91, 215–20
Bottomley, Gillian, 124–25, 134, 144, 248n18

Brodkin, Karen, 13, 91, 146, 232–33n9
Broumas, Olga, 168, 196–97, 246n5

Callinicos, Constance, 19, 249n7; *American
    Aphrodite*, 97, 114–28
capitalism: and antimodernist nostalgia, 223;
    critique of, 200–206, 253n2; and exploitation
    of immigrants, 204; impact on Dodecanese
    Islands, 179, 199–200; and individualism 57
Chock, Phyllis, 87, 102–3, 246n5
Chouliaras, Yiorgos, 144
Clifford, James, 30, 33, 145, 147–48, 150, 196, 213
Constantakos, Chrysie, 99–100, 113
Cowan, Jane, 118, 124
cultural studies and analysis of white ethnicity,
    29–30

dance (folk): and Greek American identity,
    247n16; and patriarchy, 118, 122–23; and
    women's community, 124–25
di Leonardo, Micaela, 9, 55, 57–59, 98, 126,
    215, 218, 242–43n23
Dorson, Richard, 19, 33, 34–41, 70–71, 117,
    134, 216, 235–36n5
Doumanis, Nicholas, 178, 184
Du Bois, W. E. B., 155
Dukakis, Michael, 144
Dukakis, Olympia, 76, 182, 186–87
Dyer, Richard, 158

eghoismos, 85
Ellis Island Immigration Museum, 4–6
empathy, 148, 154–61, 250n11, 250n12
ethnicization: as assimilation, 68, 83–86; of
    American society, 9, 86, 126, 144
ethnic preservation as cultural translation, 87
ethnological antimodernism, 215; and white
    ethnicity, 216–17
European Americans, 63–66

Fischer, Michael, 3, 10, 87, 110, 140–41, 240n6
folklore: as cultural production, 31–33; in
    Greece, 38, 44–46; and Greek Americans,
    33–38, 106; and patriarchy, 116–19; and
    popular ethnography, 21–22